# THE ENCYCLOPEDIA OF *YOUR* OBSERVATIONS

## A Creed for Living Life

JERRY WELCH

 www.trafford.com

North America & international
toll-free: 1 888 232 4444 (USA & Canada)
fax: 812 355 4082

 www.tuboo.me

# ACKNOWLEDGEMENTS

This is your Encyclopedia---your guide to help you unravel the complexities of life.If you are here, you arrived under the patronage of THE UNIVERSAL BODY of OBSERVATIONS. You, as humanity have written these observations. They have been gathered from the historical input of dictionaries, books, magazines and tabloids, the media, and the internet. Specific recognition is given where possible. In some instances, sources are unknown. The author can only take credit for assembling the observations, conceiving formulas for delivering their content, and introducing his own observations. This encyclopedic guide could not have been produced without the team assistance of over  fifteen college students or graduates, who, not only entered this project in the transcription process with unbelievable talent and open  minds, but also offered much needed assistance with the technical aspects of putting it all together.

# INSTRUCTIONAL INTRODUCTIONS

An encyclopedia. How boring. I'd rather be reading a good novel. But then, maybe, just maybe, when you consider "living life" as part of the title, this COULD BE interesting and beneficial. Possibly even fun. After all, I can take as long as I want to read it and never lose my place or forget the plot, or I can pick it up a year later (or at any time) for reference. In fact, I don't even have to start here at the beginning. I can start at the end, or I can choose any word in between which will catapult me to other words back at the beginning, in the middle, or in all directions. All I have to do is follow the trail of the underlined words. I could also start with those keywords in the glossary that are taken from each letter of the alphabet. They sort of condense life's basic components in helping me form my creed for living life.

Wait a minute, here's a short story, and another. Talk about entertainment. Poems? Yep, I found some. But I can only relate to outlines, graphs, and proverbs, and what do you know? They're here too. But most of the time, I will have to find my own answers and render my own opinions or judgments.

So who am I? Anybody. It is you who has to decide whether or not to agree, and you, of course, are everybody.

I'll bet my cousin in Baghdad would get a lot out of this. He has been a laborer all his life and probably wouldn't find anything too complicated to understand in this guide. I wonder if my friend who is a professor at Cambridge College would have any thoughts about this; after all, it's about thinking. But I'm the CEO of the largest corporation in the world. I know how to live life. DON'T I? Could there possibly be something in life that I've missed? I guess all I have to do is turn to words such as leader, corporacracy, or power, and answer questions in my own mind. What I'll bet you didn't realize is that I am you, you are me, we are they, they are us, us is it, it is any, and any is all. Together, we comprise a whole—citizens of life.

These are what the words (yes, look it up) are meant to do: to get in your head and guide you through this encyclopedia for the rest of your life. So pick a word that you think is relevant to living life and reference it within these covers. When questions are presented, *you* answer them, but please give thought to them first and then find your answers with **C.L.A.R.I.T.Y**. Let me rephrase that: Please give **spiritually motivated** thought to them first. Speaking of words, remember the reasoning importance of how we put into practice (or use) the actual meaning (or definition) of words. If at any time or place in this encyclopedia words are not understood, look up (find) their meaning. When we successfully accomplish that, then we can honestly claim to understand them in life.

The contents of this encyclopedia have been given in a short, concise, and pointed manner, calculated to provoke thought—to cause one to reflect and ponder until he perceives and experiences the truth of the statement for himself. Much of it is in the form of alphabetization or simplicity. No originality is claimed, as truth, being eternal, cannot have originality.

The pervading character of this encyclopedic guide is practicality. Given are many words, which, if collectively used as a daily guide in life, could lead one to the ultimate truth or at the very least would make one's life easier and happier.

I AM YOU.

YOU ARE ME.

WE ARE THEY.

THEY ARE US.

US IS IT.

IT IS ANY.

ANY IS ALL.

ALL IS LIFE.

# PROLOGUE

LIFE.

What is it?

Early theories of life were materialist. Empedocles (430 BC) held that all life is merely a complex form or arrangement of matter. Hylomorphism is the theory (originating with Aristotle, 322 BC) that all things are a combination of matter and form. A simpler present-day description of human life could be that it is composed of elements in SPACE that have come together to form a working neurological system of senses which are subjected to TIME. In other words, we can only perceive life in relation to space and time.

The Mayan culture was discovered to be very advanced for its time. The Mayan calendar represents not only the culmination of life's increasing numbers but also the acceleration of changing events that lead to an unknown but correctable fate. The manuscript of this encyclopedia was composed in the year 2012. The MC ends in the year 2012. Many correlate this to mean that the Mayans were predicting the end of the world. This, of course, is very doubtful as a perception to cataclysmic end of life.

WHAT IS THE MEANING OF LIFE?

Certain comic strips depict a guru sitting on a mountaintop and a man desperately and laboriously crawling up to his feet to ask, "O Great Master, what is the meaning of life?"

The context of the scene would suggest religions or that the guru is a high priest or an enlightened person.

A very good reason why we should not consider religion as the basis for meaning of life was expressed by Frank Cleave of Duluth, Minnesota, in an article he submitted to a Duluth newspaper. It is shown here in his words.

### Self-Righteous Dogma Carries Little Authority

If I accepted someone's advice on how to live my life, would that then somehow qualify me to tell you how to live yours?

Perhaps if I wrote an exceptional letter brimming with wisdom and insight, you might at least hear me out. However, if I simply lectured you with well-worn dogma in a decisive and condescending manner, you'd likely reject everything I had to say.

Unfortunately, many of the people who write letters to the editor in the News Tribune for the sole purpose of extolling the virtues of their religion seem to miss this simple point. They blatantly tell us their religion is right, and ours, whatever it is, must therefore be wrong. They tell us why and how they are morally superior to us and they insist we adopt their thoughts, action and beliefs or we will be directly responsible for the downfall of civilization-not to mention the assorted plagues, hurricanes and earthquakes our misguided actions somehow cause.

Often, their letters are full of fear, arrogance and intolerance. Sometimes they wildly rant on in a manner suggesting an urgent need for deprogramming.

Frequently they come across as very angry and joyless as they preach against pleasure and free will in nearly every form.

To these hopefully well-intentioned people I offer a simple perspective shared by many of us worthless, wretched heathens: If you are incapable of writing a letter that reveals at least a minimal amount of tolerance, grace and humility, that's proof enough you are unqualified to lecture the rest of us on spirituality.

That said, even the warmer, more spiritually oriented writers can seem abrasively self-righteous because the very act of publicly proclaiming the greatness and perfection o their religion is inherent on all of us.

What the guru probably said was "Go to a mirror or look at your reflection in a serene pool of tranquil water and know that life is as meaningful as you make it."

Butcher, baker, president, pheasant, chairman, chairwoman, oppressed, oppressor, rich man, poor man, taker, giver, warlord, or peacemaker—we can all identify ourselves in life and how we arrived at this moment in life.

Perhaps meaning has something to do with motive, and perhaps we can find ourselves in this encyclopedia and find a meaning to life as well.

You must know we are all very tiny bits of universal energy, but every thought, every action, contributes to the whole. Who we are and what we do is part of the entire picture that is being painted of this planet. The true nature of all things needs to be observed.

To be thrust into the realm of conscious awareness.

# KEYWORDS
A word defined can be a story to the beholder.

A. **awareness**, analyze, accept or admit, act, age, adapt, attitude, ascertain, ask

B. **balance**, behavior, belief, benevolence, **brain**

C. capacity, **CLARITY**, challenge, change, circle, center, conscious, conflict, common, cognizance, control, controversy, convenience, **CREED,** curiosity

D. **decide/decision,** define, deliberate, denial, determination, different(ces), discipline, drugs

E. **ecology**, education, effect(ive), emotion(al), ethic(al), evolve/evolution, exercise

F. fact, faith, **family**, fate, fear, flourish, focus, force, forgive(ness), freedom

G. gain, gather, give, **God**, government, greed, guide

H. habit(ual), haste, hate, help, heritage, history, **honesty**, honor(able), humans, humor, **health**

I. ideal, idea, imagination, incorporate, indifferent, individual, (inequitable), influence, information, integrity, **intelligence**, interpret

J. **judge(ment),** just

K. kill, kind, **know(ledge),** karma, keep

L. labor, laugh, law, learn, liberty, **LIFE**, listen, **live/living**, logic, **love**

M. mediate, meditate, mercy, merit, mind, misunderstand, moment, **money**, moral(ity), motive

N. **natural**, nature, **need**, negotiate, nourish, number(s), nurture

O. one, only, opinion, **opposite**, optimism, **order**, offer, **OBSERVATION**

P. participate, patience, peace, peer, people, perceive/perception, persistence, perseverance, person, personal, perspective, **philosophy**, political, population, positive, possible, power, pray(er), presume, proof

Q. quality, **question**

R. racism, rationale, read, reality, reason, relate/relationship, relevant, religion, resolve, respect/respectful

S. sacred, satisfy, science, self, senses, simple, social/society, space, spiral, stress, strategic, solutions, subconscious, succeed, story

T.  take, talk, teach, technology, theology, **think**, tell, time, touch, through, truth, **thought**

U.  **understand**, unique, unit(y), use, utopia

V.  valid, value, vary, venerate, verbal, vice, **virtue**

W.  want, war, waste, water, wealth, will, **wisdom**, words, world

Y.  Y-suffix, year (as in centuries), yearn

Z.  zeal, zest

# DOUBLE KEYWORDS
Two defined words combined can become volumes to the multitude.

A.  Almighty thought, Armageddon constants, analytical analysis

B.  bring together, basic needs

C.  conscious awareness, collectively collaborate, common sense, conjectured answer, cruel liberties, creative action, coop communities, cataclysmic event, concentrated cognizance, cultural consciousness

D.  Digital Enlightenment

E.  exquisite kindness, exponential function, economic collapse, economic warfare, ecological ruination

F.  figurative language, Federal Reserve, factual truth, free energy

G.  general knowledge, global economy, global collapse

H.  healthy systems

I.  individual perception, intellectual integrity

J.  judicial breakdown, judicial corruption

K.  know-all, kangaroo court, keep down

L.  learn logic, life's paradoxes, liberty awareness, logical analysis, life lessons, learnability index

M.  manipulative exploitations, mentally ill, meditation perspectives, monetary ruin, money power

N.  normalcy bias, natural disaster, natural balance

O.  opposite consideration

P.  population explosion, profound morality, political parties, perpetual recycling

Q.  questions everything

R.  relevant reasoning, right thing, realistic prophecy, resource depletion

S.  social system, symbolic consciousness

T.  transcendental meditation, transcendent wisdom, take care, truthful trust, toroidal awareness

U.  ulterior motive, ulterior purpose

V.  viewpoint

W.  willpower, world change, world end, world plight, worldwide calamity, white supremacy

X.  youthful yearning

Y.  zealous collectivism

# <u>A</u>

**Ability:** Since <u>society</u> regards and measures us by our abilities, it behooves us to gain <u>power</u> and the means to have skills or talents to do things. This is usually a <u>learned</u> process or a matter of enhancing <u>natural</u> talents. Consider how you can improve society through your abilities. Those who are gifted in any way should seek to <u>teach</u> others to use their own gifts. What valuable abilities do you have? How can you use your abilities to improve society? Does your ability to do something result in a negative effect, such as your ability to inflict <u>pain</u> or to <u>deceive</u>? Do you have <u>patience</u> with the lack of ability in others? Or yourself?

**Abide:** The action of abiding relates to the omnipresence of <u>government</u> and commerce since we are called to <u>honor</u> contracts and adhere to rules. Further, we can abide and <u>tolerate</u> the behavior of others. At times, this is unwise, as certain <u>actions</u> should never be tolerated, but isn't life easier when small faults in the personalities of others are best ignored? Which set of rules do you abide by?

**Abnormal:** Is it always a <u>positive</u> thing to be normal? Though you may see your abnormality as a cross to bear, have you <u>considered</u> that your abnormality is what makes you who you are? Don't seek to simply fall in line with the definitions of normalcy presented by our <u>society</u>. Can abnormal also mean <u>unique</u>?

**Absorb:** What we take in and make a part of our work, our businesses, and our play has a tremendous impact on our <u>identities</u>. We should seek to be informational sponges in our lives, constantly searching for new <u>information</u> to increase our respective grasps of the world around us. Without this, we run the risk of <u>ignorance</u>. Are you open to absorbing new ideas and experiences? Is your <u>health</u> affected by what you absorb?

**Abstain:** The act of refraining from participation in a given activity; abstaining is a matter of individual <u>choice</u> and <u>decision</u>. Should unhealthy activities be avoided by abstaining? By always abstaining, do we eliminate exposure to new <u>ideas</u> and <u>opinions</u>? If you find yourself sitting on the sidelines of life, is abstaining the best option? *When should we abstain?*

**Abstract:** The abstract is that which you can only <u>consider</u>; it is truly food for thought. The presence of the abstract denotes an active and inquiring mind not devoid of <u>emotion</u> when thinking critically. The abstract is <u>sublime</u> and cannot be described with mere words; you must seek it out and feel it, but where do you start?

**Abuse:** If you do not want to be abused, do not abuse others; this is the golden rule. It's our duty as citizens of this world to treat all creatures with <u>respect</u>, making abuse of a physical nature inexcusable. Additionally, there exists <u>emotional</u> and substance abuse. Have you found yourself the <u>victim</u> of any type of abuse? Have you forgiven those who wronged you? Can abuse progress to <u>aggression</u>?

> "For after all, the best thing one can do when it is raining is let it rain."
> — Henry Wadsworth Longfellow

**Accept, Acceptance**: In life, consider the two types of acceptance: mandatory acceptance and approved acceptance. We need to <u>consciously</u> differentiate between them, accept what cannot be <u>changed</u>, and *minimize the emotional <u>stress</u>* of *mandatory acceptance*. Always accept <u>truth </u>within <u>fact</u> and find fact within truth. Regardless of type, all acceptances are in response to an offer. For example, accepting the rule of <u>law</u> is truly accepting the offer of governance at any level of civic authority. Can acceptance be conditioned and is it always associated with or in response to an offer?

**Accolade**: As abilities become more numerous, so will accolades. Should accolades be your solitary <u>goal</u>? Our ultimate goal in development should be self-improvement— the development of our minds and <u>gifts</u>. While the <u>praise</u> of others is enjoyable and encouraging, it is better to give than receive. How do you seek to <u>encourage</u> others in their pursuits?

**Accomplish, Accomplishment**: If you go through life consciously accomplishing things or <u>achieving</u> things rather than just doing things, you will find that others will hold you in higher esteem and the words <u>self </u>and <u>achievement</u> will have greater meaning. Regardless of what you have accomplished, move forward and continue to achieve. Don't consider your victories in life an <u>end</u>. Rather, continue to seek more. Do you live through your past accomplishments or seek new goals?

**Account, Accountable:** In commerce, use <u>fairness</u> and accuracy, for in the end, we will be held accountable. People remember how you conduct <u>business</u>. Whether you do so with <u>honor</u> can make or break your career and personal life. These are among the things that people remember long after we're gone. How can you make fairness a goal in all of your dealings? Can you account for <u>responsibility</u>?

**Accumulate, Accumulation**: We often focus on the accumulation of <u>wealth</u> and possessions as they are heralded in our <u>society</u> as the foundation of <u>happiness</u>. But as the saying goes, money can't buy happiness. Additionally, the pursuit of material possessions leads to <u>excess</u>. Charge yourself with the integrity to ask, "How much is enough and how many is too many?"

**Accuse, Accusation**: Beware of false accusations. Know it to be true before accusing. We must make every stride to know all <u>facts</u> before coming to any <u>conclusions</u> in life, but this is even more important with accusations. An accusation thrusts the <u>morality</u> of another into question and could cause irreparable damage to the <u>perception</u> others have of them. Do you always make sure you know the facts of a situation before casting aspersions? (Prov. "Let he who is not guilty of doing wrong cast the first stone.")

**Achieve**: All are capable of achieving goals in life, but often we limit ourselves by seeking solitude in our work and shunning <u>collaboration</u>. Collaboration has defined human progress, from the foundations of the first societies to the mapping of the human genome. The input of others fosters progress, as new <u>ideas</u> and <u>perspectives</u> breed creativity. Do you as an individual receive more satisfaction from achieving a special task as compared with a group accomplishing something?

**Acknowledgement**: Acknowledgement comes in several forms, ranging from the acknowledgment of a stranger on the street to acknowledging the <u>success</u> of others through <u>accolades</u> to acknowledging our own shortcomings. For personal growth, this last example is the most important. Without recognizing our <u>mistakes</u> and faults, personal <u>growth</u> is impossible. Do you recognize your shortcomings and work to <u>change</u> them? Do you admit the existence of reality and truth? Do you recognize the validity of facts?

**Acquiesce**: To agree without protest. We acquiesce daily to the rule of our government, but this acceptance can be blind. Do you question the motives of leaders? Additionally, acquiescence when you are proven wrong is an important trait to cultivate in your life. You should consider acquiescence to be the fiber of character. However, how often do you find yourself arguing for the sake of arguing?

**Acquire**: Acquisition has become the cornerstone of our modern capitalistic world, leading to greed and economic uncertainty for entire nations. However, there are other types of acquisition, such as the pursuit of knowledge, which enrich our lives as well as the lives of others. How do you acquire? By learning, by purchasing, or by taking? Where does each path lead?

**Act, Action**: The very essence of the word is to start or begin. A rolling stone gathers no moss. Idleness is the mother of vice. So we must act to carry out decisions, and we must stay active to maintain ourselves. Action is a positive, inaction is a negative. However, many actions have negative ramifications. Careless action often results in consequences for either the instigator or those affected by the action. Take time to carefully consider the result of a given action to avoid ignorant damage. Should there be a plan for every action and should every action have purpose?

**Adapt**: To where or what do we adapt? If one is born into a dictatorial society, adaptation to oppression is usually not a matter of choice. In present-day society, thought must adapt to the effects of waste and pollution. Remember that most adaptation becomes a form of evolutionary or ecological adaptation. Do you seek to adapt to changes in your life or approach the world inflexibly?

**Addict, Addiction**: While issues of addiction are easily seen in our culture as pertaining to drugs and alcohol, addiction takes on other forms as well. Addictions control our lives; they can come in the form of gambling or even something as simple as television. Consider your life and the comforts to which you have grown accustomed. Are we all victims of addiction in one way or another? Everyone can look deep into themselves and discover pleasures and conveniences that have possibly gone beyond deserving the name "habit." We must change our thinking to consider addiction as an illness requiring medical attention. What role does dependency play?

**Addition**: By adding to our knowledge, we increase our understanding of life. The multitude of cultural beliefs and attitudes creates a near infinite total amount of knowledge. This means we should always be students of other perspectives and ideas in an effort to increase our intellectual grasp. Do you constantly seek to add to your knowledge?

**Adept**: To become highly skilled in any arena takes years of practice. In a way, by reading this book, you are seeking to become adept at living life. What does it mean to be adept at life? Does this mean happiness, security, prosperity, a good family? The answer is different for each of us. How can you better use your skills to help others?

**Adequacy, Adequate**: We are constantly telling ourselves that we are not adequate for the obstacles that face us, that we are not beautiful enough or smart enough or capable of succeeding. Self-doubt is natural and can lead us to work harder to accomplish the things we wish to accomplish. However, at a certain point, it becomes a hindrance, preventing us from seeing the right answer to a problem because our minds are clouded by self-deprecation. How can we convince ourselves of our self-worth and stop the defeatist circle?

**Adhere, Adherence**: By living in a society, we have all agreed to adhere to certain standards of behavior—the laws that make our society a relatively safe place in which to live. Are we even conscious of all the values and social systems to which we adhere? How can we make ourselves more conscious of our adherence to certain value systems on a daily basis? Additionally, we adhere to certain standards of behavior in our relationships—agreements between people based on trust. We are faithful to our significant others, we choose to not speak ill of our friends behind their backs, and in doing so, we maintain these relationships. Have you ever lost a relationship by ignoring things such as these? Have you sought to make amends?

**Administer:** This word has two meanings: either running a business or administering the assets and laws of our society. While these two things pertain to commerce and governance, respectively, they also pertain to morality. Corruption, in either form of administration, wreaks havoc on our society and should be uncovered. Rather than simply accept poor administration, do you seek to find the truth behind the motives of corporations and governmental bodies?

**Admissible**: Simply because a thing can be done doesn't necessarily mean that it should be done. What kind of behavior is admissible in our society that may not be good for us? What things are admissible that shouldn't be, and what isn't admissible that should be? These are questions to consider in everyday activities. It's admissible to drive your car to work, but wouldn't mass transit help reduce pollution? It's admissible to relax leisurely, but wouldn't this be more satisfying after hard work?

**Admission, Admit:** We make admissions and take admissions in many senses. How can we be more humble in admitting when we've made a mistake? Alternatively, if we gain admission somewhere, should we ask ourselves why? Was it through hard work, or was it simply given to you because of the means into which you were born? Who in our society is not granted admission? Getting accepted to college through hard work and study is admirable, but simply accepting opportunities offered by some notion of birthright teaches us nothing. Admission shouldn't be accepted if others are excluded based solely on their station in life, as this leads to class struggle and elitism.

**Advance, Advancement:** Society defines advancement in several ways, whether social, economic, or technological, but how might those ways be harmful to us? Social advancement aids in a comfortable life, but is there more to life than advancing in your job and your paycheck? How can you spiritually and emotionally advance? Try to remember that a comfortable life isn't necessarily a happy one and can lead to complacency. Always set spiritual and emotional goals that keep you moving forward.

> *"The only good thing to do with good advice is pass it on; it is never of any use to oneself."*
> — *Oscar Wilde*

**Advantage:** As with many things in life, this word has two sides. The first is positive: If we see opportunities to better our quality of life that are moral and hurt no one, wisdom is found in taking advantage of them. Do you actively seek to take advantage of the opportunities presented to you? Have you missed opportunities in the past and learned from these moments? The other side is negative: Many in our society seek to take advantage of the naïve, generous, or ill-informed. Are you taking advantage of someone else, or is someone else taking advantage of you? Be mindful of the subtle forms of manipulation humans utilize, sometimes without knowledge of their actions.

**Advice, Advise, Advisement:** When another person seeks you out for advice, it shows their respect for you and the way you live. Do not take the responsibility of counseling others lightly. Additionally, think through all advice you are given before acting on it. If the advice you receive is something your advisor wouldn't do in their own life, you run the risk of following the words of a hypocrite. How do we connect with people through giving them advice? What advice from this encyclopedia would you give to others?

**Advocacy:** How can we advocate for others who can't speak for themselves in our daily lives? By coming from a position of privilege, we have a responsibility to aid those who do not. There are many groups in our society who lack a significant voice for any number of reasons. One can spend their entire lives attempting to help as many groups as possible. Rather than doing that, try to find one group, with whom you feel a particular connection, that you can help. Imagine a world in which all of us did just that much. What is our social obligation for the advocacy of others? Can you think of a disenfranchised group in our society to whom you feel a connection?

> "Just remember, when you're over the hill, you begin to pick up speed."
> — Charles M. Schulz

**Affect**: Affect is an important word in both its verb and adjectival sense. Every day through our smallest interactions, we affect the people around us, and we should be conscious of this. But affected also means disingenuous; how are we affected in our interactions with people? When are we not honest in our emotions and words? If you are affected, what caused this to happen?

**Affection**: Does affection cease beyond the range of lovers, immediate family members, relationships, and pets? Who else might be deserving of our affections outside of these groups? Is there a sense in which strangers and the world more generally deserve our affection?

**Age:** As we age, we're supposed to grow wiser. But is this always true? Unless life is lived with the intention of learning, wisdom will not be achieved. What have you learned as you've aged? What do you observe about older people, and how does our behavior indicate what kind of age we are? Further, we must seek to accept the onset of age. For many, this process is difficult to accept; our bodies slow, we tire easily, and our minds are not as sharp. Denial of these things will not lead to happiness, however. Do you accept limitations or stubbornly deny they exist? Conversely, do you accept limitations before they need to exist, causing inactivity and unhealthy neglect? What do you observe about elderly people? What can you learn from them?

**Aggravate**: Aggravation is an emotional state that, if left unchecked, can have significant problems in our personal and professional lives. Aggravation can lead us to angry outbursts at those who we think annoy us, but the one who truly loses in those situations is you. Therefore, it is wise to try to keep these feelings in check. Given the incidence of emotional tension and differences, have you considered all areas of provocation? Do you recognize that aggravation has as much to do with you as it does the source of your enervation? Can you admit when you've made matters worse?

**Aggression**: When we find ourselves stressed, aggression is often a means of negative release. We snap at friends and family, we perceive insignificant insults and respond harshly, and we alienate those who care the most. When these things happen, do you just accept them? Or do you look internally to find the source of your negative response? Have you alienated those you care about through aggression?

**Agnostic:** The inability to <u>decide</u> whether or not God exists is prevalent in our culture and an example of <u>human</u> nature. Though agnostics cannot prove that God doesn't <u>exist</u>, they believe something might exist. Perhaps this is indicative of a <u>desire</u> for the divine to be a part of our universe, even if those who hold this view do not feel affected by that <u>presence</u>. God doesn't need to be traditional. Is he to you? Do you believe in nothing? Or do you think there may be a divine presence of some type in the universe? How does this affect your daily life?

**Agree, Agreement**: Have you ever placated someone by simply agreeing with them despite continued disagreement? Do we sometimes agree with them because it the easier thing to do and not the right thing? Always remember that this is not <u>true</u> agreement. True agreement comes about through extended <u>discourse</u> and true <u>understanding</u> of the multiple perspectives of a given <u>conversation</u>. We cannot agree with that which we do not understand. Do you seek clear comprehension before you agree with others? Are you capable of agreeing to disagree, that is, allowing someone to hold a radically different viewpoint without letting that difference cause a lasting divide?

<u>Air</u>: Air is birthright to all, yet we are rarely consciously <u>aware</u> of it. Do you ever think about breathing, or do you take it for granted? This <u>casual</u> approach to the atmosphere of Earth has led to rampant <u>pollution</u>, leading to a world in which one cannot assume each breath is healthy in the long term. What can we do to <u>repair</u> this damage and prevent this sort of oversight from repeating itself? What else in our lives escape our daily consciousness, though it is integral to all we do?

**Alcohol**: Alcoholism is rampant in our culture and often glorified by the media, but the reality of it is far more <u>tragic</u> than many realize, <u>affecting</u> friends and family tremendously. Alcohol exists as a legal means of mind-altering diversion. But like all diversions, without moderation, <u>excess</u> is destructive. Soon, the diversion becomes more important than small things in your life, and then it surpasses larger things until nothing in your life is as important as your <u>dependency</u>. Have you recognized alcohol as mind altering and consequently affecting your life in a negative way?

**Alienate:** We alienate those around us carelessly sometimes, and without even trying to do so. Perhaps your sense of <u>humor</u> is offensive, or people <u>perceive</u> silence as <u>rejection</u>. Have you learned to read <u>social</u> situations so as to not <u>offend</u> those around you? Additionally, our <u>society</u> alienates those who lack a voice. Their needs and concerns are not addressed by the <u>political</u> leaders of our country,

leaving them feeling dejected. Are you a part of such a group? Do you work to <u>help</u> groups who have been alienated unjustly?

**Alike**: We often assume others to be alike when they are not. Large entities, such as <u>governments</u> and <u>corporations,</u> seek to categorize people to generalize a <u>population</u>, making them easier to <u>manipulate</u>. Why do we assume likeness when people are in fact <u>complex</u> and <u>different</u> and accept this categorization when done by others? On a more positive note regarding this word, when we find those in our lives with whom we <u>share</u> traits and interests, it can lead to some of the most rewarding <u>friendships</u> of our lives—lasting and supportive. Who do you <u>connect</u> to in life? What is the common ground on which these <u>relationships</u> are built?

**Alive**: If you are reading this book, you are alive in the <u>literal</u> sense, but isn't there more to this word <u>figuratively</u>? To feel alive implies that one is living their life to the fullest. We do this through seeking new experiences and learning new things. Doing things that are foreign to us gives us a rush beyond the daily grind of our workweek and makes us remember what it is to be human. This feeling can't last, but we can find ways to make it return again and again. When was the last time you felt alive? What did you do that gave you that emotional and spiritual rush?

**All:** All is any, everyone, and everything—the whole amount. Political figures are constantly seeking to capitalize on the things that divide us as a society and globally as a species. While these differences are difficult to ignore and exist between all humans, we are undeniably part of a whole—a species—and as such, we share certain traits and needs. We need food, water, sleep, and social interaction. These should not be confused with the things we desire—the things that divide us as a species. By focusing on maintaining the needs of our species, can't we find that we have more in common with one another than we generally think? Additionally, humans are part of an even greater whole: the full spectrum of life on planet Earth. As a part of this grand whole, don't we have obligations to consider as we live our lives?

**Alliance:** Alliances are the backbone of quality diplomacy and are formed when multiple parties are united in one cause. This cause can be economic, political, or militaristic, and much good has come from such alliances. The Allied forces of World War II were able to stop the tyranny and oppression of Nazi Germany, saving the world from the chaos that would have abounded if that power went unchecked. Conversely, forces can ally themselves to mislead and manipulate the public. Are you careful to scrutinize political leaders, looking at what companies fund their campaigns? Do the words of that politician line up with the desires of their backers, or are they words designed to tickle your ears?

**Allied:** While this word is obviously related to the previous entry, take a moment now to consider who you are allied with personally and professionally. As members of a society, we work to find our place socially and economically. We ally ourselves with friends, and we ally ourselves with the employment we obtain or seek. While these alliances may improve your standing in the world, be cautious to not sacrifice your integrity for social or economic gain. Are you proud of all your associations? Do you ever find yourself ignoring the immoral qualities of others to improve your status?

**Allow:** Be mindful of the things you allow to happen in your life. While many allowed occurrences transpire with our knowledge, others pass by with no thought or consideration on our part. Our silence does as much to condone the activities of others as our advocacy. Do we allow our leaders to take advantage of us? Is there a way in which their luring rhetoric blinds us to the truth?

**Alone:** It's important to be content when we're alone. However, prolonged loneliness can be a crippling force in our lives. Have you at times felt isolated in life? How did it affect your ability to be productive? Additionally, there are times in life where we are tested, where we must stand alone and face trials either personally, professionally, or politically. Yours may be the only voice of reason in a room, but still, it must be heard. Do you speak out even when in the minority?

**Almighty:** This word is typically applied to deities—that which is all-powerful and divine. Regardless of your religious thoughts and beliefs, there are ways to incorporate divine ideals into your life. Forgiveness is a wonderful example of this. It's an act valued by many religions and one that will enrich your personal life even if you believe in nothing. Do you strive to incorporate divine philosophies and actions into your daily life? Do these teachings influence your moral compass?

**Alter:** While altering something may improve it—altering perspectives and views, for example—it can also be a destructive force. This arises through the creation of unnatural substances that cannot return to their natural state. Just because science is capable of producing such things doesn't mean that it should be done. Do you consume such products? Would it improve your health to seek natural solutions? Additionally, and most dangerously, this word also pertains to the mistake of altering the mind with chemicals that ultimately and permanently damage our brains. Do you abstain from such substances?

**Alternative:** One of the goals of this book is to present alternative perspectives on the words that define our lives. We are often trapped in our own perspective, leaving the alternative out of our minds. This sort of thinking breeds miscommunication, confusion, and eventually conflict. Aim to listen to the perspectives of others; it's these sorts of discussions that bring about resolutions. Do you try to consider the perspectives of others? Think of a time when you didn't consider another's perspective. What was the result? How could have the result been different if you had seen the situation through another's eyes?

**Altruism:** When we seek to help others with no thought of personal gain, we act altruistically. This is one of the defining aspects of humanity—the ability to help those who are less fortunate than ourselves. With that in mind, how often do you seek to help others? It needn't be monetary aid; it could be offering your time as a volunteer for any number of organizations. Can you think of anywhere in your community where you could offer help? Additionally, beware of those who appear to act altruistically but only seek praise from others for their actions. Do you know anyone who helps others disingenuously?

**Ambiguity, Ambiguous:** Ambiguity is an unavoidable part of life. In reading this book, you've probably taken note of the way most words have multiple meanings, some positive and some negative. However, ambiguity in our language and relationships can lead to confusion in our relationships and it serves us to clearly define things between those with whom we interact so that all expectations—both yours and theirs—are met. Do you seek to define your relationships with clarity? Do you speak clearly and make your expectations known to all those around you?

**Ambition:** Ambition is the driving force behind our decision-making processes, whether the ambitions are our own or the ambitions of others to which we are subjected. While this pushes progress forward, thereby creating new technologies and generating wealth, it also serves as justification for vast amounts of wrongdoing. Consider corporations who have knowingly poisoned the air and rivers simply to turn a higher profit. Ambition without morality is bereft of societal value. Do you let your morality guide your ambition? Does your ambition supersede your integrity?

> "At the age of six, I wanted to be a cook. At seven, I wanted to be Napoleon. And my ambition has been growing steadily ever since."
> — Salvador Dalí

**Amenable:** We cannot progress in life without the counsel of others, but if we are deaf to the advice of others, if we aren't amenable, it's all wasted. Do you readily listen to the advice of others? Do you truly listen to what others say, or do you simply hear it and ignore what could be wisdom?

**Amend:** While this word pertains to correcting errors in a written text, we all have errors and faults in our lives that we need to fix; nobody is perfect. The key is in realizing that these faults exist, finding them, and working to correct them. How do you amend problems in your life? Are you able to cope with these <u>issues</u> in a healthy manner by yourself, or do you <u>need</u> others?

**Amenity**: In our modern world, convenience is everywhere, from the running water at our fingertips to knowledge of the Internet. Do you confuse amenities with needs? These conveniences certainly make life more comfortable, but don't let them create a sense of laziness in you. Always remember what is necessary in life and what an amenity is. Keep a firm grasp on the difference between the two.

**Amiable, Amity:** Without amity, compromise and understanding can never be reached. It's sometimes difficult to maintain an amiable spirit when faced with those whose views differ from ours, but taking the moral high road and treating them with kindness is always best. Do you treat others with amity, even those whose views oppose yours?

> "Anger is an acid that can do more harm to the vessel in which it is stored than to anything on which it is poured."
> — Mark Twain

**Amputate:** This word has two meanings, the literal and the figurative. Given the first, how do you <u>interact</u> with those who have been injured or disabled in life either through illness or accident? They are humans just like everyone else and should never be treated <u>differently</u>. With the figurative, one can amputate <u>relationships</u> and other aspects of their life when those things become toxic. Can you recognize when such toxicity is reached? Do you hold on to the poisons of your <u>life</u> longer than you should against the life of others?

**Analogy**: Analogies are present everywhere, helping us see the <u>connections</u> between <u>situations</u>. They allow us to explain things clearly to others when <u>comprehension</u> of the literal situation is too difficult for both parties. What analogies can you find in the world around you for your life? What analogous equivalents exist between words and experiences?

**<u>Analysis, Analyze</u>:** We are bombarded daily by a constant stream of data and <u>information</u>, and the only way to make sense of all of this is through careful consideration and analysis. Without analysis, our <u>decisions</u> are hasty and ill-informed. However, the <u>consequences</u> of such hastily made decisions can be long lasting. To do this, you must look carefully at the words utilized by others and the <u>perspectives</u> from which others speak. Do you analyze <u>situations</u> before making decisions?

**Anew:** To <u>begin</u> anew, one must disregard the weight of their past. You must throw off old <u>habits</u> and start over. What do we have to gain by beginning anew in our lives? What might we stand to lose?

**Anger, Angry:** Anger is an <u>emotional</u> reaction to an external event which we dislike. How will you act upon the anger? Will you let it fester within, lash out verbally, or go to the very extreme of resorting to physical <u>harm</u>? Have you <u>rationally</u> considered your justification for any action (above) against another life

form? Though we are mostly only troubled by superficial <u>stress</u>, more often than not, we get angry. While we may think that our anger accomplishes something, the poisonous nature of it is generally more harmful to us than to the object of our <u>rage</u>. Anger can be consuming and can lead to a <u>desire</u> for revenge. Isn't it just a waste of <u>energy</u>? It is not a matter of right and wrong. It is how we manage anger that is most important. Should we avoid it? Wouldn't the better choice be relief through resolution? When does <u>annoyance</u> become anger?

**Anguish**: Many suffer but few understand the cause of their anguish. We often feel a sense of malaise for no obvious reason, but there's always a source to be found. What causes most people to be unhappy? Are their lives truly lacking, or are they just unable to be content with what they have?

**Animal**: Is man an animal? What separates him from the other animals on the planet? Could it be his conscience? His ability to feel guilt? Regardless of the answer, our place at the height of evolutionary development carries great responsibility, and we should not use that position as a rationale for the destruction of the planet we share with all animals.

**Animosity**: What causes animosity between people? Is it true opposition or simply misunderstanding? The root of this word is related to the previous entry: animal. When we experience these strong sensations of anger and revulsion, are we not reduced to an animalistic state? As humans, we should be above such emotions. They may be unavoidable, but we can suppress them and rise above them before we make costly errors in our personal and professional lives. Do you work to overcome the animosity you feel toward others?

**Annoy:** How many trivial things do we let annoy us? Annoyances are inevitable in life. Even those who don't annoy us generally can rub us the wrong way on a bad day. The important thing to remember is to not act on those things which annoy us. We all undoubtedly annoy others at some point in time and would prefer it if we weren't constantly berated for the minor things we do wrong. Treat others accordingly, and try to overlook such minor slights. What things annoy you on a daily basis? Wouldn't we feel better about ourselves and the world around us if we were to just let them go?

**Anomaly:** We find anomalies regularly in our lives—occurrences that defy explanation by passing outside of predictable circumstances. We have to react to these things accordingly: Analyze the new situation and respond after careful thought. What anomalies do we find in our day to day life? What do these anomalies tell us about the nature of the world around us and its predictability?

**Answer, Answerable**: All answers originate with questions. When you look for an answer to your question, you should look for facts. Where facts are not available, you should consider all the possibilities. What questions remain unanswerable in your life and in life more generally? Can the answers that determine your approach to life change as you grow?

**Antagonism:** Why do we antagonize others? What do we stand to gain from this kind of confrontation? Approaching any situation from an antagonistic perspective is rarely productive as it determines your responses before a situation has developed. Antagonism blinds you to reason. Would our lives be easier if we ceased to antagonize those around us because of our own unhappiness and let them be?

**Antecedent**: What came before you and was your antecedent? How does understanding our antecedents help us understand ourselves? We can't truly understand our place in a society historically unless we understand the past. Furthermore, without this comprehension, we risk repeating the mistakes of those who came before. Be mindful of this—that which preceded you has formed you more than you realize.

**Anthropoid:** Anthropoids are human-like, but they are not quite human. What defines someone as human? Their physical features? Consider that this definition is outlined less by appearance and much more by identity. It is our own identities that separate us from others.

**Anticipate:** All our actions are based on some form of anticipation. We anticipate needs that will exist based on past experience—the need for money and food, the desires of partners, the social demands of friends—and do what we can to satisfy all those things. Do you anticipate what others will want and need? Do you prepare to give them those things in advance? Don't become so rigid in your anticipation that you cannot adapt when unexpected situations arise.

**Antisocial:** The antisocial surround us, infecting others with misanthropic tendencies. Why do we have antisocial tendencies? How does the antisocial behavior of one person affect society as a whole? There will always be times when we seek solitude, but remember when you commit yourself to a social situation that you should act accordingly. Consider your mood before committing to such gatherings. Spending a night in is better than alienating your social circle through antisocial behavior.

**Antiquated:** What about our society is antiquated? Which laws and customs do people cling to even though they should be done away with, dismissed as a relic of the past? While old approaches lacking relevance should be discarded, we should also pay mind to what valuable concepts the past holds. Age does not denote antiquation, but irrelevance in the present does.

**Antithesis**: An antithesis is an opposite, and we find ourselves surrounded by opposites in our daily lives. But how might things that seem like antitheses actually not be in reality? How might these binary oppositions be more unstable than they seem? Be mindful to not be swayed by those who seek to paint others as antithetical to your own position, as common ground can always be found.

**Antonym:** Continuing with opposites, antonyms are like antitheses between words. How are antonyms working as you read this? Can you think of antonyms for the words in this volume and how they too relate to life?

**Anxiety, Anxious:** Many spend their lives overcome by anxiety, incapable of moving forward because they are paralyzed by fear. But why are we anxious? Fear of embarrassment, or the judgment of others? Is there not something of vanity in anxiety, the fear that all attention is focused on yourself?

**Any, Anybody, Anyhow, Anything:** Any offers us a dizzying amount of possibility, discarding all restraints. Any can be anyone, anywhere, in any way. Because it is so open to everything, it also includes everything, everyone, everywhere. What other possibilities does "any" offer us? Do you find that these seemingly infinite possibilities can limit us rather than liberate?

**Apathy**: Apathy destroys our ability to progress in any arena of life, whether personally, emotionally, or economically. How can we overcome apathy to be more productive in our lives? Apathy is often bred by sensations of ineffectiveness within a role—a citizen who feels the government doesn't care about his vote becomes apathetic toward politics. The things we do always play a part in how our world progresses, so these sensations are false. Maintain an interest in all the areas affected by your actions. Apathy will always be regretted in the long run.

**Apocalypse:** If the apocalypse were truly impending, what would you do? How would you wish that you had led your life differently? It is human nature to examine our conduct only at an ending, but the better response is examination at all times so as to approach any end confident in your life. Additionally, consider the possibility that the behavior of our society is bringing about such a cataclysmic event. Do you work to respect the environment, preserving our planet for future generations?

**Apologetic, Apology, Apologize:** Apologizing implies repentance and self-awareness that you have done <u>wrong</u>. This response is often halted by <u>pride</u>—only the <u>humble</u> can truly accept when they have failed others. Additionally, it takes a gracious heart to accept the apologies of others and grant <u>forgiveness</u>. How can apologizing set us free from what we feel guilty for in our lives? Do you forgive others readily or hold a <u>grudge</u>?

**Apostasy, Apostate:** Often in our lives, we turn away from the <u>religious</u> institutions of which we were once a part. While dogmatic <u>differences</u> provide an appropriate <u>reason</u> for apostasy, careful consideration should be involved in any <u>decision</u> to abandon our past notions. When we turn away from one religion, though, we often turn toward another, and sometimes that religion is money, power, and greed. What is your religion, and what ones have you turned away from?

**Apparent:** We are often ruled by what is apparent, rather than by what actually is. The <u>façades</u> of others are easy to accept at face value, but behind some lies malicious and duplicitous intent. How can we transcend appearances to <u>comprehend</u> <u>reality</u>, and what is truly valuable in life? Do you make your own views and <u>expectations</u> apparent to others? Or do you hide behind a mask?

**Appeal:** What appeals to you in life? That which appeals to us is based on our perceptions. If you are reading this book, chances are you <u>desire</u> self-improvement. However, not all desires are as productive as this; some of our desires would destroy our lives if <u>acted</u> on. Consider the case of <u>lustful</u> attraction. Actions based on these sensations can destroy relationships and families. Exercise self-restraint when considering that which appeals to you. Do you <u>consider</u> the <u>consequences</u> of seeking out those things which appeal to you before pursuing them?

Do you pursue those things which would be productive?

**Appearance:** Looks can be deceiving in life. Throughout history, people have sought to put on a show to attain those things they <u>desire</u> politically, professionally, and romantically. We must always <u>examine</u> the <u>motives</u> behind someone's <u>actions</u> before accepting what could be nothing more than honeyed words. Additionally, if you wish to lead a happy life, presenting yourself to others genuinely is key. Our <u>relationships</u> with others are only as genuine as the effort we put into them. Do you look past appearances to see motives? Do you present yourself to others genuinely?

**Appease:** Too often, it is easier to appease those in <u>power</u> than it is to go against them and do what is right. Doing what is right isn't always easy; sometimes we risk negative <u>consequences</u> as a result of our resolve. Don't shrink back from these situations; respond to them with <u>integrity</u>. Have you ever appeased others in your life just because it was easier? How can you gain the courage to stop appeasing and to instead act on what you feel to be right in life?

**Appertain:** To appertain is to relate to something else. We may not feel like <u>political</u> problems in another country appertain to us, but their ramifications could indeed. As you live life, look for these larger <u>connections</u> to your world and seek to make the connections positive if you can. List a few external connections to your life. Are they <u>positive</u> or <u>negative</u>? Do you have agency to change those that are negative?

**Applicable:** The words in this encyclopedia are meant to be applicable to life; through careful thought and reflection on observations they'll help you find answers. With this word, it can be taken to mean "<u>relevant</u>." Consider your work; it would be unwise to bring up irrelevant topics in meetings as you would waste the time of others and appear unprofessional. Or privately, if a friend seeks advice, only words which are applicable will matter. Do you maintain relevance in your words? Do you have difficulty communicating as a result of tangential dialogue?

**Application, Applied, Apply:** To succeed in life requires application—application of talent, effort, ethics, and empathy. Relationships, jobs, and endeavors all require these things. When we succumb to apathy, we cease the application of these things, leading to failure and loss. Where have you failed to apply yourself when you should have done better? Do you learn from the mistakes of your apathy and apply yourself now?

**Appraise:** How we appraise the things around us is often influenced by our culture. Certain values are more highly prized than others, leading us to judge others. Some of these judgments are necessary; if someone is considered dishonest, an appraisal of their character would be subpar. However, others are superficial and based on appearance rather than the integrity of a person. How do we assign value and appraise things in everyday life? Are we aware of the values informing our appraisals, or do they remain unconscious to us? Do you try to avoid superficial appraisals?

**Apprehension:** This word has a positive and negative connotation. To be apprehensive is often wise, as it can prevent loss. However, opportunities are often missed as a result of apprehension, as we lack the courage to take a leap of faith. Try to find a way to balance these two sides of this word by analyzing a situation as best as you can before choosing action or inaction. What opportunities have you missed out on in life because you were too apprehensive to pursue them? What have you lost as a result of taking risks?

**Appreciate, Appreciative**: How often do we fail to appreciate what's been given to us?

Some take for granted their wealth in family members and friendships, while others spend all their time and energy appreciating money and feeding their greed. Gratitude for the things we have leads to a content life, and showing others that you appreciate them will bring them happiness. How can we shift our values in what we appreciate? Do you take the time to make your loved ones feel appreciated?

**Approval:** By informing others of their value or quality of their work, we give them our approval. For many, seeking approval is one of the most motivating factors in life, but living life solely to please others works to our detriment. We can be seen as sycophants by others, and disingenuous. Be careful in granting and seeking approval; too much of either puts your life out of balance. By constantly seeking the approval of others, are we ever not true to ourselves? What happens when we seek the approval of those in power? Do we end up reinforcing power structures that leave some disenfranchised?

**Aptitude:** Everyone possesses some kind of aptitude, whether it is for music, math, organization or art. But not everyone uses their aptitudes for the greater good. Additionally, many allow their talents to go to waste through lack of use. How can we use our strengths and aptitudes for the general benefit of others?

**Arbitrator, Arbitrate:** Arbitrators are always needed in times of conflict. The responsibility of an arbitrator is considerable, and one should always remain unbiased when mediating disputes. How are you able to act as an arbitrator in your day-to-day situations, such as conflicts among friends? Do you more actively try to resolve conflict as an arbiter, rather than taking sides?

**Ardent:** Many people are ardent about the values they hold, refusing to relinquish them even when they no longer make sense. But that is not to say it is always a <u>mistake</u> to hold strong ideals and <u>values</u> ardently. Do you hold your beliefs ardently, or allow yourself the room to question them as well? Is a belief that cannot be questioned <u>healthy</u>?

**Arduous**: Life's many tasks can be arduous. But that does not mean that they are insurmountable. The day-to-day can always grow tedious, but rather than shrink back from these <u>tasks</u>, we should pursue them with <u>perseverance</u>. Do you try overcome arduous tasks through concentration and <u>empathy</u>? Do you face <u>challenges</u> with diligence?

**Argue, Argument:** Many arguments spur from selfish reasons, and we often let <u>anger</u> get the better of us. Consider whether or not your argumentative approach to a <u>situation</u> is productive. While strong beliefs and opinions can lead to arguments, the better approach is to reach a place of mutual <u>understanding</u>. Do you try to see the perspectives of others when arguments arise? Do you argue to win, or do you try to engage in productive conversation? What causes are worth argument? Social inequality? Environmental abuse?

**Arrogance:** Some are arrogant enough to believe they know what's best for others, but are <u>blind</u> to their own arrogances. We've all had moments in our lives where we've considered ourselves superior—in <u>intelligence</u> or in <u>ability</u>—but those who hold this to be the case at all times make themselves unteachable. We can only <u>learn</u> from a position of <u>humility</u>. In what aspects of your own life are you arrogant, believing yourself to be more capable and successful than you

> *"Work is what you do for others . . . art is what you do for yourself."*
> — *Stephen Sondheim*

really are? Do you recognize these aspects in yourself and seek humility?

**Art:** Art offers a means of emotional and intellectual <u>expression</u> of the human condition. Elements of life are brought out through great works, showing us things that all humans have in common. Even beyond the masterworks, art as a <u>hobby</u> can be rewarding and therapeutic, giving us joy in the <u>act</u> of creating something entirely new. Do you take time to appreciate art in all its forms? Do you share the artistic interests you have with others? Do you make art of your own?

**Artificial**: Much in our present age is artificial, from our food, to our clothes, to even sometimes our bodies. This goes against the natural order of the world and leads to a shallow outlook as we become more obsessed with <u>vanity</u> and easy <u>consumption</u> rather than character and <u>environmental</u> <u>understanding</u>. Do you seek out things that are made naturally? Can you think of some ways your life would be improved by using these organic solutions?

**Ascend, Ascent:** To ascend we move upward, overcoming <u>obstacles</u> and transcending what tries to drag us down. This can happen personally, professionally, and even mentally. By reading these pages, you will hopefully gain a measure of ascension, answering <u>questions</u> and broadening your <u>perspective</u> on life. How can you ascend the obstacles in your life? What are some obstacles in your life? Should they be approached with careful thought, perseverance, counsel from others, or all of the above?

<u>Ascertain</u>: We are in a constant process of ascertainment—to seek out the definite <u>truth</u> of a given matter. But sometimes this process is difficult, with so many different sources telling us different things. What do you <u>listen</u> to when you're in the process of ascertaining what <u>choice</u> is right or wrong?

The media, the government, or your own conscience? Never ignore your own moral compass in these situations. If a choice seems immoral to you, falsehood is likely close behind.

**Ascetic:** An ascetic tries to live his life without the usual comforts and amenities, sometimes for religious reasons. Obviously, this lifestyle isn't for everyone, but there are lessons to be learned from this behavior. In our consumer-driven culture, we're constantly being told that we need things that we simply do not require. What do you think you could do without?

**Ascribe:** We often ascribe certain attributes to people without really thinking them through. This is at the heart of prejudice and racism and should be avoided. When people are judged, it should be based on their character and actions and nothing else. Have you ever misjudged someone, ascribing to them characteristics that they did not in fact possess? Why?

**Ashamed:** A sense of shame fills us when we do something wrong, even if we are not entirely sure what we have done. What is the purpose of this shame? We can allow it to direct us to make amends with those we have wronged, but dwelling on these sensations and letting them fester is never healthy. Do you seek to resolve feelings of shame? Do you try to make amends when you have wronged others?

**Ask:** In order to learn, you need to cultivate a healthy curiosity; with that comes a desire to seek answers. When we ask for things we expect answers, but this may require personal effort. At times there may be no one to answer our questions, leaving us with the weight of personal discovery on our shoulders. Regardless, we must continue seeking the truth. Do you ask questions in a constant effort to learn?

**Aspect**: When solving a problem, we must assess all aspects of it. The temptation to view things one-sidedly is ever present, but only creates more problems in the long run. What does it take to view all the different aspects of everyday situations in life? Do you attempt to view things from all sides, analyzing situations critically after enough information is known?

**Aspiration, Aspire, Aspiring**: Aspirations are dreams and hopes for what we hope to accomplish. These goals help keep us driven and may be separated into short-term and long-term goals. Don't be afraid to overreach in setting goals; the process of learning in the attempt is valuable in and of itself. What do hope for yourself? Are your aspirations selfish desires, or do they benefit others as well?

**Assert**: An unexamined assertion is worth little and can even be harmful to others. They can damage the characters of others or disenfranchise groups in our society. With this in mind, make sure that all of your assertions are based on careful examination. Have you ever asserted something you have no way of knowing? What foundations do most of our assertions rest on?

**Assimilate**: We often feel pressure to assimilate into our surroundings and become like everyone around us. There's comfort in this, but in many ways, comfort can breed laziness and apathy. Consider this before becoming part of a herd mentality, always keeping critical thought in the front of your mind. What value is there in individuality and being different? Is an unassimilated mind necessary to be able to think for yourself?

**Assist, Assistance, Assistant:** We begin life dependent on the assistance of others, but are quick to forget it once we no longer need that help. Do you strive to help others in your daily life? How have others assisted you? Consider how you can assist life in all forms, such as by helping an injured animal or watering a plant. These things may seem small, but the world would be better if more people did so. Additionally, if you need assistance, don't let pride get in the way of asking others for help. If you get help sooner, you can often avoid even greater hardship in the future. Do you let others help you when you need it? Do you recognize when you need assistance?

**Associate:** Who we associate with says a lot about who we are as individuals. If you keep the company of immoral people, others will judge you based on that before even getting to know you. While we must be accepting of the faults of others, don't let such associations hinder you in your life. What do your friends and associates say about you? What are their goals and values?

**Assume, Assumption:** Too often, we assume without knowing all the information affecting our decisions. With people, assumptions regarding character and personality are a form of judgment. Rather than making assumptions, it's better to ask questions and learn something of others before making assumptions; by doing so, character and expectations are made clear. Do you often make assumptions? Do you ask questions to ascertain the truth instead?

**Assurance, Assure:** Everyone longs for assurance in their lives—to be told that they are doing the right thing, with the right person, and generally good people. Do you provide people in your life with assurances in order to give them comfort? Conversely, when might it do more harm than good

to assure someone? Be mindful that the assurances you offer are genuine.

**Astute:** The astute reader of this book will begin to see how each word fits with the others, how every word is interconnected. Even if you don't consider yourself astute, you can develop this trait by constantly seeking to analyze situations as they present themselves. Without astute observation, it becomes difficult to make the right choices. Are you astute in your observations? Do you think your past choices could have been better through more careful analysis?

**Atone, Atonement:** What do we seek when we seek atonement? Is it forgiveness, absolution? Or is it selfish in origin—a desire to simply remove feelings of guilt and shame? Examine the selfish desires behind the wish for atonement, as they can often be as bad as the desires that caused the initial wrongdoing.

**Atrocious:** Atrocious things in life fill us with disgust. This often brings to mind horrific acts from history, but our modern culture of consumption is authoring its own atrocity against our planet in very quiet ways. Do you make every effort to prevent such atrocities? How do you respond to such acts? Do you try to help? Or does the news of atrocities a world away pass by with apathy?

**Attention:** What deserves our attention and what does not? Often our attention is at the mercy of the media forces that direct it, regardless of how fair or unfair that may be. After all, how can we pay attention to a certain calamity or event if no source has reported on it? Be wary of how news media affect your attention. Do you seek out news outside of the mainstream media?

**Attitude:** How does attitude affect perception? How does the way we feel about something or someone influence how we see them? When a negative attitude is taken, in a situation or to a person, we close off our mind to the possible truths offered by these things. Our attitude is the lens through which we see things, and adjusting this lens allows the multifaceted nature of interaction to come into focus. Conversely, what attitudinal picture (e.g., facial or body language) do we <u>present</u> to others? Attitude is everything; you can make your own <u>reality</u> by adjusting your attitude.

**Attract:** Some people have magnetic personalities, allowing them to effortlessly attract other people. However, our modern <u>society</u> encourages shallow attraction as opposed to meaningful <u>connections</u> between people. Are you more attracted to depth, or shallow vanity? Do you seek out meaningful connections with others?

**Attribute**: Attributes can be intrinsic <u>qualities</u>, or they can be ascribed to someone else. Can you tell the difference? Not everyone can. Think carefully before you <u>believe</u> what another says about someone's attributes; they may have <u>motives</u> beyond the <u>truth</u> that serve their own ends.

**Authoritative, Authority:** The abuse of authority is a great betrayal of <u>responsibility</u>. While an authoritative presence has many positive <u>associations,</u> the ramifications of its misuse can be staggering. Have you ever bowed down to an authority because you felt like you had to? Or conversely, where do you think authority figures might <u>influence</u> your life where you don't expect it? Do you speak out against insidious uses of authority or simply let them pass by?

**Autocracy:** An autocracy gives one person all the power, and the end result can only be disaster and unfairness. Without even distribution of power, the needs of one party will always be subjugated under those of the other. While this happens most obviously on a political scale, consider other places in which it occurs. Where do you see autocracies occurring on a smaller scale? In offices? In personal relationships?

**Avarice:** Avarice is an excess of <u>greed</u> too immense to <u>control</u>. This has saturated our <u>culture</u> completely, leading to <u>economic</u> crises that continue to plague our country. This is also making an impact to us on a personal level, as materialistic pursuits affect our <u>relationships</u>. Have you ever been guilty of avarice? Has avarice in any form ruled your life at certain points and exercised too much control?

**Avocation:** An avocation is something one does outside of their regular work. This can lead to greater <u>satisfaction</u> in life, as our hobbies may not reward us financially but offer a release from the rigors of our work week. If your current full-time job is unfulfilling, have you considered finding an avocation to <u>supplement</u>? What hobbies have you enjoyed in the past but ceased to do? It's always <u>wise</u> to have hobbies; with productive <u>leisure,</u> we can return to work with a renewed vigor.

**Avoid:** It is tempting to avoid difficult things in life. Only the mature and courageous among us can stop avoiding unpleasant things and <u>tasks,</u> but their <u>reward</u> is a more productive and less anxiety-ridden existence. Few people enjoy <u>confrontation</u>, but without it, <u>problems</u> will only fester and grow more difficult to surmount in the long run. Do you confront your problems? Additionally, there are things in life—bad <u>influences</u>, for example—that should be avoided. How do you identify that which should be avoided?

**Awake**: Many live their lives without ever truly being awake and fully cognizant of their <u>actions</u> and <u>circumstances</u>. This word is most often associated with rising from sleep, but what we're referring to is being awake figuratively. If we aren't awake in this sense, we can't scrutinize that which is around us, and our <u>decisions</u> will become less productive than they could be. Do you find yourself going through the motions more often than not? Has your routine bred <u>apathy</u> in your life?

**Aware:** You have to be <u>awake</u> to be aware, and self-awareness is the key to an <u>ethical</u> and happy life and one of the things that makes us human. Too easily, we find ourselves sucked into self-delusion and selfishness, without awareness of how truly small we are in the greater scheme. Do you differentiate between <u>observing</u> passively (seeing something, but without remembering it or registering any mindful significance) and <u>conscious</u> awareness (seeing something and automatically understanding the <u>reason</u> for its existence)? Being truly aware allows us to help others in a way that would be impossible if only focused on our respective plights or <u>pleasures</u>. How can you achieve a heightened awareness in your <u>life</u>? Where might your blind spots lie?

**Axiom:** Axioms are a <u>truth</u>; they need no <u>proof</u> to show their verity but are self-evident and uncontestable. These are the sorts of truths that the founders of our country based their decisions on—truths that had been ignored until that point in history. What axioms <u>dictate</u> your life? Are there universal truths you <u>ignore</u>, either through <u>ignorance</u> or avoidance? The changes brought on by accepting such truths can be difficult, but are in the end worth the effort.

# B

**Back:** Time does not flow in any direction but <u>forward</u> into the <u>future</u>. But our minds are not capable of seeing into the future. The only direction our minds are capable of seeing clearly is backward into the <u>past</u>. As we move forward, do we forget to look back or remember where we came from? When is looking back a journey of <u>learning</u>? When is it wise and worthwhile? When is it a crippling <u>nostalgia</u> that can do far more damage than good? What do you gain from focusing on the past? How might it force you to <u>neglect</u> the present? How do you learn from the past without letting your mistakes cause festering guilt? As we move forward, do we forget to look back or <u>remember</u> where we came from?

> *"Remembrance of things past is not necessarily the remembrance of things as they were."*
> — *Marcel Proust*

**Bad:** Subjectivity makes everything's <u>quality</u> unique to every one of us. How is labeling something as bad a rejection of patient consideration or an elimination of the desire to make it <u>good</u>? One person may find a musical genre to be bad, while another finds it to be good. When you consider quality, what is the thing itself (a song, a book, a table), and what are your <u>preconceptions</u> of it? Can you <u>respect</u> the tastes of others, even when they disagree with your own? Bad can also refer to the given moral qualities of an action. Is this subjective or objective? What parts of <u>morality</u>, if any, are <u>absolute</u>? What parts of morality are <u>relative</u>? Consider the full spectrum of moral implications related to a given action before assigning a moral value to it; sometimes the ends justify the means.

**Balance**: Look at the total picture. It is the balance of life forms, power, justice, emotions. An extremely important part of living life, balance suggests <u>middle</u> ground or a positioning directly over a fulcrum. Is balancing the act of finding a working <u>equilibrium</u> between multiple objects, acts, or facets of life over that fulcrum? The state of equilibrium is dependent on the placement and weight of the <u>extremes</u> and the <u>ordinary</u>. In our lives, one is consistently required to balance work, family, lovers, and learning, but what is the right proportion of each? One can balance based on where <u>focus</u> is lacking, where <u>expectations</u> are exceeded, or how we want to present ourselves to others. One can balance based on time or resources. What is the best balance for you? What do you balance in your life? The best balance for one person may not be the best for another. Is your life balanced, or does it teeter back and forth on its fulcrum? If your life seems uncontrollable, how might shifting the fulcrum on which your life rests bring you a level-headed sense of <u>peace</u>? How might removing the unbalanced factors be equally peaceful?

**Ban:** To ban something from one's life is to <u>reject</u> it entirely, to push it out of sight and hope it never comes back. But how much of banishment suggests a lack of <u>understanding</u>? Ideas and people are often banned because they are misunderstood or disagreed with.

When you ban something, is it out of anger, confusion, righteousness, or something else? Are there times when it is better to ban things from our lives rather than let them continue to cause us <u>harm</u>? Is it better to ban a problem from your life rather than resolve it? For example, if you are being physically or emotionally abused, that relationship needs to be cut out of your life. But how might it be difficult to ban such relationships even if you know they are unhealthy?

**Bank:** In today's world, <u>currency</u> tends to serve as a measure of <u>worth</u> for many people. It ebbs and flows between people, just as water flows to each house in a city. Banks serve as reservoirs, but our society needs its citizens to direct the water to those regions left parched in this <u>economic</u> climate. How much is a bank a reservoir of <u>wealth</u>? Is using a bank a way to store and safeguard your wealth? How does hoarding wealth leave our <u>society</u> worse off in the long run, if at all?

**Barbarian:** Many advanced groups in history (the Mongols, the Nazis) have been subjectively called barbaric. Those same people considered their murdered <u>victims</u> barbarians as well. It was less in a sense of violence and more describing their victims as <u>inferior</u> foreigners. What quality does the word barbarian actually address? How is the <u>accusation</u> of a person, or a people subjective? Barbaric acts can be committed by a single person or a <u>group</u>, but only their acts should be described as such, not their character.

**Barrier:** A barrier is an obstacle that prevents an outcome. We all have barriers in <u>life</u> that we have to <u>overcome</u>, no matter its stature. It is difficult to achieve, but everyone has the <u>capacity</u> of doing this. It requires <u>determination</u>, <u>will,</u> and due diligence, among others, to achieve your <u>goal</u> and overcome any <u>obstacles</u> that might be presented to you. Have you faced a difficult barrier before? How did you overcome it?

**Base:** Without a firm foundation on which to base our <u>actions</u>, the results will not be as successful. Bases exist in many areas,

ranging from the <u>moral</u> to scholastic. A firm moral compass guides us and serves as a base for our interactions with others, without which interactions in this world suffer. An <u>education</u> also provides a base or groundwork of knowledge upon which we build our <u>perception</u> of the world. Without this base, we are ignorant and clueless to the world around us. How do the bases in your life guide and <u>support</u> you? What have you built upon them?

**Battle:** Many things in life are worth fighting for, but time must be taken to carefully consider the value of such <u>action</u>. While the ramifications of a global <u>conflict</u> are obvious, the harvest reaped of personal disagreements gone awry can have an even deeper <u>influence</u> on your daily life. When do you consider it better to <u>fight</u>, as opposed to practicing <u>tolerance</u>? If we don't choose our battles carefully, we run the risk of coming across as critical and unpleasant. How do you choose your battles?

**Beaten:** Many people give up when they are unwilling to continue or are unable to continue for a lack of <u>will</u> or <u>ability</u>. The greatest among us are never beaten, but just take another path to their <u>goals</u>. When have you felt beaten? Is it by choice or by force? Where is the next path that will lead you to your goals? What could <u>perseverance</u> help you attain, even when the odds are against you?

**Beautiful, beauty:** When someone or something is beautiful, it is easy on the eyes; it's magnificent and elegant. When we look at the <u>world</u> around us, it is filled with <u>absolute</u> beauty in all walks of <u>life</u>. But just as much as beauty can be <u>praised</u> and glorified, it can just as easily be destroyed, seen in the assault of women, the destruction of our forests, and much more. Why do people feel the need to destroy the beauty that is around us? On the contrary, what attracts you to beauty?

**Be:** Not only does this fundamental verb of existence convey the present, but also the possibilities of the future. What do you want to be in life? Whatever it is, what is your motive? There are many motives one may have for their existence, such as the accumulation of wealth, the building of a family, or advancement and visibility within their community. Are your motives selfish? If they are, consider ways to broaden your goals to include helping others, balancing your own success with contributing to humanity.

**Begin:** Everything has a beginning and an end, even if we cannot see it. To begin something is to open a new path in life that has not been tread before. When you open that path, do you first survey the landscape, or do you simply begin hacking at the brush? Walking the full length of that path allows others to follow and experience what you may create or discover. How important is it to find a balance between spontaneity and planning as we commence something new? Finishing those things we start is a testament to our respective characters. How important is it to you to finish what you begin, and how do you begin it?

> *"The beginning is always today."*
> — *Mary Shelley*

**Behavior:** The nature of your being can be discovered through your actions. That is why your behavior is your appearance to the rest of the world. People often change their behavior to appear different to different people. While modeling your behavior on another person can bring you social acceptance, be mindful not to sacrifice the person that you are in order to simply please others. What is the value in the behaviors that come to you naturally? What is the value of behaviors that are modeled of others? What are the dangers of inherently destructive behaviors? How is your behavior indicative of who you are, who you would like to be, or who you want others to see you as? How might it be changed to be more indicative of who you are, who you would like to be, or who you want others to see you as?

**Being:** You can only be if you are conscious of yourself. This awareness separates us from animals and plants. We are conscious of our actions and the full spectrum of history and time. We are even relatively conscious of how we fit into such a vast spectrum. But with this awareness comes responsibility. We must recognize the effects of our being on others, and history. What is your effect on history, big or small? What is your effect on your environment? Who you are as an entity? Who will you be?

**Belief:** Belief is based in the realm of faith, often leaving it to stray from the safety of knowledge. However, many beliefs can be based on personal and relative facts. *What are your beliefs based on*? How do you support them? Beliefs are a powerful aspect of an individual's approach to the world. The consequences of this can be beneficial or a source of malevolence, so it is important to carefully examine your beliefs through the lens of their larger effect on society. How are you able to view your own beliefs? Rationally? *In what ways are you dogmatic and stubborn?* Do you believe in **the universal body of observation?**

**Belong, belonging:** To belong is to be a part of something, either through a group or property. It's not possible to fit in with every single group or organization in the world, but don't let that discourage you. Instead, belong to something where you feel the most comfortable and can greatly strive in with others who have your same interests and passions, which requires self-awareness. What groups do you belong to? Have you ever felt uncomfortable?

**Bend:** When you bend, you maneuver in a way that gives shape or force into a curve or angle. As the saying goes, "Bend, but don't break." This is a lot easier said than done because it's <u>convenient</u> to trade in the turmoil and <u>struggle</u> of the situation for something more <u>comfortable</u>. Still, it's an achievable act and one that will lend to a stronger sense of <u>discipline</u> and self-<u>worth</u> in the long run. Do you bend over backward for someone and get nothing in return? Do you strive to bend, but not break?

**Benefaction/benevolence:** Life is a two-way street. We often <u>take</u> things from others to help ourselves, but it is equally important to <u>give</u> back. There are countless places in modern <u>society</u> that could use our aid, not only financially but also the <u>service</u> of your time. This is part of the <u>responsibility</u> that comes from living in a society. If these things are not done by you, who will do them? How do you help others in your daily life? When do you go to great lengths to make others' lives better? Do you treat life as a one-way street where you are the only person on the road?

**Benefit:** When someone benefits from something, it is advantageous for them. Some, however, aren't able to realize the reasons as to why something is beneficial for them, or better yet, they stubbornly do not <u>acknowledge</u> it. Why is this? Have you ever found this to be true from your own perspective? Benefits come in all shapes and sizes, but it's up to you to <u>recognize</u> a benefit when it springs in your <u>life</u>.

**Benign:** To be benign is not necessarily to be inconsequential, but to not <u>harm</u> others. To live life without having negative <u>effects</u> on others can be difficult. It requires you to live by the golden rule and to consistently consider the <u>consequences</u> of your <u>actions</u>. This takes careful <u>consideration</u> of the possible outcomes of a given <u>choice</u> and many lack the <u>foresight</u> to <u>achieve</u> it. In many cases, it can be easier and more profitable to live a life of malice. How does your life refrain from harming others? How much effort are you willing to put forth to live such a life?

**Best:** The "best" is <u>subjective</u> according to everyone's <u>taste</u>. The best sports car, bottle of wine, or hiking spot will be different for everyone. Be sure to not think your own tastes are so superior that tastes aren't <u>relative</u>. How might something you consider to be the best be the <u>worst</u> to someone else? It can be alienating to others if their own preferences are consistently considered <u>inferior</u>. Still, <u>superior</u> work will always be admired and rewarded, and striving to be the best in the areas you consider most important is always a worthwhile endeavor. A person can strive to be the best at what they do by delivering results to their employer or <u>quality</u> to their customers. The ability to <u>achieve</u> the highest level of performance in a field can be difficult, as it is based on <u>talents</u> and <u>skills</u>. These qualities can never be possessed by all individuals in equal amounts. How do you strive to be the best? Are you satisfied in the work you produce, and do you consider yourself the best at your job? How might others be <u>better</u> than you?

**Better:** There will always be something better. But that does not mean you cannot improve. There's constantly room for <u>improvement</u> in our lives, in the <u>work</u> we do, in how much we <u>know</u>, in how we <u>interact</u> with others. Never consider yourself to be so perfect that nothing need be improved. Your life will become stagnant if you do. How do you try to improve yourself as a person? Do you more often feel content as you are? If that's the case, how do others view your contentment? But, in this quality being a relative description of superiority, make sure to consider why something is better before declaring finality. How can what makes something "better" to you seem <u>worse</u> or even completely irrelevant to someone else? How do you <u>accept</u> the <u>opinions</u> of others? Do you accept them readily? Even when they contradict your own?

**Bias:** Everything possesses some amount of opinion. This encyclopedia, news reports, religious texts, they all include bias. But when is bias bad, and when is it good? Bias might lead people to make uninformed decisions, but it also might help them understand and see from a new perspective. What, in your life, do you insert your bias into? How does it help inform others? How does it mislead them?

**Bible:** A source of <u>inspiration</u> and <u>security</u> for many people, this book holds stories, proverbs, and direct <u>advice</u> that some see as metaphorical and others interpret literally. Regardless of whether or not this book is an historical document or allegory, the <u>messages</u> themselves are powerful and resonate just as much today as when they were first penned. How do you interpret the Bible? Should the Bible be taken as a source of <u>truth,</u> or should it be used as a <u>guide</u> for interpreting life? Even if you do not consider the Bible an historical document, what can you gain from studying its messages? How might those messages be supplemented from other experiences or texts?

**Bigot:** A person can be incredibly stubborn in their misguided <u>beliefs</u>. Can you explain all of your beliefs <u>rationally</u>? Which beliefs can you not explain? As humans, we all automatically develop individual <u>traits</u> or <u>personalities</u> within the context of surrounding social norms. These beliefs may come from indoctrination as a child, or they may be rooted in bad <u>experiences</u> with certain groups, but they are never excusable.

Views held by a bigot are those which most often hinder <u>society</u>, halting <u>progress</u> and equality. If a person is obviously <u>wrong</u> in their perceptions, how can or can they be persuaded to change their views? Are you willing to change your views if new evidence is presented?

> "The year you were born marks only your entry into the world. Other years where you prove your worth, they are the ones worth celebrating."
> — *Jarod Kintz*

**Birth:** The <u>beginning</u> of life is generally considered a sacred and beautiful event. Birth carries on the legacy of <u>humanity,</u> and our <u>actions</u> in the present shape the future of subsequent generations. How can we make life better for those who are born now and in the future? But birth can refer to any beginning of anything. An <u>idea</u> is born of ingenuity. Our nation was born of ideologies. At the root of all these things is <u>creation</u>. What do you create in your day-to-day <u>life</u>, and what will you leave behind? This needn't be anything as grand as a country, but try to let your actions leave a good reputation as your legacy. Your <u>character</u> is your first child.

**Birthright:** A claim to <u>privilege</u> based on the situation of one's birth, from a plot of land to a throne and crown. Does anyone really have a birthright? If all men are created <u>equal,</u> then should not life be the only birthright for all? Do not let the situation granted to an individual by their birth impress you. Instead, examine their <u>character</u> and <u>actions</u>. Further, consider your own position. What have you been given as a result of your birth that others have not? <u>Status</u>, <u>money,</u> or privilege? Be careful to not feel <u>entitled</u> to such things, as though you <u>earned</u> them. They are merely things into which you were born. While he was referring to the racial inequality of his day, if we are to take the words of Dr. Martin Luther King to heart, we must judge people, including ourselves, based on the content of one's character.

**Black:** This opposite of <u>white</u> is characterized by <u>darkness</u> in color or in mood. What in your life is black? What connotations does this color have for you? Are they <u>positive</u> or <u>negative</u>?

**Blame:** Scapegoats are often used for <u>problems</u>, even if the true <u>cause</u> is more distributed. Blame provides an outlet for the frustrations of a person or group in a given situation, but it doesn't provide an opportunity to solve the problem at hand. Does someone always need to be blamed for missteps? When can blame be placed on a <u>group</u> versus a person, and when should it be ignored? Very dark chapters in our history have come to pass as a result of a group being made into scapegoats, most notably the Holocaust. Consider such historical events before blaming others needlessly. Furthermore, punishment must be equally considered when blaming. When <u>crimes</u> are committed in our society, and individuals are found <u>guilty</u>, their fault must be punished. Consider how this relates to your personal life. Our legal system has established fitting punishments for the possible crimes in our country. What is your approach to punishment in your personal life? When others wrong you, how do you forgive? Or is your <u>anger</u> unbridled regardless of the perceived infraction? Should you be looking at yourself first?

**Blaspheme:** To blaspheme is to <u>insult</u> something larger than yourself, but the only apparent result is the reaction of believers. When is blasphemy simply a personal insult to believers, rather than to <u>belief</u>? How does blasphemy from an atheist differ from that of a zealot? One should always <u>respect</u> the beliefs of others. They hold to them because they value them greatly. By making blasphemous statements to such believers, they become alienated, and the entire situation becomes one of <u>conflict</u>.

**Bless, Blessing:** Blessings are often thought of in a purely religious context, but that is not always so. A household can be blessed with prosperity. A state can be blessed with peace, and a society blessed with kindness. In what ways are you blessed? Have you received <u>advantages</u> in life that others have not? If so, how can you leverage these to improve the world as a whole? Oftentimes, we think more of the things we don't have than the things we do. We are blessed in various ways—we have <u>friends</u>, we have <u>health</u>, we have financial <u>security</u>. Even if you don't have any of those things, there are undoubtedly many things in your life to be <u>grateful</u> for.

**Blind:** To be blind is not to have vision. While some have the unfortunate formality of being clinically blind, others are still dealt with blindness in their everyday life, stemming from <u>love</u> to <u>happiness</u> and everything in between. Don't let outside factors blind you from the <u>beauty</u> of the <u>world</u> and all of its intrinsic features. What blinds your life? Have you addressed this blindness or have you unfortunately had to succumb to it?

**Blood:** Literally, blood is the fluid circulated by the <u>heart</u> through the body carrying oxygen and nutrients. Without blood, we could not physically survive. But the word blood means much more than this. For many, the word "blood" means <u>family</u>. You are a descendant of you ancestors' "bloodline." We don't choose our "blood family," but these ties are unbreakable. Do you find <u>comfort</u> in the fact that there are others in this world to which you are bound by the same blood? To many, blood symbolizes the exact opposite of this blood bond though. There is a reason that many people faint when they see blood; it triggers something in our mind that makes us imagine <u>pain</u> and <u>danger</u>. If you get shot, you bleed. If you cut your hand, you bleed. If you lose enough blood, you die. Why do some people relate the word blood to family but others to pain and <u>death</u>? What do you think of when you hear the word "blood?" Are there any personal experiences that you imagine when you hear this word? What are they? How do your life experiences affect your perception of blood?

**Boast:** Accomplishments bring some of the greatest satisfaction in life. When we work toward a goal and achieve them, the reward evidences our efforts. However, arrogantly proclaiming your accomplishments to others for the sole purpose of impressing them is off-putting and alienating. How does boasting further your goals in life? Can you have achievements worth boasting about? Should you bother to do so?

**Body:** The body is composed of many different components: spiritual, physical, mental and emotional, among others. Since we only live once, it's important to take care of your health. This takes willpower and initiative, but the dividends you'll reap from your effort will be years added to your life. Do you treat your body as an object or as yourself? Is it something to be preserved and nourished, or to be used recklessly? On the other hand, a body can also describe the body of work or the legacy of an individual. What is the body of work you've added to the world? What deeds will you be remembered by?

**Bond:** A bond is a connection that ties us to places, people, and things. Whether we realize it or not, we bond ourselves to our world every day through conversation, employment, and residency. Be cautious of bonds which claim depth, but are in reality one-sided. In any relationship, depth can only be offered by true reciprocity. Do you make

bonds of worth, or bonds of appearance? Bonds of worth and bonds of appearance both often create a feeling of security. But many times, bonds can be captivating and imprisoning. How do your bonds offer you security? How do they confine you?

> *"A room without books is like a body without a soul."*
> — *Cicero*

**Book:** These compilations of thoughts, ideas, and emotions are becoming obsolete with the onset of technological development. What aspects of books are timeless and irreplaceable? How important are they to your life? What can we continue to gain from a physical text, a tactile manifestation of thought existing in a moment of time? What can we gain from simply consigning these works to the convenience of mere data?

**Boundaries:** It is important to maintain boundaries with others. Boundaries keep us from invading one another's privacy. They are an important part of relationships. But when is it important to dissolve boundaries in a relationship to give way to a deeper connection? When is it important to establish boundaries in a relationship? How do the boundaries that you create aid you? How do your boundaries hinder you?

**Boycott:** To refuse services or goods from a person can be an effective way of getting what you want. It can also be an effective way of asserting political desire as a group. Under what circumstances do you or would you boycott? When is boycotting an unnecessary act? If a problem exists and has been identified, can a solution be found by simply not being a part of the problem?

**Brain:** The control center of your body, your brain regulates everything that takes place in your body on a daily basis. Many tasks are handled without conscious thought on our part. We breathe, we blink, and our hearts continue to beat involuntarily. How much does your brain do that you don't realize? How much of its functioning do you take for granted? Are you caring for it properly? Your brain allows you to read this sentence, and it is allowing you to interpret this <u>book</u>. Some brains are capable of mathematics in multiple dimensions or memorizing all of the names of every star. Some brains are capable of <u>imagining</u> new worlds for a storybook or a painting. What is your brain capable of? Are you <u>aware</u> of its full <u>potential</u>? How can you improve its abilities and functioning? How can you improve its <u>creativity</u>? *Can the brain be thought of as the center of the <u>universe</u>?*

For another perspective on this subject, look at *Brain Change* by Dr. David Perlmutter.

**Break:** While some societal constraints and injustices should often be broken for the improvement of a <u>culture</u>, there are other things that should be protected from such an <u>event</u>. Careful consideration of the impact of massive <u>change</u> should be considered before approaching the concept of rejection, either on a social level or within the context of our personal lives. When have you broken a rule? What was the result? Do you regret it? How might it be considered a breakthrough?

**Breath:** Contemplate or meditate on the <u>act</u> of breathing. You likely take the automation of this act for granted. What else comes naturally to you despite its complexity? How might others have to exert themselves to <u>accomplish</u> it?

**Brief:** Brevity is the soul of <u>wit</u>. But how brief is it important to be? Should thoroughness be forsaken for briefness?

When can the two walk hand in hand? When does one trump the other? In your dealings with others, strive to be <u>concise</u> and <u>informative</u> rather than falling victim to circumlocution.

**Brother:** We have brothers in our <u>families</u>, but we also <u>choose</u> them as we live our lives. How do you choose your brothers? Reflect on the brothers in your life. Who have you chosen as a brother? Who was given to you as a brother? Does it matter whether a brother is given or chosen? How do you treat them differently from one another? Sometimes the <u>bonds</u> formed with those we meet are stronger than those formed

by familial ties, but do not neglect the importance of family.

**Brutality:** One needn't commit an <u>act</u> of <u>violence</u> to be brutal. Our <u>words</u> and actions can convey brutality toward others, giving the conveyor an aura of <u>cruelty</u>. These words can be just as violent as an act of brutality. When is brutality warranted, if ever? Can one be brutal and <u>fair</u> simultaneously?

**Build:** Our lives revolve around building. We build careers and <u>families</u>. We build our understanding of the universe. We build <u>relationships</u>. But building rarely comes easily and requires just as much <u>maintenance</u> as it does construction. A structure that is not properly maintained will eventually fall and need rebuilding. How much of yourself do you <u>commit</u> to construction? How much of yourself do you commit to maintenance? What are you striving to build in your life right now? What from the <u>past</u> are you trying to maintain?

**Bureaucracy:** The modern <u>government</u> is generally defined by a vast <u>network</u> of bureaus, or departments, each reserved to a different function. It is the epitome of what one would consider the diversification of labor. But what does bureaucracy <u>accomplish</u>? Are the jobs created by a large bureaucracy worth the inefficiency that comes with it? When should you look for shortcuts in a system, and when should you advocate following <u>rules</u> to the letter?

**Business:** Governing the affairs of commerce, business has become one of the most powerful forces in the world. With this power comes the responsibility to act morally. But how is this even possible when the entity of business is founded on greed? To view another aspect of this word, consider what is and what is not your business on a personal level. *Do you associate the activities and processes of living with running a business? Are you aware of what is your business? Do you get upset when others do not take an interest in your business?* How often do you tread into the business of others? When is it acceptable to infringe on others' business? What education is necessary to operate a business? Have you learned the difference between a job and a business?

# Circle
## of *Life*

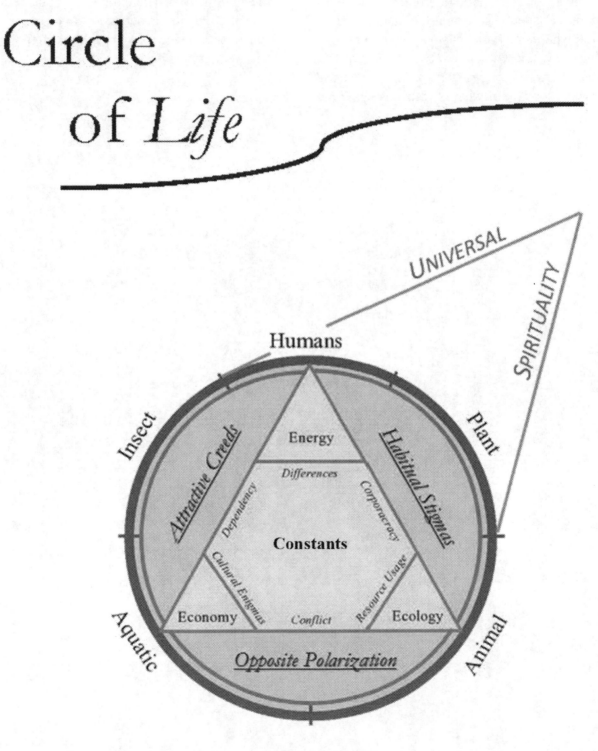

# C

**Calculate:** From the most personal of relationships to anonymous, large business and government endeavors, many harmful <u>decisions</u> are made because those involved are ill-informed. Not taking the time to calculate the possible <u>outcomes</u> can lead to poor decisions. Use all available <u>resources</u> to understand as much as possible about a given decision before making it, and do so with reason and rational <u>estimation</u>. How might the abundance of detail complicate decision making? How might it make it easier? Ultimately, the goal of calculation is to obtain the most accurate conclusion possible. What is your <u>capacity</u> for discerning what the <u>consequences</u> of your actions are and will be? How often do you use that capacity to calculate?

**Callous:** In a literal sense, this word means the formation of skin into a <u>hardened</u> layer <u>as</u> a result of repeated wear and tear. The figurative use of this word arises directly from this literal definition and means the hardening of <u>emotions</u> because of continuous hardship or <u>desensitization</u>. What makes a person desensitized to the emotions of others? What makes someone sensitized to the emotions of others? Those who are callous toward the feelings and needs of others lack <u>empathy</u> and <u>compassion</u>, two elements that are integral to living a fulfilling and positive life. To successfully interact with others, we must at least attempt to

> *"People give pain, are callous and insensitive, empty and cruel...but place heals the hurt, soothes the outrage, fills the terrible vacuum that these human beings make."*
> *— Eudora Welty*

see things from the point of view of those with whom we interact, even if it is vastly different from our own. How much are you desensitized to the plights of others? How compassionate are your for others?

**Cancer:** Too much of anything is a bad thing. Our bodies are filled with <u>cells,</u> but when some begin to take more than their share of the body, it <u>deteriorates</u>. These abnormal cells in the body grow unchecked, eventually negating the body's ability to function. What in your life spreads rapidly and destroys? What can you do to <u>mitigate</u> or avoid this <u>damage</u> all together? When is it okay to <u>control</u> the things in your life that have the potential to take that life? When do you let them run their course? Cancer is an illness, a <u>disease</u> which carries with it a different emotional stigma depending on whether you are the bearer or the observer. How might you be able to <u>clarify</u> emotions such as <u>fear</u> or <u>compassion</u> in conjunction with cancer? *Do you live in <u>fear</u> of it?*

**Capable:** To be capable of something can simply mean <u>being able</u> to do it, but we also use the word to indicate the <u>status</u> of being able to do something particularly well. What things do you find yourself capable of doing? Do you feel that some capabilities are <u>innate</u>—that we are born with—or that some are <u>learned</u>? What kinds of things would you like to be capable of? Do you have a plan for how you could become capable of <u>performing</u> them?

**Capacity:** The <u>ability</u> to <u>learn</u>, <u>become</u>, or <u>be</u> any given thing is an amazing quality of human life. We have the capacity to do so much. Consider the capacity of those among you. Municipal judges act as corporate police enforcers and have the capacity to settle disputes. Doctors save and better lives through medical intervention. Consider the capacity of certain past humans. Einstein had almost no functional schooling, but he devised most of the theories for modern physics that still shape our world today. What is the limit to the human capacity? Consider your own capacities. What are you capable of doing? How much more are you capable of? With the capacity or ability to do something also comes the <u>responsibility</u> of doing it. How do you use your capacities responsibly?

**Care:** The <u>attention</u> and <u>concern</u> that <u>humans</u> show is, in many ways, integral to humans' social interactions. How do you care for yourself? How do you care for others? When do you watch out for dangerous situations that are not of a <u>physical</u> nature? When do you predict future problems and solve them, even if they are not your own? Care is equally an <u>emotion</u> that humans have for other non-living things, such as emotions, ideas, places, and objects. What things do you care about most in life? This is a word that can be used in many ways and demands a lot of thought, especially in conjunction with <u>awareness</u>. It is important to be aware of your surroundings, both physical and emotional. Like a vigilant hiker walks effortlessly through treacherous woods, a little bit of tact will take you a long way in life. But most notably, what is really important to you? What do you care about? How do you structure your life around the things and people that you care about? How do you justify those <u>priorities</u> by which you live your life?

**Career:** A <u>job</u> is any <u>task</u> that one performs for <u>money</u> or other <u>gain</u>; a career is the work one chooses to <u>devote</u> one's <u>life</u> to. It can also, when used as a verb, mean to move violently and erratically. Do you see any kind of connection between these words? Is it possible that they are opposites? Do you feel that you have a career or simply a job? How did you, or would you, choose a career? Can something for which one is not paid still be a career?

**Caste:** It is important to acknowledge the <u>systems</u> of <u>social</u> <u>status</u> dictating both <u>inclusion</u> to and <u>exclusion</u> from certain <u>groups</u>. These groups can be strict, or they can be flexible. They can be dominating, or they can be subtle. Many times they include tiers that create a system of <u>hierarchy</u> and therefore dictate which castes are more significant than others. Which <u>divisions</u> serve a practical purpose and which were created to cause dissonance in social capital favoring one group over another? Where do you fit in within these divisions? How do you traverse the boundaries of different castes? It is important to think critically about what exactly makes someone a part of a certain group. How did they decide to be a part of the group? Did or do they have a choice?

**Cartel:** Commonly associated with the sale and control of drugs, the word cartel is actually rooted in the realm of business. It is a group of companies that join together with the purpose of maintaining <u>control</u> over the price of a product by controlling the entire means of <u>production</u>. This places an enormous amount of <u>power</u> in a small amount of hands. Unchecked and in the wrong hands, <u>organization</u> on this scale can be used to bend the legislation and <u>economy</u> of our country to the <u>selfish</u> will of just a few people at the expense of the rest of the population. How can you recognize when a small group is making self-serving decisions affecting a large amount of people? How can the concentration of power be avoided?

**Casual:** There are times for both <u>formality</u> and <u>informality</u>, and we must be receptive and tactful when deciding which to employ. But in general, life is happenstance. Why do we seek to control so much of it? Similarly, the physical world is not planned, but rather a series of perfect circumstances. How do you take the time to relax and exist as a casual being? How are you flexible when it comes to planning? How can you let chance and circumstance play a larger role in your life?

**Casualty:** Like those who are harmed or killed in an accident or a conflict, we often find ourselves victims of the actions of others in our lives, either through their deliberate actions or accidentally. It is important to internalize these experiences so as to avoid hurting others through your own externalities both intentional and unintentional. How have you learned from the times you've found yourself to be a victim? How did this make you think differently about your own actions? How has this made you change your actions so that they do not cause others to become casualties? How can you prepare yourself for being a casualty?

**Casuistry:** Some people are capable of bending and weaving words in order to placate naysayers and get what they want duplicitously. They use sly, yet faulty reasoning to prove an argument of morality. We should all be wary of those who can spin webs with such creativity. How can you readily identify the motives of those you interact with? How often do you think critically about arguments you are presented with? How often do you accept arguments without question? Are you honest and upfront in your own interactions and arguments?

**Cataclysm:** Large-scale, violent events can occur on both sociopolitical and natural landscapes with equivalent ferocity. Their frequency and intensity is most always unpredictable, but we can always make an effort to be prepared. How prepared are you for a cataclysmic event? What can you do to mitigate a catastrophe before it is too late? How can you recognize which activities are

environmentally and socially unsustainable and prevent future catastrophe? How can you change your actions after a cataclysm in order to avoid repetition of a catastrophe?

**Category:** A category is one way we divide the world into different groups so that we can more easily understand it. Do you find that categories are always beneficial, or can they have negative effects on both us and the way we treat those around us? To what categories would you say you find yourself falling into? How many of them were chosen by you, and how many of them were chosen for you?

**Cause:** Every event is preceded by something or a series of things without which it would not have occurred. These precursors are not always visible until after the event, but once they are learned and studied, they are usually used as good predictors of future events. How do you predict the future using the knowledge you have about causes? How often are your predictions accurate? When a person brings about an action or result they can also be seen as one of the proximal causes of it. Bearing this in mind, how aware are you of what you cause to exist, to change, or to be reborn? It is important to be able to gauge the degree of one's influence on the cause and effect spectrum and ascertain whether that influence registers in a positive or negative way. You must be able to realize when it is necessary to take responsibility for your actions even if you are not entirely or at all deserving of blame.

**Caution:** We must take care not to make mistakes that could lead to harmful consequences. The decision to throw caution to the wind or to proceed with discretion and care depends on your awareness of a situation; you cannot employ the right amount of caution without a coherent understanding of your surroundings, both physically and interpersonally. Do you know when to use caution? Where is the line between recklessness and necessary caution?

Where is the line between necessary caution and debilitating fear?

**Censor:** Sometimes censored ideas and sentiments shed more light on a given situation than those which are propagated. Censorship is a powerful tool, and the fact that something is censored inherently means that someone powerful enough to censor it has motivation to stifle it, whether secretly or blatantly. When someone's voice is silenced before they can express themselves, how important is it to determine who is censoring them and why? Is it right to censor them if they are wrong? When is it permissible to censor what is correct? As a society we censor what our children see on the television, the internet, and in everyday life. But how might they learn from a world without censorship? How might they be better in a world that is censored?

**Censure:** It is important to know when blame is due, but equally important to know when it is not. Offering blame where it is not warranted can ruin a relationship. How often do you make sure that you have the complete picture of a given situation before you censure others? How do you hold others accountable for their actions? How needlessly censorious are you, or are you overly forgiving of others?

**Center:** We all have priorities weighing on our lives in different ways. When these priorities are harmonious and aligned with respect to one another, life reaches a state of equilibrium. Conceptualize priorities as revolving around a center. Obligations pull you in some directions, and life's pleasures in others. Your path in life is where these

> *"There is more than one way to burn a book. And the world is full of people running about with lit matches."*
> — Ray Bradbury

> *"Chaos is the score upon which reality is written."*
> — Henry Miller

obligations and pleasures meet. As you act on your established priorities, you dictate where and what the center of your life is and what you spend the most time doing or thinking about. What is the center of your life? For some, that center is balanced. For others, it is skewed toward oppressive obligation or self-fulfillment. What qualities does your center have? Is it obligatory? Is it pleasurable? How do you keep it from consuming you?

**Central, Centralize:** When many things are brought under the control of one entity, they have the potential to be run more smoothly and uniformly. This is the key concept in systems such as dictatorships. However, when the original entity is corrupt, this umbrella of power can be harmful. Dictators, when they are not benevolent, generally terrorize their subjects and force them to live in fear. Centralization puts a large amount of power in one place, so we must be wary of whose hands in which we are concentrating this power. How do you diffuse the centralization of power? How much power do you hold yourself? How often do you give your power away in order to mitigate the effects of centralization?

**Ceremony:** A large event marking a tradition or benchmark in life, generally with an underlying symbolic or religious meaning. Often ceremonies serve to bring generations closer and to make us feel like a part of a meaningful group. What ceremonies have defined the progression of your life? What traditional purpose did they serve? Can you separate the latent symbolic meaning of a ceremony from its literal and overt manifestation? Do you understand the significance of the ceremonies in which you participate?

**Challenge:** The sore feeling in your muscles as a result of <u>exercise</u> is evidence that you have challenged yourself. You have used your muscles to the point of tearing them and now they will rebuild themselves <u>stronger</u> than they were before. Whether physical or mental, challenges help us <u>grow</u>; the <u>difficulty</u> of a <u>task</u> becomes fuel for the future in the form of knowledge, practice, and strength when we are able to <u>overcome</u> it and <u>persevere</u> despite the <u>opposition</u>. When was the last time you left your comfort zone to challenge yourself? What did you learn from that challenge? How did you change in the process? In challenging others, you are helping them to grow and change as well. How often do you challenge others? Do you provide them with the skepticism that allows them to be fully challenged by conflicting ideas?

**Chance:** Many aspects of life are out of our <u>control</u>. Life is <u>random</u> and <u>chaotic</u>. But we can improve our chances of success by anticipating possible outcomes and taking steps to improve our chances for success. How can you recognize <u>opportunity</u> for what it is? How can you <u>seize</u> it when it presents itself? What is it that you can control, what is it that you cannot? When is it okay to act without knowing the full extent of the outcome?

**Change:** Change is <u>omnipresent</u> in our lives. You cannot stop it from happening, and you must accept its power. What in your life is currently changing? What is staying the <u>same</u>? How do these changes and 'non-changes' influence your life as a whole? How do you <u>adapt</u> to these changes? We must think diligently about what we have the <u>agency</u> to change and what falls outside of our <u>influence</u>. Once you realize that you cannot change everything, you must <u>accept</u> this fact and change only what you can. What are the things in your life that you cannot change? What are the things you can change? How do you change them? Accept those things that do not and cannot be changed. To begrudge them and their place in life is to foster <u>stress</u>.

**Chaos:** As life can seem hopelessly out of <u>control</u>, it is important for us to find <u>order</u> where we can, and accept the state of chaos where we cannot. How do you actively accept chaos? Do you fight it rigorously, or do you allow it to overwhelm you with constant <u>change</u>? When things get so chaotic, do your best to <u>prepare</u> for everything. Yet, chaos is not always the opposite of order and rigidity. It is sometimes important to find the majesty in what seems to be chaos. Even the most hopelessly <u>random</u>-looking things yield to <u>patterns</u> and order on some levels. When did you last discover a pattern among chaos?

**Character:** The character of a person dictates their <u>actions</u>. Their looks and their <u>appearances</u> are trivial when analyzing the <u>moral</u> nature of one another.

Therefore, we should always <u>judge</u> others by the <u>content</u> of their character above all else. What is your character? What do you really want it to be? What <u>criteria</u> do you use to define your character? How does your criteria change when you are examining the character of others versus your own?

**Charitable:** Charity has the connotation of being one-sided, but those who are charitable <u>gain</u> a lot, too. When you <u>give</u> for the sake of giving, you will find that you take away many <u>intangible</u> things that you didn't count on. How often are you charitable? How often is being charitable hard? What do you gain from being charitable? <u>Friendship</u>? <u>Trust</u>? More charity? How do these things make charity more than just a simple monetary <u>donation</u>?

> *"I would prefer even to fail with honor than to win by cheating."*
> — *Sophocles*

**Charm:** To <u>please</u>, <u>delight</u>, <u>attract</u>, or <u>fascinate</u> can be a useful skill when used as a <u>social</u> lubricant or <u>buffer</u> in facilitating <u>interactions</u>. It can be used to win friends and to succeed at interviews. How do you use your charm? How are you successful in charming others? There is a fine line between charming to achieve an end and to <u>manipulate</u> maliciously. Be wary of those who are <u>superficially</u> charming and ill-intentioned. What are your intentions for charming someone? Are they good or bad? When have you been the victim of someone who was ill-intentioned and charming? How might it be disenchanting to find out the truth about having been charmed?

**Chauvinism:** While the word is generally associated with the idea of male dominance and gendered hierarchies, there are a myriad of different <u>groups</u> and profiles with which we can choose to <u>align</u> ourselves. These groups and profiles can be broader or even more defined than gender. What we must take note of is when our <u>attachment</u> to a group is <u>fanatical</u> or undue. It is important to take a step back and <u>examine</u> the <u>tenets</u> set forth by any group of which we choose to be a part. Many of the most heinous acts in history have been performed behind a <u>veil</u> of <u>fear</u> tactics, resulting in disproportionate support for an undeserving movement. What groups and profiles do you identify with? Is your attachment to this group or profile fanatical, based on fear, or irrational? What are your reasons for being part of this group? How can you recognize when it is time to detach yourself from a group due to its chauvinistic tendencies?

**Cheat:** Ill-gotten <u>gains</u> are not gains at all. They are the empty product of a <u>deceit</u>. To fully gain something is to <u>learn</u> from it. One gains from a book by learning a lesson or fact. One gains from another human by learning to trust, love, or befriend. One does not learn these things from cheating. How often do you <u>earn</u> and <u>obtain</u> <u>honestly</u> and <u>fairly</u>? How often do you earn and obtain with deceit? What did you learn from using honesty and fairness? What did you learn from using deceit?

**Check:** To check something is to <u>investigate</u> it and <u>assure</u> oneself that it is how one believed it to be, but it can also mean to stop or slow something. Do you see a <u>connection</u> between these definitions? Does one have to slow down in order to thoroughly <u>understand</u> its nature? Is there anything or anyone you feel so <u>confident</u> about that you feel no need to check it? How do you feel when you yourself are investigated by another person?

**Cheerful:** Being cheerful helps maintain a <u>positive</u> mental <u>attitude</u>. Studies have also shown that even <u>smiling</u> when unhappy will eventually cause your brain to excrete chemicals to make you <u>happy</u>. By acting cheerful when you are feeling despondent or unhappy, you could propel yourself out of a rut. How do you act cheerfully to fight off the blues? Cheerfulness is contagious; it has the potential to turn a close friend, coworker, or even complete stranger's day around. Do you make an effort to be cheerful and <u>pleasant</u>? How might cheerfulness lead to long-lasting happiness?

**Cherish:** The things we hold <u>dearly</u> in our lives make it <u>worth</u> living. Mimetic desire describes the phenomenon that occurs when we <u>want</u> things simply because other people want them. However, when we cherish something, it comes directly from our own <u>heart</u>, unadulterated by the <u>priorities</u> of others and fueled only by the aligning of a mutual <u>appreciation</u> in others. What in your life do you cherish? How do your priorities align with these things? What

> *"No one has ever become poor by giving."*
> — *Anne Frank,*
> Diary of Anne Frank

can you do to maximize your time spent with the things you hold dearest?

**Chicanery:** Unfortunately, we must be wary of the possibility of trickery in any form. Always make sure you understand what you are being told before you take action. Those who are the most practiced in deceit are clever; we must be aware of their methods. How can you recognize the ugly face of deceit? How can you think critically and patiently instead of being swept into a frenzy by confusing rhetoric and suggestion?

**Chief:** This person of utmost importance is the leader of a given organization, clan, or country. There is the chief of a tribe, the commander-in-chief, the Chief Executive, the Chief Justice, or of chief importance. A chief must be trustworthy and conscientious to maintain the steadfast voluntary support of their followers. Who are the chiefs in your life? How did they get there? How do they treat you as a subject? Do they deserve to be there? What are their intentions? Most importantly, how might you be a chief?

**Child, Childhood:** When we are children, we yearn to be older, have responsibility, and be wiser. When we are older, we yearn to be young and go back to the place that is marked by a sense of wonder and fascination combined with sensitivity and vulnerability. How have you changed for the better since your childhood? How have you changed for the worse? Never lose your child-like curiosity with the world, even when you grow older, and broaden your horizons while toughening your skin. How do you readily use new information to better understand the world? How do you avoid being more sensitive than necessary while using your accumulated body of knowledge to solve the conflicts in your life?

**Choice, Choose:** Your choices create the reality of your life, but the choices of others create reality, too. Before we were born, the choices of your mother affect your future health. As we speak and for all eternity, choices drive the reality in which we and all other things exist. But since we are imperfect, we may not always choose correctly. Sometimes there isn't even a correct choice. The consequences of incorrect choice will shape our reality for the worse, but the consequences of correct choice shape it for the better. How can one know whether or not a choice is correct or incorrect? By observing the impact of results? Try applying this idea of correct and incorrect to a decision you have to make. You will find that most decisions have choices that are both correct and incorrect. You may even find that most decisions have infinitely more choices than two. How do you best decide which decision is best for you? Do you fortify your choices with information and knowledge? Do you choose with your gut? When is it important to act on a whim and choose without thinking? When it is important to take your time with choices? Lastly, how do your choices affect things around you, the people, the places, and the ideas? How do your choices affect you? There is generally no way of knowing the definitive outcome of a choice. How do you you cope with your wrong choices accept wrong choices? How do and the wrong choices of others?

**Christian, Christianity:** Christianity is a religion based on the teachings, beliefs, and practices of God in three persons (the Father, the Son, and the Holy Spirit). Christianity is the world's most widespread religion and heavily relies on the Bible to guide people through their triumphs and challenges. What other writings can guide you through the rocky road of religious beliefs? Do you consider yourself a Christian or follower of Christianity? What beliefs and teachings do you adhere to?

> *"Two roads diverged in a wood, and I – I took the one less traveled by, and that has made all the difference."*
> — *Robert Frost*

**Chronic:** When something is <u>persistent</u> and <u>unrelenting</u>, it becomes a factor that needs to be dealt with. Chronic <u>problems</u> are the most <u>difficult</u> because they are the hardest to remove. Their <u>repetitive</u> nature and frustrating determination will eventually turn into <u>permanence</u>. What chronic problems are present in your life? How can you <u>mitigate</u> or eliminate these problems? How can you keep them from becoming a permanent facet of your life?

<u>Circle</u>: The circle is a <u>natural</u> <u>shape</u> and <u>cycle</u> that is characterized by <u>infinity</u> or no <u>end</u> or <u>beginning</u>. For example, nature is a circle. Death begets life and life begets death. There is no beginning and there is no end. This is the case for many aspects of life. Any series that is <u>repeated</u> over and over and ends the way it began. Even a <u>group</u> of people who share the same interest is a circle. What facets of your life take after this shape? What facets of your life have no beginning and no end? It is comforting to think of time as a cycle that repeats itself. What can we learn from observing past life cycles or cycles within our lives and applying it to the present?

**Circumspect:** We must be sure to <u>consider</u> all sides of an issue before taking action. It is important to <u>think</u> critically about all the <u>information</u> presented to us in order to make a <u>prudent</u> decision. Do you <u>explore</u> all sides of an issue before taking <u>decisive</u> action? Are you thorough in your search for answers even when they may not be the ones you are looking for? Nonetheless, remember to always be careful about your wary and cautious ways. Risks are an important facet of life, and quite often they are rewarding. When does circumspection become excessive <u>cynicism</u>?

**Circumstance:** Circumstances rule people; people do not rule circumstances. They <u>shape</u> and <u>mold</u> the <u>reality</u> in which a person exists and consequently mold the person as well. We can, however, do our best to <u>plan</u> ahead to improve our circumstances. Or, we can make the best of bad circumstances when it is not possible to avoid them. How often do you look to the <u>future</u> when you approach life, taking into account the <u>possibility</u> of malfunction? How does this affect your future circumstances? Recognize that people are a product of their <u>environment</u>. Your circumstances are different from those around you, and the circumstances in which other people find themselves can tell you a lot about why they are who they are. How do your circumstances differ from those of other people you are close to?

**Citizen:** We all have a certain <u>responsibility</u> to our <u>country</u>, which goes hand in hand with the <u>rights</u> we are afforded. These responsibilities are fiscal, moral, and demanding. They range from paying taxes and following traffic <u>laws</u> to challenging immoral laws and the domination of smaller social groups. What is your <u>social</u> <u>contract</u> with your country? How do you fulfill that social contract? What would you like to change about it? How do you react when you feel as if your rights a citizen are in jeopardy?

**Civic:** Before we can know how to act within the <u>framework</u> of a <u>community</u>, we must understand the community itself and how it relates to us. What is your relation to your <u>government</u> and your <u>country</u>? How are you doing your part to ensure that the <u>system</u> remains <u>sustainable</u> and <u>productive</u>? Has the government always held up its end of the bargain? What is your role in <u>society</u>? How do you perceive it and how are you told to perceive it?

**Civilization:** Civilization can have a fairly neutral meaning. When we talk about a <u>group's</u> civilization, we're indicating the <u>sum</u> total of its <u>thoughts</u>, <u>writings</u>, <u>culture</u>, and <u>actions</u>. But it has also historically been used judgmentally—that civilization, where people live, is preferable to the natural world, where they do not. It's also sometimes used to indicate that one group, described as civilized, is better than another one, which is described as barbaric. How do you feel these different kinds of meanings feed in to one another? Do you find one or more of them problematic? Which one do you prefer to use, and do you think about the other ones when you do so? Is civilization something one chooses to contribute to, or does everyone who lives with other people do so necessarily, whether they intend to or not?

**Claim:** A claim is a statement one makes of either belief or ownership, whether true or false. What kinds of claims of ownership

do you make over things in your own life, and why do you feel they are justified? Have you ever claimed that something is true—or false—only to later find out that the opposite is the case? How do you form judgments about the kinds of things you claim?

**Clan:** Whether the bond is common ancestry, heritage, interests, or goals, clans represent organized groups of people who choose to separate themselves in some way from the greater population. How do you separate an individual from the clan in which they claim membership? What clans are you a member of? How do these clans shape who you are? How do they separate you from others or other clans?

**Clarify:** Clear communication is the cornerstone of good interpersonal relationships. When you make your intentions and expectations as clear as possible, and act with integrity, misunderstandings are minimized and relationships flourish. How do you strive for clarity in your relationships? How often do you succeed? Do you ask for clarification when you are unsure about something? Many people also use lack of clarity as a tool to deceive and muddle their intentions, passing them off as acceptable. How can you recognize when someone is being purposefully unclear? When do you use clarity as an undignified tool?

**Clarity:** Always make an effort to achieve a state of mental clarity before you make important decisions in life. This mental state is one that includes C - common sense and awareness, L - logic, A - analysis, R - reason, I - integrity and information, T - truth, and a general Y - yearning. How can you achieve this state of clarity? What obstacles must you overcome to do so?

at many different levels. How do you concentrate on living your life in a way that is absent of evil and wrongdoing? What aspects of your life have become tainted? How can you clean them?

**Clear:** To be clear can mean to be colorless, transparent, or easily understood; it can also indicate the action of removing debris or anything else that obscures our vision or use. What do all these senses of the word have to do with feeling that our minds are clear? Do you attempt to be clear when you communicate with others? How does it affect our lives when things are unclear?

**Clean:** To be clean is to be free of what is unwanted. The unwanted can by physical, such as dirt, blemishes, or flecks. But doing things that make us feel guilty can be figuratively unclean. This carries a variety of meanings

C... Conscious Awareness of Common Sense
L... Logic
A... Analytical Analysis
R... Reason
I... Intellectual Integrity/Factual Information
T... Truth
Y... Yearning Desire

**Clemency:** We must embrace critical and rational thinking in every aspect of our lives, especially the judgment of others. We must always acquire as much information as we can about a situation before we make a judgment, offering mercy when it is possible and condemnation when it is necessary. How do you practice proper judgment? When is it proper to forgive and practice clemency rather than brutality? How might one be more effective than the other? How might one be more moral than the other?

**Coalition:** We often define ourselves by the role we play in a larger group. Life forms have always coalesced into larger groups forming ecosystems, symbiotic organizations of hundreds, sometimes thousands, of species which depend on one another for survival. As a species, humans can decide to either coalesce for what is right, or stand alone and let others do so for morally starved reasons. What groups do you claim membership in? How does your personal moral compass align with the goals of each group?

**Code:** Ideally, society and individuals would both have perfect moral codes and none of the systems trying to hold people to this standard would be necessary. Unfortunately, our moral codes are attacked each day. Think critically about your codes and their relation to the codes of others and society as a whole. What is your personal set of rules, or code, for living life? How do these rules coincide or coexist with societal codes? How do you defend your code effectively? Has your code arisen from rationality or propaganda?

**Coerce:** It is certainly a benchmark in life to realize that you alone are responsible for your own actions. Though most adults recognize their agency in decisions they make, they are susceptible to a host of morally questionable outside forces. When does someone's desire for you to do something conflict with or become irrelevant to your personal views? How might you be susceptible to guilt or chicanery as a means of goading you into doing things against your will? How do you use these practices on others?

**Cognizance:** Before any decisive action can be taken, we must be aware of the situation in which we find ourselves. Becoming informed about a decision is the first step in the often arduous process of making the right choice. An increased amount of knowledge about a given situation or decision can only help; as we learn more we gain perspective and can more easily see the problem from all sides. How much information do you seek before making decisions? How does that information influence your decisions? How can you improve your general awareness of your surroundings?

**Coincidence, Coincide:** There is no law governing our universe stating that life's problems have to come at convenient times. Often, two or more things happen at the same time and their separate inconveniences are compounded, leaving us to wonder how so many things could go wrong at once. Life has many moving parts, and sometimes these parts collide and wreak havoc upon you for no reason at all. How do you govern your life? Do you rely on coincidence or do you purposefully orchestrate events so that they coincide to benefit you? How might one solution be better than the other? We cannot always control the events that most deeply affect our life, but it does help to realize what is under our control and what is not. What in your life can be changed by our individual agency and what cannot?

**Cold:** A word with many shades of meaning, it could mean very literally the opposite of warm; more figuratively, it can mean emotionally shut off, and as a noun, it could

> *"Alone we can do so little; together we can do so much."*
> *— Helen Keller*

refer to a minor <u>sickness</u>. What does the word cold mean to you? How does that meaning affect your perception of and how you live your life? How cold are you?

**<u>Collaboration</u>, <u>Collaborative</u>:** Few people have had <u>successful</u> lives exclusively due to their own <u>merit</u>. The notion of <u>teamwork</u> has the potential to pervade every stage of our lives from learning how to share and play well with <u>others</u>, to working within <u>groups</u> of people, to make a wage and sustain your lifestyle. The best type of collaboration is that which arises from a <u>collective</u> <u>goal</u>, one that takes into account the needs and concerns of everyone involved. How have you succeeded with the help of others? What did you accomplish? How might it be more rewarding than succeeding alone? We must <u>simultaneously</u> be aware of those who collude for personal gains at the expense of others, as this kind of collaboration is parasitic. What is the difference between beneficial collaboration and morally starved collusion? Why is it important to learn everything you can about the moving parts of a situation before you collaborate with an <u>organization</u> or individual?

**Color:** Our <u>senses</u> provide us with <u>tools</u> to interact with the world; we must all embrace and take <u>pleasure</u> in the color of life. Color, though its chief connotation is a visual effect dictated by the size of wavelengths, is used to describe liveliness, <u>diversity</u> and <u>vibrancy</u> <u>experienced</u> by all of the senses. Colorlessness describes a <u>dull</u> state <u>devoid</u> of any flare or <u>interest</u>. Sometimes we must make extra effort to maintain the colors and <u>variety</u> that make our lives worth living and to stave off the colorlessness that threatens to oppress and kill <u>inspiration</u>. Where and when is your life colorful? How does that color make you feel? What can you do to add color where your life is colorless?

**Combat:** There will always be things in our lives which we <u>oppose</u> and <u>struggle</u> against. As intelligent creatures, we have the <u>responsibility</u> to determine if these things are worth <u>conflict</u>. The phrase "choose your <u>battles</u>" speaks to this point, but it is almost more important to know your battles. What do you combat in your life? How do you go about understanding all the sides of these conflicts? How might they be solved through <u>collaboration</u> rather than combat? What is a good <u>cause</u> for combat? What is a cause bred of a combative nature?

> *"The world is a tragedy to those who feel, but a comedy to those who think."*
> — *Horace Walpole*

**Comedy:** Comedy not only represents a suspension of reality in favor of <u>entertainment</u>, but also in favor of <u>circumspective</u> thinking, <u>reasoning</u>, and critical thinking about social <u>lore</u>. It has the ability to remove us from our present situation, affording us an entirely new vantage point. <u>Satire</u> and parody poke <u>fun</u> at things that have been normalized in our society. By forcing us out of our <u>comfort</u> zone, comedy allows us to think critically about the <u>dogmatic</u> values that our <u>society</u> holds so dearly. What is the comedic potential in criticism? How do you take this criticism and societal reflection seriously when it comes in the form of comedy? How can you apply this criticism and reflection to your person? By laughing at yourself? <u>Laughter</u> has the power to <u>release</u> <u>tension</u>, break awkward silences, and bring people together by allowing us to let go of emotional and societal restraints that dictate the majority of our lives. When do you use comedy in your life? How do you let laughter and comedy better your life?

**Comfort:** Comfort is <u>relative</u>; what some may consider comfortable living conditions, others would describe as <u>foul</u> and unlivable. We must not take our comforts for granted, and avoid false comforts that merely cause us to procrastinate. When times are especially hard, false comforts frequently make themselves known, and real comforts prove their validity. What do you consider a real comfort in your life? What do you consider a false comfort? How does the faulty logic and purposeful blindness of empty, false comforts manifest themselves? When do you offer comfort? Do you offer it when appropriate or necessary?

**Command:** The subjugation of one over another requires dominance. A command differs from a request in that it negates the possibility of free will in its recipient; the commander, in a general sense, inherently assumes that there is no chance that the command will not be carried out. In this sense, a command dehumanizes its recipient because it discounts their ability to reason for themselves. How do you react to commands? Do you blindly follow them, or do you think critically about their consequences and the motivations of those giving them? How do you react to reasonable commands? What commands do you give to others? Are they reasonable, or are they dominating?

**Commemorate:** If we do not make an effort to figure out why things have gone wrong in the past, there isn't much hope for fixing similar problems in the future. On the other hand, commemorating those who have done outstanding good in one way or another highlights what has been done right in the past, allowing us to see what kind of behavior warrants repeating. How do you strive to understand what public figures are being commemorated for? How do you unveil obvious symbols and pageantry to discern the real lessons that should be taken from past behavior? What have you been commemorated for?

**Comment:** Often, feedback is necessary for growth. Feedback in the form of comments can be both positive and negative. They can outline faults or successes. When expressing your opinion, be tactful and mindful of those you address and what point you are trying to get across. What is the nature of your comment? Is it necessary, redundant, or combative? Comments should always be given with the goal of improvement in mind, never with the goal of insult. When do you feel comfortable with what you say or how you say it? At what times do you have to think before you speak?

**Commerce:** Our civilization burgeoned from the foundation of purchasing and selling of goods and services, especially trade between cities, states, or countries. New demand in new parts of the world and opportunistic suppliers eventually gave rise to the globalized economy today. At this point, everything is influenced by commerce, the exchange of goods and services, no matter how distant the transaction seems. How does commerce play a role in your life? How connected are you to the system of trade? When does the system become overbearing in your life? How can you prevent it from being so? In what ways does money motivate your decisions?

**Commiserate:** Even if you do not see eye to eye with someone, try to imagine how they feel, how their beliefs and sentiments lead them to react to things. To commiserate with someone is to see past all differences that do not directly relate to their misfortune and recognize that they are feeling low, regardless of justification. The right thing to do is offer untainted support and sympathy for their feelings. How often do you put yourself in the shoes of those around you? How do you understand feelings and emotions from the perspective of others? How do you show sympathy and support when your peers need it?

**Commit, Commitment:** We all make commitments of varying significance and scope; marriage is a commitment, as is an agreement between friends to meet at a specific time. The strength and responsibility wielded by a commitment that you make is dictated by the people involved and the nature of the arrangement. Abandoning commitment is always frowned upon, but some transgressions are more forgivable than others. What or who are you committed to in your life? How do you honor the commitments that you make? Perhaps you avoid responsibility. What was the last commitment you abandoned? What was the consequence? Were you forgiven?

**Common:** Noticing petty differences only yields conflict. Concentrating on commonalities rather than differences will always benefit you when dealing with difficult or awkward situations. When you take the time to really listen to others, temporarily suspending the bias of your own sentiments, you gain invaluable perspective on the inner workings of others and yourself. How often do you seek out commonality before contention? How does recognizing what you have in common with others make you feel more connected? How do differences make you feel disconnected? What is the importance of having common ideas, traits, emotions, etc. among all humans? *Do you perceive equality with consensus?*

**Communication:** It is important to make yourself clear when expressing your ideas to others. However, the key to communication is listening and thinking critically about the statements of your peers. Proper communication, through listening as well as articulating, prevents problems from arising from miscommunication which would otherwise be surmountable. Though your ideas may be clear in your mind, you must be patient with others as they try to understand what you are saying. How articulate are you? How versed are you in the art of listening? How might you improve both skills? How well do you communicate with those who are different from yourself?

**Community:** We seek refuge and understanding with those who we have the most in common. Communities are based around anything involving the interests of more than one person, but vary in their scope and involvement of members. They can be based on race, ethnicity, sexuality, gender, interest, hobbies, geography, talents, and an infinite number of more defining features. You may belong to many communities or just a few. What communities do you belong to? What are the criteria for exclusion? What are the sentiments of the community in which you claim membership? Where do you draw the line between reasonably exclusive communities and unnecessarily or maliciously exclusive communities?

> *"We have two ears and one mouth so that we can listen twice as much as we speak."*
> — *Epictetus*

We fulfill this connection in the form of communities and groups, but also through companionship. We strive to have broad connections with many people, but it is also important to have deep, intensely emotional connections with a few people or one person in particular. With whom do you choose to spend your time? What makes the people you spend time with your companions? A true companion will stick with you through thick and thin, whether obstacles are intangible or physical in nature. How do you make these invaluable bonds last?

**Compare, Comparison:** To compare is to examine two or more things and judge their similarities, differences, advantages, and drawbacks. Do you find yourself comparing yourself to others? If so, do you find that is a helpful exercise or one that makes you insecure or ashamed? How can you

**Companion:** As social creatures, humans have a strong need to feel connected to others.

41

judge whether you are being fair in the comparisons you make or whether your actions are being compared fairly against another's?

**Compassion:** Understanding the suffering of another is only one part of compassion. The trait equally suggests a desire to alleviate the suffering of others, as much as it suggests sympathy. How strong is your desire to alleviate the suffering of people you know? How strong is your desire to alleviate the suffering of people you don't know at all?

**Compensation:** No matter how you observe it, compensation is payment for something rendered and is usually associated with products or services derived from energy. It is necessary to observe compensation in terms of an exchange between a dispenser and a receiver. This exchange generally restores the relationship to an equilibrium. For example, an internship is compensated with knowledge. A crime is compensated with justice. How do you find equivalency in compensation? How does compensation better your relationships? How does it better your own character?

**Competence:** We all have talents that are the product of practice and determination. Some people can ride unicycles, and others can swim the English Channel. What are your competences? How do they help you excel in daily life? Sometimes it is hard to forgive people for ineptitudes, but we must remember to judge not solely on ability but also on effort and intention. Not everyone shares your competencies. How do you embrace the ineptitudes of others? How do you work to make your own ineptitudes into competencies?

**Competition:** As human society has progressed and become more civilized, the competition is much more convoluted. Competition breeds unwanted feelings of inferiority and resentment, and should be reserved for things that truly matter. When is it appropriate to foster competition? When is it appropriate to avoid competition? A healthy sense of competition can push us to do things we previously thought impossible of ourselves and build bonds forged by respect and collaboration. But it can also create conflict and create unnecessary rifts. What are wars if not competitions of national might? How has competition helped you grow with your achievements? How has it helped you create bonds and collaborate? How has it caused conflict and rifts between you and others?

**Compile:** The objective of compilations is more than just to stockpile information or objects. Instead, the purpose is to be able to assemble all of the necessary parts of a whole in order to view the bigger picture. For example, this encyclopedia is a compilation of observations about life, organized alphabetically, and designed to be intuitive and therefore as helpful as possible to its readers. As a whole, this encyclopedia holds the ability to provide its readers with the questions and self-reflection needed to form a broader understanding of their own life. This kind of organization can seem like a daunting task, but you will find that the resulting understanding is significantly more comprehensive. When do you take the time to compile information or objects in order to see the bigger picture? How does this bigger picture help play a role in your understanding of the topic?

**Complacent:** A state of complacency is ours to enjoy after a long journey or series of accomplishments and is not to be confused with apathy. Nevertheless, a state of complacency generally implies a veil of unawareness and naiveté. How does complacency make you ignorant of your surroundings?

**Complain:** There are better uses of your time than complaining about a given grievance in your life. Be proactive and positive in your environment. Don't waste time enumerating its shortcomings. How do you seek to ameliorate your situation before you complain about it? How often do you push your qualms with life aside to enjoy the positive things? Does this bring a much stronger sense of happiness than complaining?

**Complaisant:** If you are too eager to please, you lose a part of yourself in favor of the satisfaction of others. But refusing to make an effort to please anyone but yourself creates distance between yourself and the rest of the world. It is important to find a middle ground between these two extremes.

How often do you do things to please others? To what extent are your actions based on your own moral code? To what extent are they based on the future approval of others?

**Complementary:** To be complementary is not necessarily to be two halves of a whole, but to emphasize the strengths and successes of another. For example, it is true that combining complementary colors of light will create white light. But the primary quality of their each being complementary to the other is that they each emphasize the brilliance of the other color. What or who complements your strengths? Whose strengths do you accentuate? What is the importance of having complementary people and ideas in your life?

**Complete:** Something that is complete has been made whole; there is no need to further add to or revise it. Do you feel that one's life can ever be complete, or is there always something that can be further accomplished or performed? What kinds of things are you most proud of completing? How can you tell when something is complete?

> *"Constant complaint is the poorest sort of pay for all the comforts we enjoy."*
> — *Benjamin Franklin*

**Complex:** Complexity can be both beautiful and frustrating. It can be the intricacy of the natural, biological world, so complex that it brings many to tears. But it can also be the barrier between a problem and its solution. What do you consider complex? What makes complexity beautiful to you? What makes it frustrating? Our lives are full of complexities and connections; all we have to do is look for these kindred entities in order to gain a greater understanding of life. How do you make sense of things that are complex?

**Compliance:** Sometimes a demand for compliance is reasonable and sometimes it impedes upon your individual agency and rights as a human. It is important to recognize who administers orders, their qualifications, and their intentions. When it is important to scrutinize commands before following them? When is it important to mindlessly and blindly comply? How strictly do you adhere to your own ideas of when it is important to scrutinize and when it is important to comply?

**Complicate:** Not everything in life is as cut and dried as we would like it to be; things can get pretty messy and complicated. Though many of the complicating aspects of life are out of our control, some complications are preventable. We must make an effort to alleviate complication by communicating and accept the complexity of that which we cannot simplify. How do you needlessly complicate your life? How do you complicate the lives of others? In what way could you make it all simpler?

**Complicity:** An accomplice to a crime is generally as guilty as the criminal. When found in such a situation, it is always important to impede the immoral act. It is important to surround yourself with people who do not subject you to such a situation and thus possess a strong <u>moral</u> compass. Who are the moral individuals with whom you surround yourself? Who are the immoral individuals? When confronted with the <u>opportunity</u> to be an accomplice, what do you do?

**Compliment:** Sometimes a compliment is all someone needs to feel whole. No matter how obvious a <u>positive</u> quality may seem, your <u>recognition</u> of it will <u>reinforce</u> <u>confidence</u> not only of the person in themselves, but also the mutual <u>bond</u> you share. In what way do you let others know that you <u>appreciate</u> their qualities? Which of your own qualities are appreciated? Compliments can also be a danger, leading to arrogance and an excess of confidence. Don't mistake compliments as a reassurance of <u>superiority</u>. Their intention is only to reinforce the good in individuals. How <u>arrogant</u> are you? How do you interpret the compliments of others?

**Comport:** Before we can think critically about our own <u>behavior</u>, it is necessary to take a closer look at the <u>motives</u> of individuals and <u>society</u> as a whole. Who makes the rules for behavior? What makes you behave and act as you do? If you think critically about how you behave in the world, you will be free from <u>forces</u> of all types that wish to make you behave in a certain way for <u>selfish</u> goals. What are your own goals? How do you comport yourself in order to achieve them?

**Compose:** Take a step back and analyze the <u>composition</u> of both your own <u>psyche</u> and your <u>priorities</u> in life. What are you composed of? What is your life composed of? The composition of our lives ideally creates a <u>balance</u> between obligation and pleasure, charity and indulgence and work and play. When any of these balances are <u>skewed</u>,

*"Compromise is a word found only in the vocabulary of those who have no will to fight."*
— *St. Josemaria Escriva*

the result is stress, anxiety and cognitive dissonance. What do these balances look like in your life? How do you keep them balanced?

**Composure:** A composed and <u>calm</u> <u>mind</u> maintains a <u>balanced</u> and <u>rewarding</u> life. An <u>anxious</u> and scattered mind maintains a life of <u>stress</u>. How do you maintain composure in life, especially in stressful situations? In extremely stressful situations, the natural response is to escalate your body and brain's respective stress levels to those of the situation. However, by taking a deep <u>breath</u> and a step back from the situation, you are able to obtain a <u>rational</u> <u>perspective</u> that will aid you in making the most prudent decision. How does this rational perspective help you overcome a stressful situation?

**Comprehension:** The act of <u>understanding</u> is not always an easy feat; it is an impressive power that varies among people. How good are you at comprehending the intentions, actions, or words of others? Make an effort to <u>listen</u> carefully to all the <u>facts</u> and then <u>think</u> about them <u>critically</u> in order to gain the most coherent understanding of a given situation. How often do you make sure things are <u>clear</u> before moving on?

**Compromise:** <u>Conflict</u> can sometimes seem unavoidable in our lives but, intellectual or physical, combat doesn't solve problems. Conversely, compromise results in a <u>solution</u> often bred by critical <u>thinking</u> and <u>listening</u>. It is not until we have the <u>capacity</u> to learn from one another that we can put our own needs aside in order to see the world through the <u>lens</u> of our <u>opponents</u> or <u>naysayers</u>. When you are presented with a conflict, how willing are you to <u>sacrifice</u> something in order to achieve a solution? How ready are you to present a compromise?

**Compulsion:** We all have certain <u>responsibilities</u> and <u>obligations</u> that vary in their degree of compulsiveness. In the context of your life, recognize who creates and enforces these <u>pressures</u>. Which compulsions are absolutely <u>necessary</u> for you to live happily? Which compulsions are unnecessary and <u>imposed</u> by outside forces? Which compulsions come from within your own subconscious? How can you control or mitigate those <u>impulses</u>?

**Compunction:** Before you let yourself feel <u>guilty</u> or <u>sad</u> about something you have done, you must take care to <u>discern</u> how much <u>culpability</u> is actually yours. Guilt that is imposed by societal <u>morals</u> is not a guilt that is always warranted. How much <u>control</u> do you have over the situation? What are the other factors compounding upon your issue? What can you do to fix the situation now instead of <u>wallowing</u> in guilt?

**Concede:** Sometimes <u>admitting</u> that we are <u>wrong</u> can be difficult, and the longer we have <u>contended</u> the opposite of the <u>truth</u>, the harder it is. To concede any point shows preference for <u>critical</u> and <u>rational</u> thought over <u>pride</u>. By looking <u>objectively</u> at facts, we can attempt to separate those who simply do not like to be wrong from those whose arguments possess <u>merit</u>. How do you employ reason and critical thinking to arrive at your opinions? When you are proven wrong, what do you do? Do you swallow your pride?

**Conceit:** You will never hear someone describe someone as conceited with an affectionate tone. An overconcentration on and overinflated <u>opinion</u> of oneself is both <u>unattractive</u> and counterproductive. A certain amount of <u>confidence</u> gives people faith in you, but <u>modesty</u> shows people that you can <u>relate</u> to others and are conscientious and <u>aware</u> of their needs. What do you do to express your self-confidence? How could this be interpreted as conceited? Perhaps you do

not have a lot of self-confidence. How might you become more confident?

**Conceive:** When we <u>think</u> of anything, we are conceiving it. That which is possible to think of is conceivable. With a toolbox of critical thinking skills and a <u>discerning</u> outlook at the world, the sky is the limit for what we can <u>mentally</u> conceive. Never lose your <u>curiosity</u> about the world around you. How do you <u>challenge</u> your brain with new <u>ideas</u>? How do these challenges improve your overall brain function?

**Concentrate:** In a society obsessed with <u>immediacy,</u> our <u>capacity</u> to concentrate suffers. Multitasking is a useful skill, but it has become a way of life for us. Separate activities and decide which are worthy your full <u>attention</u>. Concentrating on <u>one</u> thing at a time instead of a myriad of different things allows us to <u>accomplish</u> that one thing more effectively. A concentration of human effort can yield truly incredible results. What is worthy of your concentration and full attention? What is not worthy? How does your concentration of energy reflect their merit of attention and effort? Be <u>wary</u>, however, of concentrations of <u>power</u>; they are <u>capable</u> of accomplishing great things. Any powerful organization should be scrutinized carefully and held accountable for all its actions. How do you recognize a concentration of power? How are they detrimental?

**Concept:** Complex, abstract ideas comprise much smaller <u>arguments</u> and <u>facts</u> called concepts. <u>Understanding</u> these smaller portions of a whole is the key to being able to <u>scrutinize</u> concepts effectively. What are the different ways you break down a concept into smaller, more digestible parts? How many parts of a concept do you need to understand before you draw <u>conclusions</u>?

**Conception:** Though human life is an incredible thing, the conception of a significant <u>idea</u>

is even more impressive because, unlike a human being, it can exist and propagate forever. What kinds of ideas exist for forever? What kinds of ideas exist for only fleeting moments? How do these ideas differ? How do they differ in their conception? What ideas have you conceived?

**Concern:** When we show concern about something, we are showing that we care about it and that we have a stake in its well-being, or an investment of ourselves in an entity outside of our body. When showing concern for people, make sure you are tactful and do not convey a disproportionate lack of faith in their abilities. How do you show concern for others? At what point does this concern consume you? How is it unhealthy to be consumed by concern? One can also have concern for much broader goals and concepts. For global issues like climate change, showing concern raises awareness and alerts others to the issue. There is no time to waste being tactful with the environment. Be forceful and vocal. How do you show concern for these kinds of broad issues? How do you share that concern with others to incite a more unified, universal effort?

**Concerted:** Collaboration and teamwork are important skills to develop even if you prefer working alone. When we put aside our differences and unite around a common goal, it is amazing what we can achieve. Concerted, human interaction and achievement is always greater than the sum of its parts. What was the last project that you partook in? How did the orchestration of all of the collaborating parts bring about a well-rounded, final product?

**Concession:** When trying to reach an accord by compromise, it is often necessary to

accept certain concessions. No one can have it all. Sacrifice is an integral part of life, whether the issue is life altering or relatively inconsequential. But do not offer concessions that are not earned or warranted. Concessions should always be reciprocal as part of a compromise. How can you discern which concessions are reasonable to make and which are exploitative? How do you accept compromise as a solution when it does not give you everything you want?

**Conciliate:** One will always benefit from being as friendly as possible with everyone they meet. One will always gain approval through friendly acts. How do you greet all those you meet? How do you treat those acquaintances who you do not seek to befriend? What are your moral justifications for getting into the good graces of others?

**Concise:** Something concise is short, to the point, and without redundant or unnecessary words. Do you consider concision a virtue? Is it always a positive, or are there times when more elaborate, poetic language is a benefit, instead? Do you feel that you are concise in your own speech and writing?

**Conclusion:** We must ensure that when we reach a final conclusion, it is as a result of critical thinking and rationality. Jumping to conclusions is easy when we are continuously faced with sensationalized information, but it is important to realize that some people stand to benefit from your mistakes. How quickly do you jump to conclusions? To what extent is it better to examine every piece of evidence before determining a final conclusion? If a conclusion is truly valid, it should be able to withstand a thorough factual examination. Those who ask questions should arrive at the same conclusion. Be wary of those who shy away from questions regarding their claims and conclusions. How do your conclusions

> *"It is better to risk saving a guilty person than to condemn an innocent one."*
> — *Voltaire, Zadig*

stand up to careful examination? How convincing are they?

**Condemn:** Because of the nature of what it means to define something as immoral, the act of condemning something is inherently polarizing and definitive. It is not something to be taken lightly. For this reason, we must take care to not take it for granted. Before you condemn something, try to make an argument for condoning it or for defining it as moral. If you can make any sort of argument for doing so, reexamine your grounds for condemning it. How much thought do you give the act of condemning? How well do you scrutinize your own condemnations? Think of something that someone once condemned that you thought was condonable. How did this dispute end?

**Condition:** Allow yourself to be conditioned to certain norms, morals, and habits. But do not forget the process by which you were conditioned. Recognition of this fact is invaluable; it allows us to relate to others no matter how different they are. It also allows us to determine the motives and intentions of the conditioner. How might your outlook on life and lifestyle be a product of conditioning? What or who is the conditioner that brought you this outlook? How do their intentions influence your conditioning? How can you change that conditioning to reflect your own intentions?

**Condone:** To condone an act is not explicitly speaking in favor of it, but it might as well be. Before you condone an action or sentiment, make sure you have explored the facts and morality surrounding it. What makes an act condonable? What is your argument for condoning things? How does this argument differ from the argument for condemning things? When might you condone something that someone else condemns?

**Conduce:** It is important to understand what in circumstances in your life are favorable to certain outcomes. Try to establish cause and effect relationships between your lifestyle and the way you feel on a daily basis. Which behaviors are conducive to feeling your best? How are these behaviors conducive to a healthy and productive life?

**Conduct:** The way you conduct yourself says a lot about you as a person. You must overtly recognize this by taking responsibility for your conduct. How do you act? What influences these actions? How are they perceived by others? How do you perceive them? How might your actions be improved? Arguably, more important than the way that you conduct yourself is the way that you conduct others. The way that you lead others will make or break you in the eyes of your peers. How do you conduct others? How do they view the way that you conduct them? What makes a good leader?

**Confession:** Though sometimes it takes a lot of courage, it is important to be truthful to yourself and those around you. We are all allowed to keep our personal lives personal, but when we are drawing conclusions and making decisions which affect others, it is important to put all of our cards on the table. How does truthfulness beget informed decisions? What examples of this can you think of? Finally, remember that a confession is not to be taken lightly. When someone confesses to you, their secrets are to be guarded and kept, not to be dispersed and ridiculed. How do you treat the confessions of others? When have you, if ever, divulged someone's secret? What were the repercussions?

**Confidant:** Trust is an extremely important part of relationships. Whether it be a family member, a best friend, or even a pet, a confidant is someone with whom we can share the burdens of our life without the fear of undue or unfair judgment or criticism.

They are someone who will help you with your biggest worries and woes. Who can you confide in? Why have you chosen them as a confidant? How do they reciprocate?

**Confidence:** You do not have to be good at everything to have confidence nor do you have to be the best at one thing. Having confidence is only about believing that you are capable of whatever you put your mind to. It is more akin to perseverance and determination than talent. For what reasons do you exude confidence? How does your self-confidence reflect your abilities? How does this confidence affect the way other people perceive you? How much confidence do others have in you? The amount of confidence that you have in yourself directly affects the amount of confidence that others have in you. But you can also have confidence in things, ideas, places, as well as people. In what do you have confidence? Have you ever been disappointed by what you have confidence in?

**Confidential:** Trust is an extremely important part of any relationship. We must be aware of which exchanges are private and confidential, and which are okay to share. Before accepting the burden of a secret, make sure you are well aware of the situation surrounding it and the implications of keeping the information yourself. How do

you evaluate the confidentiality of secrets? How trustworthy are your friends with your secrets? How trustworthy are you with the secrets of others?

**Confine:** To constrict the freedoms of a person or an idea is a crime as it stifles creativity and progress. However, operating within certain confines can foster creativity that is needed to overcome barriers and restrictions. What are the confines and restraints under which you operate? How do they inspire you or force you to think more creatively? Constraints can also function as a way of dividing and categorizing. Certain things should be kept compartmentalized to separately achieve their most optimal functionality. What things in your life are best kept inside certain limits? When do you find it useful to separate business from pleasure? How do you maintain focus when these parts of your life are separated?

**Confirmation:** Before deciding upon one path over another, it is prudent to make sure that the information you have about each direction is accurate and up to date. Measure twice, cut once. Before we make large decisions, it is important to reiterate and remind ourselves what we already know. How do you reassure yourself of the path that you have chosen or that has been chosen for you?

**Conflict:** For two things to be in conflict means that it is difficult for them to both exist at the same time because they are both attempting to occupy the same space or the same time, or because they are so ideologically opposed that they cannot both be fully true or fully implemented. Could it ever be possible to entirely rid our lives of conflict? To what extent can a willingness to compromise help to avoid or lessen conflict? What kinds of negative consequences do we suffer when we provoke or participate in conflict? How can we be as vigilant and tactful as possible in order to minimize conflict or when trying to understand the other side of one? Do you attempt to see issues from all angles and put yourself in opposing shoes? When a conflict arises, do you attempt to solve it rationally and calmly? Is conflict always a waste of time, resources, and energy, or can it be productive? Are conflicts of ideologies—whether it be two people in a relationship or all the way up to our two political parties—necessarily less destructive than when conflict escalates into war? Does the scale of the war make a difference? Are you aware and do you fully understand conflict as a constant of life?

**Conform:** Everything about <u>society</u> tends to <u>push</u> us in the direction of conforming to <u>fit</u> in, taking the most sensationalized figureheads of a given society as examples, and striving to be like those <u>revered</u> members. However, if everyone conformed, where would new ideas come from? No society is perfect, and necessary change would be impossible if the actions of those who came before in the society were simply repeated over and over again. <u>Individual</u>, rational, and critical thinking always trumps blanket appeals to conform. How do you evaluate behaviors and rules before you conform to them? What aspects of your character are the result of conformity? What aspects are the result of individuality?

**Confound:** What is your experience of confounding situations leading you away from <u>resolution</u> and <u>order</u>? What is the relationship between how <u>confusing</u> something is and how time must be spent <u>understanding</u> the <u>problem</u> itself before we can begin to <u>solve</u> it? How could it be useful to take a step back in order to see how problems overlap and make a web rather than existing as completely separate entities? How could one particularly bad problem confound others until we recognize their interconnectedness?

**Confrontation:** When two <u>opposing</u> things meet face to face; an integral part of <u>conflict</u>. What is the effect of confrontation on the amount of <u>tension</u> in a conflict? When is confrontation justified? What other options might or should be tried first? Do you think before you confront? Do you avoid confrontation when possible?

**Confusion:** Confusion describes our <u>inability</u> to <u>understand</u> something, but can also mean a general state of <u>disorder</u>. Do you recognize when confusion is used to benefit some and disenfranchise others? How are the powers that be able to use purposeful confusion for a specific end? When you are confused, where

and how do you seek answers to remedy this state? Do you have the confidence to hold accountable those who are propagating confusing information, or do you give in to <u>embarrassment</u>?

**Congenial:** <u>Agreeable</u>, easy to get along with. Do you feel that you have a <u>friendly</u> demeanor? In what kinds of situations does or could that help you? When are there times when confrontation is more valuable instead? Do you make an effort to be <u>amicable</u> instead of <u>cold</u>?

**Congratulation:** To <u>express</u> <u>happiness</u> in another's <u>accomplishments</u>. Do you consider it important to show those around you <u>support</u> and to take pleasure in their accomplishments? How important to success is the support of friends and family? Do you ever take congratulations for granted? Are you able to swallow your <u>pride</u> and congratulate an opponent on their <u>victory</u>? How could doing so benefit the both of you? If it's impossible to always win in life, what are the options you have for your behavior when you lose?

**Congregate:** A <u>gathering</u> or coming <u>together</u>. What makes people congregate? Can you recognize the root causes of the congregation of certain peoples? Are you careful to make sure you know what exactly you are congregating around before you let yourself get lost in the <u>crowd</u>?

**Conjecture:** <u>Opinion</u> or <u>guesses</u> formed without concrete, <u>explicit</u> <u>facts</u>. Have you met people who attempt to elevate their conjecture to the level of truth and facts when in reality they are nothing more than personal opinions? What factors could make it easy for people to do this? What kinds of issues are more susceptible to this? Where should the burden of proof lie? Do you think critically about the <u>rhetoric</u> of others to determine whether their statements are <u>true</u>?

**Conjunction:** When two or more things are used at the <u>same</u> time, they are used in conjunction. Do you find that most issues are <u>isolated</u> or <u>integrated</u> with others in our lives? What kinds of things, positive and negative, work in conjunction with one another to achieve different results than they would on their own? Do you look for <u>connections</u> in your life?

**Connect, Connection:** A connection is something that <u>links</u> two different things together <u>physically</u>, <u>mentally</u>, or <u>emotionally</u>. What kinds of connections do you have in your life with other people? Were they formed by choice or by luck? Are there negative connections that you have tried to erase or wish you could? What is the most important connection you feel you have, the one that has the most impact on your life, whether good or bad?

**Connive:** To <u>secretly</u> aid in wrongdoing. Are those who connive put on the face of a good person and turn around and do the opposite worse than those who are openly wrongdoers? Are you careful to beware of those who are intentionally vague about their sentiments or <u>motives</u>? Do you make your <u>intentions</u> clear? Are you wary of those who seem to have a <u>dissonance</u> between their <u>actions</u> and their <u>rhetoric</u>?

**Connote:** When one <u>word</u> contains a socially constructed <u>meaning</u> beyond its dictionary definition. Though many words have multiple meanings, a connotation is something that is <u>constructed</u> over time and supplements the meaning of a word, and may or may not be explicitly defined. Why would it be important to realize the connotations of the <u>language</u> we use? What kinds of consequences could there be if we fail to recognize someone else's <u>implied</u> meaning or if someone else fails to recognize ours?

**Conquer:** Conquering something means to put it into one's <u>possession</u> through <u>fighting</u> for it in some way. What kinds of things do you think are worth fighting for? Would you say there are things you have conquered or people you have conquered in order to <u>win</u> certain rights or privileges? What would you like to conquer next in your life?

**Conscience:** An inner ability to recognize what is <u>morally</u> <u>right</u> and <u>wrong</u>. Our conscience, past being a moral <u>compass</u>, seems to hold us accountable for our actions and sentiments. What are ways in which your conscience has informed your actions? Would you describe guilt you feel after doing something wrong as a kind of <u>punishment</u> from your conscience? What kinds of other factors or forces encourage you to ignore your conscience? Have you met other people who seem to have less or more of a conscience than you do, or even no conscience at all?

**<u>Conscious, Consciousness</u>:** The <u>awareness</u> of your <u>feelings</u> or the things around you. Though hard to nail down entirely what consciousness is for all of the <u>creatures</u> of Earth, is it possible for us to have a full enough understanding of what <u>human</u> consciousness is and therefore adequately describe it? Is it the thing that allows us to have <u>emotions</u> and to <u>interact</u> with our environment? As humans, we have the unique ability to recognize our consciousness. Do we therefore have a responsibility to question it? What additional responsibilities does our consciousness burden us with in respect to the animal world and the Earth? Though it could be defined simply as being <u>awake</u>, is it possibly preferable to evoke a connotation of consciousness which defines it as overt <u>feelings</u> and <u>sentiments</u> one has while awake, including <u>subconscious</u> feelings? What kinds of things do you think we should remember to be conscious of in our lives?

**Consensus:** The <u>agreement</u> of the <u>majority</u> or all <u>parties</u> on a given <u>issue</u>. Before you let yourself or your ideas to be overpowered by a consensus, do you look at the separate elements that comprise it? Every party could have different <u>motives</u> or <u>goals</u> which ultimately all lead toward propagating the same belief; if this is the case, do the different motivations matter? Can one have evil reasons to reach a good consensus? Do you look for further evidence even when there is a consensus?

**Consent:** <u>Approval</u> or <u>agreement</u>. Before you consent to something or on behalf of someone or something, do you consider all possible sides of the story? What arguments are being presented by both sides? What <u>incentives</u> may affect the way that issues are presented, and their ultimate goals for arguing one way or another? Do you think critically before you give your <u>permission</u>?

**Consequence:** A consequence is something which occurs as a <u>result</u> of an <u>action</u>; for something to be of consequence indicates that it is <u>important</u> or <u>significant</u>. Life would be much simpler if every action had an exactly opposite and equal <u>reaction</u> as is true in physics, but how do the consequences to our actions in life vary in severity and scope? How are consequences relative to a myriad of established facts about your life? Are more affluent individuals more insulated from the consequences of their actions? Do they suffer less for a crime or act than a less affluent individual would? Even if your action does not have direct consequences to yourself, do you realize the consequences of a given action in all respects? Do you take into account not only other people, but also animals and the <u>environment</u> you live in? Do you take <u>responsibility</u> for your actions even when the consequences do not hold you directly <u>accountable</u>?

**Conservation:** Conservation is the act of <u>preventing</u> <u>loss</u> or <u>decay</u>; it has become more generally used as a synonym for the <u>environmental</u> movement. It seems as though <u>waste</u> has only recently become an issue as it has only recently piled up high enough on a large enough scale to warrant attention. But to what extent has conserving our environment always been an issue in human history? It has become evident that our <u>planet</u> is <u>finite</u> and that we are using far more than is a <u>sustainable</u> amount; what do you believe the end result will be of this reality? Do you consider conservation in your daily life?

**Conservatism:** An <u>ideology</u> that opposes <u>change</u> and <u>reform</u>, especially in the socio-political arena. This ideology represents adherence to the status quo, though the status quo itself changes over time. What do you believe are the probable <u>motives</u> of someone who does not want anything to change? Can we assume that they are gaining something or at least are happy with the current state of affairs? How does that which is currently benefiting them compare to the costs to those who want things to change? Do you critically examine opposing <u>viewpoints</u> and do you use research to make up your mind? There is a lot of power to be had by uniting people under a single

> *"Here is your country. Cherish these natural wonders, cherish the natural resources, cherish the history and romance as a sacred heritage, for your children and your children's children. Do not let selfish men or greedy interests skin your country of its beauty, its riches or its romance."*
> — *Theodore Roosevelt*

51

ideology; do you make sure that you examine issues from all sides before you commit to an entire ideology? Do you scrutinize <u>political</u> and <u>social</u> issues before you let yourself be swayed by the <u>rhetoric</u> or <u>sensationalism</u> of one side?

**Consider, Consideration:** To experience and expand the <u>thought</u> process in an orderly manner through the acquisition and employment of <u>information</u>. Do you consider all of the changing parts of every situation in which you find yourself, with a <u>rational</u> and <u>critical</u> eye before you draw <u>conclusions</u>? Do you make every attempt to be as <u>cognizant</u> as possible about your environment, both environmentally and socially speaking? With this thinking, are you considerate of others? Do you put into action consideration of those around you?

**Console:** To console is to <u>comfort</u> a friend or loved one. Do you sometimes ignore that they have a <u>problem</u> that is clearly in <u>need</u> of fixing, knowing all that they need from you in particular is <u>unconditional</u> loving <u>support</u>? Have you been in a situation where you could recognize the <u>cause</u> of a problem, but knew your place was to comfort them in the wake of the <u>consequences</u>? Who do you turn to when you need consolation? *Are you willing to console strangers?*

**Consonant:** A consonant is a letter of the English alphabet which is not a vowel, but to be consonant means to be in <u>harmony</u> or <u>agreement</u>. What in your life seems to have reached an <u>equilibrium</u> and what seems off kilter? Is it important to you to reach consonance in your life? How could you best do so?

**Conspire:** To conspire is to <u>agree</u> with someone else in <u>secret</u>, usually to do something <u>illegal</u> or <u>immoral</u>; it forms the root of the word "conspiracy." Are conspiracies necessarily <u>evil</u>, or do you think one can conspire to perform positive works? Have you

experienced other people conspiring against you? Have you done it to others? Do you have regrets or fears about these experiences?

**Constant:** To be constant is to be unchanging. As a result, we sometimes use it to mean "faithful." There are six constants of human life: <u>changing</u> differences, <u>conflict</u>, <u>corporacracy</u>, <u>cultural</u> enigmas, <u>dependency</u>, and <u>resource</u> <u>usage</u>. Can the <u>awareness</u> and <u>acceptance</u> of these constants help us to attempt to keep them in <u>balance</u>? Does the state of their being out of <u>balance</u> cause much human injury and pain? Which of these concepts should be familiar to you, and which should be important in your life? How could using this encyclopedia help guide you through exploring these constants? (See also: *A Day of Life: Moments in Time*)

**Constitution:** In many <u>governments</u>, their constitution is a set of <u>laws</u> and <u>principles</u> that guide the functions and limits of their government. What is your constitution? What are the factors that have helped you <u>develop</u> your <u>sentiments</u> and <u>attitudes</u>? What are the laws and principles of your government's constitution? How does your government adhere to those laws and principles? How might those differ from your own personal constitution?

**Consumer:** The literal definition of "consume" is to <u>destroy</u>, though we generally use the word "consumer" to indicate someone who <u>purchases</u> items. Do you see a <u>relationship</u> between the two meanings of the word? Is there such a thing as <u>responsible</u> consumption? Do you consider yourself a responsible consumer? What steps do you take to make yourself one? Is being a consumer an unavoidable part of <u>living</u> in our <u>society</u>?

**Contaminate:** To make something <u>dirty</u> or at the very least <u>impure</u> by touching or mixing it with something else. Has it been your experience that minds can be contaminated by <u>misinformation</u> and <u>propaganda</u> in the same way that water and air can be contaminated by <u>pollutants</u>? Do you make sure you are getting good and accurate information before you draw <u>conclusions</u>? How can you avoid contaminating the minds of others with <u>sensationalized</u> yet empty factoids?

**Contempt:** A double-edged sword: the <u>feeling</u> one feels toward something that is <u>evil</u> and detestable, or being subject to this feeling. Before you decide that you have contempt for something, do you make sure you know the whole <u>story</u>? Is it healthy to have contempt for other human beings, or should we reserve it for ideas?

# 6 Constants of
## Human Life

Changing Differences
Conflict
Corporacracy
Cultural Enigmas
Dependency
Resource Usage

**Content:** The content of something is what it <u>contains</u>, though as a descriptive term, it can also describe whether a work has significance. What is <u>inside</u> something below the superficial level? What does it mean to you to consider Dr. Martin Luther King's advice to not judge people "by the color of the skin, but by the content of their <u>character</u>"? Do you avoid using <u>prejudice</u> to shape your opinions of others? What steps do you take to identify unintentional prejudice in your own thoughts and approaches?

**Contented:** <u>Satisfied</u> or <u>complacent</u> with what one has done or what one is. Does the similarity of "contented" to the word <u>content</u> indicate that our lives or actions contain something specific in order to achieve this feeling? Are you satisfied with what you have <u>accomplished</u>, or are you <u>ambitious</u> to accomplish <u>more</u>? What times in your <u>life</u> have you felt contentment? Is it always a temporary feeling?

**Contention, Contentious:** A contention is a or supposed <u>truth</u> that someone is <u>arguing</u> for; to be contentious is to be argumentative. Though it could never be <u>objectively</u> clear what too argumentative or too <u>passive</u> is defined as, do you have a sense of what these ideas mean to you? Do you strive to always argue for something that you believe in rather than arguing for the sake of arguing? What is the <u>difference</u> between being contentious and being thoughtfully <u>inquisitive</u>?

**Context:** Context can exist for many things— words, actions, situations. When we talk about something's context, we are referring to the full set of <u>circumstances</u> surrounding it, which we need to have <u>knowledge</u> of in order to fully <u>understand</u>. Have you been in circumstances that you thought of differently after you had context for what was happening? Have you been judged by others who did not understand the context for your actions? Where do you draw the line between providing context and providing an excuse?

**Continence:** Your <u>capability</u> to <u>control</u> yourself and your <u>appetite</u>. Is having self-control an important part of your experience of living life? Do you look at <u>food</u> as fuel to make your body perform as efficiently as possible, or as an enemy that <u>lures</u> you in under the guise of deliciousness and wreaks havoc on you when you are conned into eating too much of it? Do you know what you are putting into your body and in what amount? How does your diet reflect your attitude and goals?

**Contract:** An <u>agreement</u> of some kind, which states <u>expectations</u> and which implies or explicitly states that there will be a penalty of some type if these expectations are <u>violated</u>. It can be written, as a <u>legally binding</u> <u>document</u>, spoken, or even tacit. In terms of reality, a contract is meaningless and is only as <u>valid</u> as the involved parties want it to be. Are you aware of the tacit or overt contracts of which you are a part? Do you take initiative to be sure of what is expected of you? Do you <u>honor</u> contracts which you agree to? Has anyone reneged on a contract you had with them? Do you believe there is an implied social contract that every human has with the rest of <u>society</u>?

**Contradiction:** A statement that expresses the <u>opposite</u> of something. Do you recognize when someone has contradicting <u>sentiments</u>? Why is it important that we learn to recognize contradictory statements, and how do we do so? How do you educate yourself before you contradict someone's statement or <u>refute</u> a perceived contradiction? Do you approach discussions and <u>arguments</u> mindfully with a discerning eye?

**Contrary:** Something which is contrary is in <u>opposition</u> to something else, whether an idea or a person. Are you careful to <u>listen</u> to others rather than simply offering automatic <u>refutations</u> for their sentiments and <u>opinions</u>? When is it productive to hold people <u>accountable</u> for their statements, and when does arguing simply become contrarian? Have you ever discovered something to be true that was contrary to your previous beliefs?

**Contrast:** A contrast is a comparison that highlights sharp <u>differences</u> between two or more items. Can noticing differences between entities be as important as noticing <u>similarities</u>? Why is it important to be <u>observant</u> and mindful when dealing with new situations? Can drawing a contrast between a new thing and an old thing be the most effective way to <u>understand</u> it? Do you <u>compare</u> and contrast in order to understand your life?

<u>Control</u>: <u>Power</u> over something which allows you to <u>guide</u> or <u>manage</u> it. Does maintaining control of your life seem daunting at times? Do you have the presence of mind to employ self-control when possible and to <u>exert</u> power over others only when they cannot control themselves? Control can be overt or completely hidden; do you follow the chain of <u>command</u> to see who is the puppeteer at the top before you pass judgment? Are you in control of your life? Who else or what else is capable of exerting control over you? Are you aware of their <u>motives</u>? To be in control of your life, do you have to strike a <u>balance</u> between your <u>motives</u> and <u>decisions</u>? Have you experienced the sensation of them existing in <u>balance</u>? When <u>pleasures</u> or <u>pains</u> become too plentiful, can life suddenly seem out of control? Is it helpful to think of your <u>mind</u> as the control center of your body, and then <u>resolving</u> to control the <u>center</u>? *How do you deal with control garnered financially or by force?*

**Controversy:** A point of <u>contention</u> or a large <u>argument</u> or <u>debate</u>. Are you able to keep a cool head when embroiled in any sort of controversy? Is getting overexcited always counterproductive, or can it help portray your <u>passion</u> about a solution? Where do you stand on controversial <u>issues</u> you can think of? How many people have to <u>disagree</u> with a stance in order for it to be considered controversial?

*"You have no control over what the other guy does. You only have control over what you do."*
*— A. J. Kitt*

<u>Convenience</u>: Something's convenience is the measure of how <u>easily</u> it can be <u>obtained</u> or <u>performed</u>. With an increasingly <u>globalized</u> <u>economy</u>, it is possible to obtain almost any <u>product</u> or <u>service</u> that you might like; the variable is how convenient it is to do so. In a world where certain <u>goods</u> have become more obtainable, has the benchmark of status become convenience? Properties closer to hubs of activities, where convenience is increased, are more expensive, and those who can afford it often have people to perform even the simplest tasks for them to save time. Have we reached a juncture of such <u>excessive</u> convenience that it is time to ask ourselves: At what point does convenience breed <u>laziness</u>? If everything is too easy to come by, are we never encouraged to <u>work</u> hard to obtain something? While enjoying convenience, do you keep in mind that many people live in a <u>reality</u> of not being <u>able</u> to <u>acquire</u> their needs and desires as conveniently as you? *How does it relate to pleasure?*

**Conversant:** Being <u>knowledgeable</u> about something through experience or study. Do you know people in your life who you <u>trust</u>

regarding a certain issue or idea because they are highly conversant in the relevant area? How can you determine whether is truly well versed in a subject they claim to be, or hiding behind a façade of puffery and rhetoric? What would you claim to be conversant in, and how do you demonstrate your expertise to others?

**Convert:** To transform from one form or function to another or, when speaking of people, to change one's mind from one belief system to another. Have you ever found yourself converted into believing something different? What kind of formula did you use to dictate your choice, and what kinds of difficulties did you face? What was more important in your consideration—what you knew about your inner or spiritual world, or what you knew about the exterior one?

**Convey:** To transmit an idea or entity from one place or person to another. Can conveying ideas be more difficult than conveying physical things? Is it more difficult to convey ideas to someone who has difficulty understanding them or who actively disagrees with your conclusions? Do you put effort into conveying your ideas even when it seems like an uphill battle? What is the biggest problem you have when trying to convey your ideas to others? *What instruments do you use?*

**Convict, Conviction:** A convict is someone who has been found guilty of a crime by a court of law and sentenced to serve time in prison. A conviction can be either the act of declaring someone guilty or a belief which one holds strongly. Does it seem odd to have these two very different definitions linked to the same word? Or is there a way that strong beliefs can become prisonlike, in that it is hard for us to escape them, even if they are incorrect? How do you feel about the way convicts are treated in American society—is it fair or unfair? How about after they have served their sentences? Is our justice system a reasonable one, or do you see significant flaws in it?

**Convince:** To elicit the feeling of sureness in another. When you decide whether someone is convincing, are you always able to tell whether they are genuinely trustworthy and honest, or if they just seem to be? Before you are convinced of anything, do you make sure you scrutinize carefully the evidence or information that you are presented with? Do you consider yourself gullible or skeptical? How do you determine this?

**Cooperation:** Cooperation is the action of multiple individuals working together in order to achieve a common goal. Do you think of cooperation when you consider opponents in a game or activity—to what degree do they work against one another in order to beat one another, and to what degree do they have to work together in or for either side to win? Does an absence of cooperation result in chaos?

**Coordination:** The result of two or more things working together smoothly, including the different parts of a living body. How does the level of coordination affect the productivity of any group activity? What is the difference and the relationship, between cooperation and coordination? Do you effectively coordinate interactions and tasks in order to be efficient and effective in accomplishing your goals?

**Copy:** Something created as an image of or likeness to something else. It is in human nature to learn by observing the behavior of others, but this also raises the question: Who or what am I imitating or attempting to be a likeness of? Does copying something outright mean that you have skipped the process that was vital in making that original thing original? Before copying someone, do you scrutinize what that behavior means and what it will mean to others when you behave this way? Do you think before you imitate?

**Corporation:** A group of people with an established charter that gives them legal rights as a group that are usually only afforded to individuals. This heading includes businesses as well as city municipalities and state and federal governing bodies. What are your feelings on the nature and uses of corporations? Why do we have them, and what benefits do they provide? Why are some people wary of them?

**Corporacracy:** A social theory in which a separate quasi-government within a democratic society operating under a corporate structure regulates and controls civil obedience, disobedience, and commercial affairs, or acts as a lower-tiered government with minimal constitutional restraint. *It is the few controlling the many.* Under corporacracy, traditional individual powers are taken from the people and given to an elite few in the form of power, wealth, and influence. Corporacracy is, at its core, about control. It is virtually our only employer, it provides us with both basic necessities and luxuries, and it governs us. Can you recognize when a small minority is benefitting at the expense of the vast majority? (See also: *Corporacracy*)

**Correction:** The changing of something from wrong to right. Is making observed wrongs right something that we should all strive toward? What causes some corrections more difficult to make than others— degree of wrongness or degree of complexity? Do you do everything in your power to be correct? Do you correct yourself when you are wrong? Do you attempt to be polite when correcting others?

**Correspond:** Be cautious of those who have sentiments that correspond with

> *"Whoever fights monsters should see to it that in the process he does not become a monster. And if you gaze long enough into an abyss, the abyss will gaze back into you."*
>
> — *Friedrich Nietzsche*

your own, and do not disregard the views of those who don't. Challenge yourself to find corresponding elements in people whom you consider different from yourself. You will be surprised what you find and perhaps change as a result. What do you do to understand those who are not like you? How do you correspond with them? Two differing people can be linked by corresponding cooperative actions rather than qualities. What do you have in common with others? How do you keep up communication when it is expected of you?

**Corroborate:** Before you draw conclusions or take decisive action, it is important to verify all the information upon which you base your decision. If not, you risk misfortune. What kinds of questions do you ask before you draw conclusions? How are they rational and applicable to the task at hand?

**Corruption:** Sadly, we must be observant for corruption manifests in all facets of our lives. Those who begin something with good intentions and secretly begin working toward opposing goals are both difficult to identify and to stop. We must look at the behavior and motives of anyone suspect before we relinquish our complete trust. What information do you gather to ensure people are true to their stated intentions? How do you assess what true intentions are? What kinds of corruption do you unwittingly participate in?

**Cosmos:** What is your place in the universe? How do you come to understand it? We all comprise matter that was created in the universe. Therefore, we all have some of the universe in us. When we die, we will return what we have borrowed. With this knowledge, you can choose to feel insignificant and small or connected and relevant to everything around you. How do you feel connected to the cosmos? How do you feel relevant and unique?

**Council:** It is important for those who lead groups to be cognizant and respectful of the sentiments and goals of the entire population, not just especially vocal of affluent ones. A good council is objective and unprejudiced, seeking not to expand their own wealth or accomplish selfish goals, but serve the needs of the people. What councils are you a part of? How do you collaborate with other council members to better the entire group and not parts of the group? What councils speak for you? How do they work in your favor?

**Counteract:** Counteracting forces oppose your freedom or the freedom of others. What counteracts your freedoms? How can you oppose that counteraction? Countering forces can bring balance to your life. Be sure to include them whenever possible to maintain a life of equal parts intention and pleasure. How do you counteract parts of your life that are overstepping their boundaries? How does this help in leading a balanced life?

> *"Courage is not the absence of fear, but rather the triumph over it."*
> — Nelson Mandela

**Counterproductive:** Something counterproductive is something that works away from progress toward a set goal. It can be frustrating to deal with people who are habitually counterproductive; do you have anyone like that in your life? Have you found yourself acting in a counterproductive manner? What caused you to do so—was it because you didn't think through the implications of your actions or because your emotions caused you to not care that you were making things harder for yourself? How can you avoid engaging in counterproductive activities?

**Country:** It is difficult to not feel an attachment to the place in which we were reared or the nation to which one belongs. However, this sentiment can be dangerous when attachment takes on the form of blind nationalism. How does your happiness benefit from a natural environment, beyond the overt manifestations of civilization? How does it benefit from serving your country in the face of threats to its well-being? Perhaps you are angry about what is going on within your country. How does this affect your national pride? Have an open mind about other countries and approach them like new friends. What efforts do you make to discern the merits of other countries before dismissing them as inferior?

**Courage:** It is a valuable skill to be able to control your fear in the face of danger or pain. Bravery is a virtue and a quality that you should look for in friends and strive to hold yourself; you will be surprised to see what you can push yourself to do when you surmount your fears. When do you practice bravery? What do you regard as a courageous act? Do you have the courage to face your fears willingly? If you do not, how might you attain it?

**Course:** We all have a unique course through life. Your course may intersect with some, diverge from others, and maybe run adjacent to others for a time, but it will always be unique to you. Map your course thus far. What does it look like? Where do you expect it to go? How do you adhere to this course in the face of opposition? Be understanding when your goals, sentiments, or opinions do not align with those of others. It takes a special person to warrant the merging of courses. Do not rush it by imposing your course or attempt to sway someone else's course against their will. Respect the unique courses that others take in life. Whose courses pass through yours? How do they merge? How did the merger happen? Was it forced?

**Courteous:** There are various systems of etiquette, yet they are all based on treating others how you would like to be treated. But they are often subjective, irrelevant formulas used to weed out those who are not part of a group. How can you decide what courtesies are necessary and what courtesies are futile? How do you avoid those that separate others from groups? How do you make an effort to practice those that are polite and kind?

**Covert:** Always question the motives of those who choose to carry out their business in secret. What is a good reason for desiring privacy? How do some use secrecy to purposefully deceive? When is it warranted to respect privacy? When is it warranted to scrutinize secrecy?

**Covet, Covetous:** It is a waste of time to concentrate on the disparity of success or possessions between yourself and others. What can you do to increase your chances of achieving your goals? How do you avoid wasting time being jealous of the possessions of others?

**Cram:** Moderation is the key to a balanced and successful life. When we pack our lives too full of anything, all aspects suffer. When you notice your life becoming unsustainably hectic and stressful, take an inventory of all the things that you are trying to do each day. Eliminate those that are not a priority. How do you organize your time? How much commitment do you take on before you feel overwhelmed and overworked? Do your days end with a sense of incompleteness? How might organization be a successful substitute for cramming?

**Crave:** We all have cravings in various forms of varying severity. They only become a problem when they shape how we live our lives in a significant way. When you find that you cannot resist giving into your cravings, take a step back and evaluate your priorities. What is the root of your cravings? How might they be a sign of addiction? Seek help if you find yourself inescapably desiring something that you probably should not have all the time. How do you control your cravings? How do your cravings control you? How can they be overcome?

**Create, Creation, Creativity:** Creativity is an intriguing and valuable human quality; embrace this and see what you are capable of fashioning. To create life is an enormous responsibility and should be approached in a thoughtful and cautious manner. What do you create? What are the forces or actions which created you? When all is said and done, our creations are the only lasting marks we leave on Earth. Bearing that in mind, what do you add to the history of our planet?

**Credibility:** Something's credibility is the measure of how trustworthy it is; the greater the credibility, the more believable and reliable it is. How do you decide when and if to trust other people? How do they demonstrate their credibility to you? How do you attempt to demonstrate your credibility to others? If one loses credibility, is there a way to regain it?

**Credulity:** It is one thing to be a trusting person, but another entirely to be gullible. In your relationships and in your personal life, distance yourself from the willingness to believe something even in the absence of valid proof. How do you avoid being gullible? How is skepticism a tool that you use to avoid being gullible? What in your life do you believe in blind faith?

**Creed:** A creed is any statement or system of beliefs. Does it represent a summation of how you view the world and yourself? There are many different religious creeds for living life. Beware of those that require the devaluation of yourself as an individual, discourage you from learning, propagate hate for any reason, or leave gaps in moral logic. Your creed should apply to a multitude of subjects—your lifestyle (way of Life), relationships, ambition, desires, and things you cope with regularly. What is your creed for living life? What is your system of principles that are believed or professed? Can you define your lifestyle? Do you understand your lifestyle? Are you aware of your weaknesses, habits, and dependencies? Does your lifestyle display credibility? Do you give credence and respect to the lifestyles of others? *Do you impose your creed as doctrine?* Should creeds collectively become opinion or doctrine based on authority as opposed to those built on experience? Do your observations encompass faith and spirituality? *What are your spiritual and fundamental truths for moral rules of conduct?* How can/do these pages guide you in its formation?

**Crime:** Though we would like to believe that every law serves the interest of the public, crimes are subjective. The legal system deems certain acts contrary to the interest of society as a whole and punishes those who commit them by processing them as crime. What is the model society that laws are trying to protect? How does this model society compare with the society you are living in or would like to live in? Should the legal system be viewed with a critical lens rather than blindly trusting it? *Do you understand the difference between crime (laws) and civil obedience (rules/ ordinances)?* How do laws punish those who are disproportionately affected by their lack of access to resources such as education, emotional well-being, and money?

# Exemplary Creed

The most important thing we own is our energy. Guard it vigorously and use it wisely.

Live your lives faithfully to nature's laws, the laws of God, and laws that humans have agreed are necessary to balance the constants of life.

Analyze carefully the rules established by others and disregard any that take away or challenge your right to life, liberty, and the pursuit of moral happiness.

Maintain a sense of well-being for all life forms and pledge yourself to understanding the role that all life forms play in our moment (of time).

**Cringe:** Examine the things that cause you to cringe and ask yourself why they elicit this reaction. Why are you afraid or disgusted? Reduce the amount of things that frighten or disgust you by thinking about them in a rational way. Then, you can determine whether or not they really pose a threat. How are you oppressed by your fears? How do you overcome them with reason and critical thinking?

**Crisis:** Crises can come down like a ton of bricks without warning. Our fate is not defined as much by the severity of the event but by how thought-out and effective our response is. For example, the climate crisis is approaching the point of no return. Average global temperatures are getting higher and pollution is rampant. But the way we deal with the situation defines the crisis more than new weather patterns. As with any catastrophic event, we will be on the wrong side of history if we continue to cope with this crisis by ignoring it. How do you respond to crises? How do you incorporate a rational mind and a calm attitude? How does this help the final result?

**Criticism:** Aim to criticize constructively. To solely criticize creates distance between yourself and your peers and is counterproductive. Give people reasons why you find fault and suggestions on improvement. Criticism can be a valuable tool in improving your life and the lives of others, but only if it coincides with sufficient tact. What is the general intention of your criticism? How does criticism appear to you? Can you accept it without taking offense?

**Cruel, Cruelty:** Cruelty is unacceptable in any form. Cruelty should be taken as evidence of evil in a person because it is an unkindness that has no justification. Therefore, those who are cruel should not be trusted. Who do you know who is cruel? How do you work to eliminate or diminish their presence in your life? How do you speak out against cruelty?

**Crush:** Sometimes life can seem as if it is crushing us; all our responsibilities and obligations become suffocating. In those times, look beyond your subjective reality and take stock of your life. Rid yourself of unnecessary stressors. Acknowledge those stressors that cannot be eliminated entirely but can be quelled with some effort. What in your life feels as if it could crush you? How can you work to reduce things that are pressing in upon you and threatening to crush you?

**Cry:** There are many benefits of crying. It releases stress and it informs others of your feelings. There are many cultural stigmas surrounding who should cry and when, revolving around age and gender, expectations, and stereotypes. However, crying is healthy and useful. Don't let the prejudiced opinions of others stop you from expressing yourself when necessary. How do you express yourself with crying? How do the prejudices of others affect the times you cry?

**Cuddle:** Physical human contact can be extremely comforting and therapeutic. Whether it be for just a moment or hours on end, snuggling is a valuable reminder and physical manifestation of our feelings. Like an extended full body hug, cuddling is a physical reassurance of love and affection. It has the potential to express things that all the

> *"People speak sometimes about the 'bestial' cruelty of man, but that is terribly unjust and offensive to beasts, no animal could ever be so cruel as a man, so artfully, so artistically cruel."*
>
> *— Fyodor Dostoyevsky*

words and phrases and sentences in the world could not describe. When and with whom do you make time for snuggling? How does it strengthen your relationship? How does cuddling compare to all the other facets of your relationship?

**Cue:** Certain cues are overt and easy to follow while others are tacit. Be vigilant in social situations for clues which dictate the correct way to act. Cues are signals made by another to elicit a response in you. How susceptible are you to being coerced into doing something that you do not want to do? What are the motives and intents of the cues you submit to?

**Cull:** Cull through people only to the extent that you pick out well-intentioned qualities and stray from malicious or selfish ones. Culling through people as you would objects robs them of their humanity and limits them to the realm of usefulness or relevance. How do you come to recognize and value qualities in others? How do you avoid stepping on others for personal gain?

**Culminate:** The culmination of your life will not be visible until you are gone. So, there is little utility in thinking about the high point in your life while you are still living. Still, to acknowledge a high point in your own life is to acknowledge both a peak but also a resultant downfall. This attitude has the potential to rob you of the motivation to continue to succeed and reach new heights. How do you view your past successes? How might they be seen as motivation to press on?

**Cult:** Though this word has come to have a radical and negative connotation, cults can be formed around any idea or aspect of life. Before identifying yourself as part of any group, make sure you know for what it stands. How is your membership in a particular cult based on understanding? How do you educate yourself about a particular group before you claim membership?

**Cultivate:** Ideas are cultivated daily in people of all ages and backgrounds with various intentions and results. Cultivate ideas based around tolerance, equality, and the value of empirical evidence and rational thought. What do the ideas that you cultivate look like? How do they reflect your personal creed for living life? How do they reflect ideas of tolerance, equality, empirical evidence, and rational thought?

**Culture:** The goal of comprehending a culture is to understand rather than judge. Cultural customs can seem arbitrary and strange to outsiders and must be approached with tact. Equally so, your culture may be strange to those who have not lived it. A lot depends on the culture you were raised in and what you were taught to believe. How may some things seem strange to outsiders? How can you help outsiders understand the strangeness of your culture? Perhaps you are unable to explain the strangeness yourself. Remain tolerant and curious about other cultures that differ drastically from your own and differentiate between ideas that are culturally specific and those that are universal truths. How do you approach foreign cultures? How do you understand and appreciate their oddities and quirks?

**Cure:** It is important to realize that not everything is curable. Cures will vary in their effectiveness from patient to patient. We must be patient with what we cannot cure immediately while working toward long-term solutions or the abatement of pain when the outlook is bleak. What is a cure for you? What cures you of stress and negativity? How do you deal with ailments that you cannot cure?

**Curiosity:** Curiosity is what drives experimentation; it is a fuel for the engine of our lives, pushing us to explore our world and ourselves. Healthy curiosity fosters understanding and discussion. It is the foundation for scientific discovery, invention, and the exploration of the universe, and we are inherently born with it. It is hard to imagine the human race without it. How do you use curiosity to gain knowledge? What are you curious about? Remember, you should stay out of the affairs of others when they do not concern you. A good curiosity does not permit you to meddle with others. How do you deal with those who concern themselves with your affairs?

> *"The important thing is not to stop questioning. Curiosity has its own reason for existing."*
> *— Albert Einstein*

**Currency:** Currency is exchanged for goods and services, and is largely responsible for the progression of our civilization. When money becomes an end itself or is used to do immoral things, this is when it becomes evil. Superficial or material, what meaning do your goals carry? How can you recognize when others are driven by greed alone? What is the difference between the use of currency as a tool to improve society and actions motivated by pure greed?

**Current:** Something which is current is passing by right now—neither future nor past, but occurring in the present. It is also used to describe the movement and flow of rivers. Do you see a connection between the two meanings? Is it important to you to keep up with current events? Or do you focus on other times, instead—fond memories of the past or hopeful speculations about the future? Do you ever feel as though you are swept up in a current, like that of a river?

**Custom:** Different cultures have vastly different customs, habits, and traditions, all of which dictate how they act in certain situations. Comparing the customs for the same events across cultures, such as marriages, deaths, greeting newcomers, and births, aids in the understanding of cultures as a whole. How are your customs a product of your culture and not as absolute truths? How might your culture improve these customs in order to be more applicable to life?

**Customize:** The more freedom we have as humans, the more we are allowed to customize our own lives. Customizing something material serves as a manifestation of our individuality. Your ability to customize your own life is a function of your own personal agency. How do you customize your life according to your own individuality? How do you exert your own individuality and agency in order to do so? What are the benefits of that customization?

**Cycle:** People often refer to life as a cycle. Though it is hard to see our own lives as anything other than linear, looking outside our own consciousness shows we are part of a grand cycle which has been occurring for millennia. Animals are born, feed off the fruits of the earth, and then die and return to it. Where is your place in a grand cycle of living organisms? How does that perspective change how you view yourself? Are you important? The answer may be more complex than you think.

# D

**Damage:** Refers to <u>cause</u> and <u>effect</u>. It is important to pay attention to the <u>consequences</u> of your behavior; you must be constantly aware of your surroundings. On the other hand, when you sense that an outside force has the potential to damage you in some way, you must <u>choose</u> to distance yourself from it or confront the dangerous element if it threatens others around you. While the wounds of physical damage are often fast to heal, the <u>emotional</u> scars left by psychological damage can be more enduring. Remember that damaged does not mean <u>broken</u>. To say something is damaged connotes that there is a possibility that it could be returned to normal or even to a more fortified and resilient state. Hurricanes and storms ravage coastal areas, but people keep coming back with stronger and smarter structures. Just as <u>humans</u> have persevered through storms and earthquakes around the <u>world</u>, you must press through damages to your <u>life</u>, learning to be more resilient and less vulnerable to future damages. Treat damage to others with sensitivity and encouragement. Be <u>mindful</u> to help those you care about when they are damaged. Whether the damage you cause is intentional or incidental, you must take <u>responsibility</u> for it. Often, the damage we do to those around us is accidental, more the result of carelessness or neglect than <u>malice</u>. Are you aware of the <u>repercussions</u> of your actions? What damage do we do to others unknowingly? How can we decrease the damage that we do? Do you seek to help those who need it? Do you seek help when you need it?

**Damn, Damnable:** Implies a complete lack of the possibility of <u>redemption</u>. Something that is damned is beyond <u>hope</u>, so do not toss this word around lightly. At times, <u>life</u> can seem bleak and hopeless, but every situation has redeeming qualities from some <u>perspective</u>. To damn something or someone is to condemn it to stay as it is, ignoring the possibility of improvement. Before you judge and damn, take time to try to <u>learn</u> about the problem and fix it. Is there something to be gained by offering wrongdoers <u>redemption</u>? What does it take to declare something irredeemable or unable to achieve <u>salvation</u>? Before using this word, we must ask ourselves: is anything beyond hope? Why does one deserve <u>condemnation</u>?

**Dance:** Dance is used to express many different things across the vast array of cultures on our diverse planet. Some dances are <u>ceremonial</u> and hold great cultural significance, while others are purely for the enjoyment of the dancers and onlookers. The movement of the body to music can be an expression of oneself. Dancing is the <u>rhythm</u> of <u>life</u> and can be a joyous <u>activity</u>, <u>connecting</u> people to one another and to their own <u>emotions</u>. Do you let the contagious joy of dance enter your <u>body</u> and move you? How can dance be more integrated into your own life and effect well-being?

**Danger, Dangerous:** Daily, we're surrounded by dangerous situations in which we are threatened. Some dangers are obvious and a part of our daily <u>lives</u>; our <u>world</u> is dominated by the <u>power</u>-hungry and <u>greedy</u> who will think nothing of sacrificing the general welfare as a means to their end. But how might certain dangers escape our <u>awareness</u>? Are we surrounded by <u>political</u> and <u>economic</u> dangers that remain hidden? Can you sense danger?

**Dark:** The opposite of <u>light</u> and often seen as the opposite of the <u>positivity</u> and <u>hope</u> that light has come to represent. When darkness begins to creep into your <u>life</u> in the form of bad <u>habits</u>, debt, abusive relationships, or any number of negative forces, do not lie down and let it overtake you. Find the last shreds of light within yourself or within trustworthy friends and use these beacons, however small, to navigate your way to <u>safety</u>. Do not lose hope. Dark times are upon us, <u>socially</u>, <u>politically</u>, and <u>economically</u>. As Aristotle once said, "It is during our darkest moments that we must focus to see the light." When life gets you down, do you wallow in darkness or try to find the light? How can you keep darkness out of your life?

**Dawn:** It is the <u>beginning</u> of something, whether it be a thought, a day, or an entire <u>era</u>. If we think of the literal dawn of each day, it is easy to see why so many analogies stem from its qualities. It is quiet, peaceful. The <u>black</u> of the night becomes a <u>dark</u> blue in early morning before yielding to the golden dawn. Take inspiration from this beautiful, daily <u>transformation</u>. No matter how dark things get, a new dawn is coming; after the dark always comes the dawn of a new day. Perhaps the best way to get through the darkness is to focus on the impending <u>light</u>. It is easier to be a part of the necessary <u>social</u> <u>change</u> when you approach the unpleasant present with hope for the <u>future</u>. Do you consider the <u>negative</u> times of your life to be nothing more than passing phases, or does your <u>pessimistic</u> focus on the present prevent you from solving <u>problems</u>? When will your dawn come upon you? How will you emerge from the darkness into the dawn?

**Dead, Death:** A well-known lecturer who was diagnosed to die paused at the word "death"

and said, "It is not the things we have done in <u>life</u>, it is the things we have not done that we recall when approaching death." Life is meant to be lived. Death can be mourned, but life should be celebrated. What do you regret not doing thus far? What can you do to <u>live</u> your life fully so as to approach death with a sense of <u>contented</u> <u>accomplishment</u>? *How can you fully <u>understand</u> the effects of death in all life forms?*

**Debate:** A cornerstone of modern <u>life</u>. In bygone <u>eras</u>, <u>rules</u> in life have been dictated by a single individual or unifying <u>religious</u> text. There is little debate necessary in such an absolute style of <u>governance</u>. In a dictatorship or theocracy, if something is <u>condemned</u> by authority, it is deplorable; <u>morality</u>—what is right and wrong—never enters the picture. This stands in stark contrast with life in most places in the <u>world</u> today. There is constant debate raging in every corner of the world. Debate is an extremely useful <u>tool</u>; it is quite literally a <u>war</u> of <u>words</u>, in which each side is allowed to present a case and to refute the <u>arguments</u> of the other side. When watching any debate, pay attention not only to what each party is saying, but how they are saying it and what <u>motives</u> they might have for saying it. Those who have a weak argument will attempt to sway <u>opinion</u> with loud and drastic statements, but otherwise weak arguments. Those with a sound argument needn't raise their voice to make their point. Beware of those who try to excite rather than educate and scare people rather than solve problems. Lively <u>discussion</u> and <u>dialogue</u> provide the forum needed for <u>productive</u> debate that will move us toward <u>progress</u>. The most important thing to consider in debate is <u>respect</u>. Too often our debate becomes argumentative and our positions grow fortified and isolated from mutual <u>comprehension</u>. We must understand and respect our opponents before we can

> *"Each night, when I go to sleep, I die. And the next morning, when I wake up, I am reborn."*
>
> *— Mahatma Gandhi*

move forward. Do you make an effort to understand the views of those who disagree with you? What is truly worth debating?

**Debility:** Just as everyone has individual strengths, everyone has unique faults and weaknesses. Physical infirmity is obvious, but mental feebleness is seldom so readily identifiable. To overcome your own mental shortcomings, you must first identify them. A closed mind is a special type of self-inflicted handicap that can blind one to the views and sentiments of others. A lack of empathy can cultivate negative views with peers and impede social and emotional growth. What are some moral or emotional debilities that you are able to recognize? How might other debilities exist? How can you work to improve such shortcomings in yourself and in those around you? Are you sensitive about the weaknesses of others?

**Decadence:** Everyone deserves a treat once in a while, but excessive lavishness, especially when so many are in need, is unnecessary and even immoral. Is decadence the enemy of piety and truth? Material possessions can bring only a finite amount of happiness. It is fine to place value on objects, but do not let this value be overinflated by envy or mimetic desire. Maintain your individual perspective; no matter how high you rise up the socioeconomic ladder, your happiness will still be defined by your values, not by those around you. In many ways, the obsession with material possessions has overtaken relationships and experiences, as well as many other intangible, but truly amazing forces in our lives. The simpler you live, and the more perspective you maintain on your own life, and the happier you will be with what you have. In what ways are you decadent? What comforts could you forgo, and what might you learn by eliminating them? How could you help to improve the quality of life of someone else by living slightly less decadently?

**Decency, Decent:** Decency is dictated by culture, because it refers to behavior that conforms to a normalized set of values. Stop for a moment and think about all of the aspects of your daily life that are dictated by etiquette and societal conventions. Again, these rules are different in each culture, and different rules exist within each culture, but typically, it is customary to show respect and deference to elders, those of a higher rank in government, and to celebrities and sports heroes. However, decency extends beyond these rules. What shows the most about a person is how they treat those they are not required by society to treat with respect. A life lived without decency toward others will be empty, no matter how rich a person may be in other ways. At its core, decency evidences a respect for all humanity and a willingness to see all people as equals through proper and polite treatment. Everyone deserves to be treated decently; treat others the way you would like to be treated. Another interpretation of this word relates to appropriate behavior and subject matter. Indecency in speech and subject matter can cause awkward social circumstances and is often perceived as a desperate cry for attention. Do you treat others respectfully? Do you respect your company enough to avoid offending them? How do you conform to the standards of modesty?

**Deceit, Deceive, Deception:** Deceive others and you will only deceive yourself; deceit may pay off in the short term, but if you deceive to get ahead in life, you will ultimately end up alone and poorer than when you started. Beware of those who use deceit to take advantage of others or further their own goals. Self-deception can be just as harmful as deceiving others. It is worth examining your own life as you would a stranger's. Rationalization of bad behavior holds up to momentary scrutiny, but becomes obvious when you look at your life from a bird's eye perspective. Many hope to gain though their deception, but what do they lose? Do you distance yourself from deceit, both within your own mind and from others who display deceitful behavior? How do you feel after deceiving others or discovering you have been deceived?

**Decide, Decision, Decisive:** Every action or inaction is a decision. With each day, we are making hundreds of decisions; upon waking, we decide what we will wear, what to eat, what to drink, and many other seemingly inconsequential things. Decision making is an ever-present aspect of life, ranging from the miniscule to the life changing. Only in hindsight can it become clear which are arbitrary and which are life changing. A great mistake humans continually practice is deciding and acting upon pre-conceived or anticipated end results. Seek to find C.L.A.R.I.T.Y. before making any decisions, especially those that will set you on paths you have yet to travel. With clarity comes the confidence that our decisions are for the best. When you must make a decision between two options, gather all the available facts and try to see the situation from as many perspectives as possible. Make decisions after rational and patient consideration of all options and respective repercussions for all involved. Each one of your actions is the result of a decision made by your brain, whether conscious or subconscious. Be mindful of those decisions that are involuntary, as opposed to the voluntary. The only way that you can prepare to make good subconscious decisions is by building good habits and making a habit of critically thinking about all information you are presented with. Problem solving and decision making skills are not innate, but learned and practiced; the more you exercise your brain, the better equipped you will be when you are faced with any type of decision. Practice positive thought patterns; if you have a problem

> *"It does not take much strength to do things, but it requires a great deal of strength to decide what to do."*
> — *Elbert Hubbard*

steps to confront and improve yourself inside your own head. confronting decisions? Do you your decisions for all those your decisions define you daily? making decisions? Should cautiously and with the utmost make difficult decisions? How assumptions and outward decisions based on fact? What seeing how your decisions are with yourself, take tangible it; do not just continue to berate Do you seek clarity before recognize the repercussions of involved? Do you recognize that What process do you use when larger decisions be approached consideration? How do you could decisions based only upon appearances be less useful than forces are hindering you from affecting your life?

**Declaration:** A verbal or written announcement. A declaration is a strong statement, so you must be sure of what you are saying before you say it. If you constantly declare things which you are not sure about, you will find your credibility quickly evaporates. A statement as bold as a declaration should not be taken lightly. Only after extensive analysis of our thoughts and beliefs should such statements be presented to others. For example, the Declaration of Independence was written by Thomas Jefferson in 1776 before it was adopted by the Continental Congress. It outlined in uncompromising terms the independence and freedom of the United States. What can this bold act tell us about the American government today? Has the spirit of this document been lost in America? What is the purpose of declaring? What does it mean to declare something? How do you declare your decisions?

**Decline:** To refuse something, a literal downward slope, or downward trend of almost anything. To decline is to become less in some way. Examining history, we can see the rises and falls of the many empires of the earth. The nineteenth and twentieth centuries witnessed the rise of the United States. Given the increasingly ephemeral trends of modern society, is America declining in power <u>economically</u> and diplomatically? On a <u>personal</u> level, everyone faces a decline as they age, but if one declines in some ways, how might they <u>grow</u> in others? Do you realize when you begin to slope downward?

**Decontaminate:** Our minds are continually contaminated with the <u>influences</u> of <u>corporations</u> and <u>politicians</u> who don't have our best interests at heart. How can we decontaminate our minds and rid them of their influence? [I think this might be better suited to just tack onto the entry for "contaminate," just because there are so many "De-" prefix words that also could be relevant and whose counterparts appear elsewhere in the encyclopedia.]

**Defeat:** We face defeat throughout our <u>lives</u> and must come to <u>accept</u> it as a part of living. No matter how severe or seemingly crippling a defeat is, the important thing is to rise again, to stand back up, and to face your fears. You are only truly defeated when you have given up. Defeat is capable of <u>teaching</u> us many <u>lessons</u>, not the least of which is <u>humility</u>. What comes from this acceptance? What do we have to gain from <u>learn</u>ing to accept defeat?

**Defect, Defective:** The lack of something important. Objects can be defective because they do not work due to missing parts.

The process of creation can be defective or abnormal. Do you see something or someone having a <u>moral</u> or physical <u>imperfection</u> as abnormal and thus subject to replacement or distancing? Does the possibility exist to turn a defect (if considered a <u>negative</u>) into a <u>positive</u>? If defects arise in the process of <u>creation</u>, can we strive to minimize them? Is global <u>life</u> being threatened by defective parts of the whole? Can we identify the defective parts?

**Defend:** If you cannot defend your ideas or opinions, you must <u>examine</u> why you hold them. Do you have a duty to defend things and people that do not possess the <u>ability</u> to do so themselves? We have all felt defenseless and <u>vulnerable</u> in our <u>lives,</u> and it is the memory of this <u>feeling</u> that should push you to defend those in <u>need</u>. It is even more crucial to defend things in <u>nature</u> which do not have a voice of their own. We risk irrevocably losing entire species of animals and degrading our <u>environment</u> beyond its already stretched resilience. Does everyone have a <u>duty</u> to defend the disenfranchised they encounter daily? Those weaker or less powerful than ourselves <u>demand</u> our defense. How have you attempted to defend the rights of those who cannot defend themselves? How do you defend others? Why wouldn't you defend someone? What is worth defending on this Earth?

**Define, Definition:** We must <u>observe</u> in order to define; to clearly state the meaning of something. We are <u>constant</u>ly battling to define everything around us in an attempt to better <u>understand</u> the <u>world</u>. While scientific definition exists as an <u>absolute</u>, there are other definitions that <u>shape</u> your <u>reality</u>. Your definition of <u>family</u> affects the way you interact with your family, as do your definitions for countless other things. These definitions are not absolute as they vary from person to <u>person</u> and can <u>change</u> throughout our <u>lives</u>. How do you express or describe meaning? What are your boundaries? What do our definitions for others say about ourselves? Do you examine how you define yourself? How do you define your actions and attitudes? What <u>influences</u> the way we define things?

**Degeneracy, Degenerate:** A process of deterioration. When any part of you as a person begins to <u>erode</u>—your physical appearance, your mental sharpness, or your

<u>moral</u> compass—you are degenerating and risk falling into a state of degeneracy. Do everything you can to maintain a healthy lifestyle: Exercise your body and mind. Stay

true to your core principles; we all have changes of <u>heart</u> and <u>opinion</u> over the course of our lifetimes, but we must continually examine ourselves and our *motives*. Once you start <u>compromising</u> in one area, it is easier to rationalize greater and greater deviations from a healthy path in life. Do you make an effort to treat yourself and others with <u>respect</u>? Do you follow your own moral compass even when it goes against the grain and is the more difficult <u>path</u>? Are you <u>defeated</u> in your <u>fight</u>? *Is aging a form of degeneracy?*

**<u>Deliberate</u>, <u>Deliberation</u>:** One must carefully weigh all options before making an important <u>decision</u>. All aspects of a situation must be objectively weighed before the <u>best</u> one becomes clear. To be deliberate with your <u>actions</u> means to be very <u>calculated</u> and purposeful with what you do. Be deliberate with your actions and your <u>motives</u> will be clear to all. Do you give yourself <u>time</u> to work through important decisions? Do you take action confidently and purposefully when you have reached a decision? How can you <u>incorporate</u> more deliberation into your <u>life</u>?

**Deliverance:** The <u>act</u> of being rescued from <u>danger</u> or the <u>public</u> expression of an <u>opinion</u> or <u>decision</u>. <u>Examine</u> the <u>motives</u> of those who want to deliver you from a force or perceived danger. To be delivered makes you feel <u>free</u> and rescues you from whatever you may <u>suffer</u> from. For many ailments, there is no easy cure; you must look deep within yourself and to your closest friends for the <u>strength</u> to persevere and overcome your <u>difficulties</u>. Do you <u>depend</u> on yourself for deliverance from your difficulties? Do you <u>commit</u> yourself and give a <u>problem</u> your all before you look for a quick fix? Are they actually looking out for you, or inventing a danger to "save" you from it for a price? There are always those in society who desire deliverance. What can you offer them? Who do you look to as the agent of your own delivery? How can you contribute to the deliverance of others?

> *"The wise man in the storm prays to God not for safety from danger but for deliverance from fear."*
> — *Ralph Waldo Emerson*

you care about, be careful not to fuel their delusions, as it will only push them toward <u>failure</u>. Who has <u>influenced</u> your delusions? What or whom in your life could fuel delusions? The media? Untrustworthy friends? Politicians? What or who <u>exercises</u> an undue influence on you?

**Demean:** Some <u>weak</u> people demean others to feel better about themselves. This occurs frequently in <u>social</u> settings, where people will <u>humiliate</u> others in an effort to make themselves more appealing. Behavior of this type reveals more about the <u>insecurity</u> of the perpetrator than the person ridiculed; be careful not to be fooled by such actions. Have you ever been <u>guilty</u> of demeaning others? Why did you <u>choose</u> to demean someone? Did you feel better or worse afterward? Do you recognize demeaning behavior as a symptom of weakness or mental <u>instability</u> in the perpetrator?

**Delude, Delusion:** Do we delude ourselves daily, often at the <u>persuasion</u> of others? With those

**<u>Democracy</u>, <u>Democrat</u>, <u>Democratic</u>:** Democracy has been the backbone of our <u>country</u> since its inception, but how might our democratic <u>values</u> be getting eroded today? At its core, democracy offers a <u>voice</u> to everyone within a <u>society</u>, providing them with an <u>opportunity</u> to shape the arc of their country's trajectory on federal, state, and local levels. Do today's <u>politicians</u> have true democracy as their goal, motivating their every action, or are their goals more selfish than that? How are you part of our democracy? What could you do to be more active within our democracy?

**Denial, Deny:** While denial of falsehoods based on factual evidence is important, the rejection of ideas simply because they are contrary to your own hinders a complete understanding of the world. The worst denial is self-denial. We only deceive ourselves when we deny to ourselves that a problem exists. What do we fear when we participate in self-denial? Do you fall prey to your own dogmatic beliefs? Do you blind yourself to the problems of your life rather than addressing them?

> *"Many forms of Government have been tried, and will be tried in this world of sin and woe. No one pretends that democracy is perfect or all-wise. Indeed, it has been said that democracy is the worst form of government except for all those other forms that have been tried from time to time."*
>
> — *Winston Churchill*

**Depend, Dependency:** To rely on it and to be bound *you should strive to be in on no one but yourself.* part of relationships, but a only healthy variety. Avoid by those who would cling little in return. On the other of the generosity of others depend on something means to it by necessity. *Ideally, a position where you rely* Dependency is a natural balanced dependency is the being taken advantage of to you while you receive side, do not take advantage while offering them nothing. Dependency is a "*constant*" in that we have depended on certain elements such as air and water to live since the beginning of time. We depend on both man-made and natural things for our survival, like food provisions, services, electric heat, etc. Yet, to be too dependent on any one source for these things is dangerous. Do you have fail-safe alternatives for everything you depend on, should one of your sources fail? Likewise, don't forget your dependency on others and their dependency on you. Recognition of this dependency requires responsibility and a commitment to the needs of others. When do you find yourself reliant on others? When sick? Poor? Do you depend on mechanical devices? The automobile? The computer? Has an addiction become a dependency for you? Do you create dependency? Do you need to be dependent? (See also: *A Day of Life: Moments in Time*)

**Deplete, Depletion:** Whenever you are aware of depleting something in your life, your immediate follow-up thought should pertain to how you can manage your use of said resources to be more sustainable. Many natural resources are becoming tragically depleted because of ignorance and greed. Populations of endangered animals are depleted for their hides or ivory by short-sighted or just completely indifferent individuals who profit from selfish and illegal poaching. Our natural resources are both precious and finite and should be treated as such. In a trend that has only been getting worse since the Industrial Revolution, corporations and other insidious entities have been depleting our natural resources and robbing us of their value. As is often the case with natural resources, a few greedy and morally-starved individuals reap the benefits and stick everyone else with the burden of the damage they have inflicted. How can we stop this unnecessary depletion? In what ways can you modify your daily behavior to aid in conservation?

**Deplore:** To feel or outwardly express a severe disapproval of something, or a deep sadness. Many deserve to be deplored, while others suffer unwarranted criticism. Still, in other situations, the actions of a person may be deplorable while the character of the individual underlines their actions. In these situations, would forgiveness and absolution be a wiser choice than condemnation? How do you decide who deserves deploring? How do you tell the righteous from the deplorable?

**Deprave:** To deprave is to ruin, to render bad or wicked. This extends beyond the planet itself to the humans who inhabit it. How have we depraved the world around, making it into something it was originally not? Is it in our nature to be depraved, or has our modern society led to a corruption of morality? Has anyone depraved you? Is depravity inevitable as we age and learn to know more about the world? Why do we deprave?

**Depression:** The act of being very sad and gloomy. One can fall into depression because of lack of self-esteem or relationships and high stress. Is it important to reach out for others when feeling depressed in order to become mentally stable? Have you ever felt depressed? How were you able to overcome your depression? What can you do to help those who are depressed?

**Deprivation:** To remove something from someone. This action could be used as a consequence for a child or as a punishment for a wrongdoer. Have you been deprived? What are the effects of deprivation on a person? Have you experienced or considered it as a victim? How can it affect your health/emotions?

**Derogatory:** People make derogatory remarks about others for all kinds of reasons. Examine the motives and the espouser of a belief before you give any weight to their statements. Often, people insult others to feel better about themselves. Dealing with your pain by trying to inflict pain on others will only lead to a spiral of self-hatred and contempt for others. Do not go down this route; when you are inclined to make derogatory comments, instead examine yourself and resolve to improve from the inside out instead of bringing down others. How might their hurtful remarks only be hurting themselves? Have you ever found yourself making such comments?

**Desirable, Desire:** There will always be things that you desire in life that you cannot have. Acting with foresight and a sense of responsibility in the face of this desire is essential to acting as an ethical being. When you want something, the way you get it defines what type of person you are. If you are willing to work hard to fulfill your desires, you will be rewarded. If you seek to fulfill your desires through deception or cheating others, eventually your character will deteriorate beyond repair. A combination of temptation and unchecked desire has the potential to drive the weak-minded mad. Maintain a healthy perspective on the things going on around you and you will not be swept up in unnecessary fads or trends fueled by mimetic desire (only wanting things because others have them/want them). Resisting unsavory methods to obtain your desires avoids their long-term consequences and we must work daily to do so. Desire also fuels ambition, but cannot be confused with need. Use your strong desire to motivate you to achieve rather than sacrifice to get instant gratification. What do you desire? How do you manage your desires on a daily basis? Are you working toward goals that have arisen from within you or things that make other people happy?

**Despair:** This is a feeling of depressive hopelessness that can be so profound that it proves fatal for some. At minimum, despair degrades one's quality of life and often causes the afflicted to isolate themselves from other people and their help. Is despair a common feeling in your life? Through observation, have you learned the warning signs for when you are beginning to slip into depression and despair? Are you even aware of it? Do you allow others to help or do you rediscover hope on your own? If so, are you aware when others are slipping into this negative mind-set? Are you willing and able to help them to recover from despair? In life, you may find yourself overcome with despair. A loss of all hope or confidence can feel finite and absolute, but it rarely is. You must find and cling to things in life that give you hope and inspiration. Allowing ourselves to ignore those things which will improve our emotional state will force us into depression. By applying positive thinking to our situations, we can avoid depression. What gives you hope in life when despair threatens to consume you? Have you determined whether despair is self-inflicted or caused by outside forces? Is there a spiritual remedy for your despair?

> *"It had long since come to my attention that people of accomplishment rarely sat back and let things happen to them. They went out and happened to things."*
> *— Elinor Smith*

**Destined, Destiny:** Destiny is a hotly contested issue, but it is an unavoidable fate that each individual was put on Earth to fulfill. Philosophers have argued for centuries for the exclusive presence of either free will or fate. We may never know if we are simply acting out our part in a grand cosmic play or if we are constantly defining our own course. Do not confuse a sense of powerlessness in the face of an unhappy life for the whims of destiny. Often, our destiny is to change our situation; we need only make the effort to improve our lives. In many ways, we define our own destiny by striving to realize our dreams. In the end, it doesn't matter whether your life is predetermined or not, as long as you work hard for what you want and respect others. How much agency do we exercise over our destiny? Is our destiny always already decided, out of our hands? How do you approach your future?

**Destitute, Destitution:** The condition of lacking necessities to support life. As a result of increasingly severe damage to our Earth, we as humans are rendering more and more places destitute. Are sustainable practices and conservation of our remaining resources the only things that can save the Earth from complete destitution? You can help by being a responsible consumer, recycling, and volunteering for causes that work to stop pollution and environmental degradation. How are you contributing to the destitution of our planet? How can you curb the negative influence you have on the environment?

**Detail:** A particular item or idea that determines many things in life. A lack of attention to detail can result in circumstances we later find regretful. If you allow yourself to become jaded with your life, you will let valuable details slip through the cracks. View the world with a curious disposition and a discerning eye. Very small actions or attitudes can speak volumes about a person. Details are also what make the difference when you are presenting yourself or your work to others. Read the fine print before you agree to something. Can small details change an agreement or contract from agreeable to unfair? Be mindful of the offers made by world leaders to improve your life; the details will always contain what they want in return. Do you give proper attention to detail? What do we lose when we don't pay attention to details?

**<u>Determination, Determine, Determined</u>:** To make a decision and come to a conclusion. Nothing worthwhile in life can be achieved without hard work. When you feel as if your goals are impossible or that you are fighting an endless uphill battle, sometimes your own determination is the only thing that will make you continue to persevere. Is it what pushes you to start and finish something? Is there a fine line between determination and stubbornness? Determination means that you have a goal and will do anything to get it. Is it worth periodically stepping back and evaluating both your goals and your means of achieving them? How we deal with difficult circumstances is what defines us; those who persevere improve their lives, while those who lose hope or are unwilling to work must languish in perpetual disappointment. Do not live life in such a way that you wonder what could have been if only you had worked harder. How has determination guided your life thus far? How can you use determination to accomplish what you want in life?

**Develop, Development:** Developing as a person can be a confusing part of life. Don't be too hard on yourself; many people are their own harshest critic, but they fail to use this information to help themselves and instead wallow in self-hate. Focus on ways to improve and develop things about yourself that you do not like, and you will become a fine-tuned version of yourself that can make you proud. Good habits lead to good personal development. What can you start doing today to develop personally? What have you already done to develop yourself? Are you willing and able to help others develop themselves? How can we facilitate the development of institutions in our society?

**Dialogue:** Conversation between people. When opposing viewpoints are in conflict, discussion and debate are the best ways to find a solution. By establishing a civilized dialogue in which all voices are heard, we are able to move forward and make progress. How can you turn hostile situations into dialogues rather than arguments? How can we enter into a dialogue with those who oppose us?

**Dictionary:** In many ways, this book is much like a dictionary, giving the definitions of words designed to spur you into thought. How does defining words help you better understand their relations to other words? How do words and meanings structure the way we think?

**Die:** Death is a natural and inevitable part of life. As we die, we can only hope that we have no significant regrets. To "live without regret" is a tall order; we make mistakes, and sometimes these mistakes lead to a certain amount of regret. Instead of regretting, concentrate on learning from your mistakes and then moving on. What do you regret? What can you do to take a step away from your regrets and work toward leaving them in the past? What can you do now to prevent regret in the future? Are you afraid to die?

**Differ, Difference, Different:** Don't let someone tell you that being different is a bad thing. We all have strengths and weaknesses that largely define who we are as people. Before you condemn something unique about yourself, try to see it as a strength. Celebrate differences between yourself, your culture, and others you encounter; extend an invitation of friendship across any division you encounter before you make assumptions. Difference is a "*constant*" that has always surrounded us, in mental ability, intelligence, ideals, and cultures. All of mankind is a collection of changing differences, and this isn't a bad thing—perhaps our greatest hope lies in our differences. We should balance our differences, not eliminate them. How are you different from your peers? Have you accepted your differences? What can you learn by examining the differences between you and others? Do some possess traits you find admirable that you could learn from? *Do you understand how differences can lead to conflict?*

**Difficulty:** Difficulties will come and go in your life. What matters is not how severe the difficulties are, but how we deal with them and what type of person emerges on the other side of a difficult stint. No matter the size or scale, approach plights in your life with determination. Also, do not view it as a failure if you have to ask for help; help allows you to eventually defeat difficulties. Do you let difficulties overwhelm you, or do you face them with a positive attitude and tackle them decisively? How do you overcome difficulties?

**Diligence:** Life is conducted by means of diligence. Those who are diligent TAKE. Those who are not diligent FORFEIT. It's the difference between weak and strong, smart and dumb, and organization and chaos. Be mindful of those whose diligence only serves to fulfill their selfish ends. Are you diligent in those things you wish to achieve? How diligent are you? Do you find things being taken from you due to lack of persistence?

**Dilute:** To dilute is to make something weaker and thinner. Liquids can be diluted by adding more solvent just as experiences can be diluted by undesirable elements. Life is diluted with substance abuse; it becomes less vivid, less real. What else makes life less vivid? Have you found yourself in a place where your vision is blurred by the negativity of your own mind or of those around you? What can you do in these times to find clarity? How can you resolve to add things that complement your life, making it fuller and more meaningful, rather than dulling and weakening the things you experience?

**Diminish:** So many things in our life diminish over time. We sometimes let little things diminish us day by day, when by themselves, they wouldn't be significant. Additionally, with age comes a loss of physical ability, but much can be gained from aging so long as one's life has been spent seeking wisdom and truth. How can we overcome obstacles without letting them wear us down? What was the most difficult obstacle you have overcome? Why were you able to overcome that obstacle?

**Disability:** Disabilities come in many forms, sometimes physical and sometimes mental. Some are obvious, while others go unseen. How can we overcome our own personal disabilities, and how can we be more accommodating to the disabilities of others?

**Disadvantage, Disadvantaged:** When the odds are stacked against you in any situation, you are at a disadvantage. We also refer to entire groups of people as "disadvantaged." This title means that for their entire lives, they have been fighting an uphill battle to fulfill even the most basic human needs. We should learn to help others, one of life's important tasks, so we can ethically develop. Do you recognize when you are needed by others in society and your personal life? How can we help the disadvantaged around us? Have you been disadvantaged in any situation?

**Disagree, Disagreement:** There is nothing wrong with disagreeing. However, you should make an effort to solve the disagreement and refrain from judging others solely on differing views. Agreeing to disagree is better than losing friends over differing viewpoints. How can you move past disagreements in your life? What do you do when you disagree with someone? What can be gained from a careful examination of an alternate view?

**Disburse:** To pay out or distribute from a fund. Given the size of the government, it's difficult to grasp the scope of our nation's budget. Have you analyzed the way public funds are disbursed? What can be found in examining the details of our country's expenditures? Have you really thought about where your tax money is going? Do you think you would agree with most politicians' decisions?

**Discern:** To realize differences. The way we perceive and distinguish things in daily life has a direct impact on the way that we see the world and live our lives. Every act of discerning is a decision, as we choose what factors to examine and which to ignore. How can we enhance our discerning process and rid it of biased influences? Ignorance is bred by those who do not discern the world with a critical eye. Do you examine all factors in a situation before you pass judgment?

**Discipline:** Refers to a process by which someone is trained based on a punishment-reward system or the actual action used to Self-discipline is a cornerstone goals will take discipline— mental trap if you lack the want. Even something as simple time changes the amount of work Does discipline in health and fulfilling life? What discipline do better implemented in your daily encourage or curb a behavior. of success. Accomplishing your you will find yourself stuck in a discipline to achieve what you as discipline regarding your use of you accomplish on a daily basis. exercise lead to a longer, more you have? How can discipline be life? How is a lack of discipline

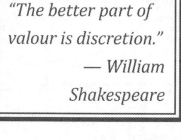

*"The better part of valour is discretion."*
*— William Shakespeare*

preventing you from accomplishing your goals right now? How has hesitance kept you from discovery?

**Discreet, Discretion, and Discretionary:**

Gossip is for lowly minds with nothing more important to discuss. Exercising discretion not only keeps your mind out of such mindless drivel, but it will also help you gain the trust of others. Where do you have discretion in your life? Where can you exert more discretion in your life? Do you find that others trust you with their private matters, or do they consider you a gossip?

*"In case of dissension, never dare to judge till you've heard the other side."*
*— Euripides*

attention, and generalizations are made about the negative aspects of a given people. What do we really gain by this? When have you been discriminated against? What could we gain by celebrating our differences and working to learn more about other groups of people?

**Discuss:** When people are open-minded and respectful of the ideas and sentiments of others, the line between discussion and debate is blurred. Debates are useful up until the point that they become two opposing sides attempting to drown each other out with their contradicting ideologies. A fruitful debate should be more of a discussion, a dialogue between two sides trying to understand each other. We achieve this kind of discussion by asking questions of those who disagree with us in order to understand to disarm their aggression. Make it your reflex to try understanding a viewpoint or argument before acting with hostility. Do you discuss before you attack? What kind of information do you discuss?

**Discriminate:** Analytical thought requires our ability to detect differences among people, things and ideas. It is only when we ignore the present in favor of the past that discrimination is a bad thing. This means that you should not let your preconceived notions stop you from gathering new information and changing your opinions. The bad kind of discrimination seeks to point out differences and portray them as something negative. By grouping people together, our society attempts to understand the needs inherent to a specific group. Such approaches fuel discrimination, as groups are pitted against one another in a quest for societal

**Disdain:** When we disdain someone, we look down on them as a result of thinking they are beneath us in some way. Consider perspective before you look down on others. Rather than simply judging their actions and life, perhaps you could learn to understand why they do the things they do. Do you analyze all the facts before you let disdain enter your heart? What right do we really have to disdain others? Have we not, at other points in our lives, been guilty of the very same sins?

**Disenchant:** To disenchant ourselves, the veil of illusion that blinds us from reality must be lifted, either by ourselves or others. It can be disappointing to be freed from comforting illusions created by many powerful figures as a means of control. When reality seems too harsh, you must ask yourself what you have to gain from pretending it isn't rather than doing something about it. If people are blinded to the truth and believe the world to be good, the status quo is easily maintained. How can we help ourselves become disenchanted, yet not disheartened that things may not appear to be as good as we believe? What ways can you help disenchant others? Would you prefer to live in a world of happy illusion?

**Disguise:** Be mindful to not only see the truth, but with every piece of information you receive, consider who might benefit from its distortion. By following the trail of interest, we can find the faces behind the masks of misinformation. The stereotypical disguise is employed by a person, but how might media information also come cloaked in disguise? Do you analyze that information with the critical eye necessary to see through its disguise, or do you accept it unquestioningly?

> *"Our inventions are wont to be pretty toys, which distract our attention from serious things. They are but improved means to an unimproved end, an end which it was already but too easy to arrive at."*
> — Henry David Thoreau

**Dispute:** Before you take issue with someone's viewpoint, examine all of the facts you are presented with. If you ask questions to gain understanding instead of making accusations, disputes can transform into discussions. Approach disputes by examining the perspectives of others rather than just your own. By considering their views, their motives will be clearer. Agreement can seem impossible—but still, how might compromise be reached through debate and discussion? Do you discuss before you dispute?

**Dissolute:** A dissolute life without morals is not worth living. Our moral structures give us purpose and frameworks for interacting with others. Dissolution can only end in distress. Does your moral compass factor into your decisions? How can you help someone who is dissolute?

**Dissuade:** To persuade someone not to do something. Politicians have been known to dissuade us from what we would otherwise know to be true. If you dissuade yourself because of logic and reason, your choice may be appropriate, but don't allow self-deprecation prevent you from taking advantage of opportunities. Do you let yourself be dissuaded by reason and logic? Besides politics, how else do we sometimes let others dissuade us from our beliefs instead of holding by our true tenets? Alternatively, do you find yourself practicing self-dissuasion because you fear failure or doubt yourself? Are you easily dissuaded?

**Distort:** To give false meaning about something. Distorting the truth is very damaging. The media distort the news through the way newscasters present information and through what they ignore. The exclusion of certain stories says as much about a media outlet as what it does report. Beware of ulterior motives to stir up fear in the public. Get all the facts before you let someone whisk you into a fearful frenzy. Are you on the lookout for the distorted misrepresentation of facts? How do the media distort the truth to fit their own agenda? Can you discern their agenda just by looking closely at the stories they tell?

**Distract, Distraction:** To divert your mind's attention from something. A life ruled by distraction will not be productive. Only with sustained attention and focus can we accomplish a task. Alternatively, distraction can also help us center ourselves when work becomes too taxing. Make sure to take breaks so you can be completely focused while working. Do you have a strategy to minimize distractions to maximize productivity? How can you rid your life of distractions?

**Divide:** Separate into different parts. A unified body of individuals is stronger than one divided against itself. So how can we avoid division? How can we band together for a cause and avoid unrest and internal divisions that will only make us easier to conquer? Do you prefer to work alone or in groups?

**Divine:** This word either refers either to something of gods or the action of intuiting something without knowing for sure beforehand. Humans may be trying to return to from whence they came: their divinity. Many neglect the divine in favor of earthly pleasures, but how is this a mistake? Where can we find the divine in the earthly, in everyday life? Do you believe in the divinity of gods?

**Divorce:** The separation of any two things, but usually refers to a married couple. Marriage is a commitment to spend the rest of your life

with someone and should be founded on trust and mutual expectations*. Divorce signifies the end of this supposedly eternal bond and can be very difficult, but is sometimes best for both parties involved. Just as marriage is an extremely important decision that should be a result of careful thought, divorce is an equally life-altering decision that should be given sufficient consideration. Could discussion and dialogue help mend the arguments we have with our spouses, while divorce merely puts an end to the conversation? How else can we use the word divorce to describe a situation?

**Dog:** Some call this species "man's best friend." First and foremost, dogs display an unconditional loyalty that is unmatched in other animal species. In addition, scientific studies have shown that dogs can recognize, interpret, and react to a wide array of human facial expressions. Anyone who has ever seen a dog do tricks knows that they can interpret verbal and physical signals. Dogs can be extremely intelligent and loving companions if they are shown the same qualities in return. Like a good close human friend, the life of an animal should not be taken for granted. Do you have a dog as a pet? How do you enjoy your dog? What qualities make canines such good friends, and what can you do to embody these characteristics?

**Dominate, Domineer:** Domination requires the submission* and subjugation of someone or something, and can be exerted in many forms. As human rights have made enormous strides in the last century and even the last few decades, domination in a human sense has been reduced but is far from completely diminished. Good examples are the fact that sensationalized gossip dominates the news and that money has come to dominate our political system, such as the influence of wealth on our legislative systems. Beyond

> *"If there are no dogs in Heaven, then when I die I want to go where they went."*
> — *Will Rogers*

this, others seek to dominate us through emotional abuse and manipulation in our personal lives. Can you think of ways that negative things dominate aspects of your life? Have you suffered under the domination of others? Have you ever wrongly dominated someone else? How do hierarchies and unfair domination hurt even those who do the dominating? How might collaborative efforts serve everyone better?

**Doom:** Destruction for objects, death for living things, or as an action, to condemn someone or something to this fate. For some, it may be inevitable, inflicted by others and inescapable. Despite the negative aspects of a given station in life or a quality of life inherited at birth, it is always possible to improve your station and avoid what may seem inevitable. How might we also be the makers of our own doom? Is death always doom? How do the choices we make affect whether we meet this kind of fate?

**Dormant:** Often our own capabilities lie dormant within in us, buried beneath insecurities and low self-esteem. These undiscovered parts of you only remain that way if you listen to nagging doubts instead of exploring your potential. Rather than ignoring urges to try new things, perhaps attempting them will reveal abilities you never knew possible. If this prospect makes you nervous, start with small actions and work your way up. And if not, what is there to lose by leaving your comfort zone? How can you explore what hidden talents you might have? What do you suspect to be lying dormant in you? Do you make an effort to periodically step out of your comfort zone?

**Dotage:** Dotage, or very old age, is a condition faced by those lucky enough to live a long life. Many things deteriorate, but what do you find gets better with age? How will you face your own dotage? With dignity, or with regret? Do you plan on living a long life?

**Doubt:** Doubt is healthy in the sense that it makes us double-check and make sure of all facts before we proceed in a given instance. It is unhealthy when you find that doubt in yourself is holding you back from trying new things or decrease your motivation to accomplish your goals. When you find yourself doubting anything in your life, do not waver in limbo; get the facts that you need to make a definitive decision. If you doubt that you have lived life fully, allow that to drive you toward new endeavors. How could you use your own doubt as a productive force in your life? Have you been doubted by others? How did you overcome that doubt and move forward?

> *"The whole problem with the world is that fools and fanatics are always so certain of themselves, but wiser men so full of doubts."*
> — *Bertrand Russell*

**Downcast:** Looking on the world with downcast eyes creates nothing but unhappiness. Optimism can require a greater amount of effort, but will make you happier in the long run, since the steady lull of discontentment can be intoxicating and painful. How can you shift your eyes upward and approach the world with a positive attitude?

**Dragging:** Time can drag, whereas it seems to race in other instances. When you decide to accomplish something, go for it 100 percent; never drag your feet when you know where you want to go. What causes the strange phenomena of dragging and racing time? Does time usually drag or race for you? How can we try to stay in control of how time passes for us instead of frequently feeling like it's out of our control?

**Draw:** Draw is a word of many meanings, and it forms many different words: drawback, drawbridge, draw out, draw up, and so on.

Yet what all the words have in common is the presence of <u>movement</u> and the insistence on <u>change</u>. To draw also means to <u>produce</u> something creatively. How can you integrate creative movement in your <u>life</u>? Have you <u>experienced</u>* any drawbacks?

**Dread:** Dread is a legitimate <u>emotion</u> we <u>feel</u> when approaching something unsavory or <u>anxiety</u> producing. Additionally, fear of the <u>unknown</u> is a normal <u>human</u> <u>reaction</u>; we seek <u>light</u> to avoid the mystery of the <u>dark</u>. However, human <u>behavior</u> in the face of the unknown has driven discovery and <u>developed</u> our species. How do you respond to the unknown or the unpleasant <u>circumstances</u> of your <u>life</u>? How can dread keep us from <u>achieving</u> what we want? Does the feeling of dread affect or health or well-being?

**Dream:** Dreaming is a necessary <u>part</u> of a <u>happy</u> <u>life</u>. Even if we don't always <u>achieve</u> our dreams to the <u>desired</u> extent, dreaming still allows us to see outside of our own <u>situation</u>. It enables us to envision life as we would like it to be, allowing us to set <u>goals</u> to achieve the idealized version of <u>reality</u> we picture internally. Is dreaming useful only because it gives us something to work toward? Do you achieve your dreams?

**Drug:** Drug dependencies are a scourge in our <u>society</u>. While the police and <u>government</u> regulate and enforce against it as much as they can, the final <u>responsibility</u> rests with each of us. While prescription drug usage for specifically medical purposes has <u>improved</u> the <u>quality</u> of <u>life</u> for many, drugs are often used as a means of <u>escape</u>—a method of coping with <u>reality</u>. While we may not ourselves be drug users, we can learn from this. Escapism is the greatest drug of all, and while it is enjoyable momentarily, its overuse can <u>blind</u> us to the <u>present</u> and become a dependency. Have you found yourself <u>dependent</u> on drugs? How do we <u>exercise</u> <u>power</u> over these kinds of dependencies in our lives? How can we <u>best</u> avoid their <u>dangerous</u> <u>effects</u> in the first <u>place</u>? *Are <u>pharmaceuticals</u> natural elements or manufactured elements?*

**Dumb:** In the old times, those who were dumb could not speak. All <u>groups</u> should have a <u>voice</u>, and should <u>exercise</u> the <u>right</u> to speak their <u>views</u> and <u>needs</u>. Nowadays, the term is used to refer to someone who is not smart or may be intellectually challenged. What would it feel like to be considered dumb? Have you used this term to refer to other <u>humans</u>?

**Dunce:** A dunce is a stupid person, one who <u>learns</u> slowly, or someone who does not fit either of these <u>categories</u> but is labeled as such. When do we unfairly assign such a <u>label</u>? At what point does such a label simply become a means for our own glorification through <u>comparison</u>?

**Dupe:** A dupe is person who easily believes <u>lies</u> and so is easy to fool and <u>cheat</u>. To dupe also means to swindle or cheat someone out of something. An <u>honest</u> person should have no need to conceal themselves from others, even those susceptible to such things. Have you ever been made a dupe? How might our <u>political</u> system conspire to make dupes of voters, and how might we fall for it? Alternatively, do you seek to fool others?

**Duplicity:** Duplicity is tricky or dishonest dealings of others. Those who <u>act</u> with duplicity <u>conspire</u> to make <u>dupes</u> out of others. How can we reveal the duplicity we find in others, and in institutions?

**Duteous, Dutiful, Duty:** Tasks that need to be completed. Everyone has duties in <u>life</u>, whether they <u>choose</u> to fulfill them or not. Fulfilling our duty not only performs a <u>service</u> to <u>society</u>, but also gives us a sense of <u>purpose</u>. We also have a duty to those we hold close to us; in our <u>actions</u>, we should be <u>honorable</u> toward them, and do right by them. What is your duty, and how are you fulfilling it?

**Dynasty:** Dynasties have often been built into <u>political</u> structures. In Chinese antiquity, for example, each son succeeded his father as emperor. In North Korea, this <u>structure</u> persists. But dynasties might also exist in America. Our <u>perceptions</u> of the familial successor of a politician will be altered by our <u>views</u> of the predecessor, but we must be <u>cautious</u> to examine all politicians regardless of their hereditary background. Right to rule should never be determined by birth, but should be based on the <u>abilities</u> of an individual. How might dynasties exist in American politics? Do you value content of <u>character</u> over heritage?

# E

**Earn:** To earn something is to <u>contribute</u> and <u>receive</u> <u>recognition and compensation</u> for your <u>work</u>. Contribution drives <u>society</u>, and <u>living</u> in a well-functioning society is inherently <u>better</u> for everyone's <u>lives</u>. Do you earn your <u>worth</u> or do you take it? Conversely, societies are often filled by those who <u>succeed</u> based on the <u>work</u> of others. This <u>creates</u> a disparity among <u>levels</u> of society; those in <u>power</u> can easily take <u>advantage</u> of the endeavors of those in their employ, reaping greater <u>benefits</u> than those who <u>struggle</u> simply because of the <u>privilege</u> society has granted them through <u>birth</u> and power. How has this sort of entitlement <u>affected</u> your life? Have others unfairly benefited from your work?

**Earth:** Our <u>planet</u> is bountiful and ripe with <u>resources</u>, but it cannot sustain a <u>philosophy</u> of want permanently. For much of <u>human</u> <u>history</u>, the <u>damages</u> being perpetrated against our planet were <u>committed</u> out of ignorance, especially in <u>situations</u> such as industrialization and commercial hunting. Now that the <u>effects</u> of these <u>practices</u> are well known, is it our <u>responsibility</u> to take <u>action</u> to <u>stop</u> them? The actions we take don't <u>necessarily</u> <u>need</u> to be grand gestures, but the simple act of <u>recycling</u> or volunteering to pick up litter

> *"We have always known that heedless self-interest was bad morals, we now know that it is bad economics."*
> — *Franklin D. Roosevelt*

in your city not only helps the <u>environment</u> but also sets an example for others. What are some ways you can help your <u>community</u> and the <u>world</u>? *How do you <u>perceive</u> this planet in a <u>spiritual</u> universe?* Sometimes the <u>task</u> of <u>helping</u> our planet seems insurmountable, but we shouldn't let this dissuade us from making efforts. The <u>result</u> of collective <u>care</u> for the <u>Earth</u> will also <u>give</u> more bountiful <u>harvests</u> to all. You do not have to "hug a tree," but just be mindful of your <u>waste</u>. When you <u>consider</u> all that you <u>use</u> and do every day, are you <u>contributing</u> to the Earth's preservation or decay?

**Earthly:** There are many things on the <u>Earth</u>— things to do, <u>consume</u>, see, and <u>love</u>—but we must <u>draw</u> the line between what is earthly and what is not. Attempt to <u>think</u> beyond your <u>senses</u> and <u>explore</u> how others may <u>perceive</u> the <u>world</u>, and how the yet-to-be-discovered <u>phenomena</u> of the <u>universe</u> may <u>affect</u> you. Do you <u>feel</u> like a tiny speck on a rock in <u>space</u>, or are you an oasis of sentience in the desert of the <u>dark</u> universe?

**Ease:** If you <u>find</u> <u>life</u> to be easy, you are likely <u>capable</u> of far more. <u>Consider</u> how you can <u>expand</u> yourself and your <u>mind</u> to have a larger <u>effect</u> on the <u>world</u>. Do you find yourself living <u>life</u> with ease? Do you <u>challenge</u> yourself every day?

<u>**Ecology:**</u> All <u>parts</u> of <u>life</u> on <u>Earth</u> inhabit their own ecosystems. We each have our <u>own</u> place within those <u>systems</u>; some are predators in the <u>form</u> of criminals, others are scavengers, and many of us are ants <u>working</u> to <u>build</u> the colony. But unlike other life forms, we are able to <u>change</u> our <u>roles</u> in that system. The only thing that <u>limits</u> each of us is our own will and <u>personal</u> <u>ability</u>, two things that <u>most</u> <u>people</u> either cast aside or take for <u>granted</u>. *Do you <u>consider</u> the <u>moral</u> implications of your ecological*

*creed?* While animals <u>act</u> solely on <u>instinct</u>, <u>humans</u> have moral agency that is lacking in the rest of <u>nature</u>. We may <u>feel</u> we deserve things in life, but if the means to that <u>end</u> affects our ecology, no amount of entitlement warrants the end. How has ecology <u>affected</u> your life? In your pursuit of <u>happiness</u>, do you take a longer route in an <u>effort</u> to adhere to a <u>sense</u> of ecological morality? Are you critical of others who rape our resources to change their <u>status</u> in society, or do you tacitly <u>consent</u> to their actions? Are you acting in the ecological role you are comfortable with and <u>want</u>? *Do you consider ecology a "<u>condition</u>" for living life?*

**Economics:** The <u>study</u> of how <u>people</u> <u>interact</u> with one another to <u>complete</u> <u>tasks</u> and <u>earn</u> a <u>living</u> is incredibly complex. There are endless variables, from a person's <u>motivation</u> and <u>ability</u> to the general <u>attitude</u> within a <u>society</u>. When you <u>look</u> at the <u>money</u> in your wallet, <u>remember</u> that it is just pieces of paper signifying the <u>worth</u> that you have earned, been given, or taken. Are you proud of how you <u>earn</u> your living? How much <u>value</u> do you place in those pieces of paper, versus the value of other things on this <u>Earth</u>? To expand further, how much of your life is dictated by existing economic <u>systems</u>? Our current capitalist <u>model</u> is built on <u>greed</u>, steering us in <u>directions</u> that often confuse what we want with what we need. What is the <u>difference</u> between <u>desires</u> and <u>necessities</u>? How do you differentiate between the two in your <u>own</u> <u>life</u>? *Is economics a "condition" of life?*

**Economy:** What do you contribute to the <u>world's</u> supply of goods and <u>services</u>? Are you, in the <u>end</u>, taking or giving <u>worth</u> to the world?

This becomes a major point of <u>crisis</u> for many as they <u>age</u>; they wonder whether they have been a drain or a spigot in <u>society's</u> reservoir of <u>resources</u>. At the end of the day, <u>ask</u> yourself what you have <u>produced</u> and consumed. Is your method of <u>living</u> <u>helping</u> or <u>hurting</u> the <u>economy</u>?

**-Ed:** *This suffix pertains to the <u>past</u>. Some* <u>people</u> *are* <u>moneyed</u> *and* <u>blessed</u>, *others are impoverished and cursed. What* <u>word</u> *would you* <u>attach</u> *to this modifier to* <u>describe</u> *your* <u>own</u> <u>life</u>?

**Edict:** When you <u>receive</u> an <u>order</u> from a figure of <u>authority</u>, how likely are you to <u>obey</u>? What counts as a <u>command</u> to you? Do you <u>consider</u> yourself a <u>follower</u> or a <u>leader</u>, and how do you <u>respond</u> to being put in the <u>role</u> that you do not <u>identify</u> with?

**Edify:** Are you a <u>teacher</u>? Do you better those around you, and do you <u>accept</u> the <u>advice</u> and <u>wisdom</u> of those who have broader <u>experiences</u> than you?

**<u>Educate, Education</u>:** <u>Learning</u> is an endless <u>journey</u> in <u>life</u>; you probably <u>learn</u> multiple things every day. Institutionalized education is a very <u>important</u> <u>part</u> of societal <u>mental</u> <u>growth</u>, outlining the basic subjects and their <u>knowledge</u> for every generation. However, this <u>wealth</u> of knowledge, important as it may be, should only be considered the baseline of learning. It's a <u>foundation</u> we should all possess and is not an <u>end</u> to our education. To truly educate oneself about the <u>world</u> and the <u>universe</u> is a thing to behold. Does education allow us to see the world in a much brighter, more pervasive <u>light</u>? Education comes in many <u>forms</u>,

> *"Education is the most powerful weapon which you can use to change the world."*
> — *Nelson Mandela*

from technical to classical to contemporary. Do you <u>consider</u> yourself educated? How can you further your education and invest in yourself more? Have you tried to <u>constantly</u> remain a <u>student</u>? Only by remaining <u>humble</u> about our knowledge can we remain teachable. *Does <u>teaching</u> and <u>sharing</u> expand our <u>spiritual</u> education?*

**Efface:** Do you often <u>find</u> yourself attempting to <u>hide</u> in the background of a <u>situation</u>? Are you <u>afraid</u> to put yourself <u>forward</u>, or do you regularly place yourself in scenarios where you prefer to go unnoticed? It is very <u>difficult</u> to <u>advance</u> oneself while effacing oneself. Attempt to make yourself a <u>person</u> who belongs at the forefront of a situation rather than in the background. On the other hand, many of us crave the limelight, often overshadowing others needlessly. This <u>attitude</u> can be incredibly off-putting for others. In <u>personal</u> <u>relationships</u>, such attitudes can make it nearly impossible to be a <u>true</u> <u>friend</u> and <u>support</u> others, as stepping back and doing nothing but <u>listen</u> proves <u>challenging</u>. How can you make yourself less conspicuous in conversation, <u>creating</u> <u>emotional</u> <u>space</u> for others or <u>allowing</u> them room to <u>shine</u>?

**Effect:** What effect do you have on the <u>world</u>? Is it a <u>positive</u> or a <u>negative</u> one? <u>Creating</u> an effect on the world is reciprocal; we all <u>grow</u> by <u>affecting</u> our <u>environment</u>. This <u>defines</u> who we are in <u>life</u> and how we <u>present</u> ourselves to others. As <u>science</u> tells us: for every <u>action</u> there is an <u>equal</u> and <u>opposite</u> reaction—<u>cause</u> and effect. Only when we act with <u>C.L.A.R.I.T.Y.</u> can we see the effects that our actions will have, and careless actions can create ripples and waves in the <u>waters</u> of life that <u>threaten</u> to swallow us whole. Do you attempt to see <u>consequences</u> before you act? How have the careless actions of others caused negative effects in your life? How have you <u>incorporated</u> those experiences and used them to <u>guide</u> your own actions?

**Effective:** Do your <u>efforts</u> in <u>life</u> <u>produce</u> the <u>results</u> that you aim for? Having an <u>effect</u> on one's <u>environment</u> is <u>important</u> to us all; it is how we are able to affirm our <u>place</u> in the <u>world</u>. Are you satisfied with the results of your <u>actions</u> and how they place you in life? While effort can be exerted to <u>improve</u> one's <u>situation</u>, it is only through effective actions that <u>change</u> can be <u>achieved</u> without <u>waste</u>. To attempt improvement without an effective <u>strategy</u> only leads to frustration, and frustration will worsen the situation, thus creating a vicious circle that impedes <u>progress</u>. Take <u>time</u> to <u>consider</u> your <u>options</u>, <u>discovering</u> the <u>most</u> useful way to <u>approach</u> a given situation before acting. Have you approached life ineffectively in the <u>past</u>? Using hindsight, consider the situation now. How could you have found the result you sought through more effective actions?

**Efficient:** Do you <u>consider</u> how much <u>energy</u> and <u>material</u> you <u>use</u> when you <u>accomplish</u> your day-to-day <u>tasks</u>? <u>Completing</u> even a major task is hardly <u>impressive</u> if it is <u>done</u> very inefficiently. This relates to the previous entries on effective actions.

**Effort:** Putting your all into a <u>task</u> is <u>important</u> in <u>life</u>; it <u>defines</u> how much of your <u>potential</u> you have <u>realized</u> and what you are able to <u>achieve</u>. When you make a conscious effort to <u>accomplish</u> something, you will <u>enhance</u> yourself. How much <u>effort</u> do you put into living your life? 'It's important to <u>avoid</u> needless effort, however, as 'it's fatiguing and does not garner the <u>results</u> we <u>desire</u>. Do you <u>look</u> before you leap, or do you carefully <u>plan</u> your <u>actions</u> and <u>apply</u> effort accordingly?

**Ego:** This three-letter <u>word</u> <u>defines</u> the <u>ability</u> to bring down the <u>most</u> powerful of <u>people</u>. It is the sense of <u>individuality</u> as opposed to the <u>idea</u> of one among <u>many</u>. But it is also a façade over our true selves that <u>helps</u> us to define who we are when we have not yet found the <u>true</u> <u>answer</u>. <u>Search</u> out what within you makes you behave as you do, and then reconcile with it to behave as you are meant to. Additionally, this word describes our self-appraisals. Unchecked and inflated, an ego can alienate others and leave them unwilling to <u>interact</u> with you. While it is incredibly <u>important</u> to <u>view</u> oneself as valuable and have a <u>positive</u> outlook on one's worth, overvaluing oneself <u>leads</u> to arrogance. Do you appraise yourself <u>honestly</u>? Has your ego been left unchecked, or have you interacted with arrogant people in the past? Arrogance can blind us all, leading us to believe we have nothing more to learn. Do you strive to maintain a humble attitude? How can humility improve your life?

**Eject:** To be ejected from a group is very disheartening. Have you ever experienced ejection? How do you deal with the turmoil produced by it? Additionally, it's important to recognize when negative elements of your life need to be removed. Too often we cling to destructive relationships because of a desire to maintain situations that were once positive. While everyone deserves a chance to make amends, if negative parts of your life refuse to do so, you must protect yourself and excise that which is toxic. Have you maintained unhealthy situations for too long in the past? Looking back, what could you have done differently to protect yourself?

**Element:** An element is a component of a greater good. We best thrive when we are in our own comfortable element, but it's important not to be sheltered in the fact that you're only exposed to your niche element. Expand your horizons, and elements for that matter, in which you are freely able to discover life. What is your element of choice when enjoying yourself? Have you tried to branch out and find other elements?

**Eliminate:** Elimination of something implies that it is unwanted. Many people attempt to eliminate unhealthy aspects of their lives, such as bad habits and poor relationships. What can you eliminate from your life? Consider the best ways of going about removing parts of your life. When should others be given second chances? Should you keep the door open for reconciliation in the future when removing negative relationships? The answers vary from person to person, and any decision should be approached with caution.

**Else:** In our lives, there is always another option to take in every endeavor and relationship. Consider this option, this "else" and weigh your choices. What choices have you neglected to consider in your life, and what forks in the road do you currently face?

**Elucidate:** The ability to make your desires, expectations, and ideas known to those around you fosters understanding between people in all areas of life. Comprehension of others comes through discussion, and vague conversation on any subject only leads to frustration, confusion, and sometimes confrontation. Sometimes confusion is accidental, and the tense situations that can be caused by conversations that lack clarity are only exacerbated by this; individuals become defensive when they feel they're being clear even when they aren't. Resolving such conflicts is achieved through patience and polite interaction. Do you make every effort to be clear in what you say to others? How can you politely request clarification from others? Additionally, be cautious of people who are intentionally nebulous. They seek to manipulate others by hiding their true motives. Do you mentally examine the motives of others and what they might attain through unclear discourse?

**Em-:** This prefix involves empowerment, embracing, and generally enhances a concept to apply it to something in practicality. How can you apply your abilities to your life, just as this prefix applies itself to otherwise lost words?

**Emancipate:** To set something free is to give it its own life and to define yourself as a liberator in the eyes of another. Have you ever emancipated something or someone from a imprisonment, either physical or not? Do you more often trap others in situations, or do you help them to live freely? Are you yourself free, or do you need an emancipator?

**Embarrass:** Embarrassment is a condition of shame for ourselves or others; it is a purely emotional concept that we often allow to rule over us. Shame derives from a sense of failure, specifically public failures. While a desire to impress others and succeed is normal and healthy, an overwhelming fear of embarrassment can cripple us at home, work, and in our personal relationships. Fear of failure prevents us from taking risks, and without risk there can be no reward. Do you often find yourself embarrassed over things that do not matter? How can you take control of situations to direct emotional charge away from yourself and others? How can you turn embarrassing situations into ones of mirth for all?

**Embrace:** To embrace something or someone is to make it/them a part of your life. We must be cautious as to what we allow to have this emotional proximity to us, as it affects our personalities and decisions more than mere acquaintance. Do the things you have embraced adhere to your moral standards? Have they continued to adhere to your worldview as you have grown as a person? As we change as individuals, so should the things we embrace. What and who have you embraced, and have you consistently held this embrace or allowed it to loosen?

> *"Unexpressed emotions will never die. They are buried alive and will come forth later in uglier ways."*
> — *Sigmund Freud*

**Eminence:** Some consider themselves above others in life. Are any of us truly better than others, especially due to our titles and official endowments? Superiority is a societal construct; in truth, all individuals are equal. However, because society generally seeks to separate individuals into groups rather than viewing us as unique entities in our own right, we are labeled according to political views, monetary assets, or skin color. These divisions create notions of eminence, and we should all work to eradicate them. How can you let self-important people know where they stand relative to you? How can you seek to avoid a sense of eminence in your daily life?

**Emissary:** Some people carry messages with them in life that they attempt to spread to others. This book, by its very nature, seeks to share a message that will allow readers to evaluate their own lives and establish their own answers. Do you feel that you have something that others should know? How can you spread this message, and how can you do so without infringing on the lives of others? It's important to recognize that as no one has all the answers, any message you wish to share with others may be the truth for you, but may not be for them.

**Emotion, Emotional:** Emotion rules all of us at times. It is a form of mental agitation or disturbance, and we recognize it in our minds as fear, happiness/sadness, love/hate, elation/depression, but do we understand how it affects our bodily health? It is the mood of the moment, but if misinterpreted and taken to an extreme, can emotion become a force that changes our lifestyle? Certainly, we should not allow it to make decisions for us. Emotions are an important part of bodily function and performance. It is important to convey to others that we understand and care for them. Learn how to change negative emotions such as depression into positive emotions such as happiness. Doing so will make everyone around you more comfortable, as emotions tend to spread. Listen to the people around you; know that you are inherently biased in judging your own emotions. Do you let your emotions dictate your actions too much or too little? What is the measure of your ability to differentiate between good and bad emotions? How do you cope with flash or instantaneous emotion caused by accidents, trauma, and other unknown or unanticipated triggers? Do you seek help in resolving your (deep seated) emotions?

Do we understand how emotions affect our bodily health? *Can emotion become a force that changes our lifestyle/creed?*

**Empathy:** Being able to understand the emotions of others is very important in day-to-day life. It is important in both personal and professional relationships, and we all must work to train ourselves to better understand those around us; to live together with the constant of changing differences and strive for happiness. How much credence do you give to the emotions of others? Are you a warm or cold shoulder to others in times of need? Relationships are built around the ability to understand and feel the emotional states of others around us, and it helps those who feel depressed and grief stricken as though they aren't alone. Empathy requires us to put ourselves aside and let others be the focus. Do you try to act selflessly to give others emotional space?

**Emphasis, Emphasize:** Everyone emphasizes things in their lives. Some people emphasize their hobbies, others emphasize work, and others emphasize exploration of themselves. What in your life do you devote your energy toward? Is it the most deserving aspect of life for your attention?

**Empty:** Emptiness is something that we must all deal with at times. It is often a symptom of missing something in our lives—success, affirmation of worth, love—but we cannot allow it to control us. All of us have something to be proud of. Find that aspect of yourself and emphasize it. Do you attempt to not dwell on those things that cause you pain? Do you attempt to help those who feel emptiness?

**Emulate:** Using others as an example can be helpful in finding the correct path to follow. But be wary of modeling yourself after

> *"When people talk, listen completely. Most people never listen."*
> — *Ernest Hemingway*

another. We are all individuals and all our lives will be different due to various circumstances. Make sure not to lose yourself as you follow the examples of others. Who do you emulate and why? Take into account that everyone has faults, including those we model our behavior on. With this in mind, avoid the faults of others, and focus on the good. Do you ever find yourself falling into bad behavior as a result of your peers?

**Emulous:** The danger that comes from emulating too much. When you find yourself jealous of another, you will forget the troubles that they experience and the obstacles that they face. Every person's experience is different, and it is important to maintain pride in yourself. Everything is relative, but be careful in comparing yourself with another. Do you follow your own path, or do you walk behind others, only following in their footsteps?

**En-:** This prefix enhances a word. Do you find yourself enthroning another person or an idea in your mind? Are you entangled within the problems that exist in your life? Attempt to emphasize yourself and the things that you love, rather than those that bring you negativity.

**-En:** This suffix involves creation; a room may seem darkened when you are sad, or you may be strengthened by your self-assurance. How can you enliven your life to explore the world as best as you can?

**Enable:** Empowerment is important. Enabling yourself and others to succeed in life is key, and we all must have our own way to do so. Embrace whatever it is that gives you inspiration and courage to do what you need to do. On the other hand, enabling poor behavior can be incredibly destructive to both yourself and others. When we see our loved ones harming themselves through drug use, alcoholism, or other unhealthy behaviors, remaining silent enables them to continue unhindered. Do you seek to encourage yourself and others to be their best? In what ways can you enable others to succeed?

**Enamor:** What captivates you with beauty? It may be another person, a profession, a hobby, or the joy of helping others. Make this entity a close part of your life; it will give you light in times of darkness and an anchor when the world is tumbling about. Be careful to not be enamored with things for shallow reasons; that which is truly beautiful exists beneath the surface. Do you find yourself drawn to the physical, or do you look inside to see the true value of that which appeals to you?

**Encyclopedia:** Having the information you need in one place is important. Life comprises chaos and order. Do we need both? This encyclopedia is a source of organized observations and knowledge. Hopefully, this one is a source of spiritual inspiration and guidance in forming or improving your creed for living life.

**End:** Nearly everything has an end (with the notable exceptions of irrational numbers and the universe). When you begin something, consider how you would like it to end and how it likely will end. 'It's only by living with a clear vision of our end goals that we can accomplish them. Do you keep long-term goals at the front of your mind so as to act in a way that makes them achievable? All our lives will end at some point, and it is important to consider how you would like your life to be thought of after you are gone. With this in mind, do you strive to live a life free of regret? Do you try to avoid hurting others daily? If you were gone tomorrow, would people look on your life and consider

you a good person? When something does end, let it be. Attempting to stretch something will only distort it into something it was not meant to be.

**Endear:** We all need warmth in our lives, especially emotional warmth. Endearing others and experiencing endearment gives us a sense of belonging, and it is important to embrace those people, groups, and things that we can share these connections with. Who and what is endearing in your life? On the other hand, endearment can also blind us; we can view those 'we've loved through rose-colored glasses, glossing over their faults and the negative impact they have in our lives. Does your sense of attachment to others blind you? Do you constantly reassess your relationships with others to see if either party could do more for the other?

**Endow:** We are all endowed with talents, skills, and connections. How we choose to leverage these advantages in life is up to us. We are also able to endow others with advantages to improve their own lives. What have you been endowed with, and what can you offer to others?

**Energy:** Energy is what drives us, our world, and our lives. On a personal level, energy can be considered where we place our efforts as well as our level of fatigue on a daily basis. In a global sense, energy can be considered that which powers our society. It is important to find the best sources of energy that we can, both in ourselves and in our world. Wasting energy is something to be avoided, as is energy that is only available through creating excessive waste. What do you use your energy for, and what do you desire in return?

**Enhance:** Improvement should be a goal for all of us. Throughout our lives, we can continuously enhance ourselves and enrich the lives of others. How do you enhance yourself every day? Do you have an end goal for who you want to be and a <u>plan</u> to become that person? Be careful to <u>avoid</u> enhancing only one area of your life to the detriment of other areas. Is it worth advancement at work if your <u>relationships</u> with <u>friends</u> and <u>family</u> suffer? <u>Consider</u> the larger picture as you improve your circumstances.

**Enigma:** Life is full of puzzles. Some of these puzzles are <u>simple</u>, and some are more <u>complex</u>. Some can be <u>solved</u> in a day or a week, while others take generations. As you <u>consider</u> the enigmatic <u>journey</u> that you will take through life, consider what is realistic to <u>accomplish</u> and what is not. <u>Striving</u> to accomplish the impossible is admirable, but often foolhardy and disappointing. Do you continually ponder the mysteries of life? Do you <u>maintain</u> a <u>sense</u> of wonder about the unknown, forever seeking to <u>gain</u> new <u>knowledge</u> and new <u>perspectives</u>?

**Enjoin:** You likely often <u>find</u> yourself being <u>urged</u> by someone—a parent, an employer, a religious <u>leader</u>—to do or not do something. How much credence do you <u>give</u> to these demands? Do you <u>expect</u> others to take your edicts with the same urgency that they expect of you?

**Enjoy:** We all have things in life that <u>speak</u> to us at a <u>level</u> beyond the mundane. The <u>best</u> way to live life is to <u>find</u> what you truly enjoy and to <u>embrace</u> it as much as possible. What is your <u>passion</u>? 'It's <u>important</u> to remember, however, that life is not purely about enjoyment. We live in a <u>society</u> where we must <u>work</u>, not only for income, but we must also put work into our <u>relationships</u>. Chasing nothing but enjoyment is, in the end, unsatisfying as it leaves other parts of our lives neglected. Do you <u>maintain</u> a proper <u>balance</u> between work and pleasure? Have

> *"Know then thyself, presume not God to scan, the proper study of mankind is Man."*
> — *Alexander Pope*

you found yourself tipping toward one side or another frequently?

**Enlightenment:** Some people look at enlightenment as a <u>gift</u> from <u>God</u> or an inherent <u>ability</u>, but true enlightenment comes from within us. It does not <u>matter</u> if someone claims to be enlightened. It matters that you <u>question</u> that person's enlightenment and validate its existence for yourself. In what ways do you <u>seek</u> to gain enlightenment? This book aims to <u>help</u> you find your own <u>creed</u> for living life—an approach to the <u>world</u> that is entirely yours, not only because it is tailored to you, but because you made it. With so much <u>chaos</u> and confusion in the world, 'isn't such clarity a form of enlightenment? How can you share your <u>approach</u> with others to help them <u>gain</u> the same understanding?

**Entitled:** To be entitled is to offer a claim to receive or do something. Some feel entitled to something, even though they did not put in the <u>work</u> needed to <u>receive</u> legitimate entitlement. Truly, it's a lack of <u>respect</u> to those who are actually <u>successful</u> and warrant entitlement. Have you ever felt entitled to something and didn't receive it? Why do people feel a sense of entitlement when they don't receive it?

**Enter:** Entering implies a new <u>beginning</u>. When you join a <u>group</u>, walk into a building, or form a new <u>relationship</u>, you are beginning a new <u>part</u> of your life. Whenever you begin something new, ask yourself, "How will this <u>affect</u> my life?" What do you <u>cause</u> to <u>end</u> as you embark on a new beginning? Have you lost <u>opportunities</u> as a result, and what have you gained to counter that loss?

**Entertain:** <u>Life</u> should be joyous. What do you like about the things that you find entertaining? If you are able to distill your pleasures to the essence of what you enjoy, you will more easily be able to find pleasure in life. Perhaps your preferred form of entertainment is bringing joy to others. Do you entertain other people? While relaxation is an important part of maintaining a healthy, happy life, be careful to not become too focused on chasing entertainment. The best approach is to use entertainment as a way to recharge oneself, allowing us a chance to become reinvigorated and giving us something to look forward to when we finish our work. Does entertainment cloud your life? Do you maintain motivation or succumb to lethargy in your entertainment?

**Enthusiasm:** Showing your enjoyment for life is important. People will be more interested in your life, and you will find that you have more enjoyment overall. Enthusiasm should also apply to how we commit ourselves to endeavors. If any task is worth doing—whether 'it's a job, a relationship, or a desire to make personal changes—'it's worth doing right. In order to have success in any of these things we must approach them with enthusiasm and, perhaps more importantly, we must constantly renew our enthusiasm for them. Do you find yourself taking on new tasks enthusiastically only to find your fervor wane as time goes on? What are some ways that you can renew your zeal?

**Enthusiastic:** Someone who obviously enjoys their life tends to be easier to work with, live with, and know in general. Positivity is infectious; if you are an enthusiastic person, others around you will find themselves enjoying life more as well.

**Entice:** Temptations are everywhere in life. You have likely found yourself tempted many times today, but you pulled through and concentrated on what needed to be done. Self-control is an important attribute that many people lack. It will make your life much more enjoyable, so that you can indulge in your enticements without guilt later. Additionally, if you find something enticing, there is likely a reason for that. Perhaps it's a sign that you're neglecting aspects of your life, or perhaps it's a new experience waiting to happen. So long as exploring these things hurts no one—including yourself—the opportunity to gain a deeper understanding of yourself through such actions is crucial. Do you find yourself drawn to things 'you've never done? Do you make an effort to avoid temptations when you need to do so?

**Entity:** It is important to differentiate between that which is real and established versus that which only exists in dreams and fictions. Which entities in your life are most important to you? What do you consider important without it being a part of your observable reality?

**Environment:** We must first learn to live in harmony in the environment that we were placed in. If we attempt to create our own environment (e.g., large cities) rather than learn to live in our existing one, we will ultimately destroy that which sustains us. While political leaders attempt to divide us on the issue of the environment, 'it's undeniable that our actions have ramifications. Worse, we 'don't reap the ill harvest of negative actions against our world, future generations do. We can wait for change to happen on a larger scale, but we can also do things in our own lives to improve how we interact with nature on an individual level. What is one thing that you could do differently in your daily life to help the environment? Could you recycle? Could you carpool to work rather than drive alone? The changes 'don't necessarily need to be drastic for you, but imagine how different life could be if all of us did something small.

**Epidemic:** Disease can come in many forms: viruses, bacteria, politics, and ideological movements. We must be careful to vaccinate ourselves against such threats, either by syringe or by using common <u>sense</u>. Keep in <u>mind</u> what your life <u>goals</u> are and whether new movements speak to your <u>logic</u> or your <u>emotions</u>. Do you tend to accept poor <u>leadership</u> from your public officials? Do you hold them accountable?

**Epitome:** It is easy to consider something or someone to be <u>perfect</u> when they hold the <u>qualities</u> that you are looking for. But <u>keep</u> in <u>mind</u> that no one is perfect; you likely epitomize something to someone, but you know your flaws better than they. <u>Additionally</u>, by placing others on a pedestal, we set ourselves up for disappointment, and we place undue pressure on them to <u>perform</u>. We all <u>need</u> room to make <u>mistakes</u> and then make amends when we do. Allow others the space to grow by acknowledging their <u>weaknesses</u> internally. Do you place others on a pedestal? Have you ever been placed on a pedestal? How did it <u>affect</u> your <u>relationship</u>?

**Epoch:** Throughout <u>history</u>, epochs have been used as reference points at which significant <u>change</u> occurred. They track our cultural <u>revolution</u> and show us <u>progress</u> or decline. What changes mark the epoch in which we live? Have these changes <u>improved</u> humanity, or do they send it down an unsustainable <u>path</u>? The <u>answers</u> to these questions can only truly be known in hindsight, but be mindful of them as they should dictate our <u>actions</u> in the present.

**Equable:** To be <u>calm</u> and stable is an admirable <u>trait</u>. We 'can't truly find <u>solutions</u> to the <u>problems</u> of our lives without approaching them with calmness and clarity of thought. Rather than reacting, we should <u>strive</u> to respond. Do you seek to find logical solutions to problems in a calm way? Consider your

> *A society that puts equality before freedom will get neither. A society that puts freedom before equality will get a high degree of both."*
> — *Milton Friedman*

<u>past</u>. Have there been <u>times</u> when your reaction to a situation has only made things worse? Would you <u>describe</u> yourself as equable or volatile?

**Equal:** <u>Fair</u> and balanced treatment for everyone would be <u>ideal</u>. Unfortunately, this is a lost <u>lesson</u> on some people. We must <u>work</u> together to <u>treat</u> one another as we would ourselves; equality can only be <u>achieved</u> by popular consensus. There are many in our <u>society</u> who seek to marginalize <u>groups</u> through inequalities, and too often we <u>accept</u> this as the status quo. How do you <u>respond</u> to these injustices when you see them? If you are subjected to inequalities either at work or in a larger <u>sense</u>, do you <u>speak</u> out against it? If you see others suffering such injustices, do you speak out even if it does not directly <u>affect</u> you? Do you <u>believe</u> you are treated as an equal?

**Equate:** What things in your life do you <u>consider</u> to be analogous to one another? Does <u>money</u> equate to <u>happiness</u>? Does <u>family</u>? What in your life do you live for?

**Equilibrium:** Equilibrium is when opposing influences are balanced; it can also lend to stable presence of mind. There are several <u>negative</u> outside <u>influences</u> that can swerve your <u>personal</u> equilibrium, and they can be of a small or large stature. Thankfully, there are <u>positive</u> influences that counter them, but you can only choose to seek out these positive influences for a stable equilibrium. Where does your personal equilibrium stand? Do you seek to add to it in hope of tilting it in a positive manner?

**-Er:** This suffix is <u>attached</u> to a word to denote someone who does something. What do you do in <u>life</u>? Are you a <u>worker</u>, a player, a trickster, or something else?

**Era:** Given the <u>size</u> and scope of <u>history</u>, we often <u>divide</u> history into smaller periods called "eras." It makes it easier to <u>examine</u> the various stages of our civilization and <u>enables</u> us to view both the <u>good</u> and bad of a given <u>age</u>. Our modern era—sometimes referred to as the Information Age— has brought the <u>planet</u> together in ways previously impossible. Our <u>connection</u> to one another and to the events of our <u>world</u> is constant, and while this has <u>negative</u> aspects, it gives us an opportunity to view the world on a <u>global</u> scale. Does this provide us with a chance to instigate <u>change</u> in a larger <u>sense</u>? Do you keep tabs on the important affairs of our world? What do you think the next era will bring, and what changes <u>need</u> happen before we reach it?

**Erase:** Erasing something implies a <u>negative</u>. We erase <u>mistakes</u>, we attempt to forget bad <u>memories</u>, and we try to wipe our slates clean at <u>times</u> to restart. But there is always a something left behind, a shadow of what used to <u>exist</u>. Do you attempt to <u>ignore</u> that shadow, or do you <u>embrace</u> it as part of your life? While we all attempt to live in ways that <u>avoid</u> mistakes, are not our mistakes as much a <u>guide</u> as good advice? Thomas Edison went through countless prototypes before achieving <u>success</u> in creating the light bulb, and each <u>failure</u> was simply reaching out into the unknown only to <u>discover</u> which <u>path</u> was not right. Have you ever made such mistakes?

**Erode:** When we think of this word, we often <u>consider</u> the scientific side of it—water and wind slowly eat away at rock and reshape it into something smooth. However, this word can be applied to our <u>personal</u> lives as well. Our <u>problems</u> can seem as unbreakable as rock, impossible to <u>overcome</u>, and immovable. How can we, with sustained <u>effort</u>, reshape the <u>difficulties</u> in our lives

to make them manageable? Additionally, even the strongest <u>relationships</u> erode over time if not maintained, leaving interactions with <u>friends</u> and loved ones shadows of what they once were. We must put in the effort to <u>maintain</u> such things, or they will be lost. Have you lost relationships simply by allowing them to <u>grow</u> dormant? How could you have <u>prevented</u> this from happening?

**Error:** We all make <u>mistakes</u>. If you dwell on them, you will find it <u>difficult</u> to move <u>past</u> them. Instead, celebrate your mistakes. Use them as learning <u>experiences</u> so that you may <u>help</u> yourself and others in the future. Have you <u>approached</u> your mistakes with a clarity that allows you to see their <u>benefit</u>?

**Escape:** We all <u>feel</u> like we need to escape some part of life at times. Perhaps it's the grind of <u>work</u>, or a <u>relationship</u>, or the same old routine. Whatever it is, escape in a <u>healthy</u> way. Many people make their lives worse by <u>escaping</u> with a "bang" and leaving a trail of debris. This often happens because we do not give ourselves time to recharge, <u>leading</u> us to make drastic <u>changes</u> to our lives. <u>Consider</u> the bridges that might be irreparably burned by such <u>choices</u>. Wouldn't it be better to escape your life with hobbies, vacations, or even a moment of meditation? Do you take the <u>opportunity</u> to do such things?

**Esoteric:** <u>Language</u> and <u>ideas</u> that are esoteric are meant to only be <u>understood</u> by a select few—those with a depth of <u>knowledge</u> and years of study most 'don't possess. 'We've all been in <u>situations</u> where others around us are speaking about things we 'aren't exposed to, whether 'it's <u>politics</u>, art, or sports. Though this sort of thing generally 'isn't <u>done</u> maliciously, it can exclude others and should be <u>avoided</u>. When you find yourself lost in an esoteric conversation, do you ask <u>questions</u> and use it as a chance to <u>learn</u>? Do you attempt to <u>convince</u> others that you 'aren't ignorant to protect your pride?

**Espouse:** It is <u>important</u> to have a <u>cause</u> or central idea in life; it gives us something to <u>identify</u> with and stand beside. Do you <u>advocate</u> for something or someone?

**Essence:** Everything has a basic <u>form</u> to it. Our essence is what defines us; finding it is how we <u>define</u> ourselves as people. It allows us to distill all our <u>experiences</u>, genetic urges, and <u>instincts</u> down to an entity that is us. What is your essence? In reading this book, you are searching for <u>answers</u> 'and trying to <u>find</u> your <u>creed</u> for living life. Is not this the essence of your <u>approach</u> to life?

**Essential:** Those <u>parts</u> of us that make up our essence are indispensable to us. For an athlete, the <u>body</u> may be essential. A philosopher is nothing without a strong <u>mind</u>. For others, 'it's family or friends. What essential to you, and how can you preserve it? Do you put in the <u>effort</u> to make sure the <u>important</u> people in your life 'don't feel taken for <u>granted</u>? Such effort goes miles to proving the <u>worth</u> others have to you.

**Estate:** Some of us leave more to our <u>loved</u> ones than others after we have lived our lives. In our consumer <u>culture</u>, we often place money and objects on a pedestal. We work our entire lives to accumulate <u>wealth</u> as though it is the most <u>important</u> thing to leave behind. While granting your loved ones financial security is of <u>value</u>, there are other more intangible things that one can give. Is the accumulation of wealth so important that it is <u>worth</u> neglecting your <u>family</u>? <u>Consider</u> the <u>memories</u> you will leave behind as much a <u>part</u> of your estate as your savings. What will you leave? Will your loved ones consider <u>money</u> and land to be the most important, or something very <u>different</u>?

**Esteem:** To hold something in high esteem means to <u>respect</u> it. We can hold art and <u>opinions</u> in high esteem, but most importantly, we can hold people in high esteem. What is <u>necessary</u> for you to regard someone with <u>respect</u>? Is it the same standard that you use in assessing yourself, or is it very <u>different</u>? Do you give others to <u>hold</u> you in the same esteem that you hold yourself? We must all be cautious, however, that in respecting others we do not <u>blind</u> ourselves to their faults. It is possible to respect the <u>work</u> ethic of an <u>individual</u> or their <u>intelligence</u> while still acknowledging that they are not perfect. Perhaps their life at home is not what it should be or they are prone to <u>anger</u>. Do you attempt to see the whole picture of a person?

**Eternal:** Given the brief <u>nature</u> of our time on <u>Earth</u>, the concept of the eternal is <u>difficult</u> to comprehend. How can we strive toward the eternal though? Obviously, our <u>actions</u> in life will only have a <u>brief</u> lasting impact after we are gone, but by keeping our eye on the bigger picture, we gain a greater <u>appreciation</u> for long-term consequences. Do you live your life with this in <u>mind</u>?

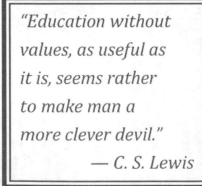

*"Education without values, as useful as it is, seems rather to make man a more clever devil."*
— *C. S. Lewis*

<u>**Ethical, Ethics:**</u> What is <u>right</u> and what is <u>wrong</u>? Different people will produce different answers to this <u>question</u> in varying <u>situations</u>. It is important to be able to weigh how a decision will affect everyone, including those people that you may not see. Many ethical dilemmas involve hurting people that you do not <u>communicate</u> with, and including them in your decision can require <u>empathy</u> that you do not normally <u>exercise</u>. One of the <u>goals</u> of this book is to help readers examine their lives in a larger sense, so that their decisions may be wise. In order to live ethically, one cannot simply attempt to avoid hurting others. A sad truth of humanity is that it is impossible to <u>avoid</u> damage to others. However,

consider romantic relationships; if a relationship is not beneficial for the two involved, is it not ethical to break ties so that each may have a chance at greater happiness? This requires foresight and the willingness to make an ethical, albeit painful, decision. Do you shy away from difficult decisions even though they are ethically proper? How has such behavior played out in the past for you?

**Etiquette:** We have established many norms for performing tasks and behaving among one another. It is oddly important to understand these norms because it can be the only outward impression that others take from you. Most important in this is perception. While we may intend to present ourselves in a certain way, the way others perceive us is in many ways more crucial to quality expression and mutual understanding. Do you consider how others might perceive your actions, even if they are not intended in such a way? Have you misunderstood others simply because they didn't follow our norms of behavior?

**Eu-:** This prefix denotes pleasantness. We use euphemisms every day to soften the tone of our speech, and we strive to live our lives with a feeling of euphoria and accomplishment. What in your life do you "eu"?

**Evade:** We live life in the pursuit and avoidance of various things. You likely pursue comforts and success while avoiding discomfort and disaster. What else do you evade? Do you pursue association with the right people? 'It's incredibly easy to avoid that which is unpleasant, even if it is necessary. An obvious example is confrontation. Sometimes confrontation is unnecessary and will do nothing but alienate others. At other times, it's important to stand up in support of important issues. Do you shy away from such things? What are other things that are difficult to deal with, but 'shouldn't be evaded?

> *"Man's mind, once stretched by a new idea, never regains its original dimensions."*
> *— Oliver Wendell Holmes Sr.*

**Evaluate:** Evaluation requires a metric to check against. When you evaluate yourself and others, what metric do you use? Is it too high or too low? Does it compel you to strive to be better and to support those that you care for? Be sure to exercise fairness in your evaluation and that any assessment, if asked to be shared, is constructive rather than hurtful.

**Even:** We all want our lives to be in balance—not too much work, not too much indulgence —but it is often difficult to even things out. What we can really strive for is to even things out in the long run. Every day need not be a balanced affair as long as the years are consistent. Does your life feel off-kilter? Do you work to regain balance when it does while maintaining patience?

**Event:** An event is an occurrence of something that happens. There can be a lot of stake for any given event, resulting in emotions being paramount. Don't let your emotions get the best of you when you're caught up in the competiveness of the event. Have you attended an event as of late? Were you extremely invested in it?

**Evil:** True evil can be very difficult to identify. Just as with the snake, it may disguise itself in many forms, and it may have a silver tongue. Be wary when things seem too easy to accomplish or unexpectedly pain-free. Assume that you will have to give something to get something. At times the evil in our world can be incredibly disheartening. News of shootings in schools and strife throughout the world—pain inflicted by humans on one another—can break the spirit of even the most optimistic of <u>individuals</u>. What can we do to stop such evil? Perhaps you see solutions, but others 'don't. Wouldn't it help all of us if you <u>shared</u> those views? Even something as simple as talking about the <u>issue</u> goes toward finding a solution.

**Evidence:** Evidence is a body of facts and information that serve as an indication if the results hold true. There are thousands and thousands of people are put in jail without proper evidence being <u>presented</u> in trial. On a lesser scale, we all have <u>personal</u> evidence that lends to the fact that we're a good person, but other people are not made aware of this evidence and therefore, they don't know how you truly are as a person. Do you try to give as much evidence as possible when presenting yourself to others? Do you shelter evidence?

**<u>Evolution</u>:** The <u>idea</u> that our <u>world</u> is shaped by <u>chaos</u> rather than careful manipulation. Life comes from a natural state of <u>adaptation</u> and <u>change</u>. Our current <u>environment</u> came about through the interaction of too many variables to <u>measure</u>, and it is still changing. Consider ways you have evolved in your own life. When you' start a new <u>job</u>, isn't there a period of change? Did you adapt to those changes easily, or do you find such things <u>difficult</u>? Of utmost <u>importance</u> in this is flexibility. As we encounter new things in the world—people, places, ideas—we must remain flexible in <u>order</u> to take what is <u>positive</u> and learn. Do you strive to be flexible as new ideas are <u>presented</u> to you?

**<u>Evolve</u>:** It is <u>important</u> to continually <u>change</u> in life, just like the <u>environment</u> has changed to become what it is now. How can you evolve over your life to become who you <u>want</u> to be? Do you <u>desire</u> to become a predatory hawk, or a peaceful dove?

**Exact:** Very few things in life are quite as they should be. Attempting to <u>achieve</u> <u>perfection</u> will be an <u>exercise</u> in frustration. However, in all things <u>improvement</u> should be the <u>goal</u>. As you read this text, you seek to find <u>answers</u> and improve your life. Do you <u>approach</u> other <u>parts</u> of your life in the same way? Do you <u>maintain</u> the status quo or attempt to make your life and the world better? Even if perfection is impossible, is there not something noble in attempting to ameliorate one's <u>world</u>?

**Exaggerate:** Everyone exaggerates. The key is <u>knowing</u> how much to exaggerate. When you are striving to be the <u>best</u> of the best, there will be many others who <u>claim</u> to be as <u>good</u> as or better than you. Are they just putting on a better façade? When in your life has a competitor bested you out of <u>merit</u>, and when have you been bested psychologically? Additionally, if you become known as a person who exaggerates, others will begin to <u>doubt</u> your claims. Be wary of using the superlative or saying something is "the best" or "the worst." Do you <u>avoid</u> hyperbolic statements? Are you wary of others who only <u>speak</u> in such terms?

**Exalt:** We all <u>praise</u> something. Perhaps you praise <u>God</u>, self-worth, or sound <u>Philosophy</u>. Such things are a <u>part</u> of your <u>identity</u>, and they say a lot about the person you are to others. If your <u>focus</u> is religious, are you not held to a higher <u>moral</u> standard than others? Do you take into account how others will <u>view</u> you based on these proclamations? In all things, we must <u>strive</u> to make sure that our <u>actions</u> align with what we profess to the <u>world</u>.

**Examine:** Always look closely at life. There are many things and people that <u>pretend</u> to be something they are not. Look for the cracks in the <u>stories</u> of others, check the varnish on the chair you are about to buy. The devil is in the details. Truly, by seeking answers and establishing your creed, you are in a <u>state</u> of self-examination. 'Shouldn't we also <u>apply</u> such vigorous appraisal to the <u>world</u> around us? 'You've already turned your eye inward, but as no one is an island, do you also balance this action with the examination of what is presented to you daily in our society?

**Example:** An example characterizes or illustrates a general rule or guideline. Oftentimes, we let an example stand as an end-all, be-all in demonstrating an issue or whatever is being argued. Rather, it should simply represent a singular entity, with more examples yielding more accurate results and responses. How do you use examples? Do you welcome them into your thoughts?

**Exasperate:** We all lose our cool sometimes. It is important to maintain control of yourself and look at the situation objectively. What is it that makes you frustrated or angry? Realize what that is and you will be able to harness your emotions more readily. Additionally, have you ever found yourself to be exasperating to others? Many things can cause this, such as a desire for the spotlight or perfectionism. It's important to make note of it when things like this occur in order to prevent the alienation of others. Are you mindful of ways you might exasperate others? Do you make changes according to how others respond to you?

*"An early-morning walk is a blessing for the whole day."*
*— Henry David Thoreau*

**Exceed:** Always defy expectations. There is something that everyone is better at than everyone else. Find out what that thing is and push beyond the limit of what seemed to be possible. Do you know what it is you are best at? Do you constantly seek to improve in that field? Additionally, it's important to recognize what others have to offer as well and encourage them in that. All too often, we allow ourselves to rest on our laurels rather than seek to improve ourselves. Can you put your pride aside and encourage others when they are better than you? Do you allow them

to push you to be greater, or do you grow bitter?

**Excerpt:** We often judge things based on less than the sum of their parts. When you open a book on a bookshelf, you likely read a few sentences without absorbing the full story. When you give someone an excerpt of work, which is the representation that they have, they will judge the overall work on that. Are you displaying your best work? Do you strive to gain a full perspective on things before making judgment?

**Excite:** Life is best with some excitement. What makes life great for you? After you do what needs to be done every day, consider how you can live life the way that you want to. This not only includes short-term diversion, but also long-term goals. 'It's never good to focus solely on that which excites us, but by striking a good balance between obligations and distractions we live richer lives. Do you maintain this balance? Do you find it easy to put your distractions aside and focus on your obligations, using them as a reward for your hard work?

**Excuse:** There are many things that we consider "acceptable" and "unacceptable" without thinking about them. You have likely had to excuse yourself in the past. What do you consider an inexcusable offense? On the other hand, this word can be used to describe the explanations we offer to explain failings. When you perform below expectations, do you pass blame to extenuating circumstances, or do you assume responsibility?

**Execute:** When you carry out a task, do you do so with utmost precision and care, or do you allow nature to help decide its course? Many people stress themselves over executing tasks that are impossible or planned in a roundabout fashion; think about how realistic your task is before executing it. When we approach situations with foresight, we can execute tasks in a much more productive manner, leading to better results and less stress. How much time do you spend planning your endeavors? Do you rush to the finish line, or calculate a strategy?

**Executive:** People under the "*constant*" of *corporacracy* are bestowed with enormous power over others. However, this title does not make these people any more infallible. Some people in positions of power have earned their place through strong leadership and work, while others have simply taken credit for the work of others. What sort of role would you prefer? Are you known for leadership and work? (See also: *A Day of Life: Moments in Time* and *Corporacracy*)

**Exercise:** The equivalent of energy and movement. Exercising one's mind and one's body will maintain health and lead to a happier life. Exercising allows one to reach physical limits which can then be pushed. This should be a central part of your life rather than an everyday chore. It seems that we often put more effort into taking care of our possessions than we do our bodies, leading to sedentary lives that are shortened by disease. Do you make strides to exercise several times a week? Do you have forms of exercise you enjoy? Oftentimes, 'it's easier to find success in this area by exercising with a friend, so be sure to seek out others to take part in exercise with you.

**Exert:** It is important to push yourself every day. Exert yourself in maintaining relationships, in completing work, and in exercising your body and mind. We grow through exertion, and life is all about growth. Without this, our lives lack forward momentum, and we begin to feel listless in the routine of our work and actions. Where do you place your efforts? Do you balance them between life and work?

**Exhibit:** What we show to the world is what other people see us as. The impressions others have of us are lasting, and they determine how the rest of the world responds to us and the opportunities we receive. We often exert ourselves greatly at the outset of anything new, such as a new job or new relationship, only to grow complacent as time goes on. Do you always seek to exhibit the positive traits you have daily? How can you put your best foot forward even in situations in which you've been for years?

**Exist:** Existence is a precious gift that we must all cherish. By taking things for granted in life, we waste the precious element of our existence daily. Do you seek to honor that which you have? Do you behave in a way that shows others you appreciate what you have, whether it's your job, your friends, or your family?

**Exotic:** Everything is exotic to someone else. Travel to a foreign country and you will find out just how exotic you are. We are all the same in how different we seem to one another. What do you consider exotic, and why? What's most important here is to consider what we can learn from these different cultures and incorporate into our own view of the world. Are there aspects of other cultures that you consider superior to our own? Do you integrate such things into how you approach the world?

**Expand:** To expand is to simply become larger. For example, when there is applied pressure to an object, it expands further and further to the point of possibly bursting. The same holds true for your individual life; the greater the negative influences you have infiltrated throughout your life, the more that pressure and anxiety could cause your life to spiral out of control and eventually burst. Seek to expand your life's balloon to the biggest size possible in a healthy manner. What do you want to expand upon in your life? Does your life's balloon expand too much?

**Expect, Expectation:** We all have expectations in our lives. How realistic are yours? To expect beyond reality usually results in disappointment. While expectations are a part of every 'human's experience, we should avoid considering our expectations something we deserve. Additionally, unless expectations are made clear to others, can we really be upset when they are not met? Only through careful and clear communication can we make our expectations known to others. Do you communicate what you want to others? Think about past experiences. Has there been a time when your expectations were not met? How could you have communicated them more clearly?

> *"Life's under no obligation to give us what we expect."*
> — *Margaret Mitchell*

**Expediency:** We often try to do things as quickly as possible. Take a look around and consider whether or not expedience is really necessary. Take care in the work that you do and do not rush yourself. Have you given into the temptation to rush through work in the past? Were the results positive or negative for you, and how could patience have affected the outcome?

**Experience:** An experience is a practical observation of facts or events. A great feeling can come about from a positive experience, whether that is shared with friends and family, or shared internally. Some have a specific destination where they feel they can garner the best experience possible. Do you have a vacation spot like this? What makes an experience worthwhile to you?

**Expert:** We often trust experts to know a lot about things we do not. This is appropriate. But we also often trust experts to know a lot about things that they may not know. When listening to an expert, make sure that you consider their credentials. Have they seen success in their field of expertise? Have their ideas proven to be right in the past, not only in the short term, but also the long term?

**Expire:** Everything expires eventually. Take note of time and enjoy what presents itself as it comes. If we focus too much on the future, we lose sight of 'what's important in the present. Are you mindful of the future but not at the expense of the moment?

**Explanation:** We often need to supply explanations for how to do things and why to do things. When explaining something, think about how it sounds to yourself as well. Would you understand your explanation if someone used it on you? As with all things in life, clarity is of extreme importance. Are you clear in how you explain things to others? Additionally, sometimes we require explanations for things we do not understand. The only way we can be taught and learn about new things is if we lower our pride and allow ourselves to be willing to receive instruction. Do you do this when you need help? Do you seek instruction when you lack understanding?

**Explicit:** Explicit instruction carries more value than most people realize. Vague wording and subtle hints will often go misunderstood; attempt to be explicit as often as possible. Also, be mindful of those who attempt to be vague. We often see this with political figures—they seek to be vague and avoid true explanations of their plans, actions, and ideology. Are you clear in your own explanations? Do you scrutinize vague explanations?

**Exploit:** We all explore loopholes and take advantage of opportunities in life. But do not let exploitation become a philosophy. It may serve you in times of need, but if we all exploit when we can, there is little honesty left. This word can also be used to <u>describe</u> how we treat the Earth. By stripping the <u>planet</u> of its natural <u>resources</u>, are we not exploiting what 'we've been given? Do you seek to <u>approach</u> things thoroughly, or do you take shortcuts? Take <u>pride</u> in what you do, and avoid such things.

**Explore:** To explore is to travel through in the hope of learning something new. The world serves as a magnificent venue for exploration, but some seclude themselves to exploring <u>new</u> areas in our home country, rather than exploring unfamiliar horizons and terrains overseas. Altogether, the <u>ability</u> to explore is synonymous with the ability to be creative and <u>think</u> outside the box. Where do you explore? What kind of <u>feelings</u> do you have when you explore something new?

**Exponent:** What do you exemplify? When we truly <u>believe</u> something, we are exponents of that <u>idea</u> or belief. It becomes a <u>part</u> of us and should be <u>shared</u> with others. Is there something that people know you for, and do they <u>celebrate</u> it or <u>discourage</u> it? Do you share your beliefs with others, or do you <u>hide</u> your <u>thoughts</u> from others?

**Expose:** <u>Truth</u> is needed in life. Living with a <u>knowledge</u> of only lies and half-truths is impossible, and so we all have the <u>responsibility</u> to continuously expose that which is fact. This can only be <u>accomplished</u> through careful <u>consideration</u> of that which is presented to us through conversations with others or <u>media</u> outlets. Do you carefully <u>examine</u> that which is presented to you? Do you attempt to find clarity in the <u>motivations</u> behind half-truths?

*"More than any other time in history, mankind faces a crossroads. One path leads to despair and utter hopelessness. The other, to total extinction. Let us pray we have the wisdom to choose correctly."*
*— Woody Allen*

**Express:** There are endless ways to express yourself. We express ourselves through <u>art</u>, words, <u>dance</u>, and more. Everyone has a preferred method. Find out what best represents you and <u>embrace</u> it. By doing so, we <u>lead</u> <u>happier</u> lives in the long run. What are some of the ways in which you express yourself? What hobbies and <u>interests</u> do you have? Do you make <u>time</u> to engage in those pursuits?

**Extinct:** Many things can die out—animals, <u>ideas</u>, and <u>cultures</u>—but we work to <u>remember</u> all of them so that they are not forgotten. Of <u>course</u>, there are many that we miss; many <u>ideas</u> die with their creators. How can you make sure that your <u>legacy</u> and that of your <u>loved</u> ones never go truly extinct? What ideology can you pass on? Does your <u>own moral</u> compass guide what you <u>seek</u> to leave behind?

**Extra:** There are many things in life that are unnecessary— <u>material</u> goods, extravagant meals—but we <u>care</u> for these things despite knowing that we do not <u>need</u> them. We can <u>improve</u> the lives of others by forgoing some of these luxuries, and you will likely find altruism more rewarding than <u>greed</u>. Can you distinguish between things you want and things you need? Do you <u>strive</u> to live simply, excising that which is unnecessary?

**Extraneous:** It is often <u>difficult</u> to discern which elements of <u>life</u> are <u>important</u> versus which are unnecessary. It is easy to <u>place</u> importance on things which do not truly matter, but which we <u>develop</u> attachments to anyway. What in your life is extraneous, and what is <u>integral</u>? How could your life be <u>improved</u> by removing what is extraneous?

**Extreme:** Moderation is key—moderation in consumption, behavior, and our views of others. Taking things to the extreme is almost never the appropriate course of action, and it is often caused by a misguided sense of self-righteousness. Today, we live in a world of extreme pollution, noise, and haste. Attempt to live not only within your means, but within your needs—going to extremes will not help you, except in your ambition. Do you find your responses to situations to be tempered or extreme? In considering past reactions that 'you've had, how could they have been improved by calm consideration?

**Extricate:** It is very normal to find yourself in a situation that seems inescapable, whether it is trouble at home, stress at work, or discontent with society. But remember that you always have the power to remove yourself from these things one way or another. Be sure to communicate problems with others, and try not to solve too many problems at once. Have you found yourself in toxic situations from which you needed to extricate yourself? Have you found yourself clinging to unpleasant circumstances simply because they are familiar?

**Extrinsic:** This word applies to things that are not essential to us, but they still play a role in influencing us from the outside. It 'shouldn't be difficult to identify things like this in your life, but consider what they truly offer. Our society offers us security and opportunities, but are those truly essential to life? Consider what is most important. What do you truly need?

**Exult:** This word applies to a feeling of happiness and excitement. What do you celebrate in life? Do you take time to celebrate not only your success, but also the success of others?

# F

**Fact:** It is important that you take care to <u>think</u> critically about every supposed fact presented to you. What are the characteristics of fact? Must it exist as something done; something proven to be true and accurate? <u>Listen</u> closely and ask <u>questions</u>; this shows your <u>interest</u> and <u>builds</u> your <u>knowledge</u> around valid facts, and causes <u>opinions</u> put forth as facts to unravel before your <u>eyes</u>. Are facts enhanced by the <u>ability</u> to <u>communicate</u> or present them? When listening to others, take into consideration their credibility about the subject and as a person before determining how factual their statements are. What constitutes a fact—actual and certain evidence of an occurrence? Are you <u>capable</u> of <u>separating</u> fact from opinion and conjecture? When a statement is determined to be fact, do you base your <u>decisions</u> and <u>actions</u> on them?

**Fail:** It is not enough for a <u>man</u> to know how to ride; he must also know how to fall. You can fail a test, a <u>friend</u>, or a life goal. Also, brakes and organs can fail. This is the dramatic superlative that we use when we are disappointed in ourselves or others. We will fail at the time we think we will fail. When you are inclined to say you have failed, look at what you have <u>gained</u> as a <u>result</u> of this supposed "failure;" you will find that it is hard to do anything in <u>life</u> without <u>learning</u> something; learn from <u>mistakes</u> and <u>grow</u>. Do you own your failures or do they own you? Do you <u>judge</u> others as failures? Do you accuse the <u>government</u> and other entities of failing you?

> *"Facts do not cease to exist because they are ignored."*
> *— Aldous Huxley*

**Fair:** An action that is fair is considered <u>just</u>, equitable, unblemished, <u>clear</u>, <u>good</u>, favorable, and maybe even beautiful. Being fair is being honest and unbiased. As we <u>judge</u> who or what is fair, do others judge us also? Do fairness and equalization demand agreement? Do you apply the same fairness to living <u>life</u> as you expect back? How have you been treated fairly or unfairly?

**Faith:** A <u>belief</u> in something that does not require proof of any <u>kind</u>. Our daily interactions with strangers are made possible by our faith in <u>humanity</u>, faith that we are surrounded by decent people and faith that we live in a <u>society</u> that protects us against those who mean us <u>harm</u>. Faith in a higher <u>power</u> presents <u>issues</u>: <u>Wars</u> are waged over conflicting beliefs that have no <u>resolution because they are</u> based on empirical <u>ideologies</u> and therefore can never be unequivocally proven one way or another. Faith should be a <u>personal</u> matter; you have your faith for subjective <u>reasons</u>, so <u>understand</u> when someone else doesn't share your faith. Do you have faith in humanity? Do you respect the faith of others? Is faith in yourself the most important? Should faith be abstract or should it be the next step beyond <u>analysis</u> and <u>reasoning</u>? *Is your faith directed by you, by <u>religion</u>, or by society? Does your faith embrace spirituality?*

**Familiar:** Familiarity is a derivative of use; the more you <u>experience</u> or use something, the more familiar it becomes to you. What in your <u>life</u> is familiar and what is <u>foreign</u>? Familiar things can make us feel <u>safe</u> and <u>comfortable</u>. How we deal with unfamiliar things <u>shapes</u> who we are and how we live. Enjoyment found in the familiar must not take priority over enthusiasm for new experiences and knowledge; it is tempting to settle into the solace of predictability, but overindulging this pleasure breeds a static lifestyle and with it a lack of progress. Do you take pleasure in, yet make an effort to break away from the familiar and well-worn parts of your life? Do you try new things? What and where is familiar to you?

**False:** Anything that is not as it has been claimed to be. Though false teeth are relatively inconsequential, false love or friendship can be devastating. Be sure to avoid using deception to achieve your goals and be wary of it in others. Do you regard facts you are given with respectful scrutiny? Has betrayal shaped your life long after you were wronged? In what ways can you let go of your fears and trust again?

**Family:** *The foundation of life.* Family exists in many shapes and sizes, is not always based on blood relations, and above all should never be taken for granted. You must take care to respect and love all the members of your family; they will catch you when all other safety nets fail. You will encounter challenges in your life which you cannot face alone and likewise, your family members will confront challenges of their own. Who do you consider your family? Why do you consider them family? Many different types of bonds forge families and should be regarded with respect, even in the absence of understanding. Family should be cherished and maintained, even when we must make sacrifices in order to do so.

> *"What can you do to promote world peace? Go home and love your family."*
> — *Mother Teresa*

*Bumps, dust, and potholes were fare for that day of excursions in Copper Canyon, reputed to be the longest canyon in the world, located in the states of Sonora and Chicueequ, Mexico. While there, I found myself to be one of a few foreigners among several Hispanic school children from Napoli, Mexico.*

*Wanting to practice my very limited Spanish, I attempted to engage a young man who appeared to be fourteen or fifteen years old in conversation. My mouth dropped when "Como está usted?" was answered with: "I am fine. How are you?" A very pleasant dialogue ensued and wanting to be philosophical in time with my writing, I asked a question that I was sure would be answered with the words "My health." The question was "What is the most important thing in life?" I was mildly surprised when he quickly answered, "My family," but then I repeated the same question, changing one word: "What is the most important thing to life?" After brief contemplation, out came, "My health."*

**Fantasize, Fantasy:** To use your imagination to create plausible or completely unrealistic situations and possibilities. A healthy amount of fantasizing helps you orient yourself with respect to your goals and aspirations. Unmitigated fantasy can begin to take over your life; if you find yourself often escaping the reality of your life through fantasies, it is time for a change. Do your fantasies consider any degree of peacefulness, spirituality, evil or any combination thereof? About what do you fantasize? Do you use your fantasies to motivate or escape?

**Fate:** A concept situated opposite of free will on the spectrum of how much control we have over our lives. Fate represents a predetermining force that governs the way our lives unfold. A belief in fate can be a way of comforting ourselves when things go wrong or a way of relinquishing personal responsibility for our lives. Try accepting both of these concepts; our lives may be predetermined, but the way you treat others and carry yourself (as a creed) has immediate consequences even if they are not capable of disrupting any big-picture plan that an inconceivable force may have in store. Look for blessings in disguise; though it may seem as if fate has dealt you a bad hand, you will generally find positive aspects of your situation. If fate throws a knife at you, there are two ways of catching it: by the blade or by the handle. Do you assume responsibility for your actions and recognize your agency to enact positive change in your life? Can fate be altered by perception? Do we fear what we are in awe of?

> *"Never esteem anything as of advantage to you that will make you break your word or lose your self-respect."*
> — *Marcus Aurelius*

**Favor, Favorable:** Being unfairly nice to a specific person. Also, doing something nice for people that they need done. Do you favor one person over another? Why? Do you seek many favors while bestowing few? Are your favors freely given? Do you recognize the practice of favoritism? Are your favorable intentions helpful intentions or conditional intentions?

**Fear:** Fear is an emotion; fear is the feeling that one is vulnerable or in immediate or inevitable danger. In our lives, fear can be debilitating if we feel as if we cannot escape the cause, and invasive if used by others as a means of control. Should fear be used as a justification for violence? In those situations which involve the possibility of violence, rational thought should take precedence over raw fear in decision making processes. If we always react to our fears, we never get the chance to surmount them. Does an increased working knowledge of the world around us serve to abate fears through explanation of the unknown? Is created fear a significant weapon, and should fear be challenged rather than succumb to it? As H. L. Meneken once said "The one permanent emotion of the inferior man is fear—fear of the unknown, the complex, and the inexplicable. What he wants above everything else is safety. However, if we choose to never gamble with our safety for the sake of opportunity we will never progress in life." Do you face or challenge your fears? Do you think rationally before you submit to your fears? What are you afraid of?

**Feat:** An accomplishment that requires great determination and skill. Feats can operate on many levels; if you challenge yourself and succeed, you have completed a feat. Always be sure to push yourself to new heights; you will be surprised at what you are able to achieve. Do you strive to accomplish feats of any kind, or are you content with operating at or below what is expected of you?

**Feel:** To be aware emotionally or physically of the presence of something. Just as we extend our arms in front of us to feel our path in a dark room, we must use our emotional intelligence and intuition to discern things about those around us. Sometimes people are unfeeling and don't pay much attention to other people's affairs. We can't cultivate genuine relationships with others if we lack empathy. Our friends and family deserve this connection, and if we deny them that we run the risk of making them feel taken for granted. This extends to strangers as well; we can't hope to solve the problems of our society without compassion for others. Are you sympathetic to others while still being aware of your own thoughts and feelings? Do you treat others compassionately? Do you feel for people when they have bad luck? Do you put all of your observational skills to use in feeling your environment and those in it?

**Feeling:** The sense of touch or intuition which we can use to learn about our environment and situation. Explore feelings and express your feelings openly. Don't jump to conclusions based on feelings alone; feelings should be used as tools to obtain answers through further investigation. Do you trust your feelings? Are you open about your feelings toward others while still maintaining a proper amount of tact? What intuitive feelings have you had?

**Fetish:** Anything that a person is devoted or drawn toward too strongly to an exaggerated or obsessive degree. When a part of your life becomes so important that it takes precedence over all other activities, it is time to step back and evaluate your interest in this object or activity: is it healthy and sustainable? At what point do our interests become fetishes?

**Fidelity:** Loyalty and faithfulness are qualities that we should strive to embody every day. Surround yourself with those who show the most genuine fidelity; sometimes we need to lean on others for support in life and like anything meant to support any kind of weight, these people need to be trustworthy. Do you do your best to make your decisions and take action with fidelity?

**Fight:** To work hard to overcome something; the connotation suggests that violence is involved, but violence is not necessary to constitute a fight. What in your life have you fought for? Do you look for fights or fight only as a last resort? What is worth fighting for? When does fighting lead to battle and war? Do you have the courage to back away from a fight? Do you fight fairly?

**Figurative:** Using a word outside of its literal meaning in order to create a vivid image in the mind. Figurative language is part of what makes communicating with words possible, not to mention interesting. Figurative language fills in the gaps between existing words and their root intentions, by stretching the meaning of words in order to encompass

new or different situations. Our ability to discern between figurative and literal language gives us the unparalleled ability to share abstract ideas and describe things for which there are no sufficient words. Do you understand figurative language? How do you use figurative language?

**Filibuster:** A colossal waste of time and impediment to progress. When people are forced to talk over you in order to prevent you from winning an argument, their speech usually does not have merit. Are you aware of those who attempt to overshadow good arguments with empty talkativeness?

**Final:** Something that comes at the end of a progression. You might play in a final game of a competition in which the game decides the winner, or you might take a final exam at the end of a semester or school year. What important finals have you participated in? Have you always succeeded during these finals? What have you learned from the mistakes you may have made during these finals?

**Finalize:** The final form of an agreement, including all the details. You might also make a final decision about an important topic, which took time to realize and think about all the facts. What have you finalized in your life? Have you made any final decisions which you regretted making afterward? Were you able to change your finalized decision or agreement afterward?

**Find:** To discover or come upon something by chance. Before we can find anything, we have to be open to the possibility of new experiences. Sometimes we find things without looking and other times we can search for an eternity and never find what we are looking for. Freeing ourselves from doubt and opening our senses to new experiences is the important part of the journey while the actual 'finding' is a byproduct. What new experiences have you found or participated in? How did discovering these new experiences <u>change</u> your <u>life</u>?

**Finish:** To come to an <u>end</u> of something or <u>complete</u> an <u>activity</u>. The <u>word</u> is also used in terms of <u>perfecting</u> something or putting the finishing <u>touches</u> on an <u>object</u>. What have you finished? Once you <u>start</u> something, do you always finish it? If something gets too <u>difficult</u>, do you stop before you have finished?

**Finite:** Having <u>clear</u>, discernible <u>limits</u>. While <u>life</u> itself is finite, it contains many things that are <u>infinite</u>; the amount of <u>love</u> you can feel for <u>family</u> and <u>friends</u> or <u>potential</u> <u>music</u> which has not yet been <u>created</u>. Our <u>universe</u> is both infinite and expanding, but our <u>home</u> <u>planet</u> is not so <u>lucky</u>; it is equipped with only a finite amount of <u>resources</u> that are used by a continually growing <u>population</u>. <u>Understand</u> which resources are finite, and <u>support</u> renewable <u>options</u> when possible. Are you aware of the finite <u>nature</u> of our planet's resources? Can you picture infinity?

**Fire:** The <u>light</u> and <u>heat</u> emitted by something that burns. Fire is formless and forceful; it can be extremely useful or devastatingly destructive and capable of eluding <u>control</u> depending on how it is employed. Fire has forged our <u>civilization</u> via cooking, <u>war</u> and <u>natural</u> <u>disaster</u>; fire served as the first

> *"We must accept finite disappointment, but never lose infinite hope."*
> — *Martin Luther King Jr.*

<u>incentive</u> for <u>people</u> to <u>gather</u> for meals, fostered <u>sharing</u>, and promoted a <u>group</u> mentality. Despite this, fire continues to be used to hurt <u>people</u>, whether through <u>human</u> <u>action</u> or at the <u>mercy</u> of Mother Nature. Do you <u>understand</u> the symbolic <u>responsibility</u> of being capable of controlling fire as a human? How and when do you use fire?

**First:** Coming before all other <u>people</u>, things, or <u>experiences</u>, or the <u>beginning</u> of something. We tend to <u>remember</u> our first <u>time</u> doing a given <u>activity</u>. It is significant because our expectations are faced with <u>reality</u>; after the first time, the reality of the <u>situation</u> will overtake any preconceived notions we had. In the first experience, we are still very <u>aware</u> of the <u>differences</u> between what is and what we thought was. Before you do something for the first time, <u>learn</u> as much as you can about it. Do you <u>prepare</u> adequately for the "firsts" in your <u>life</u>? Is it always possible to prepare for every "first" we have?

**Flexible:** <u>Life</u> is unpredictable; it is <u>important</u> to be able to <u>bend</u> yourself to unforeseen <u>problems</u> without letting them break you. Inflexibility breeds an aversion to new <u>experiences</u> and makes it a chore for others to <u>interact</u> with you. If you are inflexible because you are uncomfortable with <u>change</u>, take steps to get used to it; it is essentially unavoidable in life. Do you make an <u>effort</u> to be flexible? How flexible are you?

<u>**Flourish:**</u> To <u>grow</u>, be <u>healthy</u>, <u>success</u>. Surround yourself with rather than stagnate your <u>life</u>. you need to flourish, fix <u>problems</u>, set yourself up to flourish? Do type of <u>environment</u> do you need

> *"When we are born, we cry that we are come to this great stage of fools."*
> — *William Shakespeare*

or prosper. Set yourself up for people who help you flourish Give yourself the <u>time</u> and space and don't make excuses. Do you you continue to flourish? What in order to flourish?

**Focus:** Can either be the <u>figurative</u> <u>interest</u> or the <u>literal</u> <u>concentration</u> point. Focus on <u>relationships</u> with

focus of a <u>group</u> or <u>individual's</u> of rays of some type on a <u>specific</u> <u>friends</u> and <u>family</u>, meet new people, and have new experiences; do not fall victim to focusing on things that will only help others. That is not to say that you should not act charitably and perform selfless acts, but rather to emphasize the importance of recognizing when someone stands to benefit from shifting the focus or putting it out of focus altogether. We must obtain all the information we can, look at the bigger picture, and then decide which things are worth our focus. Do you think before you focus? What do you focus on the most? What do you see as the focus of our society's attention? Is this focus worthy of our time and energy?

**Foil:** To stop or thwart anything. We must be conscious of the evil and immoral things which exist in the world, and do our best to stop them from happening. If people are being hurt or wronged, it is part of our responsibility as a member of a common species and society to do what we can to help them. Opinionated morality should not be imposed on others; we should simply strive to help the helpless whenever possible. Have you helped the helpless? When have you needed help from others?

**Folk:** Anything common to the cultural heritage of people in a given region or country. Folk music, folk dance, and folk stories all play roles in defining culture; many cultures do not have carefully written histories contained in books but rather interactive and boisterous histories contained in song and dance and passed down by mutual experience and oral tradition. What in your life is a result of experiences being passed down by your ancestors or fellow community members? Do you participate in folk music, dance or stories?

> *"The best way to keep something bad from happening is to see it ahead of time... and you can't see it if you refuse to face the possibility."*
> — *William S. Burroughs*

**Follow:** To go after. You can still be your own leader even if you follow in the footsteps of those more experienced than you; following their advice is merely a means to an end. When you are following someone, you should always have your wits about you; like following someone in a car to a new place. It is easy to turn your brain off, stare at the license plate, and let them take you to where you want to go, yet you arrive and are unaware of how you arrived or how to return. We must be cognizant and mindful of our surroundings, critically thinking about everything we encounter in order to determine what it means to us instead of taking someone else's word for it. Do you scrutinize even when you are following and blaze your own trail when you can? Are you a follower or a leader?

**Fond:** Tender and loving; cherishing. Let yourself be drawn to the things of which you are fond. Evaluate your feelings about what you are fond of will allow you to seek out more things you will like, and rid yourself of unhealthy interests or activities. What do you cherish? Why? For what or for whom do you feel affection? What is it about these things which are attractive or comforting to you?

**Foolhardy:** Rash; bold and daring, yet foolish for some reason. Make sure you think through your decisions before you take action. Sometimes it is necessary to take decisive action immediately, but the majority of the time, it is possible to delay a decision in order to learn more. It is better to act tardily than foolishly. Do you explore you options before acting? Do you act foolhardily?

**Forbearance:** The holding back from doing something or saying something. Make sure you know as much as you can about your situation before you act rashly. Do you have self-control? When was a time where you acted out of control? What can you do differently the next time you are upset?

**Force:** Energy or power that is capable of creating, controlling or changing. Forces of good and evil shape the world in which we live; we need to recognize each for what it is and support or combat it accordingly. Speaking generally, there are two forces that steer us through life; one we can control and the other we cannot control. Some forces are outside the realm of human influence, and others stem directly from it; when thinking about a force that comprises humans, make sure you hold each accountable, scrutinizing their motives and incentives to act as a part of this force. What forces shape your life? Do you recognize which forces in your life are beyond your control and which you are capable of contributing to or resisting? Do you base these categories on rational thought or spirituality?

**Forego:** To go before. We must familiarize ourselves with historical facts, not sensationalized false rhetoric that has been brought about by those who stand to gain from its propagation. Keep in mind that those with the most influence and control are the ones who have the loudest voice both in the present and from decades or centuries ago. Only settle for unadulterated facts about the past and look at both sides. Are you aware of what has become before you? What was the most important historical event that has affected your life?

**Foregone:** When it is possible to know beforehand or what is foretold. Our future as a planet and as a species is has yet to be concretely defined, though a cursory glance at our history and current state of affairs offers some dismal clues. The foregone conclusion to our society's romp on Earth, it seems, will be our own doing, either from harming the environment past the point of no return, permanently changing the climate and making the planet uninhabitable, or some sort of self-inflicted nuclear holocaust as a result of warring countries. Do you use clues from the past and present to speculate about the future? Are you able to foretell events that occur?

**Foreign:** That which is unfamiliar to us. Avoid xenophobic attitudes; if you discount something simply because it is foreign to you, it is time to evaluate how you are observing the world. It is short-sighted and counterproductive to judge anything purely based on its foreignness. Some people will use this attitude to fuel hate and morally starved actions. Embrace the unfamiliar; you will always learn something about yourself or the world. Do you approach foreign things with curiosity or disdain? Have you been immersed in what is foreign in order to expand yourself?

**Foreknowledge:** The knowledge of something before it occurs. We can never be sure of exactly what the future holds, but we can use our intuition and past experiences to evaluate the present in order to get a better idea. Think critically about all of the moving parts of the situation you are embroiled in; research similar situations and look inward for answers. What do you know about the future? Do you have foreknowledge?

**Foremost:** First in time, place, or importance. People inevitably change and for this reason, it is worth periodically reevaluating your priorities and goals in life; gravitate toward progression and steer clear of deterioration and regression as they manifest themselves in your decisions. What is foremost in your life? Family, friends, education, work, fun?

**Foresee:** To observe something in the future either literally in a vision or premonition or figuratively in an accurate prediction. What do you foresee in your future? How does your <u>knowledge</u> of what the future holds <u>affect</u> the way you live your <u>life</u>?

**Foreshadow:** When one <u>event</u> suggests that another might <u>follow</u>. Look for patterns in the <u>world</u>. <u>History</u> is often likened to a <u>cycle</u>; pay <u>attention</u> to <u>lessons</u> that can be derived from the <u>past</u> and <u>apply</u> them to your <u>life</u>. What patterns in the world have you found? How has history cycled within your life?

**Foresight:** This gives us the <u>ability</u> to <u>plan</u> for the <u>future</u>. Your foresight is shorthand for your ability to <u>recognize</u> what <u>direction</u> things are heading in and where you fit into things. You cannot have foresight without <u>sight</u>. Do you <u>educate</u> yourself in order to plan for the future? What is your <u>current</u> plan for the future?

**Forestall:** To <u>prevent</u> something from happening, when you see <u>potential</u> for a harmful <u>event</u> to take place. Before you are able to forestall something, you must have the <u>foresight</u> to <u>recognize</u> it will happen at all. Do you keep your <u>eyes</u> on the horizon for signs of <u>trouble</u>? Do you do

everything you can to get ahead of harmful events and <u>stop</u> them?

**Foretell:** To indicate what the <u>future</u> will be like. Bad <u>decisions</u> and <u>conditions</u> now foretell a dystopian <u>future</u>. If nothing is done about the <u>problems</u> which exist in the <u>world</u> <u>today</u>, can we <u>hope</u> to live in a <u>better</u> world in the future? Can you foretell your own future?

**Forethought:** The <u>result</u> of <u>foresight</u>; once we <u>realize</u> that there is a <u>problem</u> in the <u>future</u>, we are able to scrutinize our <u>relationship</u> to this problem and how we can ameliorate it. Do you <u>plan</u> for your future? How do you <u>work</u> around problems you come across?

**Forget:** <u>Forgive</u>, but do not forget. Your <u>memory</u> is your mental <u>encyclopedia</u> of <u>observations</u>; all your memories give you <u>information</u> with which you <u>structure</u> your <u>world</u>. To forget is to remove <u>supports</u> and braces from this <u>structure</u>, leaving you with an incomplete and dilapidated schema of <u>thought</u>. Do you easily forget? What have you forgotten? Is there something you wish you could forget? Do you ever feel forgotten?

> *"Forgiveness is the fragrance that the violet sheds on the heel that has crushed it."*
> *— Mark Twain*

**<u>Forgive, Forgiveness</u>:** To excuse, <u>pardon</u> or to give up being <u>angry</u> or the <u>desire</u> to punish someone. Is forgiveness one of the most <u>valuable</u> things that you can <u>offer</u> someone? Is it the <u>responsibility</u> of someone who has wronged you to try to make things right by <u>apologizing</u> and undoing their <u>wrong</u> as much as humanly <u>possible</u>? We cannot go back in <u>time</u> to fix our <u>problems</u>, so the most we can do when we <u>realize</u> that we have erred is to <u>acknowledge</u> this <u>fact</u> and then try proactively to make it right and <u>hope</u> for forgiveness. Error is inevitable and if an insurmountable <u>conflict</u> was created every time someone made a <u>mistake</u>, our <u>society</u> would have little time or <u>energy</u> to <u>progress</u> in ways which matter. Forgiveness can be <u>hard</u> to <u>give</u>, so does this mean that it is always the right thing to do? In some instances, forgiveness depends on the <u>perceived</u> <u>sincerity</u> of those who offer an apology for their wrongdoing. Forgiveness can be <u>coerced</u> or <u>forced</u>, but seldom is this <u>form</u> <u>genuine</u> or permanent. As Gandhi said, "The <u>weak</u> can never forgive. Forgiveness is the <u>attribute</u> of the <u>strong</u>." Have you forgiven others? When have you been forgiven? Do you <u>feel</u> like a <u>weight</u> has been lifted off your shoulders after being forgiven or forgiving others? What do you require to forgive someone? What does it take for you to receive forgiveness from someone else?

**Form:** Can mean the <u>shape</u> of an <u>object</u> or the <u>way</u> in which a <u>person</u> is standing. Can

also mean the way in which something is made or the <u>mode</u> used. How do you create impressions of others? How do you form appropriate sentences? What can be improved upon for the form of your stance?

**Fortitude:** Courage and calmness in the face of frightening or painful events. A valuable quality that should be respected in others. Though you should rely on your friends and family for support, surviving through or simply facing adversity requires a certain amount of understanding and acceptance of yourself and your situation and courage to face reality. Be true to yourself and your situation. Do you face adversity with courage and determination? Are you calm during frightening or painful events?

**Fortuitous:** Accidental; happening by chance. It is amazing how relatively small, random occurrences can significantly shape our lives. Be an opportunist; you never know when a new experience could change your life, so say yes to new things and try altering your daily routine however subtly or overtly you can. Treat every situation as an opportunity. Do you approach each day with curiosity and an open mind? When was the last time you experienced something new?

**Forward;** To move in a progressive direction, either in a physical sense or relating to life goals and becoming successful. Sometimes people must move forward on their own in order to accomplish their goals. Always try to move forward in life instead of moving backward. Do you strive to better yourself and move forward in life each day? Have you ever moved backward in life?

*"People demand freedom of speech as a compensation for the freedom of thought which they seldom use."*
— *Soren Kierkegaard*

**Foundation:** To have a foundation is to have a base in whatever you're dealing with. The stronger your foundation is, the less you'll succumb to the terror and pressure that aims to break your foundation. However, if your foundation is mentally and physically weak, you're opening yourself up to a world of hurt and difficulty. How strong is your foundation? Have you tried to build up your foundation?

**Form:** A form is an arrangement of parts; how something takes shape. Life can come in many different forms, sizes and shapes, and each of us has the capacity to change the forms in our life to best fit our needs and desires. What have you formed your life around? How do people see you in your form?

**Fraud;** Is fraud negativity and evil? Is it deceit or trickery to gain unfair or dishonest advantage? The types of fraud include actual, constructive, extrinsic, intrinsic, intentional, and unintentional. Is fraud defined and regulated by law and the legislation that creates law? Can fraud be more than just a civil wrong for which a remedy may be obtained? What part does misrepresenting the truth or concealment of information play in your life? How does legislation involve fraud as a deception against the public? Do you deceive or cheat others?

**Fray:** A noisy quarrel or fight. You should only enter a fray if you are trying to break it up. Fights occur when temper trumps communication. Do you attempt to communicate before entering a fray? Have you ever broken up a fray?

**Free, Freedom:** The condition of not being subject to the control of any other. There are many freedoms, including freedom of assembly/movement, speech, religion, the press, the city, information, oppression, political, intellectual, and all choices. Do not take your freedom for granted; fight tooth and nail to maintain it. There are many who stand to profit from slowly and secretly or suddenly and overtly restricting your freedom; be on the lookout for such people in all contexts and scrutinize the justifications of freedom limiting mandates to their rational end. Free your mind from the influence of ill-intentioned individuals and organizations; examine every piece of information you encounter with a critical eye. Do you maintain your mentality through critical thinking? Do you value your freedom enough to stand up for it? *What does it mean to you to be free?* What is a threat to your freedom? Has there been a time when you felt you were lacking freedom?

**Freethinker:** Someone who forms their own ideas about the world rather than falling victim to outdated dogmatic teachings. Everyone should aspire to be a freethinker; we can still be free thinking and agree with others. Anyone who seems to want you to accept what they are saying as true without scrutinizing it is suspect. If they are correct in their sentiments, then you will arrive there yourself with rational deduction; if they are incorrect, then you will realize when you acquire more information. Why would anyone have reason to force you to believe something without thinking? Are you free thinking? Do you persuade others to believe you?

**Free will:** Freedom to live and act as you wish, which comes with the responsibility to act appropriately and do what is right. Those who attempt to discount their own agency in their actions are weak and wily. Do you exercise your free will? Do you take responsibility for your actions?

**Fret:** To wear away by rubbing; worry. Before you fret, be sure that you know as many of the facts about the situation as possible. Fretting is a waste of time if there is something that could be done to alleviate the problem at hand. Be proactive in relieving your worry and stress. Even if something is legitimately worth worrying about, you can still concentrate on positives and take action against your worries. Do you fret frequently? What do you fret about?

**Friend:** Someone who you know well and like and feels the same about you. Good friends are the most valuable things that you can acquire in life. Do not take your friends for granted. Show your friends how much you love and value them every chance you get. How many friends do you have? Do you prefer quantity over quality when it comes to friends? Are you a good friend? What

> *"Don't walk behind me; I may not lead. Don't walk in front of me; I may not follow. Just walk beside me and be my friend."*
> — *Albert Camus*

kind of a friend are you? How do you choose friends?

**Friendship:** A good friend will fit you like a ring to your finger. Friendship is the cornerstone to a happy and fulfilling life. Friendships can grow to inhabit the space that family inhabits—the closest space to your heart. This status akin to family is the natural pinnacle of a friendship. You cannot choose your family and though you may not take them for granted, they seem to be an omnipresent force; this fact is what makes friends special. They are family members in the sense that you feel as if you have known and loved them forever, yet they are a result of your own actions and your interaction with the world. Do you value your friendships? Do you understand the importance of friendship? How do you create friendship?

**Frugal:** No matter how much excess you can afford, it is always advisable to be frugal. If you save when possible by giving up or forgoing a few unnecessary things, you will be surprised how much extra accumulates; it is much more satisfying and rewarding to use all the excess at once for one good cause whether it be helping others or giving yourself a well-needed <u>break</u>. Do you <u>save</u> when you can in order to <u>spend</u> when it counts? Are you overly frugal?

**Fruition:** Completion of a task. There is no <u>feeling</u> quite like <u>working</u> toward a <u>goal</u> and finally <u>achieving</u> it; the more <u>challenging</u> a given <u>task</u> is, the more rewarding it is when it comes to fruition. Challenge is <u>important</u> in our <u>lives</u>; without it, the fruition of your goals will mean increasingly less. Do you challenge yourself to the degree that the fruition of your goals continues to be <u>satisfying</u> and <u>fulfilling</u>?

**Frustrate:** To <u>prevent</u> someone from doing or getting what they <u>want</u>. Frustration in any <u>situation</u> is the <u>result</u> of a discrepancy in <u>expectations</u> between involved parties. <u>Avoid</u> frustration by making your intents and expectations clear to everyone with whom you <u>interact</u>. Trace your frustration to its root, then <u>concentrate</u> on <u>communicating</u> your <u>issues</u> to those most <u>relevant</u> to this root. Additionally, consider ways to alleviate frustration in your <u>life</u>. If you don't find a means of doing so, your frustration can become <u>dangerous</u> to those around you, leading to outbursts of <u>anger</u> with <u>friends</u>, <u>family</u>, and coworkers. It's easier to avoid such outbursts than make amends after they occur. Do you use critical <u>thinking</u> to surmount your frustration or let it <u>dominate</u> your <u>emotions</u> and <u>behavior</u>? How do you alleviate the <u>stress</u> of frustration in your life?

**Fulfill:** To fulfill is to complete and achieve something in its entirety. If you've ever aimed to fulfill something, you have certain <u>expectations</u> that go along with this. Fulfilling something for someone else yields even more expectations. Do you feel pressure when you <u>commit</u> to fulfill something? What was the toughest <u>task</u> that you fulfilled? Did you have a sincere feeling of <u>accomplishment</u>?

**Function:** As we have <u>advanced</u> as a <u>species</u>, our catalog of functions has <u>grown</u> considerably as a <u>result</u> of new <u>ideas</u> and <u>technology</u>. Human function in the context of <u>time</u> seems to be first to <u>maintain</u> ourselves, <u>body</u> and <u>mind</u> alike, then to reproduce, then to generate means of survival for more than just ourselves by producing <u>goods</u> or <u>services</u>, and lastly socialize and <u>teach</u> in order to keep the <u>cycle</u> going. In each of these areas, there is huge potential for positive <u>action</u> and huge <u>potential</u>* for destructive action; ultimately, we <u>choose</u> what our function is. What is our function as <u>humans</u>? What is your function? How is what you do a function of who you are? Do your actions reflect your <u>moral</u> compass?

**Fundamental:** Basic; <u>parts</u> that constitute the basis or foundation of something. Always be <u>honest</u> to yourself and others; keep <u>expectations</u> and <u>intents</u> out on the table and no one will be <u>surprised</u> or disappointed. Get back to the basics; when you are <u>unhappy</u>, look at the fundamental things your <u>body</u> <u>needs</u>. When your <u>life</u> seems insurmountably complicated, these are often the things that are first to go, and incidentally the most <u>important</u> to the sustainable and <u>normal</u> <u>function</u> of your body. We get so used to the simple parts of life that sometimes we take them for <u>granted</u> and let them go by the wayside. Do you take time to <u>concentrate</u> on the fundamental and <u>necessary</u> <u>elements</u> of your life? Are you getting enough <u>sleep</u>, <u>exercising</u>, and eating <u>right</u>? What are the fundamental elements of living a <u>happy</u> and fulfilling life?

**Funny:** Anything that <u>causes</u> laughter and <u>smiles</u>; <u>humorous</u>. A <u>sense</u> of humor is <u>important</u> in <u>life</u>; taking yourself too seriously is <u>counterproductive</u> and off-putting. In some <u>situations</u>, only certain <u>types</u> of humor will be appropriate and <u>appreciated</u> and in others none at all; be tactful. Humor can be a way to <u>connect</u> with those who you have nothing else in <u>common</u>

with; <u>sharing</u> laughter with a stranger can be a <u>bonding</u> <u>experience</u>. Funny things diffuse <u>tense</u> situations and offer a respite from an otherwise bleak outlook. A <u>good</u> bout of laughter can be rejuvenating and cleansing; surround yourself with <u>people</u> you can laugh with. Before <u>speaking</u>, do you make sure what you <u>think</u> is funny is actually funny rather than offensive to those you are with? Can you laugh at yourself? Do others think you are funny?

**Future:** What is yet to come and what will <u>happen</u> <u>soon</u> or next. We are unable to <u>predict</u> the future, but we can prepare ourselves for what the future might bring. It is <u>important</u> to make <u>decisions</u> with the future in <u>mind</u>. What are you <u>hoping</u> for in the future? How are you <u>planning</u> to make that happen? What will you do in the future?

# G

**Gain**: Some would say life is about gaining—money, possessions, higher degrees. But what do we lose in this constant race for gaining objects of prestige and ostentation? What else do we stand to gain spiritually if we focus less on ourselves? What are the gains offered by our materialistic society, and how long do they last? What kinds of gains could we have from the way we conduct ourselves in our personal and public lives? Where else in your life can observations transform into gain?

**Gamble:** Gambling deals only sometimes with money, but always with the outcomes of events involving chance. Has gambling become more of a gambit (where one seeks to gain an advantage) for the corporacratic elite or money manipulators such as Wall Street insiders, bankers, governments, and CEOs? Is it always a gamble to pursue the things you want in life? Can we achieve anything truly great without risks? But likewise, when is it better not to gamble? Given that gambling can be addictive and damaging to our lives, when should it be considered a misuse of money or resources? Is it wise to gamble when you're unsure of all the factors and stakes?

**Games**: A game is usually understood to be any activity we do for pleasure, but a game can also be when someone treats their own life and those of others as though they have no real meaning. Have you encountered those who play games with the emotions of others in order to increase their own self-esteem? Have you ever played games with the emotions of others? How can we avoid this kind of deceit in our daily lives?

**Gang:** The kinds of gangs that recruit lost and desperate people are a scourge on society, inciting death and organized violence in cities across the country. Avoid these groups, if they're in your area, and their totalitarian structure. What could drive someone to make the choice to progress to jail and death? What more positive kinds of groups could fill that need or desire?

**Garbage:** Garbage is composed of anything we find to be unwanted or unneeded. Do you think about the impact garbage has on our environment? Hundreds of thousands of pounds of it are produced each day; where does it all go? How can you minimize the garbage you create in your own life? How does the physical garbage we produce reflect on the emotional or spiritual garbage in our lives?

**Garden**: A garden is a place of land where one grows plants or uses as a place for relaxation. Gardens have all sorts of associations, from the Garden of Eden to the flower plot in your own backyard. But at the heart of all gardens is the idea of growing things and creating life. How can you grow things of beauty and nourishment in your own life—not just literally, but metaphorically as well? Gardens, like all worthwhile endeavors in life, require effort, time, and nourishment to grow. In what ways do you seek to nourish those with whom you share relationships?

**Gas**: A gas is a state of matter that is infinitely flexible in shape and volume, but we also use the word as a term for fuel, an abbreviation for gasoline. In modern America, how necessary has gas become to our everyday existence? How can we tell when we are misusing the elements we have been given? How many lives are lost over battles for oil? Yet don't we often take it for granted? Should we?

**Gather**: To gather is to bring something together, as when groups of people gather, or to bring something new into our lives, as we do when we gather information and ideas. We can also gather when we harvest, whether that harvest is of food or other rewards for our efforts. Gathering can be good for us and those around us, but when can gathering lead to problems? Does it ever become a chore? How do these different kinds of gathering—people, ideas, and resources—relate to one another? What kinds of things do we gather in our lives that are of value only to us, and what kinds of things do we gather that are also important or relevant to other people? Is it possible to gather information or ideas in a destructive way?

**Gaze**: The gaze is not only something that we use to understand the world—gazing on it to gather information—but also the way we are understood by those around us. We are always subject to the gaze of others. Would they always approve of the way we live? What social function does their judgment have? Might it be a way of keeping us in line and forcing us to be productive members of society? What function and effects does our gaze have when we let it further fall on others?

*"The most tragic thing in the world is a man of genius who is not a man of honor."*
*— George Bernard Shaw*

**Gender**: Gender, a concept we can use to language, bodies, or brains, is the way we think about what creates a difference between women and men. It is often a dividing line in our daily activities, separating the sexes in all they do. Gender has long been associated with discrimination; do you see this issue continuing in the present day? How do gender relations impact your daily life? How can awareness of gender roles spark more cognizant interactions in life?

**General, Generality**: Something that is general means that it is applicable to or describes an entire category of things. What is problematic about mistaking a specific incident as being indicative of a generality? How do stereotypes fit into this equation? How have you fallen prey to generalities in your life? How can we better recognize harmful generalities for what they are?

**Generous, Generosity**: To be generous is to give abundantly to others. How many social bonds can you think of that are made through acts of generosity? The generous giver, you will often find, is far richer in return than the person who receives. They reap the benefit of knowing they have done the right thing. How can you be more generous with others in your everyday life? What kinds of generosity have enriched your life, either by giving or receiving?

**Genius**: The idea of who or what embodies the idea of genius is a difficult one to pin down; we sometimes use it to describe things that involve high levels of intelligence but sometimes to describe originality. Have you met anyone who you would describe as a genius? Do you feel as though this word has become devalued in our culture? How often do you see it used simply to describe things in the arts that we admire and enjoy rather than any quantitative value, importance, or influence of a given work? Be mindful of those who would claim genius. Do they make this claim themselves, or do others make it for them? What can those who reach such intellectual heights teach us about ourselves? What can we learn from the lives of Einstein and others?

**Gentleman**: Different societies have used different criteria to determine just what a gentleman is, though it always indicates a man with desirable qualities. Do you find the term archaic? How would you define what a gentleman is, and what fundamental attributes one must have in order to be one? What makes your list— kindness, politeness, courtesy? Do you try to exhibit these qualities to others? How can you, regardless of gender, better incorporate these into your own life?

**Genuine:** Something genuine has no falseness to it. Do you feel that today's society surrounds us with imitations and counterfeits? Has authenticity receded into myth? Where do you see the genuine around you? Where and when do you feel genuine emotion, and feel grateful for it? When you find genuine people in your life, do you hold on to them and cultivate relationships with them? Who do you know you can count on? How

> *"Gentlemen, be courteous to the old maids, no matter how poor and plain and prim, for the only chivalry worth having is that which is the readiest to pay deference to the old, protect the feeble, and serve womankind, regardless of rank, age, or color."*
>
> *— Louisa May Alcott*

can we recognize the genuine from the disingenuous?

**Get:** To get something can simply mean to receive it, but it can also mean to understand something or to acquire it after active pursuit. Is your life focused on getting things? What negative effects might this constant quest for accumulation have? What might be lost by focusing on getting, and what might be gained by turning our thoughts and actions in other directions?

**Gift:** A gift is something we present to another person without expecting compensation in return. Not all gifts are physical objects; can you think of gifts you have received that were intangible moments or otherwise difficult to touch or hold? When do you give gifts to others? Does it make you feel good to do so?

**Give, Given:** Giving is to make a present of something, to put something we have into someone else's possession. We have all heard the saying "Give and you shall receive." What statement does this proverb make about our culture's approach to generosity? Do you feel that many people seek to give to others for their own benefit? Without receiving recognition for our good deeds, do you think people would perform them? Why do we want people to think us good Samaritans? Why do students list volunteer work on college and scholarship applications? While their deeds may provide help for others in society, wouldn't a genuine approach be more worthwhile? Do you perform generous acts from a recognition of your own privilege in society? When we truly understand that our needs are met and those of others are not, is generosity an inevitable response? Did you reach the place you are in your life alone, or were there were mentors, friends, family, and a society that helped you along the way? Have you considered ways in which you can give back to others? Do you try to give back regularly? Do you accept it when others give to you?

**Glad:** Gladness, or contentment, is a decision, not something that will simply happen if the conditions of our lives are perfect. Do you find that those who fail to realize this spend their lives in constant regret for what they do not have? How can this attitude be reformulated? How can we teach ourselves to be glad for what we have already achieved or obtained?

**Goal:** A goal may be many things: a state we want to achieve, an object we wish to have, or a place we want to be. What are the goals you have in different areas of your life? Do your spiritual, material, and ethical goals match up with one another? Are all goals positive? Have you ever had a goal become so important that you hurt yourself or others trying to attain it? What kinds of goals have you set for yourself? How have you decided what goals are appropriate or worthwhile? How can we be careful to make sure that our goals do not become destructive?

> "No one is useless in this world who lightens the burdens of another."
> — Charles Dickens

**God**: God is a spiritual entity beings, which exists across implanted in the minds of human religions, as in the forms of Christ, Buddha, Allah, idols, and pagan gods. Is there a need in human life for God, an anchor for living with hope and a potential answer to unanswerable questions? For those who believe in God, does he become a part of our being through our experience of what it means to have a soul? Do the words "become an instrument" mean of God or religion? How do our minds conceive the image of God? Is your conception of who God is and what God wants the same as that of people you have voted into office, cheered at a game, or adored at a concert? In most societies, God equates to and is associated with good. So why is there so much evil performed in his name? In a final analysis, can God ever be anything more than what each and every living human perceives him to be? When do we need a God? When do we become dependent on God? How can you bring God more directly into your life? Where might His presence be in you? *How does God relate to spirituality?*

**Gold:** Gold is how we often measure wealth among ourselves, though the metal is of questionable value in and of itself. Have you seen others ruined because of their pursuit of gold or experienced that yourself? What other riches are there to be found in life? How can you let go of a lust for gold and wealth in your own life, and be happy with what you have? *How does gold equate to money?*

## Three Observations on God Written by Three Observers

1.  *How can we observe God when no one is truly sure of God's nature or existence? Billions of people believe that God created everything that we perceive, that God is the ultimate entity from whom all came and to whom all returns. There are so many unanswered questions about God, most of which we will never be able to answer. The anonymity and enigma that shrouds God are exactly the qualities that make God powerful and comforting at the same time. God is everywhere; God knows everything; God controls everything—and yet we, as humans, still hold the power to choose whether we want to believe in God or not. The point is that God does not have to be some shadowy, bearded figure with his eye watching your every move, waiting for a slip-up to make you feel inferior. God is nature; God is science; God is the human mind. God is hope for a better life for us and our family. God does not give handouts, but rather grants opportunities. People have different definitions of what God is to them and there is no correct answer, so consider what places, people, and things you cherish most. Whatever God may be, does he play a role in your life?*

2.  *As religion pervades an increasing amount of society, it is difficult to separate the society itself from the beliefs which it hold; conflicts arise from differences which could never be settled because they are based on faith rather than fact, and have no conclusions drawn from empirically measurable reality. The concept of "God" can represent a variety of things to different people, but a common thread is connectedness and purpose. Do you understand your relationship to and place in the universe? Do you trust the source of information regarding your place in the universe? Can you sympathize with those who have different or opposite beliefs from you?*

3.  *It is necessary for all of us to feel a connection to something larger than ourselves. Without any connection, we feel lost in such an impossibly large world and universe. For some, that connection may be to the Earth; for others, it will be to the universe as a whole; and for many, it will be to God. The concept of God is different to many people around the world. He takes different forms, explains ideas in various ways, and tells different stories in different cultures. In turn, he is worshipped in a multitude of different ways. But one thing is similar among us all: we have a connection to God, whether he is experienced as within us, around us, or both.*

**Good**: Good has a wide range of meanings depending on the object or person being described: We can use it to mean we find something superior in terms of morality or physical quality, but also to mean something is dependable, like a contract being good. Do you believe the concept of good and <u>bad</u> is inherent in humans, or must it be taught? How <u>subjective</u> do you think goodness is? Are there some things that are objectively good, regardless of who is performing the judgment? Our consciences guide us toward appropriate behavior in <u>public</u> and <u>private</u>; what kinds of temptations overpower what we know to be good? How can we <u>strengthen</u> our <u>resolve</u> and <u>develop</u> an unyielding concept of good? Are you wary of those who <u>possess</u> lightweight consciences? What is the possible danger they represent?

**Gospel:** The origin of the word gospel is from the sense of it meaning "good news," but we generally use it to indicate the first four books of the New Testament and sometimes use it as a synonym for <u>truth</u>. Even if you don't believe in the <u>divinity</u> of Jesus or Allah, what <u>relevance</u> might his <u>teachings</u> still have in your <u>life</u>? Is gospel essentially <u>religious</u> <u>belief</u>? Do you think of this <u>guide</u> as gospel?

**Gossip:** To gossip is to spread rumors or facts about another person's life. Have you engaged in gossip or found yourself being gossiped about? What were the resulting <u>feelings</u> or <u>consequences</u>? Can one gossip productively, or is it always a <u>negative</u> <u>activity</u>?

**Govern, Government:** To govern implies <u>ruling</u>, but in a <u>democracy</u>, ideally, this rule should only come through the will of the people. Are you careful to <u>scrutinize</u> the <u>motivations</u> of <u>politicians</u>? How can you tell whether they are acting in the interest of the people at all or by their will? Does a dictatorship pervert government? Has governing transcended to an exercise of <u>authority</u> rather than administration of <u>public</u> affairs? Is government nothing more than CORPORACRACY, a *constant,* and how can we <u>reform</u> it?

**Grammar:** A grammar is a <u>system</u> of <u>rules</u> for speaking and <u>writing</u> a particular <u>language</u>. Even if you only understand English, are you aware of knowing multiple English grammars? Do you speak a different kind of English to your friends than you do to your professional colleagues? Do you write differently for yourself than you do when writing for others? Sometimes one judges or may be judged by others for the grammar they choose to use. Have you found yourself in this situation? What are your experiences in discovering ways that grammar can <u>govern</u> the ways we <u>interact</u> and <u>think</u>?

**Grant:** To grant is to give, whether it be a tangible object or something more abstract, like permission. We are granted many things in life—some <u>deserved</u>, some not—but how we choose to <u>receive</u> them is entirely up to us. Do we take them for granted, let them <u>overwhelm</u> us, or are we <u>grateful</u> for what we have and not <u>greedy</u> for what we don't?

**Graph:** A graph is a pictorial representation of numerical information. By putting <u>numbers</u> into graphs, can we actually show things like <u>progress</u> and <u>change</u>? Can some of the most important parts of <u>life</u>, such as <u>love</u> and friendship, ever be quantified, and should they be? Have you ever fallen into the trap of trying to measure them and place them on a

> *"Great minds discuss ideas. Average minds discuss events. Small minds discuss people."*
> *— Eleanor Roosevelt*

graph? What kinds of intangible qualities in your life defy quantification?

**Grateful, Gratitude:** To be grateful is to feel thankful for things we perceive as being beneficial to us. What are the things or people in your life for which you feel most grateful for or to? Does one always have to be grateful *to* a specific individual or entity, or can one simply have a grateful feeling in general? Can one only feel grateful for good occurrences, or can bad ones also be sources of gratitude?

**Gratify:** Gratification is the fulfillment of a want or need. What things do you think are worth waiting for? How does our desire for instant gratification impede our progress toward them? Many are quick to gratify their every desire, but what can be gained by delayed gratification? What is better about waiting to obtain what we desire?

**Greed:** Greed is the desire to accumulate prizes merely for the sake of accumulation, not because there is any real need to do so; it is the act of confusing need and want, and doing so to the point of hurting others and ourselves. Have you known people, including yourself, for whom greed has caused misery or consumed their life? Are the greedy ever satisfied, or is that impossible simply because there is always something else to be sought? What is the most insidious kind of greed—that for fame, sex, money, prestige, or something else? How can we avoid greed, learn to be happy with what we have, and recognize when the pursuit of our goals becomes harmful? Is greed a vice?

> *"I will not say, do not weep, for not all tears are an evil."*
> — *J. R. R. Tolkien*

**Grief:** Grief is the intense sadness we feel after experiencing a loss. It is a form of mental agitation or disturbance; are you always able to recognize this fact? Have you found grief confusing? Is it the cause or result of mental anguish for you? When a loved one is lost, grief is understandable; is it at that point also useful because it allows us to process the intensity of our pain? It is deprivation increased by dependency. How stressful is it for you to feel? Only you can define the level at which you perceive it; do you ever find yourself turning grief into a grievance? How do you deal with things you cannot spiritually control? Have you encountered those who let grief consume them, allowing it to rule their lives instead of learning to move past it and be happy? Have you considered how the ones you have lost would want you to live? Grief is associated with death; can we counterbalance it with support in life from friends and relatives? Have you thought about investing time in new activities and interests to help yourself cope with the effects of grief? To what extent is the way we experience grief defined by how we perceive it? Think of all the different factors that can affect the way you perceive something—the people around you, your personal belief, and the wills of others. Do you experience grief because it is expected of you? Does this cause you to hold onto your grief for longer than is necessary? How might grief become unhealthy? Where do we draw the line and say "enough is enough?" Do you wear grief in accordance with how your friends or others think it should look?

**Grievance:** A grievance is a complaint we bring or hold against another, whether justified or unjustified. If a grievance goes either unsaid or unsatisfied, it can fester into a grudge. Do you consider the validity of all circumstances before regarding them as just cause for protest against someone—a friend, a neighbor, or perhaps even God? How do you feel you need to address the grievances you have or have had? What would be the benefits of attempting to satisfy your grievances as opposed to the benefits of letting them go?

**Group:** A group is a number of people joined together in some purpose; it can be small, or it can be as large as a <u>throng</u>, a <u>mob</u>, or a <u>crowd</u>. Sometimes these groups are <u>social</u> or <u>political</u> in nature, or sometimes both. What are the dangers of allowing yourself to simply become swept up in a crowd or movement because of its size? While large groups often represent the voice of a multitude, are the views they wish to share necessarily in the best interest of all? What about joining a group makes it worthwhile for you, and what price are you willing to pay for that association?

**Grow, Growth:** To grow can mean for something to get larger physically, but it can also describe emotional or psychological development. Do you try to remain aware of the role that water plays in the physical world and our dependency on it? Our existence as human beings depends on plants, and plants depend on good seed in good soil, but what would those plants do without water? We cannot grow by ourselves. We require all these aspects in order to grow our bodies through the physical acts of toil and <u>harvest</u>. How does this interconnectedness of the physical world carry over into how we can understand growth on a figurative level as well? Our emotional and intellectual growth depends in part on our own personal experiences and observations, but how much of our growth depends on and affects others' experiences? How can we allow ourselves to be teachable for this to happen? Have you found yourself acting in ways that negatively impact your growth or that of those around you? By holding on to old patterns and misconceptions, do we prevent the growth of others in our lives? How can we provide <u>space</u> for growth in the lives of the ones we <u>love</u>? How might we seek to develop ourselves as people while gaining <u>knowledge</u> through personal observational <u>experience</u>— our observations—and the experiences of others?

> *"And the day came when the risk it remain tight in a bud was more painful than the risk it took to blossom."*
> *— Anais Nin*

**Grudge:** A grudge is a resentment we have toward other people for wrongs we feel they have performed against us. Can a <u>grudge</u> can be <u>poison</u> to a person? Who is more likely to be harmed—the one holding the grudge or the one against whom the grudge is held? Do you try to let go of those things that poison you and be <u>careful</u> that your grievance does not *cause* <u>pain</u> or <u>anguish</u>? Some <u>spend</u> their whole lives bearing grudges against those who have <u>wronged</u> them; is this a waste? What other <u>goals</u> and <u>dreams</u> might grudges prevent us from pursuing?

<u>Guide</u>: A guide is anyone or anything that helps us to reach a destination, whether that destination is a <u>physical</u> or intangible one. This book is meant to serve as a guide for living your own <u>life</u> and <u>building</u> a <u>creed</u> to live by, but where else can we find guides in our lives: the <u>gospel</u> or other books? While those you <u>admire</u> have doubtless done many things to gain your admiration, no one is <u>perfect</u> and they <u>possess</u> <u>faults</u> as well; do you keep this in mind when you observe your guides? Who do you consider a guide in your life—an elder, a friend, a sibling? Who do you consider a mentor? Are you able to see their faults and weaknesses as well as their positive qualities?

**Guilt, Guilty:** Guilt is a self-inflicted phenomenon in which we cannot stop mentally punishing ourselves for wrongs we have committed. Feeling guilty can make us feel <u>bad</u>, but are there ways in which guilt can be productive or <u>positive</u>? Do you feel your guilt indicates that you are an evil person for doing what you feel guilty about or that you are a good person for feeling guilty about it? Has guilt ever made you frustrated enough to attack people who had good intentions when talking to you about your problems?

**Guru:** A guru is a leader who is highly respected by a group of followers. With such respect comes great responsibility. How does one gain the respect of those who follow them? How can you cultivate this kind of respect in your own life?

# H

**Habit**: A habit is something we <u>perform</u> repeatedly simply because we are used to it, not because we <u>consciously</u> think it is <u>good</u> or useful. Do you believe that we do many things without even realizing it because we have made them into habits? What are the dangers of developing <u>latent</u> habits of thought? What is their relationship to our attempts to gain <u>balance</u> in our lives? Have you discovered <u>stubborn</u> mental habits in yourself? We typically think of habits as <u>negative</u> things, like biting your nails or swearing; however, can we turn habits into <u>positives</u> as well? Have you ever attempted to adopt positive habits—for example, make it a habit to be <u>courteous</u> to other people, to help others who are in need, or to spend more time with your <u>family</u>? Have you done positive things enough times that they become second nature and you don't think twice about doing <u>positive</u> things for yourself and others? What habits do you have in your life that you have found to be positive and helpful? How can you further <u>develop</u> them? What habits in your life have you found to be destructive or problematic? Are there positive habits you could develop in their place? *Should we be wary of characteristic items of <u>behavior</u> becoming <u>addictive</u> or <u>obsessive</u>?*

**Hallucinate**: Hallucinations, at their core, are things that do not exist in measurable <u>reality</u> but which we still see or hear. Is it a prerequisite to be <u>sick</u> before seeing or hearing things that are not? Can we so casually disregard the experiences of so many <u>religious</u> figures who saw or heard things others could not? Is it possible there are some outside forces that we have yet to discover which would show us that hallucinations do not equal <u>insanity</u>? What is the difference between a hallucination and an epiphany, a new realization about the nature of reality?

> *"We first make our habits, then our habits make us."*
> — *John Dryden*

**Hand**: A word of many meanings. It can refer simply to the physical body part or refer more metaphorically to our actions, as in we say we need a hand. The <u>significance</u> of the word lies in how we use it. Have you slapped or struck another? Have you pulled a trigger, or have you <u>caressed</u> and greeted in friendship? What great things in this world have been done with the use of hands? How do you use your hands in a <u>positive</u> way? How much do you think of them as representing yourself or your actions?

**Handicap**: A handicap is anything that makes <u>progress</u> or success more difficult, whether it is <u>physical</u> or not. Handicaps take on various forms and levels of severity. Is life is about <u>circumventing</u> our personal handicaps to find areas in which we shine? Can what is now your handicap be <u>transformed</u> into a personal <u>strength</u> when adapted from a <u>negative</u> to a <u>positive</u>? How would you think of addressing your own handicaps? Is it possible to address a handicap in a negative way so that it becomes an excuse? How can we avoid that?

**Handiwork**: Handiwork describes anything we create through our own <u>labor</u>, whether it is a physical object or a more abstract goal we have achieved. Is the <u>ability</u> to work with one's hands taken for granted in today's computerized world? Have you experienced a <u>fulfilled</u> feeling gained from creating or crafting things with your own

123

hands? What can you accomplish with your handiwork?

**Handle**: Handling an object or a situation implies careful control and management; it is also the part of an object which is designed to allow us to have a firm grasp on it and make it more useful or transportable. How does our understanding of what handling is begin with the way our parents handle us as infants? In what way do you handle delicate incidents? In what ways do situations present ways for us to grasp them and therefore handle them?

**Happen**: Something that happens is something that comes into being that did not exist before. How important is it to be proactive in order to have desirable things happen? Are you able to make things happen once you know what you want? How much effort do you find worth it to do so? Do you allow unexpected complications to dissuade you from achieving your goals? Do you stand idly by or do you take action and make things happen? Are there actions you could take in your life to help your desires happen? If you're not already taking those actions, why not?

**Happiness, Happy**: We can experience happiness in many different forms. It is the pleasant feeling we have when we experience positive emotional sensations. Do you treat happiness as one of your ultimate goals in life? We dedicate much of our lives to the pursuit of it, but how often do our personal definitions of happiness change? Can relief bring happiness? What are the different possible avenues from which happiness can come—humor, smiles, and aesthetics? Since happiness is usually derived from pleasure, should we not analyze the source of pleasure? Is it acceptable when someone feels

> *"The most important thing is to enjoy your life—to be happy— it's all that matters."*
> *— Audrey Hepburn*

happiness after causing another person harm? When you find that elusive feeling, are you consciously aware of the benefits and effect of being happy, such as attitude and consideration for others? Is happiness we receive from physical sensations as worthwhile as happiness we gain emotionally? Do you seize opportunities to spread it to those around you? What makes you happy? Are you generally and genuinely a happy person?

**Harass**: To harass is to intentionally torture and exhaust those around you with your words. Is harassment is a projection of what others dislike about themselves? What are the consequences for both aggressor and victim if the victim takes harassment personally? What could happen instead if the victim chose to see it as an opportunity to help the harasser? If you do not want to be harassed, why would you consider harassing others? How can you best respond to the harassment you receive from others?

**Hard**: The strong resistance we encounter when we try to break through hard surfaces reminds us of how difficult it also is to break through emotionally hard experiences. When difficult situations arise for you, do you find them incomprehensible and unmanageable? Hard times hit all of us at some point in our lives; could hard work be the antidote? Is it worth the blood, sweat, and tears to put in the effort and the energy to overcome? How do you think you can best prepare yourself for hard times? Are there people around you who can help in times of crisis?

**Harm**: Harm, which can be both the act and the effect of injury, can come in many forms, including physical and emotional. When someone is harmed, how much does it matter whether that harm is intentional or unintentional? Have you been the <u>victim</u> of harm in your life? In what ways can you prevent harm in your life and in the lives of others?

**Harmony**: Harmony is <u>agreement</u> in <u>ideas,</u> <u>attitudes,</u> and <u>behaviors</u>. Are you able to find harmony in a <u>variety</u> of things around you? Have you experienced being at <u>peace</u> with your <u>identity,</u> your beliefs, and how you live your life? At times, life can get so hectic that harmony seems impossible, but does it help to dwell on this fact? How can you take steps to encourage harmony in your life? How long and hard are you willing to <u>work</u> for it? What brings harmony to your life?

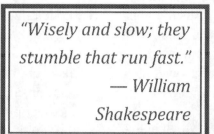

*"Wisely and slow; they stumble that run fast."*
*— William Shakespeare*

**Harvest**: To harvest is to <u>gather</u> in the rewards from one's efforts, not just in terms of actual crops, but other kinds of results as well. When it's time to gather the fruits of your <u>labor,</u> is there any greater joy? Is the essence of harvesting about finishing what you've started? Is <u>hard</u> <u>work</u> and dedication only worthwhile when you are able to harvest <u>positive</u> rewards, or can they be ends unto themselves? Have you finished what you've started? Have you reaped what you've sown? What kinds of seeds are you sowing now?

**Haste**: Haste involves not just doing something quickly, but doing something so quickly that it results in more <u>negative consequences</u> than would have occurred if the same task were performed at a slower speed. <u>Speed</u> is often equated with <u>skill</u>, but when can we tell when we are reckless and moving too fast without the necessary skills? Is it when we find ourselves actually making careless <u>mistakes</u> or only when we are not doing so through sheer <u>luck</u>? What <u>traits</u> or <u>evidence</u> should you rely on when attempting to find a <u>balance</u> between reckless haste and <u>idle</u> laziness? Have you ever felt that you were moving recklessly? How could you check whether you were moving too fast? What <u>ideas</u> or methods could you use to slow yourself down?

**Hate**: To hate is to feel extreme dislike toward someone or something. Is hate a purely <u>negative</u> <u>emotion,</u> or can anything beneficial or <u>positive</u> ever come from it? What kind of toll does feeling hatred take on your body and mind? When you have feelings of hate, do they embed themselves into your <u>mind</u> and remain bottled up within you? Have you hit the breaking point, had your <u>damaging</u> disposition spill out, and then had to deal with the consequences? Is it possible to completely avoid hatred, or is it an inevitability in our lives? How could you deal with your strong feelings of hatred the next time you encounter them? Should hatred be expressed or allowed to fester in our minds? Have you ever felt a deep hatred toward something or someone? How did it make you feel?

*"All your life, you will be faced with a choice. You can choose love or hate...I choose love."*
*— Johnny Cash*

**Haughty**: A haughty person is someone who considers himself or herself "high and mighty" above everyone else. It is important to be confident as you live your life, but how can you tell when you've taken it too far, to the point of unearned <u>entitlement</u>? Are there people who you assume you are better or smarter than? What led you to that assumption? Are you willing to address that assumption?

**Havoc**: Havoc is <u>destructive</u> <u>chaos</u>. Does it inevitably have <u>negative</u> consequences, or can it ultimately result in a <u>positive</u> outcome? Is it unavoidable? How can we prepare ourselves to handle it appropriately? When have you experienced havoc? How did you handle it?

**Hazard**: A hazard is a danger we cannot completely avoid, even if we are able to see it coming; it can also mean a risk we willingly take. Are you aware of the hazards around you? What aspects of those hazards are you able to control and which can you not? Are hazards entirely negative, or can they act as tests that ultimately improve us? How do you deal with hazards that you come across?

**Head**: One's head, as the body part which holds and protects the brain, is central to human identity. We also use the word to indicate that someone is in charge of something; the head of an organization, for example. Are these two definitions in total agreement? Is the head always in charge of who we are? Is it a control tower of the self? Considering the value of the other parts of the head, such as the eyes, ears, mouth, and nose, do you take appropriate care to protect yours? We sometimes talk about thoughts and feelings coming from either the head (intelligence) or the heart (emotion); is this an artificial distinction? Is this division present in your thoughts?

**Heal**: Healing is the act of taking something that has suffered harm and making it whole again. This can be a body or a mind, but also something more intangible, such as a relationship. Healing is generally a result of medical practice, but what about the power of the mind? Is it possible that many medicines that have been labeled placebos actually help to heal our bodies, because we believe so firmly in them that our brains help our bodies heal? What other ways can we heal ourselves? How could we use these ideas to heal others? How is healing a sick body like healing a sick relationship?

**Health**: Life as it relates to health is subject to three conditions or setbacks: your genetic makeup, physical injury or trauma, and, finally, disease and the subsequent use of internal or remedial medicine. The first of these is highly controversial because it involves manipulation before life begins, assuming we enter this world with good or average genes. The second begins with our ability to avoid injury and ends as a measure of how well we repair our minds and bodies. The third, if not genetically steered in a negative direction, is simply a matter of *what enters our bodies*; for example, making the conscious decision to inhale smoke despite our knowledge of its cancerous effects. Here, it is important to differentiate and point out that we are not only affected by what we take in with our mouths but also what we absorb via our other senses. For example, witnessing violence with our eyes can disease our brain by desensitizing us to violent acts. Likewise, listening to abrasive or subversive speech can cause disease by instilling us with negative values. Have you considered what role habits and addictions play in the regular function of your body? What decisions can you make today to improve your health now and in the long run? Do you consider exercise as being taken into the body? How does stress enter the body and what effect does it have? Can you conceive a total picture of what is possible in the broadest sense to take into your body and affect your health?

> *"Let food be thy medicine and medicine be thy food."*
> — Hippocrates

**Hear**: Hearing is one of the five main senses in our bodies in which our ears pass on audible information to our brains. We learn to talk by hearing sounds and mimicking them. How important is hearing in other aspects of our lives? How does attentive hearing affect our formal education in school, and our more informal education of observing the world? What is the difference between hearing a sound passively and actively listening in order to gather information and learn from it? How can you best use your hearing to advance your own life and those around you?

**Heart**: In merely physical terms, the heart of any organism is the engine that pumps blood through its body in order to allow it to function. In more symbolic terms, it is spoken of metaphorically as the part of the human body that feels love, affection, kindness, and empathy, and also the most important part of something, as in the heart of an argument or an organization. Do you take care of your physical heart? How about your emotional one? Do you ever feel as though there is a tension between what your head wants and what your heart wants? How have you resolved this? What do you consider as being at the heart of your life and your beliefs?

**Heat:** Heat is warmth in the form of energy, anything raising the temperature of a substance. It is necessary for human life, and we heat our homes and ourselves in a variety of ways. How do you obtain heat? Do you consider the effects on the environment as you do so? Is considering the sources and effects of our heat usage only a practical issue, or is it also a moral one?

**Heaven**: The idea of heaven is, in Christian mythology, the place inhabited by God, the angels, and the souls of the righteous; other religions believe in similar places where celestial deities reside. Because of some beliefs about the nature and location of heaven, the word "heavens" is also used more poetically to talk about the sky and all it contains. What do you think about this connection between heaven as a physical place and a state of being? Have you contemplated the nature of what truly lies beyond our earthbound perception? Is there a master creator living in the beyond that watches us and sends us to heaven or hell? Or is it just nothingness, a black empty sea devoid of any form of matter or existence? What is heaven for you? Is it hope for a better life after this one? Is it motivation to discover what is truly out there? Is there a spiritual heaven?

**Hell**: The polar opposite of heaven, Christian mythology holds that hell is the realm where the souls of the evil go after death. Some Christians would contend that hell is a finite, physical place located deep beneath the ground in the fiery core of the Earth; others would claim that hell has the potential to exist anywhere you make it. Do you believe that any place of misery or pain can be considered hell? Have you been through any experience so terrible that you would describe it as hell on Earth? Did you enact some positive changes to appease your misery or pain? What is your idea of a personal hell? Is there a spiritual hell?

**Help**: Helping is a display of appreciation, kindness, and conscientiousness. The golden rule tells us to treat others as we want to be treated; do you believe this to be good advice when you consider helping those around you? How much of helping others is a give and take process? If you spend your life constantly taking and never giving, how do you think that will affect others' willingness to help you? What if you instead give help without hesitation or ulterior motive? What are significant ways others have helped you in your past? What about significant ways you have helped others? Which do you think is more valuable—ways to physically and materially help others, or ways to emotionally and spiritually help them? Do you ever find it difficult to accept help or admit you need it? How can you help someone else today?

**Heresy**: Heresy is any belief that is against the stated belief of a particular religion. There are an immeasurable amount of beliefs on this planet, so who is to say who is right and who is wrong? Tolerance is a valued virtue in today's world. Is there a place for heresy in a <u>democracy</u>? Should it be a punishable offense? How do we tolerate the intolerant? Should we?

**Heritage**: Heritage consists of both <u>tangible</u> and <u>intangible</u> things that are handed down through generations of <u>family</u> members, and can consist of things as varied as genetics, <u>traditions</u>, <u>language</u>, <u>culture</u>, <u>beliefs</u>, and <u>physical</u> <u>possessions</u>. Do you believe your heritage is what makes you who you are? How <u>responsible</u> is it for the foundation of your <u>identity</u>, <u>beliefs</u>, and customs? How much <u>honor</u> and <u>respect</u> do you give to your heritage? Are you proud of your heritage? How do you think about the <u>relationship</u> between yourself and your ancestors, without whom you would not be here? Would you fight for your heritage? What do you plan to or what would you like to hand down to <u>future</u> generations as your <u>participation</u> in the transmission of heritage? Is it irresponsible to not participate?

**Hermit**: A hermit is someone who intentionally shuts themselves off from other <u>human</u> beings. Do you <u>enjoy</u> <u>solitude</u>, or do you like to be around others? Life can be awfully lonely without any contact from other people, but would you be able to live comfortably without any solitude at all? Can you dwell on how you would live your life as a hermit? What personal <u>motivations</u> do you think might <u>cause</u> you to become one? Do you think you would survive?

> *"I hold that a strongly marked personality can influence descendants for generations."*
> — *Beatrix Potter*

**Hero**: A hero is usually seen as someone who has done something brave and noble in the face of <u>fear</u>. Does a hero necessarily have to do something noble and brave? Can a hero instead be one who achieves <u>good</u> by doing something small and unnoticeable? Are those who do good things without expecting <u>recognition</u> the <u>true</u> heroes? Who do you consider a hero in your <u>life</u>? What have they accomplished to gain that title?

**Hesitate**: To hesitate is to wait to act in response to a situation. Hesitation can be a sign of doubt and fear, but can it also be a calculated maneuver to avoid a bad situation? When was the last time you hesitated before doing something? Did you save the moment or did your hesitation cause you to miss out on an <u>opportunity</u>? What kinds of <u>dangers</u> to yourself or others cause you to hesitate?

**Hide**: To hide is to put something intentionally out of <u>sight</u> in order to conceal it from others; we can hide things as <u>physical</u> as our own <u>bodies</u> or as <u>intangible</u> as our <u>thoughts</u>. Sometimes in life, we get scared or discouraged and go into hiding to <u>protect</u> ourselves; is this a healthy response? When is hiding actually the best <u>option</u>, and when is it simply delaying the <u>inevitable</u>? Have there been times when you were tempted to hide but instead chose to confront your situation and deal with it to the best of your ability? What forces in your life have you been tempted to hide from? How have you or could you convince yourself to face them?

**High School**: High school is, in America, the final phase of <u>publically</u> accessible and legally required <u>education</u>. As high school typically overlaps with middle and late adolescence, it is often figured as simultaneously formative, fun, and difficult. Was this representative of your experience? What were experiences you had in the first time in high school? Did it feel differently from previous schooling you had gone through? What did you learn in your high school days? Did you learn more in high school from your classroom experiences, or your social ones? How has that shaped your life to this day?

**History**: History is the human record of the past. How important is history as a teacher for humanity? Do we give enough attention to it and its lessons? Should we always contemplate and consider past actions and events before making decisions affecting the future? While there may be only one version of the past, there can be many versions of history. How do we decide which ones are worthwhile or trustworthy? If history is only what we choose to remember, what kinds of actions and inactions become part of the record and why? Has your history been something you've tried to forget or escape? How can you attempt instead to learn from it?

> *"If you don't know history, then you don't know anything. You are a leaf that doesn't know it is part of a tree."*
> — Michael Crichton

**Holy**: That which is holy is something that has special or unseen significance, generally connected with our idea of religion. But can non-religious things also be holy? For example, can you think of family as being holy, as family provides a special bond between those that love us unconditionally? What is holy in your life?

**Homage**: Paying homage is showing respect or reverence to a person who is deserving of such respect. Who do we generally believe deserves homage? Do those people actually receive the homage they are due? To whom do you pay homage in your life?

**Home**: In generic terms, a home is simply the place someone lives. But what is the most important quality of a home? Is it where we live, where we sleep, or where we feel the most comfortable? What do you think is the most important aspect of home for you? What do you believe is the difference between a house and a home? Where do you call home? How many times has your idea of where home is changed?

**Homicide**: A homicide is the killing of one human being by another.

How do we as a society show that we consider killing someone to be one of the most heinous crimes a person can commit? While the victim of the murder is the one most wronged by the crime, how many other victims are created by a homicide? What could motivate someone to commit such an act? Is it possible to erase homicide from this world?

**Homosexual**: Homosexuality is the state of being attracted to someone of the same sex. Many people object to homosexuality for various reasons, such as believing it is immoral or unnatural. Where do these beliefs come from, and how valid do you believe them to be? Should we embrace who we are and let ourselves flourish without trying to please or pander to the wishes of others? When should we display our true selves without worrying about offending others, and when do we need to restrain ourselves? Do you present yourself accurately to the rest of the world? Is it better to disguise our feelings rather than subject them to ridicule?

> *"Honesty is the first chapter of the book wisdom."*
> — Thomas Jefferson

**Honesty**: Honesty is being truthful and trustworthy while refusing to lie, cheat, or steal. Is honesty often taken for granted in everyday life? Should we exalt honesty as the golden standard to which each person should aspire? Have you witnessed people being pressured to lie or cheat to benefit their own situation or to protect another person's situation? Does society appropriately celebrate those people who uphold the truth even in the face of danger or loss? Is honesty relegated to any specific time or place? Does it come and go, or is it permanent? Are you sometimes frustrated by lack of honesty? Are you an honest, just, and impartial person? How can you work toward being more honest?

**Honor**: Honor can be defined as showing respect for an individual and recognizing them to a certain degree above the societal norm. Giving higher honor to an individual comes about from what our society dictates and regulates. The more honor you possess, the more value you hold within society. Individuals begin to look toward honorable people with the end goal in mind of gaining some sort of valuable utility that, in turn, will allow themselves to increase their own reputation and honorable status. Is honor rewarded externally or internally? In other words, does it suffice for someone to simply believe they carry honor throughout their life, or does it need to be validated by the outside world? When you respect another individual, is that automatically reciprocated with honor? What is the rite of passage one needs to gain honor? Is it achieved through actions, words, or both? More so, is honor automatically attributed to an individual, or does it need to be earned through the various rites of passage? Where do you draw the line in assigning honor? Can it be to your neighbor down the street, or is it simply dependent on a title that our society holds in higher regard? How do you deal with honor? Do you differentiate between honoring pacts and contracts, or honoring promises and handshakes?

**Hope**: To hope is to want events to work out for the best and in the way you would like. It is to wish for a better tomorrow and a feeling of desire for something to go well. However, wishing won't get you anywhere without a little hard work and effort. If you want something, you have to work for it, but hope is often the first step to reaching your goal. What do you hope for in life? How has hope helped you advance in your life? What can hope help you achieve? Are you a hopeful person? Does hope in fact spring eternal, or can it be suffocated by the constant denial of fulfilment? Is it possible that the main reason hopes fail to come to fruition that they are based on unrealistic expectations based on faulty thinking?

**Hour**: An hour is one way that humans divide up time in order to make our lives more convenient; we count twenty-four hours each time the Earth turns fully on its axis. What determines how much can be accomplished in an hour? In the grand scheme of things, does an hour seem like an insignificant sliver in a lifetime? Does each hour count the same in life so that what you do with your time on Earth matters all the same? What can you accomplish in an hour?

**House**: A building in which we live. Is a house merely a shell used for shelter until we have made it a home? When does a house become a home? Is it the way we decorate it to our liking, or is there something more fundamental that needs to be present or needs to be changed? Would you consider your house to be a home?

**Hug**: A hug is a loving embrace shared by two people who care for each other. How important is it to you to hold and be held by someone that you truly care about? Do you find a hug to be a simple and easy way to tell somebody that you are here for them and that you want to be near them, or do you find giving hugs more complicated and difficult? Who do you want to hug?

**Human**: Human beings are members of one of the only species on this planet that is fully self-aware and has a concept of the past and the future. Is it these characteristics that make us humans so special? Are the emotions of human beings particular to us? How many of them might we share with other species? Can we feel love, pain, pleasure, and remorse in a complex way that other living things have no concept of? What special skills, emotions, or abilities define you as a human?

**Humanity:** Humanity has two important meanings. First, it is used to refer to the sum total of all human beings, and second, it can be used as a synonym for kindness. Do these two meanings together imply that it is human nature to be kind? Does this match your observations of how you have seen other human beings act? Is it useful to think of all human beings as being part of the same group, or does that deny too much of humans' individuality?

> *"A true genius admits that he/she knows nothing."*
> — *Albert Einstein*

**Humble:** To be humble is to know your weaknesses and faults without letting your pride disguise them. Is humility always positive, because it means we are not being prideful or demanding? Can humility be negative when it becomes self-deprecation, or is it at that point no longer humility? What kind of experiences and knowledge do we need to have in order to be capable of humility? Do you live your life with humility?

**Humiliate:** To humiliate someone is to strip them of their pride and dignity, and to make them feel ashamed. Is humiliation one of the worst feelings possible? Should we ever make it our purpose to deliberately embarrass someone, or is that indecent? Is it ever deserved? Have you felt humiliated? By whom, and why? How did you decide to respond?

**Humor:** Humor is anything that makes us laugh; it is often based on a situation's lack of logic or the difference between what we expect and what actually happens. Do you find that humor is a quality that has the power to brighten your day in an instant? Do you believe that laughter helps us to live longer lives? Do people who can make anybody laugh have a special skill that commands the room and brings entertainment and enjoyment to all? Would you consider your personality a humorous one? If you can't make people laugh, how else could you bring enjoyment to others?

**Hunger:** Hunger is a discomforting feeling that we get when we need food, though we can also talk about our need for other things as a kind of hunger. How drastically do you believe help is needed for those who are hungry in the world today? Do we also feel hunger for what motivates us in life? When you know what you want but have yet to grasp it, do you feel it in your body as well as your brain? What do you hunger for in your life? How can you help someone else who is hungry and in need?

**Hurry:** To hurry is to attempt to move or work faster in order to accomplish something more quickly. Do you sometimes find yourself hurrying through life? While sometimes it is necessary to move quickly, is it equally important to slow down and take a break every now and then, as well? Do you find that you move too fast at times and end up acting in haste?

**Hurt:** To hurt can be either to inflict or receive injury or pain. Hurt is an inevitable part of life, as it is impossible to go through life without disappointment or injury, but is it also a necessary in order for us to truly live? How can it be beneficial to our lives to deal with hurt in a positive way? How do you deal with hurting in your life?

# I

**Icon:** An icon is a simplified picture that represents a more complicated thought or image. In the Greek Orthodox Church, an icon is an image of a holy figure and could be used as a focus to contemplate God. Today, however, this word's meaning has been extended to pop culture figures, and politicians. What icons do you hold in your life? Why are they important to you?

**Iconoclast:** An iconoclast is a person who is against the worship of images. In a religious context, this means someone who is against the worship of images of religious figures, but how might this extend past religion? Though this may seem insensitive or disrespectful to the religions of others, an iconoclast is also capable of examining the ideology of a group and judge it solely based on the merit of the ideas, rather than adhering to views because of the blind worship of images. How in our life do we substitute the worship of icons for the careful adherence to certain values?

**Idea:** An idea can come from anywhere and be the result of any random train of thought or chance occurrence. Ideas facilitate growth and development, both of ourselves and everything outside of us. Yet ideas, thoughts, and words are only as good as their route of progression. If they are stalled at conception or not nurtured, they become stagnant, wither, and die. As intellectual property, can ideas be compromised or stolen? Do you have any ideas that you hold to dogmatically? Would you ever be willing to

> *"No army can withstand the strength of an idea whose time has come."*
> — *Victor Hugo*

question them? How might you benefit from doing so? How can you welcome these trains of thought into your own life, and be more open to new ideas? Can ideas come from another spiritual dimension? Are they prevalent at any particular state of being, such as at rest?

**Idealize:** Idealization is mentally creating a perfect picture of something for ourselves that does not reflect the flaws that a thing or person has in reality. To move past idealization to reality, we first need to understand what we idealize and then discover why we idealize the things we do. Idealization can also precede disappointment when the reality of a situation does not measure up to the image we had in our minds. To avoid this, seek to accept things as they are—both people and situations—and don't ignore aspects of anything simply because they distract you from your preconceived notions. What do you suspect you idealize in your life when it may not actually be as perfect as it seems? What possible harms could you be causing yourself and others by idealization? Do you engage in frivolous idealization?

**Identify:** Identifying something means being able to recognize it either as a specific entity or as being able to group it with other similar things. To achieve anything in our lives, do we first need to identify our goals and the obstacles that may be preventing us from reaching them? Is identifying these things simple or difficult? How can you improve your ability to clearly identify your goals and obstacles in life?

**Identity:** Who or what you are constitutes your identity. But are identities ever simple, or are they thousands of little facets that come together to create each person's unique identity? Do you ever find yourself generalizing or idealizing others? How might this deny them an individual identity?

**Idiosyncrasy:** An idiosyncrasy is a peculiar and unique way of being or behaving. What idiosyncrasies have you encountered in your daily life? Do you have any of your own? How can we appreciate others' idiosyncrasies rather than judging them for their quirks?

**Idiot:** Idiot is a common pejorative term that criticizes someone's intelligence. But is it truly fair to judge someone for their intelligence alone? Wouldn't it be fairer to place our value of a person in their work ethic, their moral standards, or their capacity to love?

**Idle:** To be idle is to be without activity or work. Do people generally have good excuses for idleness in their lives? How can you avoid idleness in your own life? Even if you don't need to work to survive, couldn't your efforts be well-put in volunteering some creative endeavor? Can idleness lead to indifference? How can you determine whether you have achieved a balance between work and leisure?

> *"Idle hands are the devil's workshop."*
> *— Proverbs 16:27*

**Idol:** An idol is the image of a god to be worshipped. In Biblical times, Moses forbade the Jews from worshipping false idols, but how might the concept of idols still be relevant even today? What superficial idols do we worship, such as movie stars or sports heroes? Where else could our spiritual reverence be better directed?

> *"Never touch your idols: the gilding will stick to your fingers."*
> *— Gustave Flaubert*

**Idolize:** To idolize is think about someone or something with such admiration that we ignore their faults and flaws. Do we often idolize what isn't presently there? What is it about distance that makes idolizing easier? Is it that, when things are far from us, we can imagine them how we would like them, instead of how they actually are? What dangers could there be in idolizing others?

**Ignoble:** Something ignoble is not honorable or respectable, but instead dishonest or shameful. Have you ever been guilty of an ignoble act? How have you tried to repent for it?

**Ignominious:** An ignominious act causes shame or disgrace; it is an ignoble act made public. Is it worth risking the public shame of ignominy? Would it help to think of the ignominy our acts will cause before we commit them? How can we develop this kind of foresight? Do you consider the ramifications of all actions not just from an internal perspective, but also the external, as in what views will others have of your behavior?

**Ignoramus:** While everyone is ignorant of something, an ignoramus is someone who is overly ignorant. In today's hyper-connected world in which everything is online and a Google search away, does anyone have an excuse for being an ignoramus? How can we use tools like the Internet to educate ourselves about important issues? What are the potential consequences of our continued ignorance?

**Ignore:** To ignore is to choose to not recognize a person, situation, or fact. Do we often ignore our problems in hope that they'll go away? Is this path actually harmful to us? What do we lose by ignoring our problems instead of facing them head-on?

**Ill:** When you are ill, you are unhealthy or have a mental or physical disease. Certain illnesses are obvious, but how can illness persist in more subtle ways? Can we be <u>morally</u> ill, or ethically unhealthy? Do you know someone who is ill? Illness can dramatically decrease the quality of life of an <u>individual</u>. Consider ways in which you can <u>help</u> those who suffer from illness.

> *"Everything you can imagine is real."*
> — *Pablo Picasso*

**Illusion:** An illusion is something that we perceive to be true but isn't. If illusions blind us to <u>reality</u>, would we do well to destroy them? What illusions do you hold? How do they affect your <u>judgment</u>?

**<u>Imagine, Imagination</u>:** Imagining something involves being able to see in one's mind something that does not, or does not yet, exist. Is imagination at the root of all <u>ideas</u>? What kinds of problems do you think an open imagination can solve once it has been cultivated by developing solutions that have not been <u>thought</u> of yet? Of what might your own imagination be capable? How do you think you can cultivate it? Is an open imagination a <u>luxury</u> we <u>indulge</u> in or a <u>responsibility</u> we have toward ourselves and the <u>world</u>?

**Imitate, Imitation:** An imitator is never <u>genuine</u>, but only pretends to be something he or she is not. Imitators are everywhere; how can you separate them from what is genuine? What do we lose of ourselves when we seek to imitate rather than approach life in our own way? How can you adopt the traits you find admirable in others without losing sight of yourself?

> *"Imitation is the sincerest [form] of flattery."*
> — *Charles Colton*

**Immediate:** Something that is immediate happens without delay. Is immediate gratification often the reason we cannot accomplish our <u>goals</u>? Is it always easier to satisfy our present pleasures than to put off the gratification of our long-term goals? But how can we learn to ignore our immediate desires in favor of our long-term goals?

**Immerse:** To be immersed is to be fully covered <u>physically</u> or, more metaphorically, to be fully involved in an activity or an <u>idea</u>. If we become immersed in something not of our own choosing or something that is <u>negative</u>, is that immersion necessarily overwhelming? If we become immersed in something we <u>enjoy</u>, is it always a rewarding experience? What sort of things have you chosen to

immerse yourself in? Have those immersions been <u>positive</u> or negative for you?

**Imperfection:** An imperfection, is, of course, anything that keeps a person or an object from being <u>perfect</u>. What are your imperfections? Do you worry about them, or do you think that possibly imperfections are impossible for human beings to <u>avoid</u>? Should we strive to rid ourselves of our imperfections, or <u>accept</u> them?

**Impetus:** An impetus is the push we need to get going and go forward. It is the <u>force</u> that begins momentum, without which movement would be impossible. How can we gain the impetus we need in life to get going on our <u>goals</u>? Can certain people or events act as an impetus? Are there people in your life for whom you could be a catalyst for <u>positive</u> change?

**Importance, Important:** Something that has significant value or use. How do we decide what is important for our lives? Are the small parts of a process as important or more important than the larger <u>goals</u> or needs we have in <u>mind</u>? What do you consider important in your life? Have your <u>ideas</u> of what is important changed over time? When you act, do you stop to consider what is important to others, as well?

**Imprison:** To hold someone against their <u>will</u>. Are all imprisonments necessarily <u>physical</u>? What other forms can an imprisonment take? Do you feel imprisoned by <u>forces</u> in your life? How do you think you could <u>work</u> toward either actually freeing yourself from them or feeling less imprisoned by them?

**Improve, Improvement:** To make better, to gain in quality. Is improvement a major <u>goal</u> in your life? What would you like to improve about yourself or your situation? What steps do you think you could take to help yourself <u>accomplish</u> these improvements? Are there people around you who could <u>help</u>?

**Impulse:** An impulse is a <u>wish</u> or urge we have to do something, usually one we have based on our emotional state, and often one we have suddenly. Why impulses are so often tempting? Is it because they appear to be in line with our instincts? What factors cause us to have either <u>positive</u> or <u>negative</u> impulses? For example, what is your impulse when you

> *"If moderation is a fault, then indifference is a crime."*
> — *Jack Kerouac*

speak to someone with whom you disagree about a fundamental <u>belief</u> that you hold? Do you find yourself impulsively liking them less or thinking them to be <u>stupid</u> or <u>inferior</u> to yourself? While this is <u>common</u>, does it seem like a useful or <u>compassionate</u> way to treat other human beings? How could you keep track of and overcome these kinds of impulses?

**Incentive:** An incentive is anything that encourages us to act in a certain way, often in situations where something difficult or unpleasant must be undergone. What sort of incentive would you need in order to change your life? To change the way you <u>thought</u> about the world and your <u>relationship</u> to it?

**Incidence:** An incidence can be anything that happens. Yet every incidence involves an incredible conglomeration of different factors, including people and things—human life, <u>technology</u>, <u>animals</u>, <u>plants</u>, insects, elements, etc. How can you nurture an <u>awareness</u> of each element that goes into every incidence and thereby understand them better? To what extent can an <u>effect</u> be understood without understanding its <u>cause</u>?

**Incorporate:** When we incorporate something, we make it a part of ourselves. This <u>book</u> is meant to help you develop your own <u>creed</u> for living, a set of <u>beliefs</u> that you can incorporate into your own life. How do we incorporate sets of beliefs, however? How do we make something a part of ourselves and our daily <u>habits</u>? 'Wouldn't we need to see it clearly first? How could we begin to <u>investigate</u> how different facets of a situation interact with our beliefs before making decisions?

**Inculcate:** When we inculcate something, we fix it in a person's <u>mind</u> (including our own) by <u>teaching</u> it over and over again. What personal <u>beliefs</u> have you inculcated, and how was that process performed? Once an <u>idea</u> has been inculcated, is it ever possible to forget it or alter it in some way? Or does it enter the fabric of our <u>subconscious</u>, forever a part of the way we approach situations?

**Indecision:** Indecision is the inability to choose between multiple options. Many are <u>paralyzed</u> by indecision, making them incapable of <u>action</u> and of moving forward with their lives. How can we find a balance between indecision and <u>impulse</u>? Is it equally problematic to act too slowly as it is to act too <u>quickly</u>?

**Independence:** Independence is defined by the <u>freedom</u> to act without being prevented from doing so by others. In 1776, America fought for independence from England, but today some say that <u>freedom</u> is again under attack. Yet this time, it comes not from any colonizing force, but rather in the form of <u>manipulative</u> <u>corporations</u> and lobbyists trying to <u>influence</u> and <u>corrupt</u> our <u>government</u>. Would you agree? How can we win back our independence? In what ways have you taken your freedom for granted, and does this cause <u>apathy</u>?

**Indifference:** Indifference is a failure to care, one way or another, about the outcome of a situation. How do you feel about the <u>attribute</u> of <u>neglect</u>? Is there anything, good or bad, that doesn't need conscious attention? How can you <u>best</u> decide how much attention to devote where? Where are you indifferent where you shouldn't be in life? What is the effect of indifference on our personal <u>relationships</u> and those we care about the most? Have you ever found yourself feeling neglected by your <u>friends</u> and <u>family</u>? Have you ever made others feel neglected? How could you make these situations better?

**Individual, Individuality:** An individual is a single person, as distinguished from the various groups they could be identified as belonging to. Do we need to be individuals in our <u>decision</u> making, and to have a sense of who we are? Do you find that you are too willing to ignore your individuality in an attempt to fit in? What kinds of physical or <u>moral</u> dangers are there in simply following the crowd? How can we also make sure we are not blinded by assuming our way is the absolute best—not just insisting on our own individuality, but also being willing to accept the opinions and <u>ideas</u> of others?

> *"The most courageous act is still to think for yourself. Aloud."*
> *— Coco Chanel*

**Induce:** To induce is to lead or <u>persuade</u> a person into something. One could argue that much of politics is an act of inducement, as each <u>politician</u> tries to <u>convince</u> and <u>entice</u> a voter into believing they are right. How can we <u>avoid</u> the insidious influence of these people? Have you found yourself misled by someone who speaks well but who lacks <u>ideas</u> or content?

**Indulge, Indulgence:** To indulge is to give in to the <u>desires</u> of ourselves or others. Many are quick to indulge their every whim, but how could doing so ultimately lead to <u>harm</u>? What kinds of indulgences are present in your life? Have you harmed yourself or others through them? Have you been harmed by 'others' indulgences? How could you put an end to these <u>negative</u> outcomes?

**Indurate**: To make something <u>hard</u>, callous, or enduring. It can also mean to be unfeeling, obstinate, or indifferent. Usually, this word is used in reference to the processes involved in hardening metals like steel and gold jewelry, but we can think of it as applying metaphorically to the changes people put themselves through. Have you ever tried to "melt" yourself to <u>change</u> some aspect of your life? Why do people feel the need to do this? Do you try to act in a way that your soul says you should, or do you let others melt you and shape you to society's <u>expectations</u> of what you should be like? If society looks down upon you for something, do you change that aspect of your life? Or do you make yourself indifferent to the <u>thoughts</u> of society and endure the looks and words of discouragement knowing that that aspect of your life is who you are inside?

**Industrial Revolution:** At the turn of the nineteenth century, the nature of human life and labor changed from being based on what we could do with our bodies to being based on our use of machinery. Since that industrial revolution, our dependence on machines has increased to the point where much of our lives would be impossible without it. The unfortunate side effect of the convenience of modern technology is the damage to the natural resources of our planet; are the advancements we have made worth the cost? How can we adapt to this new form of existence, and how can we transcend it to remember things like nature?

**Inevitable:** Inevitable things will happen, whether we want them to or not. While many things are out of our control, such as aging, how many more can be affected by our actions? How can we distinguish inevitable events from those in which we have agency?

**Inexorable:** That which cannot be stopped, altered, checked, etc. What in life is inexorable, and what remains under our control? It's common to feel powerless in the face of the inexorable, but is this sentiment one shared by mankind? Would it be comforting to know that fear of the inexorable is one in which you are not alone?

**Infallible:** One who is infallible is incapable of being morally or factually wrong. Have you met those who would like to believe that they are infallible, when in reality they are anything but? Can any human, belief, or system of beliefs be infallible? Or is infallibility something reserved for only God?

**Inferior:** Inferiority describes something that is, at best, worse than average and, at worst, worthless. How much is our judgment of what is inferior based on fact, and how often is it based on personal prejudices and preexisting ideas? Is it moral or reasonable to think of one human being as being inferior to another? What are your standards for deciding whether something is inferior? Have you questioned how you developed those standards to make sure they are good ones? When you do find something that is inferior, how do you deal with it?

**Infinite, Infinity:** Something infinite is never-ending and unimaginable within the normal human mind. Space and time are frequently understood as being infinite. What else could be? Emotional states like pain and love? Can potential be infinite? What else defies human comprehension, too infinite for our understanding?

**Influence:** Influence is the power to persuade, sometimes to the point of controlling one's actions or ideas. Should we always regard influence cautiously, or are there situations in which we can automatically accept that it working positively? What are the major influence on your life, and why? How can or has your life impacted others'? Have you considered the way that you are influenced by major forces around you, such as how corporations and political figures speak through the mass media every day? Do you attempt to avoid these influences, or simply to be aware of them?

**Inform, Informative:** To inform is to provide knowledge. A well-led life is an educated one. Can one only be educated by informing oneself widely? Is it our duty to inform ourselves about the nature of national politics and government? How can we determine what is most helpful for us to learn? Is it best to focus on one thing deeply and then use our knowledge to educate others in that area or to try to educate ourselves a little in many areas of knowledge so we can understand its diversity? Is there a balance between the two? How can we inform others as well while still allowing them to think for themselves?

> "Knowledge is of two kinds. We know a subject ourselves, or we know where we can find information on it."
> — Samuel Johnson

**Information:** Information is <u>knowledge</u> we gain about ourselves and the <u>world</u> around us. Does one acquire wisdom and knowledge by restricting inputs, or by adding to them? Must information be retained and sorted in order to become <u>knowledge</u>? When knowledge is truly <u>internalized</u>, can it be examined with clarity and thereby lead to informed <u>decisions</u> and perspectives? How can you better handle the barrage of information facing you daily? How can you determine whether the information you encounter is reliable, biased, or <u>important</u>?

**Ingenious:** Ingenuity describes <u>genuine</u> originality; either a person or an invention may be ingenuous. You do not necessarily have to be a genius to create something ingenious, only <u>open</u> to <u>creativity</u>. But does bringing ingenious <u>ideas</u> to fruition also require hard <u>work</u>, dedication, and innovation? How can <u>perseverance</u> allow the initial seed of an <u>idea</u> to grow to its full potential? How can you encourage or develop the ingenuity within yourself?

**Inhuman:** Inhuman <u>acts</u> are cruel, heartless, or unfeeling. This word implies that what in fact makes us human is our ability to be kind and feel <u>pity</u>—do you think that this is true? Is it natural human <u>instinct</u> to act with pity? If this is so, why have so many rejected pity in favor of <u>violence</u> throughout <u>history</u>? How can we combat the inhumanity of humans on a daily basis?

**Iniquitous:** Iniquitous acts are very wicked or unjust acts. What could be the motivation for an iniquitous act, and what are its potential <u>consequences</u> for all those involved? Have you ever been <u>guilty</u> of such an act? How have you repented?

**Inordinate:** Too much or too many. Does <u>greed</u> lead to an inordinate amount of <u>wealth</u> or possessions? Inordinate is so excessive that it is considered out of bounds or unacceptable; how can we tell when this boundary has been crossed? Where have you crossed this boundary in your life? Does the accumulation of wealth <u>blind</u> us to the needs of others? Could you <u>help</u> others with what you have acquired?

**Inquisitive:** Inquisitive <u>minds</u> are ones which ask questions. How might being willing to ask questions lead to <u>creative</u> <u>ideas</u>? How can it benefit you to be more inquisitive? How can it lead to you being better informed about the world around you? How could you <u>teach</u> yourself to increase this quality?

**Insatiable:** To be insatiable is to have a <u>need</u> or <u>want</u> that cannot be satisfied, always demanding more. If you give yourself over to <u>greed</u>, how likely is it that you find your greed becoming insatiable? How can you <u>avoid</u> giving in to insatiable <u>desires</u> and the <u>havoc</u> they wreak on your life?

**Inscrutable:** To be inscrutable is to be mysterious or confusing. Are we surrounded by inscrutable objects that <u>transcend</u> our understanding? What do we have to gain by discerning the true nature of what we first find to be inscrutable? How could we attempt to do so? Are there some inscrutable things that are better left alone?

**Insecurity:** Insecurity can be an emotion we have in which we do not feel safe, but it can also be a physical <u>reality</u>, as when a building is insecure. What kinds of things make you feel insecure? Is your feeling a <u>genuine</u> reflection of the situation you are in, or is it based instead on other <u>emotional</u> <u>issues</u>? Insecurity is generally a <u>negative</u> feeling. How can you help yourself <u>avoid</u> it when it's not justified by the <u>reality</u> around you?

**Inspire, Inspiration:** An inspiration is the seed for an <u>idea</u>. Inspiration can be difficult to come by at times. Is it available in many forms and places if we remember to continue looking for it? Where in your life do you find inspiration? How could you inspire others through your <u>actions</u> and words?

**Instability:** When things are not stable, they are also often unpredictable. Are you comfortable with some instability around you, or do you find that you usually need everything to be in order? Can some instability be good because it leads to change, as in the case of some political instabilities? How do you cope with the instabilities you experience?

**Instill:** Like inculcate, instilling is the process through which a certain belief becomes a part of us and our belief systems. What beliefs have been instilled in you and by whom? How do the beliefs instilled in you help you understand your relationship to the world? Is it problematic to revere beliefs based on their source rather than their actual content?

**Instinct:** This is when creatures act without thinking, but instead because of qualities they were born with. Are human beings creatures ruled by instinct, as much as other animals are? Some instincts are passed down through millennia of evolution, but can an instinct be something we learn as well? Is it right to give into our instincts? Would we be better served if we were rather ruled by reason? How could you tell the difference between the impulses you have, whether they are prompted by reason or by instinct? Is your mind aware?

**Instruct, Instruction:** Instruction is the act of passing on information. Many cite the obvious venues of instruction in teachers, professors, and parents, but who or what else instructs us? Is there a sense in which the constant barrage of advertisements we see daily also instructs us? How can you judge the quality or truthfulness of the instruction you receive? What knowledge can you acquire that will help?

**Instrument:** An instrument is not only something that we use to produce music, but any tool which we use to complete a task. Is man's greatest privilege to become an instrument of God? Have you achieved this privilege? How would you be able to tell?

**Insult:** An insult is some kind of criticism, usually written or verbal, that is not meant to be helpful, only hurtful. Why are we so often insulted by, and why do we choose to insult, those whom we hate or are hated by? When have you insulted those around you? Do you regret those insults? How have you felt in the past when others have insulted you?

**Insupportable:** Something that is too much in quantity or too immoral in quality for it to continue to be supported in its current state. Many are coming to slowly accept that our current economic and environmental system cannot be sustained forever. How can we avoid the disaster that awaits us if we choose to continue ignoring the environmental and economic crises already upon us? How might we act otherwise?

**Insurance:** Insurance is generally a legal contract by which a business agrees to reimburse someone in case of loss, but we also use it to describe any kind of backup plan we make in case our first plan fails. We buy insurance in case of emergencies or things we don't expect and for which we can't plan. We buy insurance for our house and our cars, but what might we be forgetting? How can we insure relationships and the other intangible things that are important to us? Have you lost any of these intangibles in the past that you could have taken steps to "insure" in a different way?

**Insurmountable:** To be insurmountable is to be something that cannot be solved or overcome. Why do we often give up and decide that an obstacle is insurmountable before we have even really tried? What do we lose by behaving this way? What do we miss when we decide to not even try? How can we encourage or teach ourselves to avoid these losses?

**Intangible:** Intangible items are ones we cannot touch or hold. Are the intangible things in life, such as love, friendship, and trust, the most important? In a sense, that makes them more fragile, but can it also makes them capable of _transcending_ distance, time, and even the most incredible _obstacles_? What are the valuable intangibles in your life? How do you protect them?

**Integral, Integrity:** Does having integrity mean you are _honest_ and trustworthy in everything you do? If someone truly has integrity, does that mean their _moral_ compass will not allow them to stray off course in their attempt to live an upright life, including the realms of _habits_ and _work_? What kinds of _behaviors_ or qualities could you have that would encourage those around you to have _faith_ in you? What does it mean to live and work with integrity, in practical terms, each day?

> _"It is not that I'm so smart. But I stay with the questions much longer."_
> — _Albert Einstein_

**Intellect:** Your intellect describes your _ability_ to think. Do you think you have a well-developed capacity for understanding? How can careful consideration of information help you develop your intellect? Why would people consider not doing so—is it possibly because of the time and patience it requires?

**Intelligence:** Intelligence does not refer to how much we know, but instead to our _ability_ to acquire _knowledge_ should we have the _opportunity_ to do so. Lack of intelligence leads to gullibility and _belief_ in _false_ statements, an inability to appropriately acquire new knowledge. Intelligence leads to _truth_ and the ability to act responsibly. Intelligence is personified with many special abilities such as math, composition, and design, and it can be acquired easily with _C.L.A.R.I.T.Y._ Do you consider some forms of intelligence superior to others, or does that result in us unfairly _judging_ those _different_ from ourselves? Is anyone capable of being intellectually self-sufficient? What is the value of allowing the intelligent views of others to intersect with our own? How can relying on the intelligence of others allow us to _achieve_ an informed perspective? What kinds of intelligences do you consider yourself to have, or what kinds of things are you intelligent about? How do you depend on other 'people's intelligences and for what kinds of things?

**Intend, Intent, Intentions:** An intention is something we _plan_ to do, regardless of whether we are able to _perform_ it. How much do our intentions speak about who we are as people? Is every act, everything we are consciously aware of doing, judged by our intention in doing it? Why, in our legal system, is intent taken into account when _guilt_ is assessed in a crime? What do your intentions say about you? Do you approach people with an open and warm _attitude_, or do you approach them with suspicion, looking for ways to take advantage? Do you _analyze_ your intentions before doing something? Was the intention itself clear in your _mind_? Is there such a thing as hidden intention, which others might perceive or observe, and you don't? Conversely, are you sometimes aware of intentions that others may not or cannot understand?

**Interact:** When two things interact, they engage actively with each other. Is life mediated through a _constant_ series of interactions with others? Is it impossible to _avoid_ these interactions? Should we even attempt to do so? If interactions inevitably lead to _relationships_ with other people, is it these relationships that make our lives enriched? How do you find yourself interacting with others? Is your approach well received? How can you _improve_ your interactions with others or better understand why they react to you the way they do?

**Interest:** To encounter something that is interesting means that it awakens our _curiosity_. Do you find that the most intelligent people are not always the most interesting ones? Is believing otherwise a common mistake to make? Think of the interesting ideas you have encountered; what about them appealed to you? How about interesting people you have met; was it their differences from you or their similarities to you that made them interesting to you? Some combination of both?

**Internet:** The Internet, the global network that allows computers worldwide to connect with one another, has vastly changed the way we acquire, understand, and use information. The new skills needed and new opportunities offered by the Internet have effectively created a new age. There is a catch, however: Millions are inhabiting the net as if it were a real place, replacing real-life interactions with online ones, to the point where Internet addiction has become a common phenomenon. Are those who are unable to keep up with changes in technology, whether through economic or other reasons, being left behind? Are we using the Internet responsibly? What might responsible Internet use look like? Are online interunderline{actions} inherently less valuable than ones we have offline, or can they be genuine replacements? How can we continue moving into the future of this technology without sacrificing too much of the past?

**Interpret, Interpretation:** Interpretation is how we process what we see, hear, and read. Is interpretation a matter of who is right or wrong, or of what each individual perceives as right or wrong? How much is perception influenced by personal interactions and observations, directly or indirectly involving gain or loss? How does your own moral code, as well as past experience, determine your interpretations of the world around you? How do you interpret your own actions? Do you see yourself as a moral individual? How does your understanding of the kind of person you are cause you to interpret the actions of those around you?

**Intimate, Intimacy:** To intimate is to hint or speak indirectly; to *be* intimate is to be in a close, personal relationship. Do these two possible definitions seem related? Do you speak differently to those with whom you have an intimate relationship? Are all intimate relationships positive ones, or is it possible to force intimacy in a case where it is unwanted so that it becomes unpleasant? Does all intimacy need to be between two people, or are there other kinds of ways to be intimate—for example, with oneself or via a religious experience? Are you satisfied with the kinds of intimacies currently in your life? Is positive intimacy something we need as humans, or something we can do without?

> *"At times you have to leave the city of your comfort and go into the wilderness of your intuition. What you'll discover will be wonderful. What you'll discover is yourself."*
> — *Alan Alda*

**Introvert:** Those who are introverted have difficulty spending large amounts of time with others; often it proves too stressful for them. Do you believe this isn't necessarily a bad thing, as people should be allowed to live as they choose, either socially or in seclusion? How can understanding and accepting people who are introverts help us get along with them better? Do you find yourself judging either those who retreat from human company or those who seem to need it constantly? If so, what about their behavior gives you this impulse?

**Intrude:** An intrusion is an unwelcome demand on someone else's space or time and often leads to dire consequences on the part of the interlocutor. How can we avoid unnecessary intrusions? How can we learn to know when we are welcome and when we are not?

**Intuition:** An intuition is a gut feeling, something one knows by instinct to be wrong or true. Many ignore their intuitions because there is no logical reasoning behind them, but how might this be a mistake? Should we reconsider listening to our intuitions, as they can be indicating that our body is trying to tell us that something is right or wrong?

**Invent:** Inventions are new objects or processes, the results of creative ideas and ingenuity. Can we trace the development of our most creative inventions to a single dream or stray train of thought? Inventions also aren't necessarily physical. They can be stories we invent to amuse our children or new ways we think of performing basic activities in our lives. What kinds of ideas have you invented?

**Investigate:** Not all information is freely given to us; some we must seek out or investigate. How can careful investigation help us discover the sources behind the information we consume on a daily basis? How can you investigate the sources behind things like your news sources, advertisements, etc.?

**Involuntary:** An involuntary act is not done of your own volition, but rather something you must do by the force of another. What acts are involuntary, and which ones do you have control over? Can thoughts be involuntary? Do we ever pretend to lose our agency when in fact it remains within our control?

**Involve:** To be involved is to be included in something, whether the one being involved is an object or a person. Why is it easy to become involved in things when we don't suspect the true consequences to which they will lead? How can we be more careful about what we choose to get involved in? Are there things you are involved in that enrich your life?

**Irrefutable:** Something irrefutable cannot be proven wrong. Why do we often think that certain facts are irrefutable when in fact they are nothing of the sort? How can we daily reexamine what we think to be true, thereby always keeping in touch with reality? How can we be thoughtful when confronting others about ideas they believed to be irrefutable?

**Islam:** Islam is a major world religion founded in the seventh century by the prophet Mohammed, who had visions revealing the true nature of God (Allah) from the archangel Gabriel. The religion's followers are Muslims, and their main sacred text, the Quran, details how faithful Muslim should worship and live their lives. It rivals Christianity as one of the largest religions in the world. Yet, much of the Western world remains ignorant of Islamic beliefs and edicts. How much do you know about Islam? Do you have stereotypes of it? How can we benefit from more cross-cultural dialogue?

**Issue:** We frequently use "issue" as another word for problem. Issues surround us—in the news, in our work, and in our family. Is it harmful to avoid these issues because they are difficult to resolve? How might avoiding these issues be hurting us? What is keeping us from addressing them?

# J

**Jargon**: The language specific to an activity, group, or trade, which is often difficult for outsiders to understand. Have you seen others use jargon to exclude those who are not familiar with it to inflate their own self-importance? Can you see through jargon by paying close attention and asking questions? Why do you think someone would refuse to elucidate their language? When do you employ jargon? Are you intimidated by jargon or confident in your ability to communicate in and understand it?

**Jealous**: We are jealous when we desire something someone else has so much that we begin to resent them for it. Do you question yourself when you feel jealousy rising in your chest? Why are you jealous? It is one thing to be jealous of a friend for going on vacation when you have to work, but what about when you resent them for it and hold it against them in the future? Do you manage to rejoice about the accomplishments of friends? Though it can be aggravating to see enemies succeed, is it healthy or justifiable to be jealous of them? Take your jealousy and use it to examine your life; what can you do to achieve that which made you jealous?

**Jesus**: A man who lived to teach others about the concepts of morality and social responsibility. In Christianity, he is regarded as the Messiah and son of God. What has your experience been of Jesus? Have you read his words in the Gospels? Does one have to accept his divinity in order to appreciate his teaching? Do you consider Jesus to be the only spiritual way to wisdom or the only avenue in religion?

> *"Jealousy is a disease, love is a healthy condition. The immature mind often mistakes one for the other, or assumes that the greater the love, the greater the jealousy."*
> — *Robert A. Heinlein*

**Job**: A job can become a task we perform on our own or official employment for which we receive monetary compensation. Do you differentiate between jobs you do for yourself or jobs you do for others? When does a job become servitude? When you unwillingly work for little monetary compensation because you have no alternative or when you unwillingly work for little satisfaction because you have no alternative?

**Join**: To join is to bring together and to make yourself a part of a greater whole. Does being a part of something give life meaning? Humans are social animals; do you deny yourself the benefits of working together with others and being part of a group? Have you seen introverts be shunned or seen as strange because they do not integrate into groups? Have you seen rumors form around them, which lead to negative judgment? Though these are unfair judgments, if you usually find yourself more comfortable working alone, why not reach out? What could you gain by joining with other people, and what could you stand to lose? How can you join into a positive collective effort?

**Journal**: A journal is a personal record of one's life which is usually kept on a daily basis. Does life seem to move too fast sometimes?

How could keeping an account of your days be helpful? What could you gain by being able to look back on things you might otherwise forget? Is it valuable to measure your current self against your past ideas, or does that encourage negativity?

**Journalism:** Journalism is historically a professional business in which writers seek out trustworthy sources and then publish or speak their findings about the world for others to learn from. Because of the Internet, much of journalism is changing away from professional journalists and toward independent writers and bloggers. How vital is journalism to our understanding of the world? Is it good that more and more people are able to act as journalists, or is it problematic that they are not bound by official journalistic standards? How can we use journalistic tools to address injustice while at the same time ensuring that we do not accidentally create more injustice through sloppy or unethical reporting?

**Journey:** A journey is a trip from one place to another, usually a long or difficult one; the trip is not necessarily physical, but can be intangible, as in an emotional or spiritual journey. How do you evaluate whether a journey you are about to undertake is worthwhile? What kinds of benefits do there need to be in order to outweigh the risks or the difficulties? What parts of your life do you experience as having been journey-like? What kinds of journeys, physical or not, do you plan to or would you like to take in the future, and why are these compelling or necessary ones for you?

> *"We should not judge people by their peak of excellence; but by the distance they have traveled from the point where they started."*
> *— Henry Ward Beecher*

**Joy:** Joy is an emotional state of exceptional happiness. Should we think of our joy differently depending on its cause or source? Do you consciously differentiate between joy derived from greed as compared to that based on a sense of accomplishment? Is joy based strictly on pleasure a valid or substantial joy in your mind? To what degree do you manifest joy emotionally?

**Judge:** Every society has people who decide the fate of others and settle disputes, positions which are particular to each culture. In ours, those people are selected based on their education and professional history, rather than simply social status or age. But it is still possible for the temptation of corruption to sway judgment. Is it also the duty of a judge to interpret and oversee the letter of the law, or serve as a referee who makes sure that a jury functions properly? Given the fallibility of judges, should we always accept their decisions so that the law is upheld, or should we challenge and question them when we feel that justice is not being done? *How quick are you to judge? How often do you judge what you observe without facts or truth?*

**Judgment:** Judgment can mean either a careful decision made based on available evidence or forming an opinion—usually negative—about other people. We pass judgment every day. We judge others, situations, and history. But be careful not to judge too quickly. It is easy to judge without having all the facts, and things often become far more complex when all information is available. How and why do you believe judgment can become corrupted? How can we protect the integrity of our judgments, or fix them when they have become compromised? Do you often make the easy decision to avoid the rigor of investigation, or do you examine all of the evidence? Are you willing to change your judgments when presented with evidence to the contrary?

**Just, Justice:** Guided by <u>truth</u>, fairness, <u>law</u>, or religious beliefs. Is justice a <u>moral</u> <u>principle</u> that can be displayed individually through <u>words</u> and <u>actions</u>? There are a variety of <u>perspectives</u> from which to analyze any situation, and what seems just from one may seem unjust from another. Does justice serve the common <u>good</u> rather than the interests of a single individual or does it serve both? Are unjust laws to be ignored? But how do we <u>measure</u> whether or not something is just? How have you been treated unjustly? What <u>creed</u> do you use for justice? What is your principle for moral rightness or equity? Is it your right to receive justice? Do you expect or rely on receiving justice from the court system?

# K

**Karate:** A self-defense method originating in Japan based on one-on-one combat without a <u>weapon</u>. What kinds of steps have you taken or do you take in order to be able to <u>defend</u> yourself? Do you consider yourself a weapon?

**Karma:** Karma is a concept originating in Eastern philosophy, which states that we experience <u>negative</u> or <u>positive</u> consequences because of our previous immoral or <u>moral</u> actions. What degree of <u>relevance</u> do you place on karma? Do you feel that we do in fact receive the consequences we deserve, or is the world ultimately more unjust than karma holds to be true? If you do not believe in karma, do you think you would you live your life differently if you believed that karma could change it significantly?

**Keen:** If something is keen, that indicates that it is sharp, which can mean <u>physically</u> sharp, as in a blade, or <u>mentally</u> sharp, meaning either intelligent or eager. How can you <u>cultivate</u> a keen mind in yourself or others? Is it something that can be <u>learned</u>? Are there particular <u>ideas</u> or <u>topics</u> that you are keen about?

**Keep, Kept:** What in your life is worth keeping around? Maintaining bodily <u>health</u> as well as healthy <u>relationships</u> can be challenging, but it is of the utmost importance. Are you able to <u>commit</u> to such <u>promises</u> that you make to yourself and others, or do you forget to keep them out of <u>convenience</u>?

What do you truly <u>own</u>, and what do you <u>share</u>? Are you withholding something that belongs to others? Have you <u>considered</u> other <u>connotations</u>? What kinds of things are <u>healthy</u> to keep, and which are unhealthy?

**Key:** The <u>physical</u> object of a key is something we use to open a lock; a key can also be more metaphorical, referring to an <u>important</u> part of something or to a concept or idea which, once understood, allows us to access other ideas. How is a physical key similar to the kinds of keys that we access <u>mentally</u> or <u>emotionally</u>? What would you say are the key <u>concerns</u> in your life? What are the key strategies that this <u>encyclopedia</u> encourages you to use or <u>develop</u>?

**Kill:** To take a life. Killing is so physically easy that it would be trivial if not for the <u>laws</u> governing our <u>society</u> and the <u>morals</u> governing ourselves. However, killing is done constantly for reasons of <u>religion</u>, survival, <u>revenge</u>, <u>greed</u>, and even <u>pleasure</u>. The mass killing that occurs in <u>war</u> is generally done by people who were dragged into danger, while the powerful people who initiated the conflict bear no cost. Contemplate the <u>reality</u> of causing something to <u>die</u>, to be destroyed or defeated, or just to cease operating. Is it unthinkable for you, or can you <u>imagine</u> yourself killing another <u>human</u> being? What do you think of the idea that we all kill something almost every day of our lives, like other life forms or even time? Do you think maybe more <u>conscious</u> <u>awareness</u> is needed of these killings? What or who is being killed? Where and when? And, most important, why? What is the <u>motive</u>? In what ways can we kill? Do you feel <u>guilt</u> for the killings you are responsible for?

**Kin, Kinship:** The idea of kinship was based originally on those to whom one was related to by <u>blood</u>, but we can also <u>feel</u> kinship with those to whom we are not related. Do you feel as though you have a special <u>relationship</u> with your <u>family</u> that is not possible to feel with those who are not actually your kin? How does feeling kinship with another person either enrich or complicate your life? Are you capable of feeling kinship with humanity as a whole, or are there some people who you simply cannot bring yourself to feel related to?

**Kind, Kindness:** To be kind is to show compassion toward those around you. Compassion is the cornerstone of life. Does a random act of kindness mean more to you then a deliberate act, especially on a particularly bad day? If you help others to enjoy their lives, will you enjoy yours more? Do you carry out acts of kindness without thinking of a reward? Is kindness the action part of thoughtfulness, consideration, and understanding? How do you describe kindness, and where do you classify it in your life? Is kindness a virtue? Do we need to be taught kindness, or is it in human nature to be kind to one another?

> *"Be kind, for everyone you meet is fighting a hard battle."*
> *— Plato*

**Kinds:** To be of a kind means to belong to a particular group. There is an enormous amount of variety in the world. People, places, and cultures come in all shapes, sizes and colors. How many different ways can you think of dividing the world into kinds? Are all distinctions between kinds artificially created, or are some natural and inevitable? Have you ever had the experience of something seeming common and proper to you, but which was foreign and strange to someone else? When you encounter unfamiliar things, do you discount them as strange and harmful, or do you seek to explore and learn more about them?

**Knowledge, Know:** To know is to be able to understand the world around us. But true knowledge comes only from facts, not assumptions. Humanity's greatest resource is the ability to think and reason. The human mind is capable of dealing with logic and reason in an abstract and intangible way that is unmatched in any other life form. This unique ability to appreciate and catalogue the world around us as well as to contemplate complex ideas that only exist in our minds should be used to improve the world we live in. Reach for the stars, and understand everything you can; knowledge is a universal currency. To know is to be informed and educated. Do awareness and observation precede knowledge? What and how much do you file in your memory, and is there always room for more? Is knowledge the best tool for coping with all of life's problems? Do you learn more than you teach?

**Koran:** The sacred book of Islam, regarded by Muslims as the foundation of religion, law, and culture. What do you know about the creation and contents of the Koran? Can a religious text for a religion you are not a part of still be useful to you in formulating a personal creed? What other religious texts have you explored, or would you like to explore?

# L

**Label:** A label is a short description of a <u>person</u>, <u>place</u>, or <u>thing</u>. What is your experience with being labeled by others or choosing to label others? When are labels <u>helpful</u>, and when are they <u>harmful</u> or <u>limiting</u>? Is choosing whether to label someone or not simply a practical choice, or is it an <u>ethical</u> issue as well?

**Labor:** Labor is always <u>hard</u> work, though it can be either a <u>positive</u> or <u>negative</u> experience. Should labor always be associated with <u>money</u>? When we exert <u>energy</u>, is that always a kind of labor, or are some exertions of energy <u>better</u> defined in another way? Is it possible to achieve any endeavor without labor? How can we know if our hard work is misplaced or misdirected? Do you know exactly what you are working toward and what your labor is contributing to?

**Laity:** The laity, or laypeople of a <u>religion</u>, are differentiated from its clergy—they are the <u>common</u> folk. Should the opinions of laity be given equal weight as those in the priesthood? In the <u>universal</u> body of <u>human</u> <u>observers</u>, are we all laity, or all clergy? Are we guided <u>spiritually</u> by a <u>God</u> in our observations?

> *"Laughter is surely the surest touch of genius in creation."*
> *— Christopher Fry*

**Lament, Lamentable:** Something lamentable deserves deep <u>sorrow</u> or <u>regret</u>. What has been lamentable in your life? How can you move past endless lamentation and toward a better <u>future</u>? When is lamentation and <u>grief</u> <u>healthy</u> or appropriate, and at what point does it begin to make us <u>sick</u>?

**Language:** Any way we <u>communicate</u> with one another—<u>speaking</u>, <u>writing</u>, <u>drawing</u>, facial <u>expressions</u> and <u>body</u> <u>movement</u>—is a kind of language. Does language <u>mediate</u> everything we do? How often are we aware of its presence or the ways in which it <u>limits</u> our <u>thoughts</u> and <u>actions</u>? How often do we instead <u>ignore</u> it, <u>pretending</u> that it doesn't matter?

**Late:** Lateness is <u>subjective</u>; anything that does not happen when we <u>want</u> or <u>expect</u> it to is something we consider late, though other people in the <u>situation</u> might feel differently. Does an arrival after the expected time directly affect the <u>event</u> itself, <u>negatively</u>, or does it directly affect the well-being of another <u>individual</u>? Are you ever <u>deliberately</u> late? If so, what <u>motivates</u> you to do so? Have you considered all the <u>consequences</u> of that <u>decision</u>?

**<u>Laugh</u>**: Laughter is the response our <u>bodies</u> have when we find something funny, but also sometimes when we are <u>happy</u>, or frightened, or disgusted, or even <u>angry</u>. What would your <u>life</u> be like without laughter? Do you take the <u>time</u> to laugh with those you <u>love</u>? How could you make that time in your daily routine? Have you ever laughed at someone in a <u>cruel</u> way, that made them uncomfortable or <u>humiliated</u>, or been laughed at yourself in such a way? Is your laugh accompanied by a particular body movement? Can you laugh at yourself, irony or bad times?

**<u>Law</u>**: The word law can be used either to describe the <u>rules</u> a <u>society</u> agrees to live by—established either by them or their <u>authorities</u>—or it can refer to the <u>order</u> of how things happen in <u>time</u> and <u>space</u>. What do you <u>believe</u> "<u>natural</u> law" to be? What is its relationship to laws formed by humanity? Should the letter of the law be <u>obeyed</u> if the law is unjust? When have certain laws been proven to be unjust, such as during segregation? How can we discern between just laws and unjust ones? How do you regard law—as a decree to be obeyed explicitly or a societal guidance to be scrutinized carefully? What is the difference between rules and laws? What are the types of law, and does law control order? Do laws spring forth from <u>custom</u>, <u>government</u> <u>legislation</u>, or are they self-imposed? Could law exist if we did not collectively agree to it? What is the best way to challenge law as an <u>individual</u>? How can we <u>change</u> law? Without law, would we have <u>chaos</u>?

**Leader, Leading, Leadership:** Leadership is the <u>ability</u> to <u>influence</u> or <u>coerce</u> others to <u>follow</u> or do something. In present-day societies, it is most prevalent in corporate structure. Has <u>corporacracy</u> become a constant of life? Do leaders in our <u>country</u> lead us in the right direction? Is our election process more <u>complex</u> than we would like to <u>believe</u>? How can we <u>choose</u> the right leaders for our country? How can we see past <u>political</u> propaganda to vote for the right candidate? Do the abilities of a qualified leader live or die with his <u>motives</u>? How can we determine whether a political leader is <u>genuinely</u> interested in the good of the people they represent or only interested in personal <u>gain</u>?

> *"Once you learn to read, you will be forever free."*
> — *Frederick Douglass*

<u>**Learn**</u>: Learning is the act of gathering <u>information</u> through our <u>senses</u> and retaining it in our <u>minds</u>, whether we are taught it by someone else or seek it out on our own. How do we decide to act <u>responsibly</u> on what we have learned? Learning and development take time, but can <u>change</u> occur more <u>quickly</u>? Have you experienced <u>difficulty</u> from trying to <u>grow</u> around impatient people or finding it hard to grow up because there is no one to <u>teach</u> you? When we <u>divide</u> learning into <u>categories</u> like classroom, <u>books</u>, <u>Internet</u>, and vocational, does that <u>limit</u> our <u>understanding</u> of it too much? Can you learn from failure and negativity without imitating them? How does learning follow <u>observation</u> and <u>conscious</u> <u>awareness</u>, and how is it implemented by them? Should the subject matter of what we learn be <u>prioritized</u>?

**Legacy:** A legacy is anything that is handed down to us from the <u>past</u>, or something that we in turn pass along to those who come after us. What kinds of legacies have you inherited from your <u>family</u> or others? Do you feel that you have used those legacies in a way that <u>honors</u> and <u>respects</u> the <u>efforts</u> of those who gave them to you? What kind of legacy would you like to pass on from your own <u>life</u>?

**Legend:** A legend on a map or diagram tells us how to read it; a legend can also be a <u>story</u> we tell ourselves or one another about <u>history</u> that we cannot <u>prove</u> to be <u>true</u> but which we find meaningful regardless. In what ways do legends, in the sense of stories we tell, work like legends on a map? Do they <u>interpret</u> <u>information</u> and <u>guide</u> us in the same way? Is it problematic to place <u>belief</u> in legends rather than more verifiable history? In what ways can we <u>discover</u> truth through stories which are possibly <u>false</u>? What kinds of legends do you think are worth passing on?

<u>**Legislate**</u>: The national legislature constitutes an entire third of the American government in the form of Congress, with the other two-thirds being the executive and the judicial branches of government. Democratic legislatures are meant to pass <u>laws</u> based on a consensus of their own viewpoints, which in turn are supposed to reflect the <u>will</u> of the people. But does this actually happen, or are many legislatures instead infiltrated by the interests of lobbyists and bent to the wills of the <u>wealthy</u> and

those in <u>power</u>? How can we <u>determine</u> whether a legislature is acting in our best interests or instead working for themselves? To what degree do laws need to be passed to protect people from one another, and to what degree should we be free to <u>decide</u> for ourselves how to act?

**Lesson:** A lesson can be <u>information</u> we <u>learn</u> through formal <u>education</u> and schooling, or information we <u>gather</u> more informally, such as through our own <u>observations</u> or <u>wisdom</u> that others choose to share with us. What do you think are the most important lessons you have learned? Are they ones that you <u>discovered</u> by yourself, or were they passed on by others? Are there some lessons that are only available through our own observations and experiences, or is it possible for everything to be taught to us by others? What do you think is the most valuable lesson that you could pass on to those around you?

**Liberal**: When not used in a <u>political</u> sense, to be liberal simply means to be <u>generous</u>.

Politically, the words "liberals" and "liberalism" refer to either those whose main political concern is the preservation of <u>individual</u> <u>liberties</u>, or it indicates parties and policies who are invested in progressive political reform. The term "liberal" is sometimes used as an insult by conservative pundits; does this seem reasonable? Based on your <u>observations</u>, what aspects of liberalism do these pundits seem to think are worthy of insult? What parts of liberal ideology do you yourself either <u>approve</u> or disapprove of? Is liberal ideology always adhered to by citizens and politicians who accept the label of "liberal," or is there a mismatch between theory and reality?

**<u>Liberty</u>**: There are two essential aspects to liberty: First, the <u>freedom</u> *from* <u>acting</u>, meaning that we are not being compelled by institutions such as <u>government</u> to commit acts against our <u>will</u>. Second, there is the freedom *to* act, meaning that we are able to do as we choose without being restrained or <u>prevented</u> from doing so. What kinds of <u>limitations</u> do you think there should be on liberty? What kinds of justifications could there be for forcing someone to act or for preventing someone from acting? Who should be in charge of setting those limitations and making sure they are enacted? How precious is your liberty to you? Are <u>wars</u> and battles for liberty worthwhile given the potential cost in human lives? What have you done to <u>protect</u> and promote your own liberty? What would you be willing to do to <u>defend</u> your liberty? Do you consider liberty a social right?

**License**: A license represents a permission either from an official <u>authority</u> or a more informal body or entity to do something. Do we have a license as human beings to act as we choose? What would constitute an <u>abuse</u> of this license? How can one use their own license to perform <u>good</u>? How do we <u>give</u> license to those around us to act freely?

**Lie**: A lie is any <u>story</u> we tell about the <u>world</u> which we know to be <u>false</u>. Is lying an inevitability of <u>human</u> <u>interaction</u>, or is it a

sign of <u>personal</u> <u>moral</u> weakness that must be dealt with swiftly and harshly? Are there lies which we can c<u>onsider</u> to be <u>positive</u> ones, ones that we tell to spare one another's <u>feelings</u> or to take some other sort of moral action, or does the <u>evil</u> of a lie negate any positive outcomes that might come from telling it? Are all works of fiction essentially lies? What kinds of lies have you told in your life? In what ways have they <u>helped</u> you or <u>harmed</u> yourself and other people? *Has lying become <u>habitual</u>?*

**<u>Life</u>**: The idea of just what defines life is a <u>complex</u> one. If we rely only on the fields of biology and chemistry to tell us what life is, then we may be able to tell what things are alive—from bacteria to human beings—but may lack a way to talk about whether and why. Philosophy may offer many more possibilities as to how we might choose to <u>define</u> an <u>individual</u> life, ranging from the <u>mental</u> and <u>emotional</u> collection of all our experiences, to a <u>god</u>'s miraculous <u>creation</u>. We even sometimes talk about life as being a kind of excitement or fulfillment, as when telling someone to "get a life." When you <u>consider</u> all the possibilities about what it means to be alive or to have a life, which definitions seem to match up with your lived <u>experience</u>? How much of our lives are dependent on what we <u>observe</u> through our <u>senses</u> in relation to <u>space</u> and <u>time?</u> What kinds of definitions help us to develop regard for other forms of life? How <u>important</u> is it for us as human beings to <u>remember</u> that we are not the only living beings? Is it <u>dangerous</u> to manipulate life on a biological level? What about on a <u>social</u> or <u>emotional</u> level? What <u>responsibilities</u> do we have to preserve life, and are there ways to destroy it beyond simply <u>killing</u>? What do you feel is the <u>relationship</u> of your life to God or a spiritual dimension? Is life an identification of existence? *What is your <u>creed</u> for it?* (See also: Prologue)

**Lifestyle**: Your lifestyle is the sum total of all the <u>actions</u> you take to live in the way you do— your <u>habits</u>, <u>beliefs</u>, <u>economic</u> situation, and so forth. What <u>different</u> kinds of lifestyles have you experienced yourself or have you watched others live in? Do any of them seem to you to be more or less <u>moral</u> than other ones? More or less practical? More or less rewarding? Do you believe there is such a thing as a "<u>normal</u>" lifestyle? To what extent do you believe your lifestyle now will <u>determine</u> your life later? Are you doing all you could be to ensure your <u>health</u> later, or are you giving into <u>immediate</u> gratification instead? Are you able to cope with the <u>influence</u> of your <u>social world</u>? Does lifestyle mimic <u>creed</u>?

> "Life is like riding a bicycle.
> To keep your balance,
> you must keep moving."
> — Albert Einstein

**Light**: Light can refer to something that <u>weighs</u> very little and is therefore easy to lift and carry; it can also be the <u>physical</u> phenomenon of illumination that allows us to see objects. Metaphorically, this <u>ability</u> to see means we often think of light as being associated with <u>truth</u> and <u>morality</u>; it certainly shapes our vision and how we <u>perceive</u> the <u>world</u>. Do you see a <u>relationship</u> between the way light is used to describe weight and visibility? How can you find the light in your life, the <u>tools</u> that will illuminate the <u>reality</u> around you? Do you see light as <u>freedom</u> from darkness? Are there ever times when you <u>dread</u> light and desire darkness instead, when light becomes uncomfortable or painful to experience?

**Like:** The idea of "like" encompasses both the <u>possibility</u> of two things being similar and to <u>feel</u> <u>fondness</u> or <u>affection</u> for something. Do you feel as though these two <u>definitions</u> overlap in your life? In other words, do you <u>enjoy</u> or <u>appreciate</u> other people more when they are similar to you? Do you differentiate between liking things and people? What are your <u>standards</u> for doing so? Who or what do you want to <u>simulate</u> or be like, and what do you want to be characteristic of or likened to? Do you always choose to <u>associate</u> with the people and things you like, or do other factors sometimes become more <u>important</u> than your personal preference? If you like something, does that <u>cause</u> you to have <u>trouble</u> recognizing its faults and flaws? What kinds of things and people do you dislike, and what would you prefer not to be associated with? Are your likes and dislikes <u>rational</u>, or are they based only on your <u>feelings</u>?

**Limit:** The point at which there is no beyond, at which there is an end or negative reaction, a reversal of action. Do you limit yourself in <u>virtues</u> and things of a <u>positive</u> nature while allowing no limits to <u>vices</u> and <u>negativity</u>? Do you adhere to the limits of <u>law</u>? Are you confined beyond your <u>ability</u> of <u>acceptance</u>? When can limits be <u>healthy</u> for us, and when do they become destructive?

**Listen:** Hearing is an involuntary physical response to noise; we have very little control over what we hear. To listen, however, is to choose to actively pay attention, and it does not necessarily need to be with one's ears. Do you have a sense of an inner voice to which you listen? Does it urge you toward actions that seem to be good? Does it sometimes recommend harmful actions? How do you attempt to determine the difference, and when do you decide to listen to that voice? Do you feel as though you listen responsibly to people around you? Who do you choose to listen to, and who do you choose to ignore? Do you take the time to listen to the sounds of the world, the sounds of nature? What might be gained from doing so? In what ways could listening be related to your health? In what ways does listening enhance your sense of life? How can we listen more actively to those we communicate with? What are the benefits of *active listening*? How do you perceive active or conscious listening? *Do you feel that you usually understand the true and intended meaning of what you hear?*

**Literal:** When we say we are being literal, we mean we are using a word or describing a situation without exaggeration. It can also be used negatively; a literal individual is sometimes said to be someone without imagination or who is incapable of poetry. What are the potential benefits of using or understanding language literally? What are the potential drawbacks or weaknesses of doing so? Is there a balance to be achieved between the two? Is insisting on absolute truth always the best foundation for living life? What could be lost if we were always literal all the time?

**Live, Living:** Living is the process of experiencing or creating a life for oneself. Can you say you live life to the fullest each day? As you move through your life, do you consider the fact of your own mortality? To what extent do you consciously allow it to affect your thoughts and actions? How can you live with more awareness? Do you live for pleasure, convenience, and instant gratification? Do you strive to balance the complexity of all 'life's different aspects, or do you live a life of extremes? Can you adjust to living under the circumstances you were born into or that are thrust upon you? Is it more important to embrace our right to live as we please or to accept the responsibilities we have to other people to live our lives in certain ways? *Do you maintain your creed for living?*

**Location:** One's location is simply the place in which they are situated, though this is not necessarily only in the physical sense. To what degree do you think of your location as being your tangible place within the world, and to what degree do you think of

> *"Live as if you were to die tomorrow. Learn as if you were to live forever."*
> — Mahatma Gandhi

your location as being a space you occupy within a spiritual universe? Do you ever feel as though your spiritual or emotional location is uncertain? Does it feel similar to being physically lost, or is it a unique experience?

**Logic:** Logic is essentially the science of studying how evidence leads rationally to knowledge. How much would you say you value logic over other human abilities? Is it in line with human nature to act logically? What kinds of motivations or conflicts can cause us to act irrationally? How can we examine each decision we make, analyzing each factor to discern the logic behind it? How could we discipline ourselves to act more logically? Do you believe that different people, using the same evidence, can arrive at different logical conclusions? How are you able to cope with differences in logical thought when communicating with another person? Do you have patience with others' behavior when you perceive them as behaving illogically? Is there sometimes value in choosing to act illogically?

**Look:** Seeing is passive; we see anything that passes in front of our eyes. To look, however, is to be actively engaged in noticing what we see or to seek out something in particular. An even more involved way of seeing is observation, which involves carefully noticing and analyzing the details of the world around you. Are you one of the many who look but do not really observe? What do you think might cause you to do so? How can we teach ourselves to look at things more discerningly—not only to see things, but to really understand what we see?

**Lord:** We can use the word "lord" to talk about any kind of male authority, but for many people, there is only one Lord—a supernatural being who has authority over earthly lives. Do you associate the word with the lords of corporacracy who attempt to control so much of our society or in terms of spirituality? What is your personal opinion about the existence of an omnipotent Lord?

> *"You know you're in love when you 'can't fall asleep because reality is finally better than your dreams."*
> *— Dr. Seuss*

Is religion something that might make you a happier, more fulfilled person, or is it something that you feel has greater potential for harm? Do you associate "the" Lord with God as a spiritual entity, or as a religious entity?

**Lose, Loss, Lost:** Loss is something we can experience physically, as when we fail to keep something in our possession or when we become lost on our way to a destination. It can also, however, indicate the failure to win a competition or a prize, or be used as a synonym for grief. Is losing something or someone a condition of life? Do you feel that you are sometimes lost in another world or dimension, or just lost in thought? How have you handled being lost or experiencing loss? Are those experiences major factors in how you live your life? Does the way we handle loss become a major factor in how our lives are lived? How does placing a value on your loss affect your emotions and your reactions?

**Love:** Love is a state of being, an emotion of fondness that is more profound than simple affection. When you find yourself loving or in love with another, do you view them differently from other people? Does it affect your experience of the rest of the world, as well? Do you find yourself in and out of love with others, or do you feel that once you fall in love with someone you remain that way, regardless of any other emotion you might be feeling about them? How much of your experience of love has been about you wanting to fulfill your own need to be close to others, and how much of it has been about wanting to fulfill the needs of those you love? What do you feel is the relationship between how much love one gives, and how much love one receives?

- My dad was the embodiment of love. He spent the last week of his life (when he wasn't sleeping) sitting his frail body up in bed, gazing into the eyes of my mom, brother, sister, and me with a huge smile, and *saying* I love you. That was mostly all he said those last days—that was all that needed to be said. It was a summation of his ninety-one years: I LOVE YOU. Actually, it was those first two words that made his life so rich and magnificent—I love. My dad did. He loved everything. He loved life, he loved his work, he loved his family, he loved the grocery store clerk or butcher, he loved the morning, he loved the afternoon, he loved the evening—he just loved. No, he didn't go into the grocery store and tell the clerk or the butcher that he loved them, and early in his years, he didn't reiterate the words to us either, *but we all knew.* The smile on his face and the way he carried himself was convincing to all. Each day is the perfect time to recommit to love— not just romantic love, but love in every aspect of your life. So in the spirit, here are four powerful ways to let love lead your life:

1.  When faced with choices and decisions during your day, ask yourself, "What would love do?" Love is the most powerful and wisest guide I know. For example, if today you are alone and longing for your partner, chances are good that love would tell you, "Love everyone and everything, especially yourself, right now."

2.  Breathe in and out of your heart. The heart is the seat of your soul. By focusing your attention there and imagining that you're inhaling and exhaling through the center of your heart, you will feel more connected to your <u>spirit</u>. Your heart will open, and there is even strong science showing that it's good for your <u>health</u> and well-being.

3.  Look for what you appreciate, admire, or love in each person you meet. Sure, it may be easy to find flaws in people, but you'll feel so much more joy in life if you focus on finding what's special about each person.

4.  Look for reminders to put love front and center in life (a gift given or received, a strangers' smile, or a hero's action).

TRUE LOVE HAS NO <u>MOTIVE.</u> If you are questioning love, consider the opposite—<u>hate</u>. Is it easier to hate and harder to love or vice/versa? Given your answer (or choice), what are the rewards or benefits (of each)?

If you want to <u>understand</u> or <u>enhance</u> love, have you weighed in such words (thoughts) as <u>respect</u>, <u>consideration</u>, <u>forgiveness</u>, trust, and <u>desire</u> to please?

Love is not tangible. You can't buy it, sell it, steal it, but you can give it freely—even if someone does not want it.

So, love for no particular reason, but rather for every reason.

**Loyal:** To be loyal involves being faithful, refusing to leave one person, ideology, or thing in favor of another. Is loyalty a necessary component of friendship? How important do you consider loyalty when you think about who your true friends are? How can we demonstrate our loyalty to others, and discern those who are loyal to us and those who are not? Can loyalty be a negative or destructive force? How do we determine who or what is worthy of our loyalty, and what is not?

**Luck:** Good luck is when events that depend on chance appear to occur in ways that are beneficial to us; bad luck is when chance occurrences appear to harm us instead. How much do we owe to the force of luck in our lives and how much to hard work or poor choices? Do you find yourself thanking or blaming luck for situations that are in actuality dependent on your own actions? Have you become absorbed with a false dependency based on luck?

**Lure:** To lure is to attract someone into a situation that may or may not be harmful to them. To what extent are advertisements simply lures on the part of corporations that end up injuring us? Why do these strategies work, and how can we avoid being lured into their trap? How might others in life be trying to us into relationships under false premises?

**Lust:** Lust is generally thought of as intense sexual desire, though it can describe other kinds of strong appetites as well. What is the difference between sexual lust and love? Have you ever mistaken them for each other or seen others do so? Can one feel lustful about someone they love romantically, or are the two mutually exclusive? Is lust a vice or a part of the human experience which can be indulged in or celebrated?

**Luxury:** Luxury is a form of indulgence, a quality or quantity of goods over and above what we actually need. How important is luxury to you? Do you feel you might value it more than is appropriate? Have you sacrificed other parts of your life to achieve luxury or seen others do so? How can we abandon our desire for luxury in favor of more important things?

# M

**Machine:** Machines can make our work and lives easier. Each one of us plays a role in a larger machine, whether it is the people we work with, our family, or, on a larger scale, society as a whole. If we do not do our part and pull our weight, the machine groans and creaks, and if enough gears jam, it ceases to function. Are you a team player? What can you do individually to make things run more smoothly in the machines of your life? To what extent have we become dependent on machines? What machines are you dependent upon?

**Mad:** Anger is an emotion that should be avoided when possible. Being mad is poisonous to those around you. To concede to it and let it control your actions is to lose control of yourself. Look at which forces make you mad and try to examine why they elicit such a strong reaction. Striving to understand will abate your anger, even though it can be difficult. Do you keep a cool head, or do you let impulsive anger dictate your actions? When is the line crossed to areas of mental disturbance, dementia, or even insanity?

**Maim:** To cause grievous injury to another person is to take away the most important thing in life: health. Always take care when you are doing something that could hurt another person. Do you take care in dangerous situations and make an effort to be aware of your surroundings? Have you ever hurt someone very badly?

> *"People speak sometimes about the "bestial" cruelty of man, but that is terribly unjust and offensive to beasts, no animal could ever be so cruel as a man, so artfully, so artistically cruel."*
>
> *— Fyodor Dostoyevsky*

**Maintain, Maintenance:** To cause something to stay in an existing state. Just as automobiles must receive routine maintenance, so too should the body and mind. The successful maintenance of the body and mind leads to increased longevity and a better quality of life. What do you do to maintain your quality of life? Do you pay enough attention to your own maintenance, or do you sometimes let it fall by the wayside?

**Malice:** Desire to hurt or harm someone else. Have you ever felt an urge to inflict injury on someone? Did you allow yourself to carry through with that urge? How can we decrease malicious urges?

**Manage:** Many parts of life must be actively managed, or they risk falling into disrepair. How you manage your affairs will determine the course of your life. The more effective you are in your management and the sooner you are able to solve life altering issues, the more successful you will be in all aspects of life. Time management is very important in order to fit everything in during a limited amount of time. When faced with a difficult situation, do you panic or begin thinking about how you can manage different aspects to fix it? How can you better manage things like relationships and friendships? Are you able to manage your time well?

**Mandate:** A mandate is an <u>order</u> or <u>command</u>, particularly one in writing. Yet it can also be <u>interpreted</u> as the <u>will</u> of the <u>people</u>, assuming that it was put in place by a <u>vote</u> or by an <u>individual</u> that was put in place by a vote. How have you mandated your <u>opinion</u> through your vote? How can you <u>effectively</u> <u>communicate</u> your <u>own</u> mandate through means other than voting?

**Manifest:** To be <u>clearly</u> <u>perceived</u>. We must <u>strive</u> to let our <u>true</u> <u>colors</u> manifest themselves on the surface, both <u>verbally</u> and through <u>body</u> <u>language</u>. How are your sentiments manifested in your <u>behavior</u>? Is it an accurate reflection of how you <u>feel</u>? Do we <u>reveal</u> to those around us our <u>trust</u> or mistrust, our likes or dislikes, or our <u>joy</u> or <u>anger</u> without having to <u>speak</u> <u>words</u>, just by <u>thinking</u> (or obsessing) about it? Does something which is <u>chronic</u> manifest itself in another <u>form</u>?

**Manipulate, Manipulation**: <u>Politicians</u> and <u>corporations</u> constantly try to manipulate <u>public</u> <u>views</u> through <u>persuasion</u> and an <u>influence</u> on our <u>laws</u> and <u>media</u>. How can we <u>recognize</u> and <u>resist</u> this manipulation? Can you recognize manipulative <u>behavior</u> in those with whom you <u>interact</u>? How can we see <u>past</u> attempts at <u>control</u> and <u>learn</u> to <u>think</u> for ourselves? Do you manipulate others?

**Man, Mankind:** The <u>history</u> of mankind is as littered with <u>wars</u> and <u>violence</u> as it is with <u>progress</u> and technological <u>development</u>. What does this say about the <u>nature</u> of mankind? Do we have an <u>equal</u> <u>capacity</u> for <u>good</u> as we do <u>evil</u>? Do you have a conscious <u>awareness</u> of who we are relative to other <u>life</u> <u>forms</u>? Where do we fit into <u>time</u> and <u>space</u>?

**Manner, Mannerism:** Each <u>individual</u> has a set of their <u>own</u> distinctive mannerisms, but everyone must <u>adhere</u> to a certain <u>code</u> of manners if they want to be <u>socially</u> <u>accepted</u>. Be <u>aware</u> that your mannerisms say a lot about what you are like and who you are as a <u>person</u>. With this in <u>mind</u>, wouldn't it be better to accept everyone, despite <u>strange</u> mannerisms? Do you have <u>good</u> manners? What do your manners say about you as a civilized <u>person</u>?

**Many:** Many is not <u>all</u>, although it may sometimes be the majority. Should we always <u>obey</u> what the many <u>think</u>, or should we reserve the <u>right</u> to think for ourselves? What value does the majority <u>opinion</u> carry? Does the <u>fact</u> that an opinion is held by many automatically make it correct?

**Marketing:** Many <u>people</u> see the <u>world</u> through the lens of <u>products</u> and <u>possessions</u>, and it can be <u>hard</u> to <u>escape</u> the reach of advertisements in this modern <u>era</u>. More generally, the word means <u>influencing</u> <u>perceptions</u> about something. Every day, you market yourself through your actions, <u>attitudes</u>, and <u>appearances</u>. Many people and things are competing for our <u>attention</u>. How have you marketed yourself to the <u>world</u>? Do your <u>actions</u> accurately <u>portray</u> who you are? What about your perception of others? Do their actions accurately portray who they are? Do you blindly <u>trust</u> the messages you <u>hear</u> or <u>analyze</u> them for hidden <u>motives</u>/<u>meanings</u>? Is it possible that our actions are influenced by what others think of us?

**Marriage, Marry:** <u>Take</u> as husband or wife, <u>join</u> in wedlock, or <u>enter</u> into matrimony. Marriage is a very big <u>commitment</u>, which most <u>believe</u> to be a lifelong <u>decision</u>. Are you married? Do you <u>plan</u> on getting married? Do you believe marriage is about <u>love</u> or is just a <u>part</u> of <u>life</u>?

**Martial, Martial Law:** Anything having to do with the military is considered martial. Martial law is imposed during a <u>time</u> of <u>war</u> when the military is occupying a certain <u>region</u>. No such kind of <u>rule</u> has been implemented in the United States since the Revolutionary War, yet it is often the norm in less developed countries. Can you imagine what martial law must be like for the citizens under its control? Where does martial law stop and oppression begin?

**Mass Media:** Unfortunately, this remarkable network of information collection and distribution has become largely geared toward the goals of a few selfish individuals at the expense of the majority. It is important to gather facts from multiple sources and to question everything we are told. In light of this corruption and transformation from information dissemination to "selling something," how can we be more responsible consumers of news? How can we overcome these influences to obtain an unfettered news source? How can you take control of the news you are personally exposed to?

**Master:** Someone who is the owner or boss of something or someone else, or as a verb, to become an expert at a given skill. Anyone who has complete mastery over something must thoroughly understand it in order to control it. One can have mastery over a skill or piece of machinery, though a person can be mastered as well. While taking stock of the things you have mastered, ask yourself: What has mastery over you? What habits or influences are you a slave to?

**Mastermind:** To devise and oversee the completion of a plan. It is rewarding and inspiring to conceive an idea and carry it through to its realization. Don't be afraid to pursue new endeavors, but keep in mind: You should aim to finish what you start. What can you claim to have masterminded in your life? How much of your circumstance has been in your control, and how much has been out of your hands?

**Material:** The substance for which something is made out of or what can be made into

something. Do you construct objects using materials, or do you purchase everything you own?

**Matrimony:** Matrimony is a sacred vow of commitment to another person to be taken seriously. Why is it that so many marriages end in divorce? Do those people not take their vows seriously, or is it that they refuse to work through their problems once they arise?

**Matter:** Any physical substance; what we're all made of, or a measure of significance. It is easy to get mired down in small disappointments, but keep track of what matters most to you in your life. The things important to us are what make life worth living. Like the matter that physically defines an object, things that matter define our perspective. What is important to you? How can you keep tabs on those things that are important in your life? How can make sure that you are keeping them in your priorities, and not letting them slip away?

**Mature:** Maturity can be measured in many different ways and for every person, the rate of maturation is different. Overall, it boils down to your ability to understand and take responsibility for an increasing amount of aspects of your life. Be cognizant and aware of your surroundings, and you will know when it is time to accept responsibility for the problems and obstacles in your life, to stop relying on or blaming others. Can you claim to have reached maturity in your life? When did you become mature?

**Mayhem:** Chaos, disorder. Keep in mind that there are many degrees of mayhem. Though your situation may seem bleak, it is important to look for order and comfort where you can. When mayhem strikes, do you let it sweep you up in its panic inducing arms, or do you hold your ground and try to

> *"Age brings maturity, experience ripens it."*
> — *Vimal Athithan*

return to order? Do you keep your wits about you and react appropriately to mayhem? How can you avoid mayhem?

**Me:** One must escape and go beyond the "me syndrome," (an overconcentration on oneself that causes one to lose sight of one's surroundings) in order to broaden the spectrum of thought. If we are locked into an overly self-centered mind-set, we limit our conception of life to human life. We should unlock our minds in order to broaden the spectrum to all forms of life—human life, plant life, and animal life. Does the key to life then become an awareness and acceptance of the concept of living in harmony with all life? How connected are you to plant and animal life? Are you very focused on yourself or are you aware of your surroundings?

**Meaning:** You decide whether life has meaning. Everything should mean something, and every item and article should have a right and proper place. Seek meaning beyond superficiality. How do we make things meaningful? How do we keep meaningful things close to our hearts? Do you strive to find meaning through observation and critical thinking? *When you have formed your creed, have you found meaning?*

**Measure:** There is no one way to measure anything in life. Humans have invented various units of measurement to make our lives easier and to maintain consistency. Even when our units for measuring the same thing differ among groups, we can use unit conversion formulas to understand one another. It gets more complicated when we measure things such as personal qualities and less tangible attributes. Our individual subjectivity will cause us to measure things like these in vastly different ways; we all

value things differently and measure the worth of other people and things in different ways. It is important to know what you are measuring yourself against before you decide whether you are successful or not. Do not let others measure your worth absolutely. Take opinions of others into account, but also realize that you must create your own personal set of values by which you measure yourself. How do you measure yourself? How do you measure others? Do you measure others by the same standards you measure yourself?

**Mechanize:** Some would say modern life has become mechanized past any kind of organic recognition. How do you think we've lost touch with nature in modernity? Do you feel connected with or estranged from nature? How do you think we can reconnect?

**Meddle:** It is a healthy and desirable attribute to want to be helpful, but make sure your help is wanted before blindly injecting yourself into another's tribulation. Who meddles in our everyday affairs where we are perfectly capable of dealing with things ourselves? Have your affairs been meddled in by the government, politicians, co-workers, or even friends? Do you tactfully deal with unwanted meddling? Do you meddle in others' affairs?

**Media:** There has been an explosion of new types of media in the last few decades. Sometimes it can be overwhelming to know which media outlets are trustworthy and worth listening to, but it is worth consuming a variety of different types before you decide which ones you trust. Where the media errs in its content is airing their own press or other person's opinion rather than reporting factual news. Do you examine the media you consume before blindly trusting it? What media do you trust the most?

**Mediate, Mediation:** Sometimes an agreeable compromise simply cannot be reached between two parties. It is useful to have an unbiased third party, which serves as a mediator and helps to reach a fair conclusion. To mediate is to act as a judge or go-between in trying to settle a quarrel between persons or sides, and it is also a big <u>responsibility</u>. It is <u>important</u> to <u>examine</u> both sides. <u>Avoid</u> <u>biased</u> mediation, and don't mediate when you are biased. How can you act as a mediator in everyday <u>disputes</u> between your <u>friends</u> and <u>family</u> members? How can you act as your own mediator in your internal disputes?

**Medicate, Medicine:** There is a myriad of medicines on the market today. Though there are <u>government</u> safeguards to ensure they are <u>safe</u>, it is still of utmost <u>importance</u> to know what you are putting in your <u>body</u> and what the <u>potential</u> <u>effects</u> are. Certain medications are <u>necessary</u>, but sometimes the <u>temptations</u> to self-medicate are unbearable. How can we <u>resist</u> self-medication through <u>drugs</u> and <u>alcohol</u> and instead <u>work</u> through our <u>problems</u> ourselves? Have you <u>considered</u> <u>extreme</u> and <u>opposite</u> <u>aspects</u> of medication to your <u>health</u>? Do you over-medicate yourself?

**Medieval:** Much has <u>changed</u> since the medieval <u>age</u>. Certain <u>technologies</u> have been <u>developed</u>, and <u>political</u> <u>systems</u> have <u>progressed</u> significantly since the period. But what has remained the <u>same</u>? How can comparing those <u>times</u> to these <u>help</u> us <u>understand</u> our <u>own</u> times and the <u>fundamental</u> things about <u>life</u> that never change?

**Meditate:** It is crucial that we take <u>time</u> for <u>quiet</u> reflection in our <u>lives</u>. <u>Life</u> moves fast, and as we get <u>older</u>, it only moves faster. It can be <u>therapeutic</u> and some would say <u>necessary</u> to <u>clear</u> your <u>mind</u> and <u>align</u> your breathing on a regular basis. In the fast-paced world we live in, you will <u>benefit</u> from slowing your own <u>personal</u> <u>world</u> down, even if only for a <u>brief</u> few minutes. Don't use the <u>time</u> to <u>focus</u> on the <u>negative</u> <u>aspects</u> of life, but seek <u>resolutions</u> in the <u>quiet</u>. Do you set aside time to be <u>alone</u> with your <u>thoughts</u>, and to <u>consciously</u> <u>relax</u> your <u>body</u> and <u>mind</u>? How and when do you meditate? Where do you go to meditate?

**Memorize, Memory:** Memories are more <u>valuable</u> than any <u>possessions</u>. They tell you about yourself as a <u>person</u> and your <u>place</u> in the <u>world</u>. Your memory also holds <u>past</u> <u>failures</u> and <u>successes,</u> which you should not dwell upon but <u>learn</u> from to move forward. <u>Exercise</u> your <u>mind</u> regularly to <u>improve</u> your memory. How do memories of past events play a <u>role</u> in your day to day <u>life</u>? Do you make an <u>effort</u> to <u>remember</u> valuable <u>lessons</u> in life? What is your most <u>vivid</u> memory from when you were a <u>child</u>?

**Mend:** When you make <u>mistakes</u>, do not lose <u>hope</u>. Even the bleakest <u>situations</u> can be mended with <u>determination</u> and <u>tact</u>. When you are faced with a <u>problem</u>, <u>avoid</u> wallowing in self-pity and instead begin <u>thinking</u> of ways to fix it. Take <u>steps</u> in a <u>positive</u> <u>direction</u>. What steps can you take to mend the problems you are facing and avoid dwelling unnecessarily? Can you mend the wounds of others?

**Mental:** <u>Thoughts</u> happening inside the <u>mind</u>. Your mind <u>controls</u> the <u>emotions</u> you have and <u>express</u>. Do you beat yourself up <u>constantly</u> for your <u>mistakes</u> in your mind? How harshly do you critique yourself? Do you <u>talk</u> to yourself frequently?

**Mentor, Mentoring:** Lead by example. Mentors <u>help</u> point people in the right <u>direction</u>, provide <u>supportive</u> <u>advice</u> from their own <u>experiences</u>, <u>listen</u> empathetically, <u>offer</u> encouragement, and <u>serve</u> as a possible role <u>model</u>. Mentoring <u>relationships</u> can take on a <u>variety</u> of <u>different</u> <u>forms</u> and can <u>work</u> with virtually any <u>age</u> combination. When you are dealing with someone younger or less experienced than you, do you <u>recognize</u> your <u>responsibility</u> to <u>set</u> a <u>good</u> example? How have you been a mentor to others? Have you had positive mentors?

**Mercenary:** A mercenary is a paid soldier who will fight for whoever gives him the highest price. This word entails greed insofar as it means that someone elevates money above all other considerations surrounding a given decision. Have you ever worked just for the money and nothing else? Does everyone have a choice?

**Merchandise:** This word can refer to actual products being sold or any action taken to increase the sales of a given product. Advertising companies spend millions of dollars each year creating advertisements designed to convince us that we need their products, whether we actually do or not. How can we avoid the lure of advertisement and think for ourselves? What do we really need, and what could be considered excessive?

**Mercy:** Compassion and empathy are cornerstones of a productive and successful life. When you are in a position of power, you must make an effort to be merciful when you can be and merciless when you have to be. Differentiating between these two responses is part of what it takes to be an effective and respectable leader. Some would say everyone is deserving of mercy. Do you agree? Do you weigh various options and the outcomes for all parties involved in a situation before you make a final decision? Who is owed mercy, and who is not? How do we decide?

**Merge:** Many things merge in life: families, individuals, even marriage is fundamentally an act of merging. Do not let your problems in life merge into one faceless mess. Instead, separate them into smaller isolated issues that you can begin to take steps to solve. How can it be good for us to merge our goals and pursuits with others? What do we lose by being isolated? How can we separate problems that are merged?

**Merit:** The amount of effort and knowledge a person puts forth to earn high grades and do well in school. America purports to be a democracy built on merit, where even the most underprivileged person is able to overcome class barriers with hard work. However, the gap between the rich and poor is growing, and many argue that social mobility is decreasing instead of increasing. Do you think it's still possible to reach a high level of success without outside help based only on your merit? What do you think is necessary today for success? How might you implement a meritocracy for the people in your own life, on a smaller scale?

**Message:** How communication occurs. A message is sent through a channel in order for two people to communicate with each other. A message can be sent verbally, nonverbally, or through technology. Are you good at sending messages and communicating with others? Are you easy to understand?

**Mete:** To mete is to distribute something out in shares or according to what is deserved by each party. It is a large responsibility to fairly distribute a prize or punishment and should be treated as such. Take all aspects of a situation into account and hear all sides of the story before you mete out anything prematurely. When you are required to mete out a reward or a penalty do you make an effort to do so in a fair and diplomatic way? Do you pay attention to who gets to mete out rulings that affect others? Who among us can claim this right, other than God?

*"It is better to risk saving a guilty person than to condemn an innocent one."*

— *Voltaire*

**Middle:** The middle is the meeting ground of two points; it is where

161

you meet someone for a compromise. It can also mean that you are within the average section. How can you find the middle ground in everyday arguments? How can you strive to obtain a balance between pleasure and responsibility in your life? How can you be better than the average person in your job and in life?

**Mind:** The mind is the seed of our intelligence, and the body is controlled by the mind. The more you explore and expand your own mind, the better your sense of self will be. One must understand what the mind is capable of doing and should train it to help it reach its full potential. Like any other part of your body, the mind must be exercised to continue to function. Do you *consciously* experience emotions, guide observations and perceptions, control actions and movement, opinionate, memorize, and retain or recall information. You must be disciplined in regards to your mind; it is not always best to go with your first impulse before examining a situation as a whole. Do you challenge yourself to this end? Do you find it hard to control impulses and urges that arise in your mind? How do you train your mind? Do you use it to observe, think, and form decisive thoughts with C.L.A.R.I.T.Y? *Does mind enhancement come from spirituality?*

**Mindset:** To be set and locked on a decision. The inability to alter or change, pre-conceived infused patterns and moral conduct. It is healthy to be firm with decisions after considering all your options. However, being stubborn and refusing to listen to others is not progressive. Are you stubborn with your decisions or are you willing to listen to other ideas? What do you have your mind set on?

**Minimum:** The least amount of something. You will not get much out of life if you always choose to do the bare minimum. Yes, it is possible to only do the minimum amount of work to get by in life, but you will only be cheating yourself out of all the things life has to offer. You will never know your full potential until you put all you have into something important to you. Do your personal standards force you to achieve more than the minimum? Do you surround yourself with those who give their maximum?

> *"The single biggest problem with communication is the illusion that it has taken place."*
> — George Bernhard Shaw

seem minute, are actually the most important things. Don't sweat the small stuff when possible; it's easy to get bogged down by small bumps in the road. However, the more you pay attention to the small things, the more frequent and damaging they seem. Instead, keep your eye on larger goals and the long-term, big picture steps you can take to achieve them. Take time to assess value. Do you appreciate the relative size of your problems to your ability to solve and overcome them? Do you view your minute problems as very large?

**Mismanagement:** To be unorganized and make poor decisions with what resources are available. The penalty for mismanagement of our resources is now coming due, and the results could be catastrophic for the whole world. Everything is priced on world availability, not just how much we have inside our border. Ernest Hemingway stated, "The first panacea for a mismanaged nation is inflation of the currency; the second is war. Both bring a temporary propriety; both bring a permanent ruin." Do you have mismanagement in your life? How can you manage your time and resources in a more productive way?

**Minute:** Sixty seconds in a minute for the time aspect, or something very small. Some things are too small to matter, but others, though they

**Mistake:** To do something that causes regret or to do the wrong thing. All humans make mistakes. You should learn from your mistakes so you don't make them again and can progress forward in life. What mistakes have you made in life? Are you able to admit when you make a mistake? Were you able to turn your mistakes into a learning experience?

**Misunderstanding:** Misunderstandings are usually a result of miscommunication or lack of communication. To avoid causing misunderstandings, make your expectations clear with clear language, and make sure you listen to what is expected of you. Ask questions if you are confused about something. The more clarification you can provide, the better. Do your best to know as much as possible about the backgrounds and sentiments of people you are dealing with before you take action. How can we overcome cultural misunderstandings, where the only obstacle to understanding is a lack of experience and time spent around one another? What steps can you take to make yourself more clear on a regular basis? What major misunderstandings have you had?

**Misuse:** Using something incorrectly causes it to sustain unnecessary wear and tear and possible damage. To avoid misusing something, you must first know the intended use. Do you take time to follow directions and make an effort to use things correctly? Have you ever been subjected to the misuse of others? How can you avoid being taken advantage of? How can you make sure that no one has control over you?

**Mob:** Mob action has caused revolutions in the past and in some ways represents the will of the people when the government will not. An "angry mob" is a classic image of groupthink that extends beyond reason and can easily spin out of control. If you ever find yourself in a mob, make sure you still are vocal and discerning about your individual thoughts. Do you avoid letting a mob mentality control your thoughts? What can be gained from being a member of a mob?

**Mock:** Some mock others to feel better about themselves. Sometimes people mock others as a defense mechanism against the exclusion and criticism of others. When you feel inclined to mock, first attempt to understand the other side of the story. Have you ever been guilty of this behavior? Does this really help in the end, or does it merely cause more distance and isolation? Have you felt the negative effects from mocking?

**Mode:** Many remain stuck in a single mode without ever examining it or wondering why they are the way they are. The more unified your behavior and mind-set is, the more cohesive and happy your life will be. It can be a chore to have to significantly switch the way we are according to different situations we find ourselves in. Do you notice yourself switching to different modes? Can you find common ground between the different modes you go into for different aspects of your life? How can you be more mindful about the way you're living your life?

**Model:** To become successful, it is helpful to have a positive role model, or someone whose actions are a good example and serve as inspiration. Oftentimes, impressionable young people choose role models like celebrities or pop culture icons for the wrong reasons. Examine and scrutinize your model before you commit entirely to emulating it. Bearing this in mind, how can you be a good role model to others? Do you have a role model? Who was your role model when you were growing up?

**Modern:** To be modern is relating to the present or recent time. The modern times are certainly overlooked in our society, but those who see the world around them in a modern view are able to stay the most current about a lot of pressing issues and debates. Are you modern? Do you know others who are modern?

**Modest:** Modesty is a respectable and admirable quality. To be modest means to keep your wits about you when faced with success instead of becoming arrogant as a result of your accomplishments. Bragging suggests a weakness or insecurity present in the braggart while modesty accomplishes the opposite. Avoid fake modesty, as it is just done to impress further. Do you respect modesty? Do you make an effort to be modest?

**Moment:** A moment is usually considered as a fleeting instant, but historically speaking, a moment can be a second, a minute, an hour, a day, a month, a year, a decade, a century, or a millennium. It is important to see beyond your individual conception of the world and appreciate the views and sentiments of others. Step outside your skin and imagine which moments might be important to others and how you might respect these moments. Also take a step outside the moment you may be stuck in; the small world you are presently in, cradled inside the immense outer world, and always remember to keep the bigger picture on your radar. Do you appreciate the importance of perspective? Do your observations correctly evaluate your moment? What have been the most important moments in your life? What have been your most memorable moments? (See also: *A Day of Life: Moments in Time*)

**Monetary, Money:** Always consider the use or purpose of money and which pattern of use you are consciously or subconsciously following. Always logically examine the alternatives before you spend. Money is a commodity, a tool—a tangible means of exchanging goods and services. The negative aspect of money lies in how it is obtained and used. Greed is an insidious and harmful disease. Money, some say, is the root of all evil, yet it can also be the root of all activity, growth, and progression. The problem is, the line between progress or improvement and excess or greed is muddled and unclear. We share, lend, exchange, and loan money. What is money worth? When should acquiring money become a motive? Can you recognize the difference between desire and greed? Can you discern between manipulative greedy people and well-intentioned ones? Do you consider wealth in terms of money? Can money be created infinitely outside of or without law and order? Does the accumulation of money drive you? How much do you value money? Do changes in the money supply determine the direction of a nation's or even the world's economy? *What is fiat money?*

> *"Too many people spend money they earned... to buy things they don't want... to impress people that they don't like."*
> — *Will Rogers*

**Moot:** Arguing needlessly is a waste of time and energy. When something is exposed as a moot point, you are only making enemies by arguing for or against it; instead, focus on problems that can actually be resolved. Do you argue for the sake of arguing or only as a last resort to solve a problem? Do you let your ego get in the way of progress or do you swallow your pride and let an argument end when a conclusion can no longer be reached?

**Mope:** Like whining or complaining unnecessarily, moping around instead of taking steps to solve a problem is a waste of time and energy. Those who mope around and complain about their problems instead of doing anything to rectify them will only cause themselves more pain and inconvenience. Be positive; learn more about your problems and take action to solve them instead of brooding about them. Do you avoid moping in favor of a more productive outlet of your frustration or pain?

**Moral, Morality:** To be moral is to do the <u>right</u> thing in a <u>situation</u>. <u>People</u> can have morals which they <u>live</u> by, or they can <u>choose</u> whether to <u>act</u> morally or not for each action. There will always be <u>arguments</u> about what is moral and what is not, because people use <u>different</u> frameworks to <u>decide</u> this for themselves. As a <u>rule</u> of thumb, <u>treat</u> others how you would like to be treated, and be <u>sensitive</u> to the wishes and <u>needs</u> of others. Whether you act morally or not may affect your conscience and if you will <u>feel</u> <u>guilt</u>. How do you <u>measure</u> your <u>own</u> morality? Can the same <u>set</u> of moral <u>codes</u> be applicable to all, or should each person and each culture make its own morality? Do you have moral standards you live by? Are you a moral person?

**Most:** Most describes having the greatest amount or degree possible. Some feel that they have "most" of their <u>life</u> figured out, sheltering themselves from learning more to grow their life's <u>value</u>. There's always an <u>opportunity</u> to build upon your <u>personal</u> value that vaults you to getting the most of your life. What do you do to get the most of life?

**Motivation, Motivate:** A drive to do something, which can come from within ourselves or from something externally. It is an extremely desirable <u>skill</u> in many <u>separate</u> <u>aspects</u> of <u>life</u> to be able to motivate the <u>people</u> around you to <u>accomplish</u> <u>goals</u>. What motivates you? Do you <u>strive</u> to <u>lead</u> by <u>example</u> and <u>inspire</u> your peers? Are you able to motivate the people around you, or even more <u>importantly</u>, motivate yourself? Are you readily able to <u>discern</u> between <u>good</u> and <u>bad</u> <u>motives</u>? Do you look to others for motivation? Does motivation have a <u>role</u> in everything we do?

**Motive:** Motive as <u>reason</u> for doing is often applicable to gaining <u>money,</u> <u>control</u> and <u>power</u>. A motive can be <u>good</u> or <u>bad,</u> and it can have a simultaneous or dual <u>purpose</u>. A motive is what drives you to make certain decisions or certain <u>actions</u>. Motive is a prime factor in criminal investigation. How <u>important</u> is the consideration of motive in <u>business</u>, <u>politics</u>, and other aspects of our <u>social</u> and <u>civic</u> <u>world</u>? What are your <u>motivating</u> factors? Do you consider the motive behind your <u>choices,</u> <u>decisions,</u> and actions? Do you seek a <u>reasoned</u> <u>cause</u> for acting in a particular way or for others acting in a particular way? Is motive a part of your <u>thinking</u> with <u>C.L.A.R.I.T.Y.</u>? Does the significance of motive take on a <u>different</u> <u>element</u> when more than one person is affected?

**Move, Movement:** <u>Physically</u> going to a <u>different</u> <u>space</u> or placing an <u>object</u> in a different area. <u>People</u> move from house to house and to different <u>countries</u> in order to <u>gain</u> different <u>experiences</u> and see <u>new</u> things. Where have you moved from and to? Do you <u>like</u> to move? What can be gained from moving often?

**Movie:** <u>Entertainment</u> in motion, which is watched on the television. Movies are <u>produced</u> and <u>shown</u>. There are many genres of movies for <u>different</u> <u>age</u> <u>groups</u> and that involved <u>specific</u> kinds of <u>content</u>. What genre of movie is your favorite? Do you like <u>watching</u> movies?

**Murder:** <u>Killing</u> someone or something intentionally, for a <u>reason</u>. Murder is <u>viewed</u> <u>differently</u> across <u>cultures</u>. Are there cases in which murder is justifiable, in self-defense for <u>example</u>? Is <u>war</u> a <u>form</u> of murder?

**Muse:** Can be someone who is an <u>inspiration</u> for <u>creativity</u>. Many artists have <u>claimed</u> that a muse inspired them, and that is why they can create such magnificent <u>works</u> of <u>art</u>. Who inspires you? Who would you say is your muse?

**Music:** Sound that has a beat, which can be <u>produced</u> by <u>instruments</u>, by <u>people</u>, or through <u>technology</u>. People can <u>dance</u> to music and can <u>entertain</u> others with music. There are many <u>types</u> of music. What kinds of music do you <u>enjoy</u>? How often do you <u>listen</u> to music?

# N

**Narration, Narrative:** An account of connected events, a story. We each tell narratives about our own life to give it meaning and coherence. Narratives occur at different scales. The universe has a narrative, as does the Earth, mankind, and each individual, landscape, and every day. What narrative have you given your life? Is it a malleable one or one that you can never see changing? What narratives are you a part of?

**Natural, Nature:** Plant life and scenery that is found on Earth. Something natural is something that is created or happens on its own without (human} interference or alteration. Is nature under serious threat from various environmental influences, such as polluting corporations and laws that do not protect the environment? Do most people pollute, destroy, or waste the environment every day by using cars that require gasoline, by buying furniture made from trees, or by taking a shower that uses fresh water? Because of exponential numbers, should we cut down on using resources as much as we can and start using sustainable measures to preserve Mother Nature? So much in life today is artificial, often while trying to seem natural. Can you tell the difference? What can we as common citizens do to combat environmental corruption? How can you help protect nature? How can you be more environmentally responsible and sustainable? How do you interact with nature daily? Do you have inherent qualifications necessary for success? *Are your moral convictions synchronized with naturalness? How natural are you in spirit and your credence in this world?*

> *"The earth has music for those who listen."*
> *— George Santayana*

**Necessary, Necessity:** Something important or vital to live. We each must decide what is necessary in our life. What contributing factors influence such a decision? Do you let yourself be ruled by the desires advertising companies inflict on you? Do you have only an eye for the things that you truly need? What are necessities in your life?

**Need:** In a sense, life is impossible without having our basic needs met. Basic needs include water, food, sunlight, air, and shelter. However, modern needs have changed; people have emotional and physical needs now as well. But can you differentiate between what you truly need and what you only desire? What are your emotional and physical needs? Are all of your needs being met? How can you help poor people receive resources to fulfill their basic needs? Does humanity need other life forms to survive?

**Negative:** Something that is not positive or uplifting and can turn people's mood into something bad. Many people let their lives be overwhelmed by the negative things. What difference can a positive outlook make in contrast to a negative one? In what ways does our outlook shape our reality and our perception in ways we don't even realize?

**Neglect:** When someone or something is not treated how it should. Some parents accidentally neglect their children by not feeding them well or not showing enough love and attention, which can inflict permanent damage on the children. It is important to understand what a person or animal needs in order to avoid neglect. Have you ever been neglected? Have you ever accidentally neglected others?

**Negotiate:** To come to a compromise or an agreement that combines two opinions, which may be in the middle of two options. We should be willing to negotiate the issues important to us and come to a compromise. Where in your life are you stubborn when you should be more flexible? Where could you help others negotiate their difficulties? Are you easy to negotiate with? Do you negotiate often?

**Neighborly:** To live next door to someone, or act as if you are very close with someone by helping others out. Do you act as a true neighbor for the people in your life? Do you help when help is needed, and do you act with kindness? Do you help out your neighbors if they ask for help or would you if they did?

**Nemesis:** An unbeatable foe, competitor, or condition of living. Have you experienced an association with somebody who was a source of your downfall or ruin, or who has inflicted just retribution? How are you emotionally dealing with it? Have you given up hope? Is it possible to change one who is a nemesis into a friend?

**Nepotism:** Having a favorite in a specific situation, which usually is within a political or business setting. Normally, a family member is treated better than other people. Many politicians and business owners have gotten by with nepotism. But does that make it right? How might we restructure our political system so that jobs were given based on merit and not on family and friend connections? Have you been involved with nepotism?

**Nerve:** Many lack the nerve to go after what they want in life. It takes a certain amount of courage to achieve your goals, whatever they may be. Do you have that courage? Do you use your nerve in a negative way to antagonize or annoy others?

**Network:** A group of individuals who have something in common or who share similar goals. It is important to network with other professionals within and outside of your field of work. You can learn from and potentially find new opportunities for employment and other experiences. Do you network well? How can you expand your network?

**New:** Something that has not been seen before and is the opposite of old. It is exciting to discover or find something new and to share it with others. You should continually seek new horizons and try new things in order to learn and grow.

**News:** News can be found on the television, social media, in a magazine or newspaper, and on the radio. News can be good or bad, and liberal or conservative. Make sure your source is reliable first before believing everything you hear. Closely examine the interests and motives of your news sources before blindly subscribing to what they say. What influences your source of news? How do you find out the news? Do you utilize multiple news sources or just one?

**New Testament:** The New Testament is Christ's edict for the world, meant to wash away the anger of the Old Testament. Where the Old Testament preaches the words of a jealous God, intent on revenge and anger, the New Testament focuses on Christ's love. Whatever your religion, what could you stand to learn from the mercy found in the New Testament? How could you make your life more Christ-like?

**New World:** America was given the term "new world" by Columbus, who was unsure of what he had found. For those back in Europe, the New World represented new possibilities, for some an entirely new future. What do you think of as your "new world?" Do you think America remains a kind of land of possibility, or has modernity corrupted it?

**Nice:** Being <u>kind</u> to others, or something that is <u>good</u>. Although it is a <u>skill</u> to be nice to someone you do not like, you should be <u>respectful</u> of everyone. What makes a <u>person</u> nice? How can you tell who is only <u>pretending</u>? And are you nice to those who are nice to you? Are you nice out of your <u>own</u> <u>generosity</u>, or because you <u>think</u> it will get you somewhere?

**Nimble:** To be <u>quick</u> or <u>light</u> on your feet or quick to <u>understand</u> something. How can you make your <u>mind</u> and <u>body</u> more <u>open</u> to adaptability? Are you light on your feet?

**Normal, Normalcy:** The <u>standard</u> or usual <u>person</u> or thing. Some people <u>feel</u> the <u>need</u> to be normal to fit in with others because they are scared they won't be <u>accepted</u> otherwise. Normalcy <u>bias</u> can <u>prevent</u> a person from <u>preparing</u> for <u>disaster</u> and calamity when they should in <u>fact</u> have more <u>foresight</u>. Are you <u>emotionally</u> and <u>mentally</u> prepared for <u>possible</u> contingencies or disasters? How would you describe a normal person? Are you normal? Do you want to be <u>considered</u> normal?

*"The more the heart is nourished with happiness, the more it is insatiable."*
*— Gabrielle Roy*

**Nourish:** To <u>provide</u> food and fulfill needs for <u>life</u>, <u>growth</u>, and <u>health</u>. We <u>alone</u> are <u>responsible</u> for nourishing ourselves, but we often <u>forget</u> some of the multiple ways in which we need nourishment. Some parents malnourish their <u>children</u> accidentally because they are not educated. Do you take <u>care</u> to make sure you nourish each facet of your <u>body</u> and <u>mind</u>? What could you <u>improve</u> upon to nourish yourself more?

**Now:** The <u>present</u>. Although you should <u>learn</u> from your <u>past</u> <u>mistakes</u> and <u>plan</u> for the <u>future</u>, it's <u>important</u> to stay in the now. We often get caught up in the past or the future, without being able to <u>focus</u> on the <u>moment</u>. How can you <u>stop</u> getting trapped in your <u>imagination</u> and instead focus on <u>reality</u>? How can you make the <u>most</u> of the now or the present?

**Noxious:** Something <u>harmful</u> or unhealthy. Think of all the noxious chemicals in our atmosphere, especially in large, urban cities. How can you <u>reduce</u> your <u>own</u> carbon footprint? Are you actively <u>practicing</u> <u>sustainability</u> <u>measures</u>? How can we decrease the amount of noxious activity <u>happening</u>?

**Number:** Numbers or a number is the <u>single</u> determining factor (common denominator) in every <u>happening</u> of <u>life</u>. Numbers become a <u>form</u> of <u>measure</u> in comparison which ultimately leads to <u>opinion</u> and/or <u>conclusion</u>. <u>Think</u> of all the ways numbers infiltrate our <u>lives</u>—stocks, bonds, laws, regulations, equations, insects, <u>time</u>, computers, distance, measurements, finances/<u>money</u>, and <u>space</u>. How do you use numbers in daily life? *Do you make wise choices when dealing with numbers? Most important, what is the impact of numbers in population?*

**Nurture:** To <u>support</u>, encourage, feed, and <u>protect</u> a <u>person</u> or <u>animal</u>. It is <u>important</u> for <u>parents</u> to nurture their <u>children</u> in <u>order</u> for them to <u>develop</u> <u>correctly</u> and become strong and <u>healthy</u> adults. Were you nurtured when you were younger? How do you nurture others?

# O

**Oath:** A serious statement made in the name of God or some other sacred thing such as the Bible that one will speak the truth or keep a promise. Have you ever made an oath to God? What other kinds of oaths have you made? Have you ever broken an oath? Did this cost you your integrity? Have others broken their oaths to you?

**Obedience, Obey:** To listen to others and follow orders. Often, we find ourselves obeying people and things that do us more harm than good, but we find it hard to break out of the mold. Re-examine your values carefully before obeying any power, even the government. To whom do we owe obedience? Whom do we obey when we shouldn't? Who has ultimate sovereignty? Who do you obey?

> *"Disobedience is the true foundation of liberty. The obedient must be slaves."*
> — Henry David Thoreau

**Obese, Obesity:** Obesity is an epidemic in America; almost two-thirds of American adults are overweight. The food industry is to blame for their peddling of unhealthy foods, as well as Americans, for their lack of self-control. Regardless of where blame should lie, take initiative for your own well-being and make smart choices when it comes to food. Educate yourself on what is healthy. Who is to blame for this problem? Are you overweight? How can you change this problem or help others with their weight issues?

**Object:** Objects have no thoughts or feelings and can be treated accordingly. But is the same true of objectified people? What ethical transgressions do we commit when we objectify people and treat them like objects? What objects do you own that are important to you?

**Objection:** Objection can be a productive way of showing displeasure and disapproval. However, there are also ways in which objections can be harmful and unproductive, such as passive aggressive comments or violent impulses. How can you object to something in a productive and effective way? What do you object to? How do you express your objection?

**Objective:** A goal, something you are trying to achieve and work toward. Courses and assignments have objectives as well. What are your life's objectives? Do you have practical means for accomplishing those goals? How are you going to achieve your objectives?

**Obligate, Obligations:** We obligate ourselves to others through promising favors or committing ourselves to others. Should we feel burdened by these obligations, or should we think of them as a necessary part of socialization? What obligations do you have? How do you carry out those commitments?

**Obliterate:** The destruction of something. Humans are responsible for the obliteration of many things: the environment, whole countries, and even one another. Is it human nature to destroy? Is destruction a result of our environment, overstimulated by violent media representation and overly masculinized by our culture? How can we stem the tide of human aggression and violence? How have you contributed to obliteration of the planet, yourself, or of others?

**Oblivious, Oblivion:** Being unaware of your surroundings. Many people walk through their lives in complete oblivion of the world around them. How can we wake up out of our oblivion and enter reality? What do we let guide us from reality and keep us in this oblivious state? Is it our mood that distracts us or our overall environment that ceases to stimulate us? Are you oblivious to the truth around you?

**Obscene, Obscenity:** Vulgar or foul language, actions, or pictures. TV, movies, and even music are filled with obscenities. Children will repeat what they see, so ensuring they don't see things that will harm them is essential. What negative effects do these obscenities have on children, arguably the largest consumers of these forms of entertainment? How can you influence what your child watches so that they are protected from these kinds of obscenities?

**Observant, Observation, Observe:** Careful observation requires awareness and the ability to recognize what you are observing for what it is. Observations can be made with all five senses, through seeing, smelling, feeling, tasting and hearing. Does careful observation help us to learn and grow, as well as to help make good decisions by considering other observations? Are you aware of all that you observe and their place in relation to you and the rest of the world? Or do you observe passively, never really understanding the things you see? Do you observe emotionally or become affected by emotional display? Does the merit of observation depend on your ability to categorize information and sift out propaganda? Is education essentially a derivative of observation? What skills and techniques have you developed for observing? How do you observe? With C.L.A.R.I.T.Y? Do you observe with a mind closed to possibilities or open to them? What are the limits of your observational ability? Do you rebel against being told what to do while at the same time fail to observe what is correct to do? The Scriptures say "…upon this rock I will build my church." You might say, "Upon these observations I will connect with my spirit." *Is it possible to observe without the distraction of opinion and/or judgment? What other baggage weighs upon us while observing: skepticism, self-interest, prejudice, denial, or the two "B" words, bias and bigotry? Would other people observe you as being observant in a bright, discerning way?*

**Obsess, Obsession:** To constantly think about something or someone. No obsession is ever healthy, no matter how rational it may seem. What do you obsess over? What have you let consume you when it would have been better left in the past?

**Obsolete:** When something is not used anymore, like how typewriters and film cameras are becoming non-existent. Every piece of technology will eventually become obsolete, yet we chase after each new bit of technology like it is absolutely necessary. What truly drives this desire? Is it a need for new technology, or our own vanity? Is there something you used to use that is becoming obsolete?

**Obstacle:** Something that is in the way of your path or in the way of reaching your goal. Everyone has obstacles in their lives. How do we deal with these obstacles? Do we let ourselves be overwhelmed and crushed by them, or do we persevere? What obstacles have you faced in your life? How did you overcome these obstacles?

**Obstinate:** Standing by your own beliefs or opinions and not changing your ideas. Some causes deserve our obstinacy, while others are lost causes and should be recognized as such. An important aspect of this word pertains to obstinate attitudes and approaches to life. We often find ourselves so entrenched in our opinions and beliefs that we are unwilling to consider other possibilities. This leads to stagnation in the political world, as compromises can't be reached. Politicians capitalize on these attitudes, furthering their careers by focusing on the divisions in our country. Healing the proverbial chasms in our country starts with us; we need to leave obstinate attitudes behind. Are you obstinate in your beliefs, or are you open to other views and beliefs? Do you try to find ways to learn from others, even if their views appear contrary to yours? How can we tell the difference and draw the line?

> *"Be of good cheer. Do not think of today's failures, but of the success that may come tomorrow. You have set yourselves a difficult task, but you will succeed if you persevere; and you will find a joy in overcoming obstacles. Remember, no effort that we make to attain something beautiful is ever lost."*
> — *Helen Keller*

**Obstruct:** To be in the way of your sight. Numerous entities try to obstruct our clear view of reality. What do you suspect is obstructing your view and why? Your own self-delusions, the interests of politicians, or perhaps the manipulations of corporations at work? How can you transcend these obstacles and find clarity?

**Obtuse:** To be obtuse means you are incapable mentally or lack the problem solving ability you need. There are many variants of obtuseness, and it comes in many different forms. Examine a problem fully to avoid obtuse reactions. Who have you noticed to be obtuse in your own life or in national affairs? What government decisions have seemed obtuse in retrospect, and how could they have been avoided?

**Obvious:** When something is very blatantly clear. Oftentimes, things appear deceptively simple and hide from us their true complexity. What appears to be unclear when the answer is actually obvious? What seems obvious when it is actually far more complex than it first appears?

**Occasion:** An occasion is a special event. Do you know when the right time is for important events in your life? What occasions do you plan or are a part of? How do you distinguish occasions from other events?

**Occupation:** Each person's occupation is dependent on their skills and abilities, though not everyone finds themselves as suitably matched in a profession as they would like to be. How can you avoid this fate? How can you better apply yourself in your current job or in school? Is your occupation reflective of your passions, or only done for money? *Is it indicative of your creed for living life?*

**Occur:** Many occurrences happen every day, seemingly without cause, when in fact their causality is merely hidden from us. What seems magical or without explanation, when really its explanation is merely something we cannot understand? What occurrences have been unique or surprising in your life? What have you learned from these occurrences?

**Ocean:** Large bodies of water. The oceans can care for themselves. Humans must stop hurting them. Have you seen or been in one of the oceans? Do you understand the importance of protecting the oceans? How can you help to protect the oceans?

**Of:** To be of something means to be from it, a part of it, or belonging to it. Everyone is of something, and those roots help us know who we are. What do you belong to? From where do you come? Are you connected to where you are from?

**Off:** To be off means to be closed, shut down, not running. It is important for everything and everyone to shut down and take a break. Are you off? Do you approach your daily activities with <u>enthusiasm</u> and <u>energy</u>, or would some people say you <u>seem</u> off?

**Offend, Offensive:** We often offend others without <u>realizing</u> what we do. Do not seek to be offensive for the sake of amusement, but <u>speak</u> the <u>truth</u> even if you <u>risk</u> offending the unjust. Have you ever been the accidental perpetrator of an offense? How can you <u>rectify</u> the <u>wrongs</u> you've <u>committed</u> against others, even accidentally? When have you been offended by others?

<u>Offer:</u> When someone offers us something, they could be giving a gift, but usually they are presenting for <u>acceptance</u> or rejection. Be <u>mindful</u> of gifts that carry <u>expectations</u>. *Do all offers carry a mandate for response*? What can you offer to <u>life</u>, this planet, and your <u>spiritual</u> <u>creed</u>? Do you consider the legal ramifications of all offers? Do you <u>ignore</u> offers from the standpoint of emotional rejection? Have you ever treated offers as unwanted <u>charity</u>?

**Old:** Aged, or something that has been around for a long <u>time</u>. <u>People</u> can <u>live</u> to be very old; many consider elders to be very wise because of many <u>years</u> of <u>experience</u> and <u>learning</u>. It is <u>important</u> to eat <u>healthy</u> and <u>exercise</u> regularly in order to live a long and <u>happy</u> <u>life</u>. How many years does someone have to live to be considered old? How old do you want to be before you <u>pass</u> away?

**Old Testament:** The Old Testament is the first half of the Christian Bible, highlighted by the <u>creation</u> of the <u>world</u> and the <u>relationship</u> between <u>God</u> and His people. There can be a lot of <u>lessons</u> <u>learned</u> in the Old Testament, even if you do not align yourself with <u>religious</u> ideology. Do you need to be of religious following in order to realize the teachings of the first half of the Bible? Have you read the Old Testament as of late?

**Omnipotent:** To have unlimited and great power. Who can <u>claim</u> omnipotence? Is omnipotence reserved for <u>God</u> <u>alone</u>?

**Omnipresent:** Something or someone omnipresent is <u>present</u> everywhere all the <u>time</u>. What is omnipresent or inescapable? What else but <u>God</u>?

**Omniscient:** Those who see everything all of the <u>time</u>. Nothing is hidden from them, and they can <u>benefit</u> from every possible <u>perspective</u>. Though the <u>average</u> <u>human</u> can never <u>hope</u> to <u>reach</u> omniscient, how might we still <u>strive</u> to make our perspective more well-rounded and inclusive? Do you try to see every <u>situation</u> from <u>different</u> perspectives?

**On:** To be held up by, covered, or <u>attached</u> to. To be 'on' something means to be on top of it, to know what you're doing and how it's going to get <u>done</u>. What are you on top of <u>right</u> now in your <u>life</u>? What have you maybe let slip where you shouldn't have and why? How do you plan to get back on top of what you want to get done?

<u>One:</u> One may seem like nothing; it may seem small and inconsiderable. But one can be everything; it can be <u>all</u>. Everything can be contained in the potential of one <u>person</u>, <u>object</u>, or <u>plant</u> seed. How can we better <u>learn</u> to <u>recognize</u> the potential in even the smallest singularity? What one <u>life</u> <u>goal</u> is the most <u>important</u> to you? How can you, as one person, <u>change</u> the world and make it a <u>better</u> <u>place</u>? What is the one <u>path</u> you <u>want</u> to take in life?

<u>Only:</u> A <u>single</u> <u>object</u> or person, meaning just one of something. Can be very <u>positive</u>, as in the only person to <u>receive</u> a high grade or reach a particular level. Can also be very <u>negative</u>, as in the only person to be disqualified from something or the only person to <u>fail</u> a <u>test</u> or class. Sometimes it is nice

to stand out and be recognized as unique. Do you have any unique skills which qualify you as the only person with those skills? Are you the only person in your family with a specific degree or talent?

**Open:** To open means to allow someone or something in or to enter something. A person can be open to new ideas or can open doors to new experiences. What new experiences have you had? Have you opened the door to allow others to have new experiences?

> *"The measure of intelligence is the ability to change."*
> *— Albert Einstein*

**Open-minded:** It is essential to remain open-minded in our everyday interactions, as well as our most important decisions. Are you as open-minded as you should be? Or do you occasionally find yourself falling back on your old assumptions? To what have you been close-minded and why?

**Opinion:** Each opinion depends on a subjectivity. A person asserting his or her own bias. Should you break from the opinions of your parents in order to create your own opinions? But are your opinions even your own, or are they just the result of your inherited beliefs from others? Have you failed to examine the core beliefs that form the foundation of your personality, or have you carefully examined each facet of the issues on which you opine? Do you seek to understand and/or respect opinions that contradict your own? Do you have very strong opinions, or are you easily swayed in your beliefs by societal factors such as politics, religion, and the media? Can you openly discuss your opinions without offending someone?

**Opponent:** The person opposite or against someone in a fight, game, or a debate. Sometimes your opponent is an obvious one, making him or herself apparent to you. But can your opponent sometimes be more insidious than that? Where might your opponents be hiding out of sight? Can you find opponents in things like advertisements on TV?

**Opportune, Opportunity:** An opportune moment offers a fortuitous opportunity. Success will lie with those who cannot only recognize such moments, but also have the courage to seize them. Can you recognize opportune moments when they arrive? What can be learned from missed opportunities? What opportunities have you taken advantage of?

**Oppose, Opposites:** Life consists of contrasts in which our imaginary pendulum swings: good and evil, positive and negative, black and white, hard and soft, clean and dirty. Happiness and well-being are achieved when the pendulum is balanced. Is it possible that many things we are told oppose us actually contain commonalities? What opposites or differences have you noticed within your family? Are you very different from your family? *Is your world, the spiritual world, and the universe polarized by opposing forces?*

**Oppress, Oppression:** A history of oppression could be written alongside human history. Where do you see oppression still today? While it may not be as overt as it was in days past, does it still persist more subtly? Are you oppressed? How and why?

**Opt:** To opt into or out of something is to make a choice. But do you consider all the options at hand having the full information at your fingertips? Are your decisions made in awareness of everything at stake?

**Optimism:** An approach to the world in which we expect a positive outcome* from situations* in our lives, regardless of how hopeless they seem. The application of this word on a small scale relates to everything from job interviews and personal relationships to larger facets of life. An optimist responds to strife and suffering in the world with the belief that over a long enough timeline, good triumphs over evil. Adopting this mind-set enables us to see negative experiences as opportunities rather than setbacks. Positive outcomes only occur when individuals place the responsibility for change on their own shoulders. We all experience grief, loss, and anguish—no life will ever be completely free of such things, but without optimism, moving past these things can be nearly impossible. While this approach fosters a lower level of stress in our day-to-day lives, it can also encourage apathy. Think back on your own life; have there been times when it seemed as though nothing was going your way, yet the eventual outcome of the situation played out in your favor? In that situation, did you succumb to hopelessness, or did you maintain a positive approach? If one is truly convinced of an inevitable positive outcome, will they seek to be a part of solutions in the world and in their own lives?

> *"How wonderful it is that nobody need wait a single moment before starting to improve the world."*
> — Anne Frank

**Option:** Your options are all your potential choices before they have been made. Do you consider each option carefully before ruling them out, or do you let yourself be ruled by your emotions? What are your options?

**Or:** Used before the second of two choices or possibilities. It epitomizes the difference between the two paths, one of which you must choose. When faced with an or, what do you do? Are you able to make decisions?

**Ordain:** When something is ordained, it is made to happen, arranged beforehand, and ordered. Be careful not to believe things are out of your control when in fact they remain of your own making. How much of your life is ordained by others? How much can you control for yourself?

**Order:** An order is the way in which objects or tasks are placed or made to follow one another. If everything is in order, it means it has found its right place and is working soundly. An order can also be a command from another, which is expected to be enforced. Is everything in your life in order? How is your life ordered or organized? How does order correlate to chaos and law? Is chaos the opposite or hindering force and law the positive or building force?

**Ordinary:** To be normal, typical or usual. Are you ordinary or unique? Do you prefer to fit in or stand out? Are you scared to stand out?

**Organization, Organize:** To separate activities and objects to allow life to be led in a sequence and orderly way. Have you actually thought about putting your life together as an orderly, functional, structured whole, arranged in a coherent and systematic form? What about the little things? Would taking the time to put them in proper places give you more time for important functions? Can organizations exist or function without being organized? Is organized good and disorganized bad? Does it require a lifestyle change?

**Origin:** The origin is the stem of existence. Things deviate from their origin, marked by positive or negative change. Oftentimes, we forgot the origin of existence, but it's advantageous to keep in the mind the roots of whatever you're dealing with to give you an additional frame of reference. What is an origin that you have dealt with that has deviated? Have you personally added something to your origin rather than let it succumb to outside influences?

**-ory:** -ory is a suffix meaning having to do with, or like. For instance, illusory means having to do with an illusion. What do you have to do with? What associations define you?

**Other:** The second of two choices, or something different. Too often, we are quick to discount the similarities and shared humanity between ourselves and those we don't know. Do you consider other people wholly 'other,' or do you take account for each person's similarities to yourself and grant them the sympathy they deserve on the basis of those similarities? Do you consider others as unlike yourself?

**Out:** To be outside is to be away from the inside, the center, or away from a certain place. You can be out of something physically, but you can also be checked out mentally as well. Are you mentally present in your everyday life, or do you sometimes walk through it like a zombie, completely checked out?

**Outcome:** An outcome is the final result, how something turns out in the end. Outcomes may not always be what we had in mind, but utility can still be derived in each and every outcome that is presented to us. Furthermore, an outcome can be more desirable if you put forth more work and due diligence. What outcomes have you experienced that have changed in your life in one way or another? Did you have outcomes that came as a surprise?

> *"He who has overcome his fears will truly be free."*
> *— Aristotle*

**Over:** Over has many meanings, from being physically over something or on top, to having over-much, being over-full. What are you over with? Are you over your previous romantic relationship? Have you finally gotten a toxic person out of your life, for instance, or do you still need to? Do you over-consume certain products, and do you need to adjust your intake?

**Overcome:** To get over something and progress positively in front of it. Some people overcome addiction and disease. Have you overcome something in your life? What have you overcome? Is there anything you have not been able to overcome?

**Owe:** Everyone owes something to someone. Give back what you owe. We must remember the things we earned from others in life and show gratitude for the things we have not earned ourselves. What do you owe to others? What have you taken for granted in your life?

**Own, Ownership:** We don't own anything; we are only allowed to use what we have in our possession under the constraints of time and commerce. Nothing stays forever in our possession. In light of this, do we simply waste time and energy in the pursuit of material objects, when in the end we can never fully possess them? What do you own? What do you hope to own?

**Oxygen:** All living things need oxygen. Oxygen surrounds us, even when we cannot breathe it ourselves. We need oxygen to live, and yet we continually pollute that oxygen with chemicals and toxic waste. How can we avoid such pollution?

# P

**Pace**: Pace is a consistent speed of movement. We each must pace ourselves in our daily lives, yet some of us run ourselves into the ground and burn out long before we should. Maintain a moderate and manageable pace, as it will follow you to see the world to its fullest extent. How can you set a manageable pace in your life and then stick to it? How can you manage your time better so that you don't find yourself in a situation where you can't keep up? Are you in sync with the pace of life around you and in the world? What can you remove to keep pace? Have you appraised accurately the pace of the world or life in your moment?

**Pacify, Pacifism**: To be a pacifist is to be against war and violence. Ghandi, for instance, was a pacifist, always choosing non-violent means for his protest against the British government. What could our government learn from his pacifist approach? Do you practice pacifism?

**Pact**: A pact is a promise made with people, nations, or organizations. It is meant to act as a guarantee that something will happen. Don't get taken advantage of when making a pact; be an advocate for yourself in solidifying that each pact can benefit both parties for the better. Whom have you made pacts with in the past? Did you make sure they went unbroken?

**Pagan**: a pagan does not adhere to the tenets of most world religions. He or she believes in nature or in other gods. Though pagans are often in the minority in terms of religious populations, how can we still treat them as a valued part of society? Is it fair to marginalize these figures simply because they are in the minority?

**Pain**: When pain is present, it is followed by discomfort and suffering, which is caused by injury or illness. Everyone suffers, and in life, whether or not you will suffer is rarely an option. Do you watch for suffering in others? The true test in our suffering, however, is how you will deal with this suffering—whether you rise above it or let it consume you. It seeks sense as it applies to various different components and levels of pain. Have you considered the different levels of pain, disregarding or ignoring the warning of discomfort or bearable pain? How can you learn from pain and turn it into a productive thing, something that helps you grow as a person? Do you fight through pain, or do you let it control your life? Pain can be the result of many things. On a physical level, it can be caused by injury, disease, or age, and on an emotional level, it can be caused by loss or dissatisfaction with our place in life. Physical pain can be debilitating. It can cause our daily lives to be a miserable process, as even small tasks become insurmountable. So too can emotional pain be, as depression removes the will to go on. The most important part

> *Pain has an element of blank;*
> *It cannot recollect*
> *When it began, or if there were*
> *A day when it was not.*
>
> *It has no future but itself,*
> *Its infinite realms contain*
> *Its past, enlightened to perceive*
> *New periods of pain.*
>
> — *Emily Dickinson*

of dealing with pain is to accept that you're not alone; you must allow others to help you in order to ease your suffering. Have you analyzed the effect of pain on your life at this moment? Is it debilitating (weakening) you? Is it destroying your normal physical or mental abilities? This of course works both ways. When we see others suffering, we should help, giving them our time and assistance in whatever way we can. Do you accept the help of others when you need it, or does your pride stop you? Do you take the time to help others when they need it?

**Pair**: A pair is two things of the same kind that are used together. Their utility depends on their cooperation, their ability to work together as part of a team. Do you have that ability, and have you found a partner? Do you prefer to work by yourself?

**Pamper**: To be pampered is to be placated, to have every one of your wishes fulfilled. The pampered never have to achieve, as all is handed to them. They go through life assuming they don't have to work for anything, feeling a sense of entitlement in everything they do. But what do you learn or have to work for when every wish you have is instantly fulfilled? Are you able to develop a work ethic and grow as a person?

**Panacea**: Panacea is meant to cure all wounds; it is intently looked at as a solution. Moreover, it is defined as a universal remedy. Is there a universal remedy? Yes, if we always seek it. Maybe, if we accept the possibility. No, if we totally deny its existence. There will always be something, mental or physical, to ail us. Similarly, no panacea exists for the world's problems. How can we deal with these things correctly when they arise? How can we learn to accept our human frailty and stop searching for a cure-all panacea we will never find?

**Pandemonium**: Pandemonium is chaos, wild disorder, and noise. We luckily avoid

pandemonium in everyday civilized society where this kind of chaos is not a problem, but what about impoverished countries elsewhere where this kind of chaos is the norm? How can we be more grateful for our own comfort and more proactive in abating the suffering of others? Pandemonium is as chaotic as you want it to be. In other words, you internalize pandemonium from the way people describe it, how society discusses it. and your own mental image and thoughts. As a result, we are not able to step back and be truly grateful.

**Pander**: To pander is to indulge or give in to. When we pander to someone, we help them actualize their own selfish desires and vices. It is also utilized for acceptance. Often, we pander to others in hopes that they will do something for us in return at a later date or because we want them to like us. But is this honest? When pandering is in effect, do both parties benefit equally and fairly? Reevaluate your motives before pandering to someone else.

**Parable**: A parable is a short, simple story that teaches morals, like in the Bible. Parables are meant to teach us how to live. They are not meant to serve as an exact road path of how to live. Have you gleaned the lessons from parables that you should have? Even if you are not religious, don't you think there are lessons you could glean from reading biblical parables or perhaps the fables of Aesop?

**Paradise**: Paradise is an ultimate abode of just. Some say a paradise is impossible, some say there is only paradise in heaven, and some say you can find a paradise on Earth. What do you think? Is paradise an unattainable ideal, already surrounding us, or something only reached through religious devotion? Better yet, can you create your own paradise?

**Paralysis:** Paralysis causes one to lose the ability to move. Often in our most important moments, we find ourselves paralyzed with indecision as we grapple with what to do next. Have you ever felt this kind of paralysis? Decisions cannot be made blindly, and inaction will inevitably lead to missed opportunities and regret. How can you overcome your paralysis and make well-informed decisions when it matters most?

**Parasite**: A parasite leeches resources and life away from someone else. Many people have parasites in their life without knowing it, someone who asks for money, time, and emotional energy far past what is acceptable. Do you have any people like this in your life? How can you rid yourself of them? Be mindful of giving too much.

**Pardon**: To pardon someone is to grant them clemency and forgive them for whatever wrong they may have committed. Once pardoned, that person is free from any further punishment. How do you know whether someone deserves your pardon or the pardon of others? Do not pardon someone then continue to punish them. How do you know when they have been punished enough and should now be forgiven?

**Parent:** A parent refers to a mother, father, or guardian. Our parents bring us into this world and raise us into adults, but do we always show them the respect they deserve? Oftentimes, we are wrapped up in our own lives to not realize how much sacrifice our parents have gone through, whether that is tangible or intangible. How can we possibly repay them for all they have given to us? And if they have fallen short of parental expectations in some way, how can we forgive them? Furthermore, are we living in a society where children place more value in what the government tells them than in what their parents tell them? What do our elders have to teach us that we haven't thought of yet?

> *"Parents can only give good advice or put them on the right paths, but the final forming of a person's character lies in their own hands."*
> *— Anne Frank*

**Part**: A part is in itself incomplete, only a piece of a larger whole. Sometimes we mistake a part for the whole, missing out on much larger entity of which it is a part. Other times, we fail to put all the pieces together into a coherent whole. How can we become more aware and better able to see entireties clearly, instead of getting bogged down in each individual part? Should we congregate different parts of the whole in our words so as to create the best picture of our world, society, or situation at-hand?

**Participate, Participant**: When someone participates, they engage in and are a part of it. As a participant, your results are indicative of your effort level. Do you seek to excel as a participant? Are you a participant in life, or do you act as a mere bystander, letting the events that surround you pass you by? If the latter, how can you change your actions and learn to participate in life in more meaningful ways? If the former, how can you shift your participation to have a more meaningful and positive impact on the lives of others? *Do you participate in negative activities?*

**Passion**: When passion is involved, it is exemplified as possessing strong and barely controllable emotion. Life without passion will seem meaningless and lacking in vitality. Seek to do things about which you are passionate, like a job or hobby. It's important to not become so passionate about something that it consumes every waking second of your life. How can you add passion to your life or rediscover what you were once passionate about?

**Passive**: When someone is passive, they allow what happens or what others do without active response. Many people are passive participants in their lives, never acting, only reacting to the things that happen around them. Are you passive in everyday situations? Can you truly complain about an end result if you did nothing to affect it? When you do speak out, is it for the right reasons and for the moral good?

**Pass, Past**: to pass is to go by, beyond, over, or through. What have you passed on in life and left behind? Passing over something is often synonymous with regret, but you can avoid those feelings by looking at each event that you "pass" over with sincere objectivity. Might passing over or on certain choices be a natural part of life's process? What have you passed on that ended up being a good decision in the long run?

**Path**: A path is a walkway or track that leads an individual from one point to another. There are a lot of paths in life, and we have the privilege of choosing our own path to a certain extent. You can choose the easiest path that your life lays in front of you, requiring little to no effort on your part. You can also choose the hardest path, one that requires a lot of work and dedication. Every path is truly tangible, but you have to have the mind-set of believing you can give yourself the best chance to succeed at whatever path you choose. What path have you chosen? Do you regret it? Do you wish to go down more paths than one to get the most out of life?

**Pathological**: something pathological is caused by or having to do with diseases; for example, a pathological

liar has a mental disease that makes him lie repeatedly. It's a constraint on someone's life because it gives them a filtered view of the world. How often do pathological diseases go unrecognized or undiagnosed? Do they grow worse over time, prompting rather immediate recognition and a diagnosis?

**Patient**: A patient is someone who waits for medical attention at a hospital. Patient can also refer to the ability of not growing anxious or frustrated with another individual. Can these two definitions coincide? Everyone is a patient in life, as we all have to wait for the next thing to happen. Yet, we have the capacity to be proactive, but can still infuse the act of being patient to get the best outcome possible.

**Patience**: When someone exhibits patience, they have the tolerance to deal with hardship without growing angry or agitated. Patience is one of the most important underlying virtues as it relates to relationships in our lives. Do we use patience in understanding and accepting the other person's perspective and opinion? Patience is essential to achieving any goal in life, as no worthwhile goal can be achieved without consistent and applied effort over an often lengthy period of time.

Have you demonstrated the patience necessary to achieve your goals?

**Pause**: A pause is a break or temporary stop in time. Every time we make a decision, we should pause and rethink our choice, because once made, it cannot be undone. Some are always in a rush to make a decision, but a pause can slow the world down around them. Do you pause as you should each time you make an important decision?

> *"Trees that are slow to grow bear the best fruit."*
> — *Molière*

**Peace**: Peace is tranquility, serenity, and is a dwelling in the self. Complete peace is our highest state and is the natural state. Peace is dwelling in the realm of all knowledge and all beauty in complete harmony. Peace is non-resistance, complete <u>acceptance</u>, and identification with all, everyone, and everything. Peace is a feeling and requires no action. Is peace in the realm of being? Is complete peace impossible in the realm of confusing <u>thought</u>? Can peace be present without a positive <u>creed</u> for living <u>life</u>? Are you attempting to analyze this dissertation, or are you at peace with it?

> *"When the power of love overcomes the love of power, the world will know peace."*
> — *Jimi Hendrix*

**Peer**: A peer is someone of the same age group or generation. If you would be <u>respected</u> in company, seek the <u>society</u> of your <u>equals</u> and not of your superiors. We have a tendency to be drawn to other like-minded individuals or group of people—our peers. Our peers say a lot about us but unfortunately, there is not always an exact match between what your peers say in person and behind your back. Do you let this affect you? We need to surround ourselves with people that <u>aspire</u> to be things greater than themselves and not people who will bring us down. What do your peers say about you? What do you say about your peers?

**Pensive**: To be pensive is to think intensely about your life; it is to be thoughtful and introspective. Do you become pensive when you should, or do you hastily make <u>decisions</u> before you think them through? It is not good to be overly pensive either, but introspection and careful <u>thought</u> is a must.

**People**: People are simply a collective group of human beings. Never underestimate the power of stupid people in large groups, as it yields mob mentality. Do you know when to consider your own needs over the demands of larger <u>groups</u> or when to sacrifice for the good of all? When people have the <u>opportunity</u> to conglomerate, the end result is not always as pleasant as one would like to believe. How can we turn those kinds of gatherings from potentially harmful situations into something more productive for <u>society</u>? *Do you consider the role you play as a <u>person</u> when dealing with the <u>constants</u> of life?*

**Per**: Per means "for each." We have a plethora of opportunities to do something for another person, whether they are a friend, colleague, or complete stranger. The act that follows largely depends on our <u>relationship</u> with the <u>individual</u>. What do we <u>owe</u> to each person? What does each person deserve?

**Perceive**: To perceive something is to <u>observe</u> it in a special way. It is to have it enter your <u>consciousness</u> and become a part of your <u>mind</u>. But think of all the different factors that can affect the way you perceive something—the people around you, your personal belief, and the wills of others. Some people have difficulty perceiving <u>reality</u> and the lives around them, so can perception ever come close to being described as a pure thing? How can you release yourself from the fetters of other people's <u>beliefs</u> and perceive things on your own terms?

**Perceptible**: To be perceptible is to be able to be seen or noticed. Do you/I hone our perceptibility by critical <u>thought</u>? What is perceptible, and what escapes our perception? Do things escape our perception sometimes out of our own inattention and not because it isn't present? Some have the ability and need to <u>lead</u>. Some are <u>dependent</u> and need to be led. Others are <u>independent</u> and seek truth by association. Where do you fit within this spectrum?

**Perception**: When one has perception, they have the ability to become aware of something through the senses. Perception is entirely individual by nature, as we all process (perceive) <u>observation</u> and <u>knowledge</u>

in different ways. Do not appraise your perception of how others perceive you. Do we all have a different capacity for <u>understanding</u> in a <u>positive</u> or <u>negative</u> way what we perceive? Is it yours to appraise how others perceive you? Worry about yourself, and if you perceive things clearly. Perception is also unique to me and you. How we record things in our own minds (usually positive or negative) are influenced by emotions, media, celebrities, etc.

**Perfect**: To be perfect is to be as good as it is possible to be. As much as we may want to reach perfection, no one ever will. How can we reach for perfection without being disappointed when we inevitably fall short? There's no shame in failing to <u>reach</u> perfection, but that shouldn't stop us from attempting. The harder we push ourselves to reach that perfect state, even if it's unattainable, the more <u>accomplished</u> we'll feel with the end result.

**Perfidious**: To be perfidious is to show treachery or betray trust. It's frustrating for someone to betray our <u>trust</u> because we put in effort to give them certain information and trust that it will be secure. On the surface, it doesn't seem difficult to uphold trust, yet it's a commonality in our <u>society</u>. Have you ever <u>betrayed</u> the trust of another? How can you make amends for the betrayal you committed?

**Perform**: When you perform something, you carry out a task. Some say <u>life</u> is nothing but a performance, an endless series of gestures made to fool those around us and even ourselves. In fact, Shakespeare famously stated, "All the world's a stage." Performance

*"We must have perseverance and above all confidence in ourselves. We must believe that we are gifted for something."*
*— Marie Curie*

**Perseverance:** Perseverance is in that one's determination

is often <u>necessary</u>—such as at work or in a sport—but how can you also remain true to who you are at your most genuine <u>self</u>? What is the environment that allows you to perform at your highest level? Along these same lines, some are afforded the luxury of performing on their own, whereas others have <u>assistance</u> every step of the way. Are people who perform on their own too stubborn to seek outside help, or are they truly sustainable to perform independently? Are people who have assistance too lazy to try and perform on their own, or do they truly need guidance to perform at their highest threshold?

**Peril**: Peril is mortal <u>danger</u>, a situation few of us will often find ourselves in. When peril does arrive, what will matter is how we carry ourselves. Will we act with grace under pressure, for instance, or will we collapse under the <u>weight</u> of the event?

**Period**: A period is the time that passes during which something occurs. Everyone has different periods in their <u>lives</u>, characterized by certain factors and <u>circumstances</u>. But how can you <u>overcome</u> one period of your life to begin a new one?

**Persecute**: To persecute is to mistreat or torment one, either brought forth by race, politics, or religion. Millions, if not billions, are persecuted worldwide by a variety of people, forces, and forms. Whom do you know has been persecuted, and what could have alleviated that <u>suffering</u>, or prevented it? Is simple <u>awareness</u> enough to spur action, or is something else needed? Being persecuted leads to several negative <u>feelings</u>, but what steps can you take to turn those into positive feelings?

closely related to <u>achievement</u> and willpower to overcome

the difficulties, obstacles, and problems in the way of maintaining one's belief or satisfying one's goal frequently creates an achievement. Does perseverance enter our psyche before or after we decide that nothing worth gaining comes easily? Is perseverance learned, or are we born with it? Do some individuals possess an innate ability to commit themselves to a specific <u>belief</u>, course of action, or loyalty with an almost absolute conviction and little to no self-doubt? If it were not for the perseverance of a few, what <u>liberties</u> would we have? Have you ever given up too soon, only to regret later what you could have obtained had you persevered? Have you endured hardship to pursue <u>achievement</u>? Have you persisted in culminating a project in spite of numerous <u>obstacles</u>? Is focusing on a long-term <u>goal</u> instead of short-term satisfaction a part of your <u>creed</u>? Early in life, many people observe that perseverance and hard work are the main components of success and achievement. Regardless of the goal, be it earning a college degree, building a company, raising one's children, taking care of those with long-term illnesses, or many other situations where the road to achievement is long, rocky, and steep, perseverance is an important human trait and has been so throughout human history. For example, do you think that without perseverance many things that we take for granted—everything from cell phones and tablets to the wheel and our ability to create and harness the power of fire—would exist? Do you think all human beings have the ability to persevere through adversity toward that which they desire? Does this hold true whether we are speaking about <u>scientific</u> and <u>social</u> achievements or those achievements that are more personal and spiritual in nature?

**Persist**: Persistence is related to perseverance; without persistence against <u>obstacles</u>, one cannot persevere. But what does it take to persist in the face of incredible obstacles? Physical <u>strength</u> or a kind of mental strength and focus that surpasses the present and the ordinary intellect? Also, know when to stop; don't persist with those around you to the point of nagging.

**Person**: Person is singular to people. <u>Personality</u>, whether that is being reserved, outgoing, happy, or sad, describes who we are as a person. It makes others like and dislike us, and it certainly guides us through our life choices as human beings. For some, the most attractive person is the one who is at <u>peace</u> with him or herself. How can we be more at peace with ourselves and with the <u>world</u> around us? The answer does not lie in an eschewal of self-criticism, but rather a commitment to a set of <u>values</u> that leaves you no room for guilt when you go to bed at night.

**Personable**: Being personable is more than just being friendly. It means being able to connect with <u>people</u> on meaningful levels. Are you personable with others, or withdrawn? Perhaps the most important ability one can have is the ability to be personable; after all, the <u>relationships</u> we <u>build</u> with others are at times all we have. Do you have good relationships with others because of your personable attributes?

**Personal**: Being personal relates to one's inner thoughts where individuality is at a premium. Some things are personal, some are professional, or so many would like to believe. But what do you do when the line between the two begins to blur? How do you deal when the separate <u>spheres</u> of your life suddenly converge, or was it never truly possible to keep them separate at all—that is, your work is subject to your personal <u>morals</u>, no matter what?

**Personality**: Personality consists of an outward appearance toward others that forms one's distinctive character. A <u>vibrant</u> personality is a person's greatest asset; it <u>communicates</u> who you are to others, just by how you interact. But it is important not to judge and be judged entirely based on one's personality; <u>people</u> have hidden depths, deeper <u>issues</u>, and beliefs than can be easily expressed in everyday conversation. As the saying goes, it's important not to judge a book by its cover. What does your personality say about you, and how much of you is in your personality? What aspects of yourself do you share with others?

**Perspective**: Perspective is how one sees the world around them. Each person has a slightly different perspective in accordance with the different experiences they have had. In addition to their different experiences, there are other outside influences that can affect one's perspective, with some having more of a traumatic, yet meaningful, impact in changing your perspective altogether. Your perspective speaks to who you are as a person, but that does not necessarily mean you should avoid introspection that might change your perspective.

**Persuasion:** Persuasion is the act of trying to convince someone that whatever claim you're putting forward is truthful and believable. We're persuaded in all walks of life, but there are scenarios when we lend to being persuaded too much. In an act of persuasion, there needs to be an open line of communication between the two parties involved to avoid any confusion or for someone to get ultimately deceived. Do you find yourself persuading a lot? When you persuade someone, are you truthful or deceiving?

> *"People are generally better persuaded by the reasons which they have themselves discovered than by those which have come into the mind of others."*
> — *Blaise Pascal, Pensées*

**Perturb**: To perturb means to make another individual feel anxious and troubled. Certain people are easily perturbed by the slightest disturbance, never realizing that their problem lies within themselves. How can you avoid the common pitfalls of being too afraid to realize when things are awry and when you're overreacting? Many people fail to realize just how much their fear limits them until it is too late.

**Peruse**: When someone peruses, they read or examine thoroughly. Great books require our careful perusal, but how many of us can say we give these books when they deserve? How much time do you spend reading a day? How much time, in comparison, do you spend watching TV? Carefully consider what you stand to gain from each activity. The 'world's great books contain some of the world's greatest wisdom. Can TV make that claim?

**Pervade**: To pervade is to spread through something in its entirety. Our culture is pervaded by a variety of deleterious influences, including drugs, crime, and biased media. It's an issue that is increasingly becoming worse as time moves on. How can we get rid of these harmful influences and stop the pervasion that has succeeded thus far? Can we rely on those with a greater social standing (i.e., politicians, city leaders) to take care of these influences?

**Perverse**, **Perversion**: To act perversely is to continue in a stubborn way to do something wrong or harmful. What perverse acts do we see perpetrated in everyday life? Crimes like animal cruelty and child abuse are replete in our society, yet don't we have the resources available to stop them. What could ordinary citizens do to help stamp out the perversity of modern society?

**Pessimism, Pessimistic**: When one displays pessimism, they expect things with the worst outcome possible; they see the glass as half-empty. Pessimism now dominates the minds of most Americans, especially during times of economic uncertainty. How can you combat this pessimism in your own mind and perhaps even the minds of others? Do you offer positive alternatives when others approach you with pessimism?

**Pest**: To be a pest is to be an annoyance or nuisance. Our <u>world</u> is filled with pests of the insect variety and otherwise. Pests are always irksome, but how can we either eradicate them or not let them bother us as frequently? Carefully <u>consider</u> whether your pests are worth the <u>effort</u> you exert in ridding yourself of them. An individual may be a pest toward you for the sole reason of wanting to perturb you and see you crack under pressure.

**Phenomena:** Phenomena are in accordance with philosophical thinking in which they reflects a person's perception. In other words, they are the events that explain <u>individuals</u>' worldly experiences. Phenomena can get someone excited about the topic at hand, marveling about the true <u>wonder</u> of its origins. They can also be tangible or intangible. But our phenomena can be distorted by an array of outside <u>influences</u>. Do you let others instruct you how to look at phenomena? Do you have an ideal vacation spot or destination that allows you to look at phenomena more in depth?

**Philistine**: A philistine is a narrow-minded person with very ordinary tastes and ideas. He or she is not interested in <u>culture</u> and <u>learning</u>. What do you think these kinds of people miss out on when they turn their backs on culture and learning? Are their <u>lives</u> in some way stagnant and <u>empty</u>? Do you try to encourage others to learn?

**<u>Philosopher, Philosophy</u>**: Philosophy entails a unique way to look at the world, highlighted by <u>knowledge</u>, reality, and existence. Some believe that philosophy is only possible for those with doctorate degrees and professorships. But is that really the case? What <u>questions</u> do they ponder? What keeps you from pondering the same kinds of questions they do, and why shouldn't you think about them in the same way?

**Phobia**: A phobia is a strong or unreasonable fear of something. What are you afraid of? Don't we often <u>waste</u> <u>time</u> and <u>energy</u> on strong and irrational <u>fears</u> when it would serve us better to let go of these fears and <u>focus</u> on positive endeavors? How can you overcome your fears?

**Physical, Physically, Physiology**: Being physical relates to the body and other senses. So much in life is governed by our physical limitations. We are, after all, physical beings <u>limited</u> by our ability to act only within a certain body. Age further hinders us by <u>damaging</u> that <u>body</u>, sometimes making mobility and thought more difficult. The longer we <u>live</u>, the more we <u>learn</u>. Learn to enjoy youth and physical agility while you still have it, and take care of your body—you won't regret it later.

**Piety**: Piety is the condition of being pious or devoted in one's religious following. Piety can also be interpreted, however, as <u>loyalty</u> and a sense of <u>duty</u> to one's <u>family</u> or parents. Don't let piety blind you. Toward what are you pious? Do you feel a sense of duty toward your family or your god?

**Pity**: If someone has pity, they feel sorrow toward others. Pity is a <u>virtue</u>; it demonstrates <u>compassion</u> and shows that you have <u>empathy</u> for others. But be careful not to give pity where it is unwelcome. Are you able to discern when it is unwelcome or is feeling pity for others strictly in your nature?

**Placate**: To placate someone is to stop them from being angry, while making them peaceful and soothed. But where can placating make some people <u>passive</u> where they should be active instead? Be wary of those placating who seek to soothe you where you are righteously <u>angry</u>. They may have an ulterior motive as to why they're placating you.

**Place**: A place holds a particular position in space. Everything has its <u>right</u> place, but few know exactly where to place them. Larger questions arise when it comes to finding your own place in <u>life</u>, where you truly belong and can be <u>happy</u> and useful. What can help you find your place—deep soul searching, introspection, and asking others?

**Plan**: A plan consists of a formula or proposal for achieving something. Every life needs a plan, even if that plan ends up ultimately <u>changing</u>. What is your plan, and what <u>motivates</u> your eventual <u>goals</u> and purpose? Is your plan plausible? Have you thought it through? Have you had to change your plan because of <u>obstacles</u> you've confronted in life?

**Planet**: Planets orbit around a star. Many take our planet for granted without realizing just how <u>important</u> it is for everything we do. How can you show your <u>respect</u> for our planet by reducing your carbon footprint? How can you reduce <u>waste</u> and be more <u>efficient</u> in what you use and produce? How can you describe the mark you leave on the planet?

**Plant**: A plant is a living organism, and its types include trees, shrubs, and herbs. We depend on plants not only for sustenance, but for the very <u>oxygen</u> we breathe every day. Yet how do we repay and preserve this incredible dependence? <u>Treat</u> plants with the same <u>respect</u> you would anyone on whom your <u>life</u> depended.

> *"Don't judge each day by the harvest you reap but by the seeds that you plant."*
> — *Robert Louis Stevenson*

**Plea, Plead**: A plea is a cry for help by someone who cannot help themselves. Who has pleaded with you for your <u>pity</u> in the past, and did you <u>help</u> them? Watch carefully for the pleas of others in subtler forms as well; not everyone who needs help will be so direct as to simply ask for it. Be careful to avoid manipulation by those who would play on your pity.

**Pleasant, Pleasing, Pleasure**: When something is pleasant, it provides satisfaction or enjoyment. What do you derive pleasure from? What some may find pleasant, others only find troublesome and obnoxious; it is always a matter of <u>taste</u>. Perhaps more importantly is to be aware of the <u>power</u> of pleasant things to hide from us the negative aspects of certain institutions and of <u>life</u> more generally. Seek pleasure when you need it because pleasure will always deter you from your <u>goals</u>. Do you let life's pleasure's get in the way of hard work and delayed gratification?

**Plentiful**: When something is plentiful, it exists in abundant quantities. We live in a time and place where <u>resources</u> are plentiful, but just because we have these resources does not mean that everyone is as lucky as us. How might our plentiful resources actually be damaging? For example, think about the plentiful <u>nature</u> of junk food, which now leads to our nation's skyrocketing obesity. How might the ease of plentiful lives rob us of our ability to work hard and efficiently?
Avoid waste in the face of plenty.

**Plutocrat**: A plutocrat is a person who has power over others because of his or her wealth. <u>Money</u> and those who have it run our <u>society</u>, but how can we put a stop to this? How much of our current <u>government</u> is plutocracy masquerading as democracy? How can we limit the <u>influence</u> of the rich on our government? How can we increase the transparency of the government so that the flow of money is clear to the <u>public</u>?

**Poignant**: To be poignant is to possess a sense of sorrow and regret. We often find the most poignant moments in the simplest things, like listening to the rain or walking on the beach. Where can you find poignancy in your <u>life</u> where you might have overlooked it previously? Finding poignancy in the miniscule moments of life can lead to a new point of view and a greater <u>appreciation</u> of things.

> *"Loyalty to country ALWAYS.*
> *Loyalty to government,*
> *when it deserves it."*
> — *Mark Twain*

**Point:** Everyone finds themselves at a time in their lives when they ask themselves what the point of their <u>life</u> is and what the point of life more generally is as well. Have you ever found yourself asking this question? Could you find a <u>satisfactory</u> answer? While it is not apparent on the surface, everyone has a point in their life; it's just a matter of <u>finding</u> what that truly is. Avoid debate that has no point.

**Poison**: Poison is a substance that has the capability to kill or injury someone. Sometimes the poison ailing us in <u>life</u> is not as easy to <u>identify</u> as we would like it to be, nor does it come labeled as <u>toxic</u>. But little things may poison us without us even knowing it, which could be a life-changing experience for us. However, it is possible to take the necessary steps in avoiding poison. How do you avoid poisonous things in your life?

**Policy**: A policy is a course of action carried out by a governing body. Our <u>lives</u> are in a sense ruled by policy, whether those policies are our own or those of others. Policies need to be changed both from society's point of view and our own <u>personal</u> view in order to keep up with the current times. How have the policies of others <u>shaped</u> your own life, and how have you shaped your own policies to follow?

**Politic**: To be politic is to be wise and clever, perhaps even too clever or crafty. Beware of overly zealous politics who wish to <u>influence</u> you; they may not have your best <u>interests</u> at heart. Are you able to discern the difference between someone who is being genuinely politic and over the top?

**Politician**: A politician resides in government and makes decisions for the betterment of society. Some would argue that the words "public servant" are not in a politician's vocabulary. Politicians are a product engineered for mass appeal. What evidence have you seen to suggest that politicians may not have our best <u>interests</u> at heart? Think carefully before believing what politicians tell you, and know to the best of your <u>ability</u> what their <u>motives</u> are. Do I/you consider politicians to be shrewd, artful, <u>prudent</u>, or <u>judicious</u>? Has politics grown exponentially with populations to become a force (of <u>government</u>) within a <u>force</u> (of <u>cultural</u> enigmas) in the constants of life? Politics dominate every realm of our lives, whether we know it or not. They govern how we drive, park, and interact with others. Yet politics can be pernicious, exerting an undue <u>influence</u> where it should not. How can we avoid the undue influence of politics on our lives? Is such a <u>liberty</u> even possible in today's <u>society</u>? (See also: *A Day of Life: Moments in Time* and *Corporacracy*)

**Politics:** Politics are an area of government that presides over debate or conflict between parties. Politics dominate every realm of our lives, whether we know it or not. They <u>govern</u> how we drive, how we park, how we interact with others as well. Yet politics can be pernicious, exerting an undue <u>influence</u> where they should not. Is this because of the media-driven society we live in? How can you avoid the undue influence of politics on your life? Is such a <u>liberty</u> even possible in today's <u>society</u>? Are you informed of the effect politics has on you?

**Pollutant**: To contaminate with the aid of harmful substances. Think about the pollutants currently swarming our environment. They are doing much more harm than good, as entire cities have been rendered dangerous because of their pollution; surely this should be one of our greatest priorities as we continue. What more could we do to prevent them, and why haven't we done more already?

**Pomposity**: Feeling a sense of entitlement and solemnity. Do not be fooled by the pomposity of others; it is a show that is meant to boost their own ego and hide their own insecurity. The pompous display of self-importance is almost always the indicator of vapidity and self-doubt. Do you have several interactions with those who are pompous? How do you handle them?

> *"There are people in the world so hungry, that God cannot appear to them except in the form of bread."*
> *— Mahatma Gandhi*

**Poor**: Lacking enough money to live comfortably. The idle remarks of the rich are taken as maxims of wisdom by the poor. Being poor signifies the lack of something, mainly attributed to money. The poor in this world are among the most disenfranchised. Do our current policies add to their plight, or do we try to empower them? Do I/ you stigmatize the poor? How can their voice in society be heard? Is being poor a stepping stone to depression and despair? What could help lessen inequality? Ask yourself the following: If I am poor, can I adjust to the lack of some things and innovate out of necessity? How do I treat the state of poorness? Am I rich in terms of money and poor in terms of wisdom and knowledge, or vice versa? What do I make of the term "poor in spirit?"

[A POOR SPIRIT IS POORER THAN A POOR PURSE]

**Populace, Population**: the populace is the general public, including everyone in a certain place or country. We each define ourselves in relation to a certain group. This then prompts certain characteristics to be attributed to a certain group in which others make their judgments and assumptions based on each group's identity. What does your populace say about you? What populace are you a part of? What do we owe the populations of which we are a part? Does the population have a voice in governance, or do leaders ponder in their marketing without following through?

**Populous**: A populous area is one that is densely populated and crowded. Sadly, some of the most populous places in the world are also the poorest, being overcapacitated with people, animals, noise and waste. Will it take population control to bring order? Have places on Earth reached critical mass? As the world's population begins to skyrocket, how can we help those in less fortunate places, especially those suffering from overpopulation?

**Portray**: To portray means to depict or represent something or someone in a particular way. People have portrayals of us, and we have portrayals of others, all of which allows everybody to form their opinion of the individuals around them. In our society, the media is supposed to portray news and events in an unbiased and complete fashion for the public to accurately detect what is going on throughout the world, but many outlets fall short of this expectation. Why does the media do this? Is it because they're lazy and don't want to put in the extra work of educating citizens? How do you portray someone? Do you do it in a kind fashion that will positively reflect on you?

**Pose:** When someone poses, they are arranging themselves in a particular attitude or position. Beware those who strike a pose instead of acting genuinely. For some, life is a series of poses, each one struck to appease the opinion of others. Moreover, some don't exhibit a constant pose, which leads others to hold a strong misconception of one's attitude and character. Can you tell the difference between a sincere interaction with someone and a strident pose?

> *"Be thankful for what you have; you'll end up having more. If you concentrate on what you don't have, you will never, ever have enough."*
> *— Oprah Winfrey*

**Positive:** Showing little to no turn out. A positive attitude attractive quality in a person. positive is that you start to see How can we change our doubt about how things will can sometimes be the most Another benefit of being the good in every situation. thinking to be more positive even when circumstances would compel us to think about the negative? Thinking positively can have an enormous impact on our mind-set and, research shows, perhaps even our health. If positive is good, is negative bad?

**Possess:** To possess something means you have ownership over it. There are countless possessions that are worthless to covet, so do not allow yourself to be defined by what you possess. Possessions are just a mere facet of earthly existence and never as important as we would like to believe. Those in pursuit of more possessions will never have enough, while those content with their lot will find true happiness. At the same time, some possessions are needed. Is possession just a temporary phenomenon? Are you possessed by irrational thoughts? What do you own?

**Possibility, Possible:** An event that could happen and possesses some sort of feasibility. We may never know what's possible until we try something we're not sure can be done. Possibilities remain until someone has the courage to actualize them and believe they can become reality. The more realistic you see a possibility, the more inept you are to evoke the nature of that possibility with more passion and drive. What have you been too afraid to try in your life? What are you doing to actualize that possibility?

**Posture:** Posturing is the way we present ourselves to others. Many posture in life, afraid of what a genuine representation of themselves would bring. Display your posture with the utmost confidence and dignity, knowing that you can be comfortable to your own skin. Can you tell the difference between posturing and genuine people? Do you find yourself posturing a certain way to try to fit in with a certain group of people?

**Potential:** When someone or something has potential, it equates to the capacity of achieving or developing something in the future. Some have a higher ceiling for potential than others but, nonetheless, we are all equipped with it, which allows us to be the best person possible in whatever facet we decide to develop. Do you feel that you have unlimited potential or are there limits?

**Poverty:** Poverty relates to those who are poor and live in undesirable living situations. Poverty affects billions on earth, depriving them of any chance to flourish in their environment. Poverty affects even the national infrastructure as well; impoverished citizens are less likely to be well educated and skilled. This puts them at an inherent disadvantage, as they have a difficult time thriving under their current circumstances and are not afforded the same privileges as others. Is this because of their own doing or their surroundings? What excuse do we have for doing nothing while others suffer in poverty? How can the inequality be righted?

**Power**: Those that hold power in society have the ability to direct and influence others around them. Some thirst after power over others, while some simply yearn for power in their own lives. You have to be able to discern the difference as to when to stand up to someone with power and when to retreat. Where do you have power, and where is it out of your hands? Where does power belong in difficult situations, and how can you regain it? When should power lie with you and when with God?

**Practice, Practitioner**: Putting an idea or principle into play. No habit will come without practice, and no routine will become normal without constant implementation. Everything must be practiced if you wish to perform at the highest level. Do you find it difficult to practice something when your interest level is not that high? On the flip side, is something easier to practice if you're passionate and enthralled about a given topic?

> *"Freethinkers are those who are willing to use their minds without prejudice and without fearing to understand things that clash with their own customs, privileges, or beliefs. This state of mind is not common, but it is essential for right thinking..."*
> — *Leo Tolstoy*

**Pragmatic**: To act pragmatically is to act practically and logically. If you wish to be pragmatic, you have to think outside the box and think about things in an unconventional manner that will yield success. While not all things are a matter of pragmatism, where could we implement more pragmatism in our lives? Can pragmatism be utilized in every aspect of our lives, or are some things delegated to easier thinking than others?

**Praise**: Praise can be displayed through an approval for what others do; it can be seen as a way of congratulating one another. The way of this world is to praise dead saints and persecute living ones. Some are addicted to praise, needing it to maintain their self-esteem. Others shun praise instinctively, terrified of appearing arrogant. Which are you? Accepting praise is not a terrible thing, but let your sense of self rest on your own self-appraisal and not the flattery of others. What is your criterion for praising someone? What do you consider acceptable criterion when people praise you?

**Prayer**: Prayer is most evident when you need a call for help or want to express thanks to a religious figure. While prayer can help bring resolution to your issues or concerns, it can also give you a sense of greater belief that your problems will subdue, even if they don't in the end. The healing power of prayer is only as effective as you believe it will be. What does this say about the power of belief? Do you predicate praying or prayer on religion? Do you consider praying simply as a form of communicating with a deity? Since praying can be construed as asking, imploring, and beseeching, what is your motive—desperation, fear, gain, salvation, control over others, or betterment? What is your best way to (start) praying? Is there an ideal time or place for prayer, and does anything inhibit it?

*A Prayer for All Faiths*

*Our Holy Spirit, who exists as a deity in another dimension which we cannot comprehend, hallowed be thy force. Make us aware of life under God's constants and help us (to) overcome the opposing forces of evil. Grant (us) an understanding of sustenance in coexistence with all life(forms). Instill a universal love that accepts forgiveness, and inspire us to use our minds with clarity.*

**Preconception:** A preconception is "a preconceived idea or prejudice;" something that hasn't been thought out and does not include evidential information to prove validity. There are preconceptions about <u>race</u>, <u>religion</u>, <u>politics</u>, sexual orientation, geography, and so much more. Preconceptions are an easy way to state your <u>opinion</u> without having to do the extra work of finding evidence and <u>facts</u> that back up your claim. Where our <u>society</u> runs into <u>problems</u> is when people don't feel the need to correct their misconceptions about the aforementioned area, meaning they don't bother looking in depth as to why their opinion is the way it is. It's important to think before you speak, especially about <u>sensitive</u> issues. Why do people feel the need to hold preconceptions? Do you hold more preconceptions than you probably should?

**Predict**: To predict something means you envision or estimate what will happen in the future. No one can predict the <u>future</u>, but we can still guess the likely outcomes of certain events. How can prediction protect against bad choices? Being able to make <u>decisions</u> based on possible outcomes is a part of reaching <u>maturity</u>, but never forget that no future is set in stone. Do you like to predict things in life so as to give you comfort within your own <u>control</u> for what will happen next? Why do others predict things in their lives?

**Preface**: A preface is similar to a preamble: an introductory note meant to contextualize what follows. Every individual has their own preface, filled with <u>experiences</u>, <u>emotions</u>, etc. Our country has its own preface, established many generations ago, but does our <u>society</u> take this as verbatim even as the times continue to change? Would it be in the best interest to change our own and society's preface to stay modern? (See also: Preamble)

**Prejudice, Prejudicial:** Prejudice often comes from misunderstanding what is unfamiliar to us, but it can also easily come from self-love and our own <u>pride</u>. We sometimes believe ourselves to be more <u>capable</u> or intelligent than others, and therefore be prejudiced against them for it, but there is no proof for this assumption. When in life has your pride blinded you with prejudice? In what context is it even acceptable to be prejudice?

**Prelacy, Prelate**: A prelate is a high-ranking member of the clergy, such as a bishop. These individuals are given a considerable amount of <u>power</u> to wield within that church's <u>structure</u>, but some may wonder whether they wield that power as righteously as they should. After all, the church has hardly had a history of impunity—think of Martin Luther's ninety-five theses, the selling of indulgences, and the more recent sex abuse scandals. Do you need the advice of these officials in your relationship with <u>God</u>? Can you have a comfortable relationship with God without the presence of a prelate?

**Preliminary**: Preliminary events lead up to the main action, acting as a kind of introduction to what <u>follows</u>. Preliminary events almost always affect the secondary ones, though these <u>relationships</u> are hardly ever a simple cause and effect. How have the events leading up to your <u>life</u> today affected your life as you now know it? Do you place high emphasis on the preliminary events with the intuition that it will have a greater difference on those that precede it?

**Prelude**: The prelude is the part that comes before or leads up to what follows. Like the preliminary events leading up to the main ones, a prelude serves an introductory <u>purpose</u>. Where can you find metaphorical preludes in your own <u>life</u>—events that lead up to later ones or introduced a certain lifestyle that you would later <u>adapt</u>?

**Premature:** A thing that is premature happens before the usual or proper time; it is too early or hasty. Think carefully before attempting something for which you are not sure you're ready; you may regret it later. Think everything through in the best way possible so as to avoid this regret. When have you attempted something prematurely, not learning until later that you were not ready for the task? Do you feel rushed when making a decision, leading you to decide prematurely?

**Premeditate:** To premeditate is to think ahead, know beforehand what you will do, or to have a plan. A good deal of misfortune in life could be avoided if we all premeditated our actions and planned them out to the fullest extent. When have you acted without thinking, when premeditation would have done you good? What are some of the things that you premeditate about?

**Premise:** A premise is a statement or belief that is taken for granted and is used as the basis for a theory or argument. Each individual has their own premise on how they should live their life under certain situations and circumstances. An examination of these premises may lead to a reevaluation of your beliefs. Oftentimes, we fail to realize just how influenced we are by intangible and illogical forces, such as cultural and familial pressures. Yet in the end, we must decide for ourselves what our beliefs are, decide their premises, and take responsibility for them. What premises underlie your most deeply held beliefs?

**Premonition:** A premonition is a feeling that something bad will happen or a forewarning. Largely, premonition is followed by anxiety and fear of what the future will bring us, which is justifiable because little is concrete enough to yield a true positive thinking. Are gut feelings meant to be trusted? How can we tell the difference between irrational anxiety and a premonition forewarning us of real harm?

**Preparation, Prepare:** When one prepares something, you take part in the process of getting it ready to the best of your ability. Any plausible plan needs preparation, and a failure to prepare is only preparation for failure. If you take the time to be diligent and thorough in your preparation, the goal or intended outcome will be extremely desirable; it's a short-term hurdle for a long-term gain. What have you done to prepare for the major events in your life, such as finding a job, getting a promotion, or starting a family? What research and planning can you do now to prevent disaster later?

**Preponderant, Preponderate:** The preponderant party is greater in number, power, importance, etc. Due to this power, they feel a certain obligation to hold this up by exerting confidence in getting what they and the citizens want. Do preponderant individuals take this power to a greater extent than what is actually needed? Who is the preponderant party in this country? The preponderant class? Isn't it strange that the class larger in population isn't the most powerful, i.e., the lower class? How can we correct this power imbalance and make the preponderate group reflect the voice of the people?

**Prescribed:** A prescription is a rule or direction to be followed. Often we are given prescriptions by doctors, bent on making us well. But what prescriptions could give ourselves to prevent being ill in the first place? Exercise, diet? Are there too many prescribed entities that hold us back, even though others claim it can help you improve your life?

> "Only someone who is well prepared has the opportunity to improvise."
> — Ingmar Bergman

**Present:** The present is a period of time that exists right now as you read this encyclopedia. Oftentimes it's tough to live in the present because our past and future dictate so much of our time, but the present is gone in an instant, compared with the time periods before and after it. Find a quiet spot and think about your life in the current moment, rather than dwell on what was or what will. How much do you think about the present? Do you ever find it difficult to do so?

**Presumptive, Presumptuous, Presuppose:** To presuppose something is to assume too early or decide before you know all the facts. We all take things for granted before we can possibly know what is right and will be best. Simply put, it's an easy path to go down, but we need to challenge ourselves to have the fullest amount of knowledge and information possible before jumping to any conclusions, which requires work. How can you avoid presupposition in your life and learn the patience to wait until you have all of the facts? Are you presumptive because you want quick action and resolution?

**Pretend, Pretender:** Someone who pretends puts on a fake appearance, suggesting one thing when in actuality, it does not hold true. Many walk through life pretending to be something they're not. Some do so because they feel the force of social pressure, others because they cannot decide who they are or want to be. Can you tell the difference between pretenders and the real thing? Do you pretend to be someone you're not when you're in a different social setting?

**Pretense, Pretension:** A pretense is a claim, usually false, and a pretentious person holds on to that pretense whether or not it is truthful or rightfully theirs to claim. For instance, a pretentious person claims to be very important, well educated, and rich, when they are in fact none of these things and have little hope to ever be. Why do individuals feel the need to act like this? Do you have colleagues, friends, or peers that are full of pretension?

**Prevalent:** Something prevalent exists or happens over a widespread area or is common. For instance, a belief can preside over a city, a state, or even an entire country. Beliefs can become so prevalent that we forget that they're even beliefs; they become a part of our social fabric, a part of what we think is fact. We get into a habit of thinking everything as fact rather than truly being able to distinguish why something is prevalent. Can you tell the difference between a belief that is simply widely held and actual fact? Why does something become prevalent?

**Prevent:** Preventing something means to stop or impede it from happening. There are a lot of factors that prevent us from carrying out daily tasks as well as those much greater in scope. Parents prevent their children from going to a friend's house because they want them to finish their homework. Teachers and professors prevent us from using technological devices because it yields distraction during their class. What is preventing you from achieving your life goals? What obstacles can you eradicate by removing certain factors from your life—certain people, habits, or behaviors?

**Pride:** Pride is a vanity, an opinion of oneself that is too high. Pride can be a very positive attribute, as it shows you take ownership of your work and feel good about this. However, pride can interfere with relationships, making others feel that they are essentially worthless. Have you been guilty

> *"The individual has always had to struggle to keep from being overwhelmed by the tribe. If you try it, you will be lonely often, and sometimes frightened. But no price is too high to pay for the privilege of owning yourself."*
> — *Friedrich Nietzsche*

of pride in the past? What ill-effects does this kind of self-love have for you later, and how does it affect how people view you?

**Primeval**: Something primeval is very old, even ancient. The primeval existed long before civilization, even before humans. When looking as something that is primeval, it's important to consider the context of the given era. Can you imagine what the world was like in its primeval state, free of pollution and human structures? How might we return it to something closer to that state?

**Principle**: A principle is a rule or truth upon which others are based. It is a rule for deciding how to behave, but it should not be viewed as an end-all, be-all for how to run your life. Principles should act as an intricate detail that makes up your overall character and how you want others to view you. What dictates how you behave, and where did your principles come from?

**Prioritize, Priority**: When you prioritize, you place high importance and emphasis on whatever you are dealing with. Everyone has priorities in life, though not everyone assembles them in the most logical way. What do you consider the most important thing in your life, and what are you willing to do to protect? Always remain conscious of your priorities and whether you're spending your time and energy where you should be; the unexamined life is doomed to failure.

**Privacy**: Privacy equates to not being surrounded by the disturbance of others. Everyone deserves their own privacy; private time is a time for introspection and to reflect on yourself, others, and your actions. Do you always respect the privacy of others, especially those you are close to? Is privacy still respected to the degree it used to be, or has the filtration of the Internet caused privacy to collapse?

**Privation**: A privation is a deprivation of things sorely needed. Billions live in desolate privation, but little is done to improve the situation. What can you do to extend your comfortable circumstances to the lives of others? Is this difficult for you to carry out?

**Privilege**: Those who have privilege have a special advantage that is only granted to a select group of individuals. Often we are blind to just how privileged we are, taking for granted the things that many others don't have. For instance, think of all the hygienic and cooking amenities in your home—an oven, shower, stove, faucet, etc.—and think about how many people are bereft of such luxuries. The ease of our lives can make us complacent. But we should let it move us to give to others. Additionally, we should be filled with gratitude for what we have, never considering that our privilege is something we are simply owed. Do you recognize your own privilege, or do you take it for granted?

**Probability**: When assessing the probability of an event, there is a likelihood and prospect of that event happening. We can never know for certain the outcomes of most situations, but we can usually develop some sense of the probability of many situations. Have you found that the probability you assign to something is either accurate or not in hindsight? Do you consider both the possibilities and the probabilities before making a decision?

**Problem**: A problem is a situation that has less desirable circumstances that may be difficult to overcome. He who has the least problems in life will be adept at anticipating and analyzing problems before they occur. Factors like disruption, tiredness, ill health. economic problems, and ecological problems all bring on larger ill effects that perpetuate conflict, anger, argument, and crime. Before you can ever expect or hope to get relief from a problem, you must first understand the driving force behind the problem. Take note of the problems in your life. Problems do not disappear or go away; you have to face a problem. They can fade or camouflage themselves, only to surface later on. How many of them have been your own doing? Poor decisions often create problems, either through willfully destructive behavior or ignorance. How can you make an effort to avoid <u>decisions</u> which create problems? How can you <u>improve</u> your ability to foresee problems before they occur?

**Process:** A process is an accumulation of events taken in order to achieve a particular outcome. You can't reach a <u>goal</u> if you slack during the process of trying to <u>achieve</u> it. In fact, the process requires far more work than the actual outcome itself, as it dictates you to pay close attention to <u>detail</u>, among other <u>tasks</u>. What process are you involved in right now? Have you found yourself looking ahead to your intended goal and therefore minimizing the process?

*"You may delay, but time will not."*
— *Benjamin Franklin*

**Procrastinate:** When we procrastinate, should we ask ourselves "why?" Does a procrastinator <u>understand</u> that the action of putting off or delaying something can become <u>habitual</u>? Are you <u>aware</u> of its effect on others? What does it do to your <u>character</u>? Do you <u>observe</u> procrastinators in a different light? If procrastination involves <u>choice</u> because of the number of tasks at hand, do you know how to <u>prioritize</u>? Do you <u>gain</u> or <u>lose</u> by procrastinating, and does it vary depending on circumstance?

**Procure:** To procure something is to obtain it for yourself and your own purposes. Some things are easier to procure than others. But perhaps the real <u>question</u> lies in the <u>motivation</u> behind your procurement. Why do you pursue the things you do in life?

**Produce, Productive:** To produce something means to cause it to happen or for it to come to fruition. Vegetation, films, and meals are produced. There's always a <u>result</u> when it comes to producing something. Yet the extent is predetermined by how productive and <u>effective</u> you are throughout. What do you produce? Whether it's a big or small project, how much <u>work</u> do you put in?

**Profane, Profanity**: Profanity is the effort of a very feeble mind to express itself forcibly. Have you ever <u>resorted</u> to profanity when other means of speech might have been more <u>effective</u>?

**Profess**: To profess something is to proclaim it out into the open. It is to make clear what was before hidden. Many times we go to the grave never having professed what we most wanted to say during our lifetimes. It may be because we were afraid of how others <u>react</u> to it. It can also be due to the fact that we never felt we had an <u>opportune</u> time to profess something pressing. What do you have sitting on your chest that you'd like to get off? Do you profess things that shouldn't necessarily be professed in certain situations?

**Profession**: A profession is a paid occupation. We hope to find a profession that <u>inspires</u> a <u>passion</u> in us or at the very least offers us a secure living. This is the American <u>dream</u>— social mobility, meritocratic advancement, and rewards for hard work. But how many people truly find that kind of fulfillment in <u>society</u>'s current state? What are your ideal characteristics of a profession?

**Professor**: Professors are first and foremost teachers; they <u>educate</u> the <u>minds</u> of the youth in this nation. They are meant to push us beyond our initial educational limits and expand them to the greatest extent to bring about achievement and <u>success</u>. But are they currently being given the <u>respect</u> and <u>resources</u> they deserve? What consequences do the recent cutbacks on higher education have for professors and students they teach, and how can we correct the inequality?

**Profit, Profitable, Profiteer**: When you make a profit, money is at the forefront. The goal of all companies is to make a profit, but what about the goals of all people? You certainly profit from living your life the right way, but this profit is much more intangible and difficult to grasp. What happens when people take on the goals of companies and become consumed by greed? How can we shift our focus from profits and on to the things that really matter in life?

**Progress, progression**: To make progress is to make a forward movement in space or time toward a destination or goal. As time has moved forward, progress has been made in a wide variety of realms. Racism has progressed from the horrible era of the 1960s. Homosexuals are being allowed to marry after being completely shunned from society.

> *"Without deviation from the norm, progress is not possible."*
> — *Frank Zappa*

Progress takes collective effort; it cannot be accomplished by a singular entity, even if it is on a much lesser scale than the aforementioned events. For yourself, what activities/issues have you helped progress? Did you feel that it made an impact?

**Promise**: When you make a promise with someone and vice versa, you expect the result that was agreed upon to go into effect. However, that doesn't always happen. You show respect to another individual when you give them a promise but when you break that promise, does that equate to a lack of respect? Do you try to make a lot of promises to your friends or acquaintances? Is it difficult to keep these promises?

**Proposal, Propose, Proposition, Propound**: A proposal is a suggestion that needs the approval of others to be put into action. Proposals can take many forms and function in relation to a variety of different things. For instance, there are marriage proposals, but also business proposals and building proposals. Proposals must be honest, however; only with clarity and awareness can we make well-informed decisions about the proposals made to us. Are your proposals well intentioned? Do you observe proposals with clarity?

**Protect, protection**: Protecting someone or something means you keep it from harm or injury. It's not easy to protect someone or be protected; it takes courage and will to stand up in the face to fear. This is why we have others in our society to take the leap of faith to protect our world and all its beautiful features. Have you ever protected someone or been a source of protection for someone else? Was it difficult?

**Protest**: To protest means professing your disapproval or objection toward someone or something. Oftentimes we tend to protest by using physical or verbal violence. We let our emotions get the best of us without thinking rationally about the situation at hand. Altogether, protesting can be a great avenue in raising awareness about a particular issue, but it needs to be constructive. Have you ever protested? Were you able to not let your emotions reign supreme?

**Protocol**: Protocols are put in place to tell us the acceptable manners and forms in official dealings. Though knowing these protocols is useful in helping us navigate difficult situations and cultural barriers, how might these protocols become stifling and inhibit genuine interaction? Do you live your life by society's protocol or your own?

**Protract**: To protract is to prolong and draw out; it is to procrastinate. What can be done in the current moment can certainly be done at a later time—at least that's what protractile individuals think. When do you protract your duties when you know you shouldn't and they could be done more quickly?

**Prove**: Everyone has something to prove in an attempt to demonstrate the truth. We grow up with insecurities about how we look, act, achieve, and it often seems that the only way to squelch these insecurities is to always try to prove to other people that we are not deficient in the areas we _fear_ ourselves to be. But can we ever prove to everyone what we wish to? What might be gained by instead pursuing a healthy regard for ourselves, independent of the standards and judgments of others?

**Provide**: When something is provided, it is done to make the entity available for us. You can provide something out of the goodness of your heart, making it a priority for it to flourish, or it can be something you simply do. Regardless, be thankful for what has been provided to you. What have you been provided over the last year? Was it extremely worthwhile, or did you not even think twice of the act?

**Prudent**: Being prudent means showing care and cautiousness for the future. Someone who is prudent doesn't advance to the future in a rush; rather, they take the time and effort to collect as much information as possible for a future purpose or event. Am I/you wise in practical matters, or are we all too careful for our own interests? Should we be concerned about our own conduct and aware of potential consequences?

**Psychic**: A psychic cannot be explained by natural or physical laws; they are laws unto themselves, touched by the supernatural. Often we like to dismiss the psychic as impossible because we do not understand it, but there are hidden messages and lessons that we can derive from a psychic. What are we ignoring that we could learn more about? Do we ignore psychics because they are stigmatized by society?

**Psychoanalysis**: This is a method of treating certain mental illnesses by helping the patient understand unpleasant memories that have been forced into the unconscious. It is difficult to revisit the most terrifying events and experiences in your life, but looking internally combined with external help can help you overcome these obstacles and struggles. Though psychoanalysis has lately fallen out of fashion, what could it tell us about psychology today?

**Psychological, Psychology:** Thinking psychologically arises from your mental senses. Everything comes back to psychology and the psychological; we could understand everything about society if we understood how the individual brain worked. Psychology explains why we do the things that we do. It even explains why we act or think in certain ways. What do you think you could gain from a basic knowledge of psychology? If you would have been taught psychology, how would your life be different?

**Psychopath**: a psychopath is a person with a mental illness, especially one who does cruel or criminal acts without feeling sorry or guilty. Psychopaths lack the empathy common to other people, instead having only a self-interested regard. While psychopaths are usually uncommon in everyday occurrences, where do you occasionally see people acting in their own self-interest, or not feeling guilty when they clearly should?

> *"To be independent of public opinion is the first formal condition of achieving anything great."*
> — *Georg Wilhelm Friedrich Hegel*

Why do people continue to fear psychopaths? Is it the uncertainty of psychopath's mental makeup?

**Psychosomatic**: a psychosomatic disease exists only in our head, all physical symptoms imagined. These kinds of diseases show how much influence the mind can have over the body—even to the point where it convinces itself something is hurting when nothing is wrong. What does this say about the power of thought? If we can think ourselves ill, does that mean that we can think ourselves well again?

**Psychotherapy**: Psychotherapy treats mental illness through professional counseling. Its proponents seem to suggest that problems of the mind can be eased through talking. What problems do you have that you think could be eased through discussion? Who do you have to talk to that you can trust? Is it constrained by the social stigmas of race, gender, and religion?

**Public**: The public is the people as a whole; it is the entity of people that make up society. The public is a strange animal. In some circumstances, it can come together to produce enormous change for the greater good, but in other situations, it can create a mob mentality that is almost assuredly damaging and dangerous to other people. The government's job is to manage the public, acting in their best interest, but also acting as a representative of their collective will. Do you think our government performs this task effectively on day to day basis? How could their work be better, and how could we facilitate that betterment?

**Publicize, Publicity**: Publicity is not a spontaneously occurring event; it comes with incredible cultivation done by public relations specialists, intent on creating a certain public perception and excitement. Their outstanding intent is to sell eyeballs instead of focusing on the true message of the content that will affect individuals. Have you ever been manipulated by publicity, or have you ever given into media hype?

**Public Opinion**: Public opinion is held by the people generally. It is meant to reflect how the majority thinks and what everyday people are thinking. Public opinion is a force that brings about social and political action; politicians care perhaps more than anyone about public opinion and the force it has on their campaigns. Is public opinion skewed at all? Do we get the biggest representation possible to form a solid conclusion aside from bias?

**Purport**: To purport something is to make a claim or to mean something, often falsely. Purporting documents or whatever is at hand can be done on small or a grand scale that yields extreme punishment. Whom do you know has purported things falsely in the past? Like pretending and pretension, falsely purporting some facet of identity is always a hollow act, done by the shallow and working only on feeble minds.

**Put**: To put something away is to place it where it belongs; it is to put something in its right place. Do you feel as if you have been put where you belong or that you are in the right place? If you don't, what actions can you take to right the mistake?

# Q

**Quake**: To quake is to shiver and shake; in people, this is usually caused by an <u>emotional</u> state, while when the ground quakes, it is caused by <u>instability</u> underground. Do these two <u>definitions</u> seem <u>related</u> to you? Can we think of both <u>kinds</u> of quaking as being outward signs of a hidden instability? What are you afraid of enough to cause you to quake? How do you bring yourself under <u>control</u>?

*There was once a seismologist in San Francisco who used to bellow out fearful rants about how the ground was constantly moving beneath our feet and that at any moment it could collapse and swallow us all. He literally quaked when he talked about quakes. He was asked, "How can you possibly fear that which you study?" He responded, "On the contrary, I study that which I fear." We can only fear what we do not know. The next time you quake with fear, stare right into the face of the beast, study it, and overcome it.*

**Qualify:** To qualify for a position or <u>role</u> means to be <u>competent</u> in all the <u>aspects</u> it requires. One can also, however, qualify something one says, which means to soften a statement in order to make it less <u>extreme</u> or unpleasant. Do these two different <u>meanings</u> have anything in <u>common</u>? Does qualifying a statement make it more appropriate or just <u>weaker</u>? In what kinds of situations have you qualified your <u>ideas</u> to make them less extreme or at least to appear that way? Do you do so in order to please other people or because you <u>believed</u> it was the <u>responsible</u> thing to do? In terms of competence, do your <u>desires</u> regarding what you would <u>like</u> to do with your <u>life</u> match up with your qualifications to actually do it? What <u>steps</u> could you take or have you taken in order make sure you are qualified for what you <u>want</u>? Have you ever <u>limited</u> or <u>diminished</u> your <u>lifestyle</u> in the process of qualification? What <u>sacrifices</u> would you be willing to make?

**Quality**: A quality may either is <u>essential</u> to its <u>nature</u>, or 'something's excellence or lack between having qualities, in being of quality, in the second predominantly on the quality of a

> *"The happiness of your life depends upon the quality of your thoughts."*
> — Marcus Aurelius

be an aspect of an item that a measure of someone or thereof. Is there a relationship the first sense of the <u>word</u>, and sense? Does your <u>mind</u> focus product or merely the price? Do you <u>consciously</u> try to <u>improve</u> your quality of <u>life</u> and the lives of others? Is it possible to improve the quality of 'one's <u>character</u>, or is character unchangeable after a certain <u>age</u>? Is quality in <u>material</u> things more important than quality of character? Where do you look for quality, and how do you <u>measure</u> it? What is the quality of your creed?

**Qualm**: A qualm is a slight feeling of <u>guilt</u> or <u>anxiety</u>; the word originated from an Old English word for <u>death</u> or <u>disaster</u>. What <u>kinds</u> of situations or events give you qualms? How do you cope with them? Is it possible to turn our qualms into something <u>positive</u>?

**Quandary**: Quandaries are particularly difficult <u>problems</u>. Do you ever feel as though your life is simply one big quandary after another? What do you generally do when faced with a quandary? Is it possible to prepare for or <u>avoid</u> them? What <u>steps</u> can you take to turn a quandary into a new path ahead? How might the principles of clarity help you address them?

**Quarrel**: A quarrel is any kind of angry disagreement. Are they an inevitable part of life? Are quarrels always a negative thing, or can they be turned into a positive? Does airing our true feelings during a quarrel help relationships or harm them? What kinds of opportunities might quarrels represent?

**Question**: To question is to seek world around us. The power and driven human existence and How does this work? Why does in the universe? What is the exists, how valuable is it to seek before turning to others? Do we answers on virtually everything? to responsibly ask questions have you fallen into the habit of question? Why would someone questions? Is there such a thing we don't want to know the

> *"Learn from yesterday, live for today, hope for tomorrow. The important thing is to not stop questioning."*
> — *Albert Einstein*

out more information about the magnitude of questions have progression for our entire history. this happen? Where are we key to happiness? If a question the answer within ourselves not form our own opinions or Do you feel that you remember about the things you observe, or accepting some things without be opposed to curiosity or to as a bad question or a question answer to? Is the culmination of

observations within these covers achieved through questioning? *Can you ultimately create your own creed for living life through the process of questions and answers in this encyclopedia?*

**Quick**: To be quick is to move with significant speed, either physically or mentally. What is the relationship between speed and skill? Must one always be able to perform a task quickly in order to be truly skillful at it? What kinds of danger are there in being too quick, and what might be gained by acting slowly? How can you become quicker at what you already do effectively? Do you give things the attention they deserve?

**Quiet**: Quietness can be either the complete absence of noise or a sound that is not very loud. All we ever wanted was a little bit of peace and quiet, right? Quietness is most certainly a double-sided coin. If you were to witness a crime in progress and you decided to stay quiet, to what extent would you be abetting that crime? Do the negatives and positives of quietness balance each other? How dependent are you on quiet when you're trying to relax or when you restrain yourself in a moment requiring tact and patience? Do you know when it is appropriate to be quiet and when it is not?

**Quit**: To give up, stop, or resign from doing something. How can we evaluate quitting as a positive or negative thing? By what standards do you examine the influence of what it is you are quitting on the way that you live your life? What are the relative impacts between, for example, quitting a bad habit and quitting a job or activity before its fruition? Have you ever quit before determining the impact of your doing so?

**Quote:** To repeat exactly the words of another. Using a quote to support your point is the equivalent of asking for outside help. Before you use a quote to make your point, are you careful to make sure you understand the context of the original quote and its original intentions? You would only call on someone to help you in an argument if they had the same views as you, right? How do dishonest individuals misuse quotes in order to portray situations inaccurately for their own benefit? Do you try to form your own ideas before you quote someone else? Do you trust quotes blindly or scrutinize their source and context? Are you careful when choosing your own words, given that you may at some point be quoted?

# R

**Race**: The concept of race divides humanity into different groups based on physical characteristics and ancestry; much racial division is arbitrary and culturally based. Do you think of people in terms of races or as mankind as a whole? When you consider your own sense of personal identity, is your race something that immediately comes to mind? Is it ever useful to think of people in terms of their races?

**Racism**: Racism is a form of prejudice that either privileges or penalizes people because of assumptions that their race makes them inherently better or worse than people of other races. Is it inherently interesting to us because of its simplicity—the ability to hate without rational thought? Is racism hate that is perpetuated by fear—fear of change, the unknown, and stereotypes rather than real people? To hate someone based on their genes is to reject an enormous portion of humanity as invalid. Do you invalidate your own credibility by subscribing to such irrationality? If you cannot explain your own prejudices, how can you rationalize your own self-worth? Have you encountered displays of racism, either directed toward yourself or someone else? Have you had racist thoughts yourself, even involuntarily? Is it possible to end racism, or will there always be this kind of prejudice as long as there are groups of people who look or act differently from one another?

**Rage**: To be enraged implies that you have lost control of yourself. If you do not have control of yourself, then what do you really have power over? Do you try to always be conscious of your emotions and try to think rationally? What are the risks and dangers of acting based on a feeling of rage? Can rage ever be productive, or is it too unpredictable to be harnessed? Do you control your emotions, or do your emotions control you?

> *"I have a dream that one day little black boys and girls will be holding hands with little white boys and girls."*
> — *Martin Luther King, Jr.*

**Raise**: To raise can be to supervise a living thing's growth and entrance into maturity, or simply to lift up. Do you perceive a relationship between these definitions? To what extent does the way you are raised dictate the way you think and act for the rest of your life? How were you raised? What about your childhood defines the way you behave today? What will you pass down when raising your children? Do you raise new ideas to the attention of others for scrutiny and scrutinize them yourself? What is beneficial about doing so?

**Rampage**: A rampage is a spree of violence, whether emotional or physical, often brought on by a cascade of emotional fury. Have you ever lost control of yourself to the extent of going on a rampage? Do you think rationally to prevent your emotions from boiling over? How do you react to others when they rampage themselves? Do you attempt to calm them, or simply avoid them? Can frequent rampages be symptomatic of deeper mental or social problems?

**Rankle**: To rankle is to irritate. What kinds of things rankle you? Do you avoid causing others emotional pain? Are you receptive to the feelings and needs of others? When you interact with other people, do you consider that what you say and do to them may have effects far beyond what you can predict?

**Rape**: Rape has different definitions depending on whether one is talking about rape as defined by law or not. Legally, rape is usually understood as being when one person forces another to engage in sexual acts against their will. Historically, rape was used to describe the act of abducting human beings, and outside the law, it can mean to destroy or steal; "The Rape of Europa," for example, is a phrase now associated with the theft of European art treasures by occupying Nazi forces during World War II. Do you believe that the significant part of rape is the violation of another person's body or the subjection of another person's will? Does the act of rape deny the victim's value as a person? Are there things we can do as individuals that help on a society-wide level to prevent or reduce rape? Do you think it is appropriate to use the word in other contexts—such as talking about feeling emotionally raped—or should using the word be reserved only for talking about the actual crime with which it is associated? What might be gained or lost by restricting or expanding the ways we use the word?

**Rapport**: Other words for rapport include correspondence, harmony, and affinity. Your rapport with your friends defines your relationship and reinforces existing bonds.

What level of importance do you place on connecting with others? What relationships do you have in which you and the other person hold mutual respect for each other and mutual trust? How important are these factors in helping those relationships to flourish? What kinds of strategies of communication do you use to build rapport? Do you hold up your end of the bargain in creating or maintaining harmonious relationships?

**Rapture**: Rapture is intense pleasure. How much focus do you put on the thrills in life, the pure joys and fountains of ecstasy? How do you make sure that when you search for such experiences, they are true? Have you experienced the fulfillment of writing a book, getting to know a person, or discovering a new hobby? There are many fountains of pleasure which only bring instant gratification devoid of lasting value. How do we recognize activities that sacrifice the future for the present?

**Rational:** When we describe a person or a decision as rational, we indicate that we believe that it is in line with the principles of logic. Do you do your best to act rationally? What kinds of forces or temptations in your life encourage irrational behavior? Have you ever had a positive result from an irrational decision you have made, or have they always turned out to be bad ideas?

**Rationale**: A rationale is the hopefully organized reason we use when putting together our thoughts in a logical way in order to reach a decision. Can you justify your actions with well thought-out decisions? Are you deciding based on emotion, selfishness, selflessness, or cold calculation? Is reasoning what makes us sentient? Do you have a common rationale for your decisions, or do you vary between compassion and coldness with each judgment? Are some rationales superior to others? Can rationales be evil, or does that cause them to be something else that 'doesn't deserve the label of rationale?

**Rationalize:** There are two major uses of this word, with nearly opposite meanings. It can mean the act of making

*"Talk sense to a fool and he calls you foolish."*
*— Euripides*

an unreasonable idea or situation conform to reason, but we more frequently use it to describe the mental process by which we pretend—often even to ourselves—that we are acting reasonably, when in <u>fact</u> we are acting according to more irrational or <u>emotional</u> desires. Have you been <u>guilty</u> of this second sense of rationalization, <u>twisting</u> <u>ideas</u> to fit a <u>personal</u> agenda? How can we best police ourselves to <u>avoid</u> doing so? What are the <u>possible</u> effects of rationalizing a situation, particularly if we do so <u>habitually</u>? Do you form negative <u>opinions</u> of others after realizing they are rationalizing their <u>actions</u> and <u>decisions</u>? How do you <u>think</u> rationalization affects 'others' views of you?

**Ravage**: To ravage is to destroy with reckless abandon or to devastate. Destruction often receives a bad name, but is it necessary in some cases? It is impossible to build anew without first destroying the old, but how do we <u>balance</u> that with the <u>importance</u> of preserving the past? How can we <u>judge</u> whether we are destroying carefully instead of carelessly? Can you <u>think</u> of a time when you were <u>controlled</u> in your destruction so that the burnt embers of the past only fertilized that which you sought to <u>grow</u>?

**Rave**: Very similar to "rage," but while to rage connotes a lack of <u>control</u> over one's entire body, to rave is to lack control over one's speech. Have you ever become so angry about a topic or at another <u>person</u> that you began raving? Do you try to be careful to <u>think</u> before you speak? What impact does <u>listening</u> to someone else rave have on you? Does it ever prompt you to listen more closely, or do you react by ignoring them until they begin acting more <u>rationally</u>?

**Re-**: When we see this prefix at the beginning of a word, it's often a good indication that it is <u>talking</u> about doing something again, as in reeducation or <u>reuse</u>. How important do you <u>judge</u> repetition to be? In what ways can it make things <u>better</u> or clearer? When does repetition turn into <u>redundancy</u>, and should we try to <u>avoid</u> that shift? Do you repeat words and <u>actions</u> in order to be careful or as a result of absentmindedness?

**Reach**: To reach can either mean to attempt to put something within one's grasp, or, in an apparent contradiction, it can mean to actually obtain what we <u>desire</u> or arrive at where we wanted to be. When you reach out for what you seek, do you try to <u>appreciate</u> the <u>journey</u> it <u>takes</u> you on? Have you ever discovered what you were looking for on your way to what you believed was your destination? Do you have the <u>confidence</u> to reach with <u>ambition</u>, or are you timid in the goals you set for yourself? Do you <u>allow</u> disappointment to discourage you from continuing to try? What are your ambitions? What steps are you taking to achieve your <u>goals</u>?

**React**: Reacting is simply any <u>action</u> we <u>take</u> in response to a <u>change</u> in our <u>environment</u>. Do you find that you have similar or <u>different</u> reactions than others when you encounter situations, <u>people</u>, and events? <u>Consider</u> the way that you interact with the <u>world</u>. Are you proactive, or have you allowed reaction to become your way of <u>life</u>? What might you <u>lose</u> by reacting to others rather than acting independently? Do you have a <u>responsibility</u> to react to others' <u>actions</u> rather than ignoring them?

<u>Read</u>: Reading is generally <u>thought</u> of as the ability to <u>interpret</u> written language, but can also apply to any <u>kind</u> of interpretation of signs; we can read a situation, or read a face, or read music. Would civilization have been <u>possible</u> without the ability to pass on <u>knowledge</u> through reading and <u>writing</u>? How would our <u>relationship</u> to <u>history</u> be <u>different</u> if we did not have access to the <u>words</u> of <u>people</u> from previous generations? Is it more valuable to you to be able to read the original words of others for their own sake or because they <u>give</u> you a foundation on which to build your own <u>thoughts</u>? How well read are you? Do you have anything to say that will be worth reading in a hundred years' time? Have

you considered reading as a product of one of the senses that form the basis of life? Are some kinds of writing evil or destructive? What kinds of things do you not enjoy reading? Why?

> *"The man who does not read has no advantage over the man who cannot read."*
> — *Mark Twain*

**Reality**: Reality is generally to fantasy or illusion—the are, rather than how they mistakenly believe them to be. existence when it is absolutely contend that reality only exists we feel is only electrical signals spoken about as being a contrast state of things as they actually appear to be or how we might Can we define the reality of our unique for each of us? Some in our heads and that anything sent to our brain as we dream endlessly; does this seem convincing to you? Others believe that we are unconsciously living within naive, preconceived limits on reality and that we are able to move mountains with our minds. Does this stance seem more appealing? Do you only accept what you can see, hear, touch, and taste? Do suggestions of a supernatural world make you uneasy? What is your reality, at this moment, in your world? Do you recognize and accept the subjective realities of others? *Can reality co-exist with God, religion, and spirituality?*

**Realize**: To realize can indicate either a sudden understanding of a situation or idea, or the achievement of what one strives for. Do you find either of these kinds of realization to be fulfilling or self-confidence boosting? Have you realized your potential? What is necessary for you to do so?

**Reason**: The human brain is trained to search for patterns in what we see and experience, a process we sometimes describe as reason. A reason can also be the grounds upon which we base our actions. Are you aware of a tendency to see the world in terms of **cause and effect**, driving you to look for the reason behind events? Do you find yourself asking the question, "Why did this happen to me?" Do you have difficulty imagining that you are not at the center of the world because you can only see it through your own eyes? When analyzing a situation, are you sure to reason with the facts before letting your emotions overcome you? Do you always use reason in your decisions? Do you utilize your full capacity in the intellectual process of seeking truth by using rational thought? Is there is a reason or purpose for every action? *If you have met people who do not respond to reason, what other factors seem to motivate them instead?*

**Rebound**: To rebound is to bounce back from an impact, both emotional and physical ones. Are you able to bounce back from the obstacles you encounter and continue toward your goals? Do you allow yourself to be slowed down when things get tough, or do you barrel through it and bounce back up when you are knocked down?

**Recall**: Recalling is to bring back, including bringing back memories. When you work to remember events, how clearly can you imagine them? Is it a realistic recall or one tinged with your own perceptions? How could you try to enforce accountability for yourself? How could you benefit from recalling painful memories, rather than trying to ignore them?

**Receive**: To receive is to have something come into one's possession, both positive and negative. When you receive a gift, do you feel obligated to return the favor, or is it taken as homage? Do you receive with gratitude, or do you take it for granted? Are you capable of receiving failure as a learning tool?

**Receptive**: Being receptive means being <u>open minded</u>. How does opening yourself to the <u>opinions</u>, <u>ideas</u>, and requests of others <u>help</u> you grow as a <u>person</u>? In order to truly progress as a society, is it necessary to <u>communicate</u> with one another and to <u>give</u> the same attention to the <u>thoughts</u> of others as you do your own? Can one be too receptive? What are the potential <u>dangers</u> and benefits of being open minded?

**Reciprocate**: Reciprocation means to return an <u>action</u> in <u>kind</u>. Do you <u>value</u> <u>proof</u> in your <u>relationships</u>? Do you <u>give</u> as much as you get? Do you follow the rules and criteria for <u>behavior</u> that you impose on others? What happens to a relationship when one party does not reciprocate appropriately? Are you careful to reciprocate generosity in all of its <u>tangible</u> and intangible forms? When it comes to bad behavior, do you reciprocate with more bad behavior, or do you express your <u>feelings</u> and <u>confrontation</u> about the problem behavior to an extent that is proportional to how much it upset you? Do you recognize that others observe and remember your <u>actions</u> just as you remember theirs?

> *"It is amazing what you can accomplish if you do not care who gets the credit."*
> — *Harry Truman*

**Recite**: Recitation involves <u>repeating</u> aloud something previously committed to <u>memory</u>. What have you committed to memory? How can being able to recite <u>information</u> prepare you for unexpected circumstances? Is it dangerous to rely too much on recitation rather than original <u>thought</u>?

**Reckon**: To reckon can be to count, to <u>judge</u>, or to believe something to be <u>true</u>. What <u>kinds</u> of estimations do you make in <u>life</u>, <u>consciously</u> or subconsciously? What kind of <u>rationale</u> do you use to make these judgments? Do you feel you are <u>aware</u> of your own priorities and <u>biases</u>? How do you make reckonings in your <u>life</u>?

**Reclaim**: Reclamation is to claim back something that was already once our property. If our <u>environment</u> is our <u>home</u>,

does that make it <u>sacred</u>? If we do not reclaim <u>waste</u> and strive to sustain ourselves more efficiently, what will the effects be on the environment? Do you properly reclaim the <u>waste</u> you produce?

**Recluse**: A recluse is someone who <u>chooses</u> to live away from <u>society</u>. <u>People</u> are social animals; is this why it is often seen as strange to shy away from others? Do you find it difficult to <u>interact</u> with others? How could you practice this <u>skill</u>? Is it <u>possible</u> for one's <u>comfort</u> zone to become too comfortable? Do you get out and experience the <u>world</u>?

**Recognition, Recognize:** Recognition is both to acknowledge someone or something one already <u>knows</u>, and to ac<u>knowledge</u> someone's work or <u>effort</u>. Do you have your hard <u>work</u> acknowledged regularly? Are you able to separate your <u>goals</u> from the sentiments and attention of others? Can you relish an <u>accomplishment</u> without recognition?

**Recommend**: When we recommend something or someone, we <u>decide</u> based on our <u>standards</u> and experiences that it is of sufficient <u>value</u> to be experienced by others. Do recommendations that we make to one another reflect our sentiments about the world? How high are your standards for recommendation?

**Reconcile**: Reconciliation is the act of making <u>different</u> things agree with one another, both objects and <u>people</u>. How important are closure and resolution to you? How do you reconcile your failures, painful experiences, and disappointments? How do you construct a view of the world for yourself? Do you ever find yourself rationalizing what has happened? How do you reconcile difficult events?

**Recover**: To recover can mean to get better after an accident or injury, or, more generally, to regain something that has been lost. When you fall down, do you focus on the fall or on getting back up? When in your life have you stumbled and fallen? How do you recover? Do you appreciate the importance of the recovery process?

**Recreation**: There are two different meanings of recreation—one refers to anything we do for enjoyment, and the other means to recreate and make something old new again. Do these two meanings seem related to you? How important is it to you to stay active? What is the impact on your body, mind, and spirit when you don't get enough recreation? Are you sure to use at least some of your time in a way that you enjoy? Do you work to live or live to work?

> *"Weekends don't count unless you spend them doing something completely pointless."*
> *— Bill Watterson*

**Rectify**: Rectification means to fix what has been broken, such as situations and relationships. When does it become necessary to make repairs to restore what once was? Do you waste time pointing fingers, or do you focus on recovering from such events and picking yourself back up?

**Recycle**: Recycling is using old materials for new purposes rather than processing entirely new products. Do you go further in recycling than just putting the right items in the right bins? Do you save yourself money and effort by reusing old materials in your home and by fixing up your old things? Do you try to recycle and resurrect old items before buying new ones? Do you consider the ways in which nature itself recycles, using things that die into preserving or creating other lives?

**Redemption**: One can redeem a promise—like one in the form of a ticket or a coupon—or redeem oneself by atoning for one's mistakes. How can you show yourself to be worthy of redemption? Do you learn from your mistakes? Do you teach others with what you've learned? When you err, is your first thought afterward about redeeming yourself?

**Reduce**: Reduction is the act of making something smaller. Is bigger always better? How could driving smaller cars and living in smaller homes benefit society as a whole? How can we reduce our degradation of the environment to preserve it for future generations to enjoy? Do you take steps to reduce your impact on the environment? Do you separate things in your life into the categories of needs and wants? What do you really need to survive, and what has been culturally constructed as a necessity?

**Redundant**: Redundant words are ones that are unnecessary because they are repetitive. Is redundancy an indication of a lack of originality? How can originality help prevent redundancy? Are you confident in your ability to express your thoughts accurately in on one try?

**Refer**: A referral involves directing someone toward their goal. When you are lost, what source of information do you refer to for guidance? Do you look to friends, family, coworkers, spiritual guides, books, or something else? What does being able to refer to someone or something allow us to do in life? What or whom do you refer to when lost?

**Refrain**: To refrain is to hold oneself back. In a new situation, are you more likely to learn more from <u>listening</u> than from <u>speaking</u> right away? How does being able to <u>control</u> your <u>actions</u> encourage others to <u>trust</u> you? Do you refrain from <u>damaging</u> activities?

**Refuse**: To refuse is to withhold something, whether it is as <u>tangible</u> as <u>money</u> or <u>intangible</u> as permission or <u>approval</u>. Do you only refuse when you have a good reason? What <u>kinds</u> of things do you refuse to do? If it is a <u>personal</u> <u>choice</u>, should others respect it? If others are involved, are you open to <u>compromise</u>?

**Refute**: Refuting an <u>argument</u> is to provide <u>facts</u> that disprove a <u>false</u> or misleading statement. Is being able to refute an <u>opponent's</u> statements just as powerful as confirming your own? Do you always research a <u>subject</u> before entering a <u>debate</u> on it and look at the situation from both sides? Do you refute with well <u>thought</u>-out collections of facts?

**Regard**: To regard someone or something is to <u>think</u> about them in a particular way. How does one earn the <u>honor</u> of being held in high regard? <u>People</u> will not respect you because you <u>command</u> them to do so; what <u>kind</u> of <u>actions</u> can you <u>take</u> in order to encourage them to do so? Do you regard others with respect?

**Regress**: Regression is to return to a previous state of being, losing any <u>progress</u> one has made. Do you find yourself tempted by the easy ways of doing <u>work</u> and deriving <u>pleasure</u>, such as laziness and drugs? Can relying on the world around you rather than yourself be <u>thought</u> of as a <u>kind</u> of regression into dependence on others? Have you ever found yourself regressing? How can you <u>keep</u> yourself from regressing? Do your <u>observations</u> <u>help</u> you progress?

> *"Adapt what is useful, reject what is useless, and add what is specifically your own."*
> — *Bruce Lee*

**Regret**: Regret is sadness we feel over things we have done or left undone. Do you feel that regret is caused by a lack of <u>information</u>? Is it ever <u>productive</u> to dwell on and regret the <u>past</u>? Do you own your <u>decisions</u> and accept the <u>consequences</u>? Could <u>planning</u> ahead <u>allow</u> you to <u>avoid</u> regret altogether?

**Regulation**: A regulation is a <u>rule</u> handed down by an appropriate <u>authority</u>. What would the world look like if it were devoid of rules? We all <u>need</u> some sort of regulation in our lives. The <u>question</u> is: how much? But who should be the one to <u>decide</u>? Our elected officials? Ourselves? How do you regulate your <u>behavior</u>? How is it regulated by others?

**Rehabilitate**: Rehabilitation is the act of restoring someone or something suffering from <u>damage</u>. Do you try to always be at your best? Is it <u>possible</u> your <u>need</u> for rehabilitation is not readily <u>obvious</u> to others or even yourself? In order to begin your road to recovery, must you first acknowledge that you have something to recover from? If you do not stare your <u>problem</u> in the face, how can you <u>effectively</u> confront and squash it?

**Reiterate**: To reiterate is to repeat a piece of <u>information</u> already <u>communicated</u> once. What causes a <u>message</u> to not sink in the first time it is said? When is repetition truly <u>necessary</u>, and when does it become unnecessary <u>redundancy</u>? Do you make your expectations clear to yourself and others?

**Reject**: To reject is to forcibly <u>deny</u> someone or something. Rejection comes in many forms—<u>emotional</u>, <u>physical</u>, ideological—but does it always result in a feeling of isolation? Do you face rejection with <u>determination</u> and courage? What in your <u>life</u> do you reject and why?

**Rejoice**: To rejoice is to experience and celebrate intense <u>happiness</u>. Do you find it easy to <u>concentrate</u> on the positive aspects of your life? Think about the essential things in your life that make you happy to wake up every day. Do you take them for granted, or do you rejoice in them?

**Rejuvenate**: Rejuvenation means to refresh and recharge. Do you take a day off once in a while to clear your head? Do you try new ways of relaxing? Might something that works for someone else work for you, too?

**Relate, Relationship**: To have relationships is to be able to find connections with people, new ideas, and places. Do new friends and places help us grow in ways that would not be possible otherwise? Although generally considered a positive, have you had experience with bad relationships? Do you have the ability to connect with a lot of people and other life forms, or are you discerning in your choices of relationship to a point of limitation? Are your logical or natural associations well intentioned and sincere, or are they self-motivated? What is the basis for a lasting relationship? Do your communication skills allow you to relate easily with others? What are you best able to relate to?

**Relative:** There are two major definitions of what it means for something to be relative. First, relatives can be connected through some sort of actual kinship either through genetics or via legal arrangement. Second, the word "relative" can describe something that changes depending on who is viewing or evaluating it at the time. Do you consider values and morals to be relative, or are they absolute? Are all humans so different that their experiences of the world are necessarily relative, or are there some ways in which we are physically hard-wired so that there are universal experiences?

> *"The meeting of two personalities is like the contact of two chemical substances: if there is any reaction, both are transformed."*
> — C. G. Jung

Do you note activities that are taxing and try to balance them with rejuvenating ones?

**Relapse**: To pick back up a habit that one desires to quit and has been trying to refrain from. Quitting a bad habit in the first place is hard enough; is continuously staying away even more difficult? Do you have friends and family members to fill in a gap in your own willpower?

Are you convinced that the world will be flung into chaos if you take some time for yourself and let things pass by? Are you able to catch up on those projects that you have been meaning to get to and appreciate what you have? Do you maintain a balance between relaxation and responsibility?

**Release:** To release is to intentionally let go of someone or something. Do you have difficulty escaping from the hectic bustle of life? Have you tried to find something that you can do every day that will give you a release from stress, such as simple things like kicking off your shoes under your desk or perhaps cooking better meals? What are the little things that help you release tension?

**Relax:** Relaxing is an emotional state free of stress and anxiety. Do you worry too much?

**Relevant:** For something to be considered relevant, it must to be meaningful to the matter being discussed. Do you always ask yourself whether information that you are sending and receiving is relevant to the topic at hand? Have you ever become frustrated with irrelevant information? How can you remember that brevity and thoroughness are not mutually exclusive? Do you keep your statements on topic and only include information that is pertinent to the question you are trying to address in order to keep the attention of others?

**Reliance, Rely**: Reliance is to have confidence that someone or something will be there when you need it. When the going gets tough in life, do you have consistent people and things to rely on for help? Do you show your appreciation for the support given to you by others and reciprocate the support when the time comes? Are you reliable? Can reliance on others be a weakness?

**Religion**: Religion comprises many different schools of thought and highly complicated social beliefs that deal with the connection between the human species and a higher power. Religions vary in their degree of involvement in life; some are composed of moral teachings only, and others have draconian, all-pervading life rules. Religions are based on beliefs about the supernatural, which are impossible either to prove or to disprove. Religions can be positive in the sense that they can create groups for social growth and give people comfort and answers to questions that would otherwise be unanswerable, such as what happens after death. They can also be negative, such as when they create in-groups and out-groups that then enter into conflicts with each other. Have you experienced both positive and negative aspects of religion, or has your experience been only one or the other? How do you think corporations and the corporacracy have affected the nature of religion? Are you wary of religious teachings that seek to criminalize certain groups or foster any type of hate? Is the primary purpose of religion to be a rite of recognizing God or as a kind of social control? Should it be a matter of individualism, or does it require community? Should God and religion be associated with government, politics, and legal disputes? Can religion reform mankind, or is religion possibly another form of slavery? Is questioning religion necessarily an attack on it, or can that questioning simply be part of a search for an explanation? *What role does religion play in spirituality? Is religion the truth of God or the truth of mankind? Is religion more than symbolic ritual?*

**Relinquish**: To relinquish is to let something go. Have you found it necessary to give up things that you hold dear, such as toys, titles, or people? How can you help yourself remember that they all play a limited role? Do you allow yourself to be defined by your possessions, or are your actions more important?

> *"When I do good, I feel good. When I do bad, I feel bad. That's my religion."*
> — *Abraham Lincoln*

learned something? Are our memories, the catalog of our experience, like muscles that must be exercised if it is to help us at a moment's notice? Do you take it for granted, or use it daily to reminisce or recall the determination it took you to get through hard times?

**Remember**: To remember can be simply to use our memories to recall past experiences, but it can also mean to recognize a situation or person we've been in contact with before or even to pay tribute to the dead. How important is your memory to you personally? How about memories you share with other people? How can memory help us learn from the past? Do you keep your mind active to keep memories fresh and keep sensory cues around you that will help you to recall the times that you relish or in which you

**Reminisce**: Reminiscing is the act of actively remembering past experiences whether silently or aloud. What do you fondly remember when you get together with old friends? Do you write about your experiences? Reminiscing makes us yearn for the past, but can it also help with the present? What was a thing the past had that the present lacks? What can you do to reclaim aspects of your youth?

**Remorse**: Remorse is the deep regret or guilt we feel as a result of wrongdoing. We all make mistakes. Do you take responsibility for your actions and do everything you can to make up for your transgressions? Do you dwell on them? How can you avoid spending a large amount of time thinking about your failures and instead look forward? How can you prevent such mistakes from occurring in the future? How can you make it up to the person you wronged?

**Renew**: To renew is to refresh or begin again. Is renewal an important ritual for you and those around you? What kind of celebrated benchmarks in life have you experienced that signify a new beginning—graduation, marriage, a new job? What events have occurred recently in your life that make you feel renewed? What may do so in the future?

**Renounce**: Renouncing involves formally announcing one's abandonment of something. Have you ever gotten completely fed up with something you used to consider important? Before renouncing something, do you weigh the positives and negatives that it affords you?

**Reparation:** Reparations represent an attempt to heal a relationship through repayment, though not necessarily in financial terms. Have you done something in your life that you must atone for? We all make mistakes; do you deal with yours in a productive way? Is there a note you need to write or a gift you need to send to repair a wrong done? Does a greater distance between the infraction and the reparation cause it to be less meaningful?

**Repercussion:** A repercussion is another word we use to talk about impacts or consequences. Have you experienced unexpected repercussions from actions you have taken? How could you attempt to avoid them in the future? How about having to try and repair a situation caused by the repercussions of someone else's actions? Is that a situation that causes resentment?

**Repetition:** Repetition involves performing the same actions over and over, whether productively or not. Does your life feel like a flurry of repetitive tasks sometimes? Wake up, go to work, come home, make dinner— are you stuck in a routine, or do you seize the day and make an effort to do something new at every opportunity? What do you gain from sticking to a routine, and what do you gain from seeking out variety instead?

**Replenish:** To replenish is essentially to refresh or refuel. When you run out of energy, you eat, but are all kinds of replenishment so simple? How can we work toward replenishing the natural world after the environment becomes degraded, filled with filth, and uncared for? Do you care for yourself and your surroundings? If we do not work to replenish our natural resources, what will the consequences be for us and other life on this planet?

**Reply:** A reply is a response to someone else's words or actions. Before replying to someone, do you think about your answer? What kind of reaction do you hope to produce, and how will your reply affect your image in the eyes of others? Do you always think before you speak, and do you reply with rationality and respect?

**Reprehensible:** Reprehensible actions or situations are things we consider to be completely repulsive and unforgivable. Are you more likely to find things reprehensible if they happen locally or on the other side of the world? Instead of being satisfied with simply condemning such events, do you contemplate why they occur and if future occurrences are preventable? How can you prevent reprehensible events from occurring?

**Represent**: A representation can be anything that stands in for something else, including language, images, and people. How do you represent the groups that you identify with? How do others perceive your groups? There are many ways to represent who you are as a person, consciously and subconsciously. Your behavior represents the groups you claim membership to whether you like it or not. Are you mindful of how your actions reflect your personality to others? Do your actions represent who you are inside? Why or why not? How can you make everything you do representative of your sentiments and ideals?

**Repress:** To repress means to keep someone or something under control, sometimes forcibly. Is hiding your emotions inherently a negative thing? Do you believe that you cannot ignore your feelings and that they will manifest themselves eventually even if you try to bottle them up? Are you able to be comfortable with yourself and accept who you are? What feelings do you repress?

**Reproach**: A reproach is a scolding given for actions performed or left unperformed. Do you logically examine the reproaches of others? Many people scold others without considering their own shortcomings; do you feel that you have done this or been on the receiving end of that behavior? Do you consider the impact you have when you scold another? More often than not, corrections and scolding are taken personally. Do you use tact when doing either? Do you often find yourself correcting others? Are you beyond reproach?

**Reproduce:** To reproduce can mean to make a copy of something, but we also use it to talk about the practice of having children. Do you have children? How do they affect your relationship with the world? Do you

> *"An imbalance between rich and poor is the oldest and most fatal ailment of all republics."*
> *— Plutarch*

> *"If one's reputation is a possession, then of all my possessions, my reputation means most to me."*
> *— Arthur Ashe*

consider children to be an extension of one's self, a chance to teach someone else how to live with all the benefits of your experience? Are children truly copies of ourselves, or is that a mischaracterization of our relationship to them?

**Republic**: A republic is a form of government in which the citizens are able to vote their officials into office. Do you feel your government's representatives truly stand for the people? How prevalent is corruption, and what are its dangers? What steps could we taken to stop it? Who are the primary people who form corruption? Who are its primary victims? Do you feel that you are living in a republic or a plutocracy?

**Republican:** In American politics, this has come to mean someone who belongs to or otherwise supports the more conservative of the two major political parties. How do you assess or evaluate the people in your life— by their political beliefs, their adherence to a party ideology or platform, or their personal motives? Do you generalize people by their political beliefs, or are you able to see them as individuals?

**Reputation:** Your reputation is how you are known and regarded by others. Reputations can be based on a variety of different things. Have you ever had a false reputation or believed false things about someone else's reputation? How do others perceive you? What can you do to change your reputation in a positive way?

**Resentment:** Resentment is a feeling of bitter distrust and anger as a result of being mistreated. What kinds of situations or actions have caused you to feel resentment?

When you feel resentment toward someone whom you are usually close to, do you express your feelings and <u>listen</u> to them express theirs? How can you work together with others to address the problem?

**Resilient:** Something or someone that is resilient is able to resist pressure, or to recover quickly after trauma or abuse. Do you ever find it difficult to stay <u>true</u> to yourself and what you <u>believe</u> in when facing adversity? The <u>world</u> is rife with temptations and false victories. Are you able to fall back and choose a <u>different</u> <u>creed</u> or <u>lifestyle</u>? Do you strive to be what you dream of in spite of setbacks? Can you measure resiliency?

**Resist:** To resist is to push back against the pressure to <u>take</u> a particular <u>action</u>. Do you find yourself tempted to take the easy way out? Have you found that the difficult path can be more rewarding? What do you <u>resist</u> on a regular basis? Do you resist unhealthy <u>temptations</u>?

**Resolution:** A resolution is a promise we make to ourselves regarding what our future <u>actions</u> and <u>behavior</u> will be. Have you made resolutions in the past, such as a New Year's resolution? Have you been able to <u>keep</u> them, or have you gone back on your promise to yourself? What kinds of <u>ideas</u> <u>help</u> inspire you to stay true to your resolutions?

<u>**Resolve:**</u> The act of resolving has multiple meanings. It can refer to making a resolution, to the <u>kind</u> of inner strength that allow us to see difficult situations through to the end, or to find the solution to a problematic situation. Do these <u>definitions</u> seem to be related to you? Does strength bring solutions? What experiences have you had in either having resolve or bringing about solutions to difficult problems? Do you add <u>resiliency</u> to resolving problems?

**Resort:** A resort, as a location, is a pleasant place of escape and relaxation. To resort to something, however, generally implies that one is taking an <u>action</u> out of desperation. Do these two <u>different</u> meanings seem to have a connection to you? In times of desperation, what do you turn to? There are many options, such as your willpower, your friends and <u>family</u>, and your <u>vice</u>. What are the different impacts of choosing between them? Do you let your reaction match the severity of the situation at hand by not employing your last resort until absolutely necessary?

**Resource:** A resource is any <u>kind</u> of supply or asset that we can use when <u>needed</u>. Do you try to be <u>aware</u> of how limited resources can be? Do you share concerns about how much of the useful parts of the planet we extract for our own wants? Can we <u>change</u> the situation by prioritizing our <u>need</u> over our wants? How do you show <u>care</u> for the resources available to you?

<u>**Respect, Respectful:**</u> Respect is both something we feel and something we demonstrate for those <u>people</u> and things who we feel have earned our admiration—or, sometimes, our <u>fear</u>. To what extent do you believe respect is a reflection of one's <u>reputation</u> and the <u>actions</u> that one performs every day? How much respect do you <u>think</u> is necessary or sufficient to <u>help</u> carry you through <u>life</u>? Is disagreement ever a good excuse for poor <u>behavior</u> and poor manners? We might all experience some frustration now and then. How do we prevent that frustration from turning into a personal attack? Can you ever feel respect in or for a community where <u>people</u> feel uncomfortable or threatened? Do you seek respect from others? Do you respect yourself? Can you find respect for failure, disability, or handicap? How do you show it? What <u>kinds</u> of <u>thought</u> trigger an act of disrespect or dishonor? Do you respect or tolerate, and know the <u>difference</u> between the two?

**Respond, Response:** A response is any <u>action</u> that happens following an action occurring in the world around us. Is one of the basic principles of <u>law</u> and order response by action? If you are attacked by an animal or another human, what will happen if you don't respond? Is the outcome as dependent on their actions as it is on your response to those <u>actions</u>? How <u>important</u> is it for us to make sure that our responses are timely?

**Responsibility, Responsible:** To accept responsibility is to acknowledge that you are accountable for your own actions; to be responsible is to be trustworthy. What are you responsible for? Do your responsibilities <u>define</u> what type of <u>person</u> you are and will become? Do you seek out more responsibility or do you run in the other direction? Are you able to <u>balance</u> your responsibilities with your <u>pleasures</u>? What happens to your <u>life</u> when you shirk your responsibilities? Are you responsible and reliable?

**Rest:** Resting can mean to stop briefly while on the way to one's destination or <u>just</u> to seek out rejuvenation through giving your body and <u>mind</u> a break. Have you ever tried to live a full, vibrant <u>life</u> without proper rest? How do you set time aside to escape from daily responsibilities? Have you developed techniques to rid yourself of stress before you get your rest for the day? Do you get enough rest? How much rest is enough?

**Result:** A result is a consequence of our <u>actions</u>, either <u>positive</u> or <u>negative</u>. How have you been able to achieve <u>positive</u> results in the past? What actions have you <u>taken</u> that produced poor results instead? What sort of results do you deliver, and what do you expect?

> *"For it is in your power to retire into yourself whenever you choose."*
> — *Marcus Aurelius*

**Retaliate:** To retaliate means to repay for an attack by attacking in turn. Before you move straight to retaliation, do you ponder how you can compromise or reach an agreement instead of simply perpetuating a cycle? Do you <u>choose</u> your battles carefully? What goes wrong to cause us to end up in extended <u>conflicts</u> where both parties wind up feeling wronged and no problems are solved?

**Retire:** Some accepted <u>definitions</u> of retire are to go away, to depart, to withdraw from something, to fall back, to remove from active service, and to <u>take</u> out of circulation. Does retirement mark the end of a career and a luxury at the end of <u>life</u>, or does it more importantly represent a new beginning? What <u>kinds</u> of activities can one do in retirement that aren't necessarily profitable, but fulfilling in some other way? If retirement is a balancing act, what are the <u>different</u> aspects we must <u>learn</u> to <u>balance</u>? Must we always leave behind associates or friends? Do we resent being taken out of circulation and limiting our active service? Do we withdraw completely, or partially? In steps or abruptly? With or without financial stability? Does a <u>positive</u> <u>attitude</u> of looking forward and making the best of your situation <u>help</u> with the balancing act? If you have retired, has it enhanced your modesty and reticence? Will/is retirement working for you? Are you taking full advantage of the resources and time available to create the best retirement scenario for your purposes?

**Retrieve:** Retrieval is the <u>action</u> we perform when we have lost something previously in our possession. How could this apply to more than tangible possessions? Are you able to retrieve your motivation, your <u>pride</u>, and your <u>health</u>, or are they too difficult to re-obtain once you have lost them? How is it <u>possible</u> to lose them in the first place?

**Reuse:** To reuse is simply to use again; it is one of the tools available to us, along with reducing and recycling, in an attempt to cut down on waste and preserve the environment. Do you make an effort to reuse items when possible? What kinds of factors cause you to do so less than you could? Is there a point at which reusing an object becomes foolish or impractical?

**Reveal:** When we work to reveal information, it means that we are uncovering something that is hidden from us, sometimes something that has been deliberately concealed. What kinds of things are worth working hard to uncover? Do you pursue facts and emphasize reasoning based on evidence? Are there some things that are better left hidden, or is it always worthwhile to uncover the truth?

**Revelation:** A revelation involves making known something that has previously been unknown, often in a dramatic way. Have you ever had a simple piece of information severely shake your personal world? What realizations in life have completely changed your outlook? Do you welcome revelations, or do you sometimes find them threatening? Do you feel most revelations you have experienced come from curiosity and a willingness to learn, or from others who are so eager to teach that they have overcome your resistance? Have your revelations led to an accurate and cohesive outlook on life?

**Revenge:** Revenge is the act of deliberately hurting another human being in response to their having first hurt us or a loved one—or at least our perception that they have done so. Do you believe that perpetuating a cycle of violence could ever lead you to peace? When another wrongs you, do you consider what future actions will help you to recover from the event? What do you believe to be the relationship between revenge and justice? Will hurting those you are angry at remove the pain you feel, or would you be more relieved by helping another?

**Reverence**: Feeling reverence means experiencing great respect. What do you have reverence for? Do your life choices lead others to revere you? Do you revere the uncontrollable forces and features, and the special people that give our world shape? Mountain ranges? Non-violent activists? Do you internalize your feelings of deep respect and make it your goal to embody qualities that you revere?

**Revert:** To revert is to return to a previous state, which can be either a negative or positive experience. Do you often revisit old friends, places, and memories? Are there occasions when you find yourself reverting to previous behavior? Before reverting, do you take the time to decide if it is a good thing? Do you find that reverting helps you to maintain fragments of your past self that seem to peel away with time, or does it bring back bad habits?

**Review:** Reviewing—literally, to view again—involves going back over a work or subject to critique or better learn it. Do you find that a second look is always warranted? Even when looking at something simple, do you, upon review, find complex patterns that did not reveal themselves before? Do you apply the same logic to people? What are the potential dangers in judging solely by first impressions? How many aspects of your life does the old saying "Measure twice, cut once" apply to? Do you review information you are presented with?

**Revise:** When we revise a statement or a work, we alter it from a previous version to better suit our purposes. What is valuable about not being satisfied with first drafts of your work? If improvement is always possible, how do we know when we are finished enough to consider what we have produced a final version? Do you take pride in what you produce and take steps to give your best product?

**Revive:** Revival involves bringing something back to life either literally or more metaphorically. Have you ever felt yourself becoming a husk of yourself? What are the forces that caused your energy and personality to deteriorate? Do you make sure to revive yourself every once in a while? Can your friends and family help with this? Are you careful to not neglect those things that bring you true happiness? What revives you?

**Revoke:** To revoke is to end the validity or operation of an ability or permission. Are you careful to remember that some of the things you take for granted are privileges, not rights? In what kinds of situations can you have either your privileges or rights revoked after breaking rules? When something is revoked, do you examine who is revoking it and for what reasons? How could you determine whether or not a revocation of something is just? Do you understand your rights?

**Revolt:** Being in revolt means to defy and act against some kind of authority. When you see injustice running rampant and unchallenged, do you rebel? Is it possible that using the pen to suppress people is more dangerous than using the sword? Is it less obvious? Are there situations against which you have revolted, or authorities you have refused to obey?

**Revolution:** Revolution is rising up and fighting an oppressive force, or the motion of turning in a full circle. Do you see a relationship between these two meanings? Do you find it difficult to reform yourself or to overthrow those ideas within you that are harmful or unfounded? When you consider the idea of oppression, do you consider whether you are already oppressing yourself mentally? How can we determine whether and when a revolution is just?

*"Better to die fighting for freedom than be a prisoner all the days of your life."*
*— Bob Marley*

**Revolve:** To revolve is to turn upon an axis, to move in a circular path, or to focus and center on something important or powerful. All the planets in our solar system revolve around the sun, the isolated source of all of our energy. What does your life revolve around? Is it your hobbies, your family, your friends, or your work? Do you orbit something you love or something that pulls you in against your will?

**Rhyme:** Rhyme is a linguistic pattern that occurs when words have the same or similar endings. Do you find rhymes pleasing to the ear, preferring poetry that rhymes to that which does not? Do you find them easier to remember? How can things rhyme more metaphorically? Do you look for patterns in the world around you?

**Rhythm:** A rhythm is a repeated instance of sound or movement. What rhythm do you live your life to? Do you march to the beat of your own drum or fall into the step of someone else's theme song? Do you let music enhance your everyday life and let it encourage and inspire you?

**Rich:** To be rich is to have acquired wealth, though that can be measured in a variety of ways. Do you work to recognize the difference between superficial and material wealth, and wealth in experiences and relationships? How do you measure your wealth?

**Ridicule:** Ridicule is the act of mocking someone else with the intention of causing them discomfort or emotional pain. Is putting down others a hobby of yours? What motivates people to derive pleasure from the misfortunes of others? Is there such a thing as productive or positive ridicule, such as for abuses of power? How do they differ from other kinds of ridicule? Do you examine not only the ridicule but also the ridiculer?

**Right:** The underlined idea of rightness is complicated; it can mean correctness, or moral worth, or something to which we are entitled, or the direction opposite of left. How do any of these definitions seem to connect to one another? Do they? Do you ever find it hard to do the right thing? Has it ever meant forfeiting benefits for yourself or others so that your conscience remains clear and someone else remains unhurt? How do you judge whether you are doing the right thing? What are your standards? In another sense of the word, what steps do you take in order to educate yourself about and assert your rights?

**Righteous:** Righteousness is a state of acting morally or justly. How subjective do you think righteousness is? Are there standards that one *must* have in order to be righteous, or are they entirely dependent on the society or religion in which one happens to find oneself? Can a society or religion be itself righteous, or is it a state that can only be achieved by individuals? Do you strive for righteousness in your life, or do you find it an unrealistic goal?

> *"The very essence of romance is uncertainty."*
> — *Oscar Wilde*

**Risk:** Experiencing risk means to be open to the chance that something will result in failure or injury. Do you attempt to avoid risk or accept it because it can also bring benefits? How do you weigh the potential for harm against the reward to determine if the risk is worth it? Do you ever risk things that do not belong to you or take unnecessary risks?

**Role:** A role is a part we fulfill, either one assigned to us or one we have chosen for ourselves. How many roles do you find yourself playing—child, parent, employer, employee? Are you aware of yourself performing the roles you have to play, or do they feel entirely natural to you? What roles would you like to be able to fill in the future?

**Roman:** The ancient Roman Empire was a massive civilization whose technological prowess and organization helped it conquer much of the known world. It accumulated knowledge from other nations it conquered and attempted to strike a balance between total obedience to the Empire and individual freedom of identity. Do you see other successful civilizations following this pattern? What does the phrase "Rome wasn't built in a day" mean to you? How do you think successful nations fail and crumble?

**Romance:** The idea of "romance" began as a term used to describe a story that is an exaggerated fantasy, though we now use it to describe the process of falling or being in love. Is it reasonable to see a connection between these two definitions or is that overly cynical? How important is romantic love in your life? Do you find romance sometimes frightening or difficult? Do you let pride or embarrassment keep you from enjoying or attempting romance?

**Rude:** Being rude involves caring so little about others' feelings that one acts or speaks in a way that demonstrates contempt for them. Have you ever been rude to someone else? What were your motivations for doing so, and what sort of response did you receive? Was it worthwhile, or did you regret it? What is your response when someone else is rude to you?

**Rudimentary:** Something rudimentary is basic, sometimes more underdeveloped than it should be. Is it more of an insult to think of something as being rudimentary, as it implies it is inexpert work, or are basics so important that the word can be a positive or neutral description? When you take on a project, do you get ahead of yourself, or do you make sure you understand each step of an important process before you proceed?

**Ruffian**: A ruffian is a violent <u>person</u> who could be described as abiding by a "might makes right" mentality. Are there times when this <u>kind</u> of <u>philosophy</u> is <u>effective</u>? If so, is it ever <u>moral</u> to use greater strength to impose one's will on another? How might it be <u>possible</u> to fight back against those who do so?

**Ruin**: What lies in ruin is beyond salvation or restoration; it only serves as a reminder of what used to be. Is ruin sometimes necessary to create new things? When is ruin regrettable, and when is it worthwhile or beneficial? What <u>kinds</u> of things in your <u>life</u> have been ruined, and do you <u>regret</u> their condition?

**Rule:** A rule is a guideline for what is and is not acceptable in daily <u>life</u>; to rule means to have the authority to set these guidelines. How can we <u>judge</u> whether rules are reasonable and <u>just</u>, or unreasonable and dangerous? What rules have you encountered that seemed to be based on obsolete <u>ideas</u> or biases? Do you believe that rules should be broken when they are un<u>just</u> or that such <u>behavior</u> only leads to anarchy?

**Rumor:** A rumor is a story passed along between <u>people</u> without any definite <u>proof</u> behind it, though it may in <u>fact</u> be true. How do you feel about rumors? Do you ever engage in gossip? Are you wary of those who tend to do so? Have you ever found yourself the subject of a rumor? Did you treat it as flattery or an <u>insult</u>?

**Run:** To run can mean to move quickly or to manage, as in running a business. Do you see a connection between the two <u>definitions</u>? You won't get very far if you walk all the time. When you get the urge to run, do you <u>give</u> in or restrain yourself? What do you have to <u>gain</u> or lose from these two <u>different</u> courses of <u>action</u>?

# S

**Sabotage**: To sabotage is to intentionally damage something in an effort to cause it to fail. Have you ever encountered someone in life that attempted to sabotage your plans? How did you persevere and combat their actions? How did you deal with the damage?

**Sacred**: To view something as sacred is to be reverently dedicated to some person, purpose, or object. Things like family and honor can be considered sacred in life; how would you give them the greatest amount of respect and reverence? The use of this word has merit in itself as it conveys our deep feelings of respect toward something or someone. What is sacred in your life—religion, money, spirituality, or God?

**Sacrifice**: Sacrifice can be considered both a positive and a negative, whereby the time and place of the sacrifice differentiates between the two opposites. A positive sacrifice is one in which you set your interests aside with the intent of helping others. For example, you might want to go out to dinner with friends, but your son needs help with his math homework. As a parent, you choose to sacrifice what little free time you have in order to assist your son. A negative sacrifice is one in the needs of others are set aside for them to serve you; you take control of someone else's interests or possessions and dismiss them in order to better your situation. How do you ensure that the sacrifices you make are for the benefit of others or a collective good? Are you appreciative of the many worldly sacrifices made by others?

**Sad**: Sadness is a human emotion felt by everyone at some point in his or her lifetime. We feel sad when we lose someone we care about or when we fail to find success in our goals. Sadness is healthy, but how does it remind you of the importance of keeping a positive outlook on life? What situations cause you great sadness, and how do you turn them into positive experiences?

> *"Every saint has a past, and every sinner has a future."*
> — *Oscar Wilde*

**Sadist**: A sadist is someone who deliberately causes pain or suffering to others. Finding pleasure in someone else's pain suggests that you are suffering as well. Do you derive pleasure from hurting others?

**Safe, Safety**: To feel safe or a sense of safety is to be free from the occurrence or risk of injury, hurt, danger, or loss. Safety can come in a number of forms, such as the comforts of your home or the company of somebody you love. Conversely, insecurity causes anxiety and can deteriorate your well-being. What or who makes you feel safe, and how do you consciously seek it out, keep it, and cherish it?

**Saint**: A saint is not only a holy person but also a person who is humble, unselfish, and patient. How do you strive to be a decent and productive person? How are you saintly in your life?

**Salary**: A salary is the monetary reward for the amount of work that you have done in a given amount of time. Do you feel your salary defines your occupation and is a reflection of its importance in the world? Money is certainly a motivator, but do you <u>love</u> what you do? Do you find that at the end of the day, you view your <u>salary</u> as your lifeline? Does it <u>allow</u> you to live the <u>lifestyle</u> that you <u>desire</u>?

**Salient**: To be salient is to stand out and be easily seen or noticed. The best qualities of our <u>personalities</u> can be considered salient as they are noticeable and enjoyable. What <u>personal</u> <u>attributes</u> would you view as salient? Others who make statements with their fashion, sense of <u>humor</u>, or <u>shock</u> <u>value</u> are salient. How can you <u>flourish</u> your personality and be more salient in your life?

**Salvation**: Salvation is the act of saving or protecting from harm, <u>risk</u>, <u>loss</u>, or destruction. How does this act <u>relate</u> to your priorities in <u>life</u>? How do you <u>identify</u> your priorities and ensure they are used to their maximum extent? If your income is minimal, is it important for you to <u>save</u> on clothes, <u>money</u>, and food? In <u>contrast</u> to salvation, we <u>waste</u> many things in life that in fact deserve to be saved. What do you <u>value</u> in your life? What things are <u>worth</u> saving to you?

> *"Life's single lesson: that there is more accident to it than a man can ever admit to in a lifetime and stay sane."*
> — *Thomas Pynchon*

**Same**: To be the same as someone is to be identical to another. Do you find it easier to mimic others than to be <u>unique</u> or be your own <u>person</u>? Regardless, we all have something about us that is completely original and unique to only us. Have you discovered what that distinctive <u>quality</u> is yet? If not, just keep on being yourself and your <u>individuality</u> will <u>shine</u> through in <u>time</u>. How are you the same as others? In what ways are you unique?

**Sanction**: A sanction is an <u>authoritative</u> <u>approval</u> of an <u>action</u> or <u>idea</u>. Sanctions can be handed out to <u>pardon</u> certain behaviors that are considered unlawful but were <u>performed</u> to <u>benefit</u> the collective good. How often and for what <u>reason</u> do you sanction another person's <u>behavior</u> whether it is in agreement or <u>disagreement</u> with those in <u>power</u>?

**Sanctuary**: A sanctuary is a place of <u>peace</u> and meditation, and should not be interrupted or disturbed. Sanctuaries are <u>safe</u> places where no emotional or physical <u>harm</u> can be done. It is a <u>sacred</u> place where one can be <u>alone</u> with his or her thoughts. Where is your <u>personal</u> sanctuary?

**Sanity**: To be sane is to be <u>free</u> from mental derangement and to have a sound, healthy mind. Have you realized or recognized your own <u>sanity</u> and consider yourself sane? Sanity is a healthy, active, and inquisitive mind; when we become aware of our <u>self</u> and our surroundings without interruption, we have found it. How have you avoided the <u>negative</u> influences in your life that can tamper with your sanity? What in life brings you <u>clarity</u> of mind?

**Sarcasm**: Sarcasm is the use of biting words that cut into our feelings and cause us to <u>hurt</u> or feel foolish. While sarcasm is usually intended to hurt people, it can also be incredibly funny and lighthearted when used to deliver a <u>message</u> in an appropriate context. Sarcasm is akin to <u>virtual</u> <u>reality</u>, where we say one thing and really mean another. Do you recognize sarcasm when it is used against you? Do you recognize the <u>emotional</u> ramifications that can occur when you use sarcasm against others? Are you careful in your use of sarcasm?

**Satan**: "Satan" is the Hebrew word for enemy and through the advent of <u>religion</u> has come to embody all that is <u>evil</u> and sinful in the <u>world</u> today. When bad things happen, many believe that Satan is the master puppeteer behind the negativity. Do you accept the presence of a spiritual Satan? What does Satan mean to you? How do you combat Satan or evil?

**Satire**: Satire is the use of sarcasm, irony, and humor to poke fun at something bad or foolish. Satire is usually employed to make fun of human negativities in current events or politics. Do you find satire humorous?

**Satisfaction**: To fulfill one's desires and needs completely is to be satisfied. Satisfaction can arise from both positive and negative situations. Therein lies the question: Do we deviate from a positive life when something negative satisfies us? Do you find satisfaction in harassing others or hurting others' feelings? If so, how would you reevaluate your situation to determine why these negative things bring you satisfaction? What brings you satisfaction, and are they positive or negative?

**Save**: The act of saving is to avoid the spending, consumption, or waste of something. Are you economical by nature and deem it virtuous? Your individual priorities dictate what you save and how much of it you save. Most would say that they try to save money and time, which are commodities viewed by some as the most valuable to man. What do you view as precious and feel the need to save?

*"Memory is a mirror that scandalously lies."*
*— Julio Cortázar*

**Schedule**: A schedule is a series of things to be done or events to occur at or during a particular time or period. Schedules are ubiquitous in our daily lives and have come to govern our way of living. They can seem to be impossible to keep up with at times. Balance is essential to any schedule; we need time for work, play, and rest. Depriving yourself of one or all of these three things can lead to excessive stress. Do you have balance in your schedule?

**Say**: Usually, to say something means to express in words, state, or declare—an action that is done verbally. However, messages can be conveyed via body language as well. How do you communicate to others with your posture or facial expressions? The things we say offer a portrait of ourselves to the outside world. How do you paint a picture with language and add nuances with non-verbal cues? Do you think before you speak, choosing your words carefully? What do want to say to the world today?

**Scheme**: A scheme is a carefully devised plan made to accomplish a goal in the most efficient and effective way possible. Planning out a scheme to complete a project is a great way to stay on track, but don't fret if the plan doesn't progress exactly how you thought it would. As the Scottish poet Robert Burns penned, "The best laid schemes of mice and men go often awry." What do you have planned for the future?

**Scandal**: A scandal is a disgraceful or discreditable action that can damage one's reputation by means of malicious gossip. Scandals arise when people do negative things and then try to cover them up or spin them positively. Do you try to avoid scandals by being honest with others and yourself? What methods do you use to stay grounded regarding your morals and standards? How do you ensure you choose the correct path to steer clear of dishonesty and scandal?

**School**: School is most often thought of as an institution where instruction is given to the young and college age alike. Learning is perhaps the most important and ongoing process in your lifetime, though it is most certainly not over when you've finished grade school or college. Life is one massive school in which we are constantly learning new things about ourselves and our surroundings. What do you still want to learn from the school of life?

**Science**: Science is factual knowledge gathered in an orderly fashion from careful study, observation, and experimentation. Science has become increasingly prevalent and pervasive in the last three centuries as humans have become curious about how and why things happen. The rapid rise in technological progression has unlocked innumerable secrets about the nature of almost everything, yet there is still so much knowledge to be reaped from scientific exploration. Has science made our modern lives much easier, creating a flurry of new jobs and new ideas for the public masses? Are there conflicting issues between science and religion? *Do you perceive life scientifically?*

**Scold**: To scold is to angrily find fault within another or reprimand them. Everyone has flaws, but some flaws can become habitual or harmful and in turn need to be pointed out by another. No one likes to be scolded or lectured, but there are times when it is necessary to sternly state your point. Do you listen to the person who is scolding you? They probably have something valuable to say. Have you ever been scolded? How did you respond or react to it?

> *"The saddest aspect of life right now is that science gathers knowledge faster than society gathers wisdom."*
> — Isaac Asimov

**Scorn**: Scorn is a feeling of contempt that you have for something or someone cruel. Scorn is a negative feeling, but it can often give rise to something positive when you recognize the reason why you are experiencing this emotion. Have you ever felt scorn toward someone and then risen above it to help him or her change?

**Scowl**: A scowl is an angry or mean look that resembles an intensified frown. Do you constantly carry a scowl on your face? How will others perceive you? People may avoid you or think of you in a negative light, so try to loosen up and smile once in a while; others will be much more friendly and receptive toward you. How do you react to someone who scowls?

> *"Every man has his secret sorrows which the world knows not; and often times we call a man cold when he is only sad."*
> — Henry Wadsworth Longfellow

**Scrutiny**: Scrutiny is a close examination, a long and careful look. Attention to detail is important in all facets of life. In order to do so, we must remain alert and enthusiastic about what we set out to accomplish. Do you scrutinize certain aspects of your life? Are you biased with **your scrutinization?**

**Seclusion**: To be secluded is to withdraw into solitude or to isolate yourself from society. Privacy and meditation are incredibly beneficial and therapeutic to your health and well-being. However, seclusion or isolation can also be detrimental to your mental health, especially when you are forced into seclusion. Humans are social creatures and are meant to be around other humans. If you find yourself in seclusion, do you relish in it, or do you miss the comforts of human interaction? *Do you choose seclusion out of spite?*

**Secret**: A secret is a mechanism by which information or knowledge is kept from outsiders by those who are privy to it. Secrets are not absolutely good or bad, but rely on the purpose for which they are used to define their quality. Matters considered in secrecy usually tend to support self-interest. Have you kept a secret for the purpose of taking advantage of another? Have you kept a secret from someone for their own good? Have secrets ended <u>relationships</u> in your <u>life</u>? Are secrets <u>stressful</u>? Do you <u>lie</u> to keep the <u>integrity</u> of a secret?

**Secure**: The word comes from the Latin meaning "<u>free</u> from care," and this definition has held true throughout <u>history</u>. Security is <u>safety</u>, <u>comfort</u>, and <u>assurance</u>. The things that we value in life, like <u>family</u>, property, and <u>liberty</u>, should be treated with the utmost <u>security</u>. What things in your life do you secure tightly?

**See**: To see something is to <u>perceive</u> it with the eyes, view, or look at it. Do you see what you desire to see or the reality in front of you? Do you see all within your peripheral vision, that is, are you overly concerned with minor, irrelevant, or <u>superficial</u> aspects of the <u>subject</u> at hand? Or are you able to <u>focus</u> and <u>observe</u> the subject in its entirety, taking each <u>detail</u> and nuance in? As you move about in <u>life</u>, are you actually alert to the people or things that are constantly around you, or does your mind often <u>wander</u> to another place?

**Seem**: Often what seems to be one way is in fact another, and reality remains hidden from our view. Can you look past what seems to be there to see what actually is? Is your reality <u>clear</u> or concealed?

**Segregate**: To segregate is to <u>separate</u> or set apart from others or from the main body or <u>group</u>, often with <u>force</u>. Segregation is part of America's past and is an excellent lesson in how injustice can persist for decades before enough people realize how wrong it is. Where might similar injustice persist elsewhere in the world, and how can we draw <u>attention</u> to it?

**Seize**: To seize is to take something, frequently from someone else. Oftentimes, seizing is stealing, and whether done stealthily or boldly, it is a <u>crime</u>. Have you ever witnessed a seizure and done nothing to stop it?

**Select**: To select something or someone is to choose it in preference to another or others. Each day, you select your choices from a myriad of possibilities and <u>hope</u> that you have chosen for the best. But what can you do to ensure the best selection? While you cannot guarantee the right decision, you can be aware enough of your options to <u>avoid</u> utter failure.

**Self**: The self is the <u>focus</u> of each <u>human</u> being. Our self-conception is what separates us from other <u>people</u>, yet it is also what conjoins us as a collective <u>species</u>. How do you think of your <u>personal</u> <u>self</u>, as in, what do you think has formed your <u>identity</u>? How do you define your "self?"

**Semantics**: Semantics is the <u>study</u> of <u>meanings</u> behind words. Language dominates the world around us, mediating every interaction we have, yet few among us ever pay close <u>attention</u> to the nuances of the words we use or how they are constantly changing. How has your way of communicating changed over time?

> *"A man's mind is stretched by a new idea or sensation, and never shrinks back to its former dimensions."*
> — *Oliver Wendell Holmes Sr.*

**Send**: To cause to be conveyed or transmitted. What do you <u>observe</u> as messages being sent by those you come in contact with? What message do you send by way of expression?

**Senescent**: Elderly; growing old. Eventually, we all age, but this is not a <u>negative</u> thing in the least bit. Many <u>positive</u> things come with age—<u>wisdom</u>, <u>experience</u>, <u>trust</u>, and <u>honor</u>—so don't despair about growing old. Instead, try to help others who don't yet possess these qualities and pass on your legacy through them. Do you fear growing older? Do you agree to it? Do you accept it? Do you resist it?

**Sensational**: Arousing or intended to arouse strong interest and excitement. Do you know how to draw attention to unfairness which you perceive in the world? Beware of those who sensationalize things because of ulterior motives; the only way to differentiate is to think critically about all of the information presented to you. Do you scrutinize sensational information?

Senses: There are five senses that we humans have in our repertoire: sight, smell, hearing, speech, and touch. These senses allow us to consciously connect our outward experiences inwardly so they affect our thoughts, attitudes, behaviors, and the ethereal entities that are our souls. These five basic senses are accompanied by many other sub-senses, such as growth, intuition and emotion, fear, movement, and energy. Senses are tuned by what we take into our bodies. When we listen in a broad sense, the sounds we hear consist of much more than mere words. When we see in a broad sense, we all see things differently and within the context of our own limits. What do you consider to be all the senses? How do you utilize those senses to your advantage? *Do you consider the senses to be the essence of life?*

**Sensible**: To be sensible is having, using, or showing sound judgment and being keenly aware of something. It is crucial to keep your wits about you and make decisions in a sensible and reasonable manner. Sensibility is a refined skill that takes time and experience to perfect. How can you be more sensible in your life?

**Sensitive**: To be sensitive is to be fresh and new, and to be quick to feel and notice and appreciate new things. As kids, we are sensitive to almost everything. As we grow, our senses become hardened by those experiences to which we have grown accustomed. Is there anything in life to which you are still sensitive?

**Sentimental**: Having sweet, gentle, or tender thoughts and feelings about times past. Even though your sentimental thoughts might seem silly to others, they hold a very special place in your heart for a reason, so never let them go. What events or people in your life make you feel sentimental?

**Sequel**: A sequel is a continuation or a new chapter in a story that has already been told.

How do you experience sequels in your life, especially when circumstances change? A new marriage or a new career can represent the start of a sequel in the story that is your life. What moments in your life introduce the continuation of your life story?

**Serenity**: The state of being calm, peaceful, or tranquil. Serenity is truly a blessing in life, and it can be quite difficult to capture at times. With the electronic world buzzing around us constantly, finding any sense of calm or peace might seem impossible. Serenity can be found in the smallest things, however, like a hot cup of tea or an interesting conversation with a friend. What brings you serenity in your life?

*"The best way to find yourself is to lose yourself in the service of others."*
— *Mahatma Gandhi*

**Serve**: To serve is to work for a prescribed amount of time in a generally sacrificial way as a servant to a master, a senator to the senate, or a soldier to an army. Concerning whoever or whatever you serve, do you exert your full effort and potential? If so, you will graduate from the server to the served. For you, what force or cause calls to serve?

**Service**: Service is work done for others, typically by volunteers. Service is incredibly helpful and friendly when it is done for those who are in need or for the community at large. What areas of life do you dedicate your services?

**Set**: Things are set when they are in the exact place that they need to be. Are you set ready for action? Being set is an indication of vigilance and preparedness. A sprinter on the track hears, "On your mark, get *set*, GO!" When they get into that set position, all other distractions fade away, and they are truly ready to put all of their hard work and training into action. Are you set to go out and accomplish your goals?

**Setback**: A check to progress; a reverse or defeat. Everyone experiences setbacks in life, but the key is how we handle them. How do you deal with a setback? Do not run from it in the hopes that it goes away, for it will often worsen if you do so. Instead, face the setback head on and use your reason and skills to solve the problem once and for all. What setbacks have you experienced in your life? Are you resilient?

**Settle**: To establish or become established in a way of life, job, or residence. Never in life should you settle for something that does not satisfy you fully. If you go through life settling for the first or easiest option presented to you, you may find yourself wanting more than what you have. Have you ever settled for something that didn't fully capture what you wanted?

**Sex**: Sex is both a necessary and superfluous act in life. Can it be considered as the active culmination of several attractions such as love, appearance, pleasure, etc.? The difference is realized in how you use sex. Sex used for nothing other than physical pleasure will eventually become an empty gesture. However, sex used for the expression of true, passionate love, and for procreation is an enriching component of a relationship. Does one ever stop and think of the specific reason for initiating the act of sex? Have you considered which passion(s) of the moment has culminated in sexual activity? We must not forget that sex is also simply a label for gender, but does not necessarily separate genders, so the final question must be: What is sex to you?

**Sexism**: Sexism is an attitude or behavior based on traditional stereotypes of sexual roles or discrimination or devaluation based on a person's sex. The belief that women are not as mentally or physically strong as men is completely erroneous and must be erased. Similarly, the notion that men do not feel sententious feelings or lack compassion is equally false. Have you ever been victim of sexism? How did you deal with the situation?

**Sham**: A sham is something false or fake purporting to be something real and genuine. Are you able to remain alert and ever watchful to detect shams when confronted with them? Shams can be dangerous to our identity and our free will, so avoiding them at all costs is vital. Have you ever encountered a sham that you thought was real?

**Shame**: The painful feeling arising from the consciousness of something dishonorable, improper, or ridiculous done by oneself or another. Shame is one of the worst emotions known to man. To feel shame is to lose your self-respect as a result of some wrongdoing. While shame is brought about by something negative, it presents an opportunity to refresh your situation and earn back your honor and respect. When have you felt shame?

> *"The books that the world calls immoral are books that show the world its own shame."*
> — *Oscar Wilde*

**Shape**: Shape is the <u>form</u> or outline of anything that exists in <u>space</u>. It also <u>describes</u> the <u>condition</u> of that thing, whether it is in good shape or bad shape. There is an <u>infinite</u> amount of shapes in <u>nature</u> and in the <u>universe</u>. What is your shape, and what kind of shape do you feel you are in?

**Share**: To <u>divide</u>, apportion, or <u>receive</u> equally. Sharing is a <u>virtue</u> in <u>life</u>. Given the current <u>economic</u> and environmental <u>state</u>, sharing will become more and more important on a large scale. As children, our parents and teachers <u>instruct</u> us on proper sharing, giving equal part and opportunity to each person with whom we interact. How often do you share with others? Does sharing have <u>value</u>? Is a <u>monetary</u> exchange more <u>significant</u> than a non-monetary <u>sentimental</u>?

**Shift**: To <u>change</u> or <u>move</u> from one <u>state</u>, place, or <u>direction</u> to another. Sometimes it is necessary to shift your goals and priorities to be <u>happy</u> in <u>life</u>. Sometimes shifts in your life will occur without your <u>consent</u>; face these times with a calm attitude and <u>rational</u> mind-set. Do you regularly <u>evaluate</u> your life and <u>shift</u> accordingly?

**Shine**: To appear unusually brightly or animated. What makes you shine? It releases <u>stress</u> and reinforces <u>self</u>-<u>confidence</u> to do things we <u>feel</u> we are good at. Take time to appreciate your unique set of skills and abilities.

**Shirk**: To <u>avoid</u> doing something or to leave something undone. Do not shirk your duties; <u>honor</u> your commitments and plan in advance for recreational and mandatory activities alike. Do you follow through when you have given your <u>word</u> you will <u>complete</u> a <u>task</u>?

**Shock**: A sudden jarring blow; also describes the <u>state</u> of someone faced with such a <u>force</u>. Shock can wreak havoc on our psyches. Be <u>patient</u> with yourself and others who have experienced a shock of some kind.

This state of mind defies normal behavioral rules. Even people you know well can be unpredictable in this state, so make special accommodations for them. Do you bounce back from shock? Are you patient with those who have experienced a shock?

**Should**: Indicates <u>obligation</u> or <u>desired</u> <u>state</u>. Do you <u>concentrate</u> on what should have happened or what you should have done, or do you look forward and <u>concentrate</u> on what you should do in the present to <u>improve</u> your <u>situation</u>?

**Show**: To display or allow to be seen. Are you <u>aware</u> of disingenuous actions only done for show? In other words, are you <u>conscious</u> of <u>actions</u> that do not <u>represent</u> anything real but give the <u>appearance</u> of actual depth? Show your feelings and <u>personality</u> whenever possible; the more you must <u>hide</u> about your <u>true</u> <u>self</u>, the more estranged you become from it. Do you show your true colors?

**Shudder**: A sudden shake or <u>tremble</u>. One of many involuntary bodily motions indicating a possible <u>problem</u>. Typically, shuddering is caused by uncomfortable, unpleasant, or <u>fear</u>-inducing stimuli. Do you <u>trust</u> your body? There is a reason it has evolved to react in this way when something has the <u>potential</u> to harm you.

**Shuffle**: To walk lazily without removing your feet from the ground; see <u>slouch</u>. How you carry yourself says volumes about your <u>attitude</u> and <u>personality</u>. It doesn't matter that you <u>feel</u> as if you defy the lazy <u>stereotype</u> of a shuffler. People make constant <u>subconscious</u> judgments based on body language and gait. Do you carry yourself with <u>competence</u> and <u>pride</u>?

**Shun**: To purposefully exclude <u>avoid</u> or <u>ignore</u>. People are shunned for a wide variety of reasons. If you <u>choose</u> to take part in the shunning, are you fully <u>aware</u> of why they are being excluded? If someone seems to be shunned unfairly, it is our <u>duty</u> to get to the bottom of the claims rather than blindly shunning. Do you shun with <u>good</u> cause?

**Shut**: To close. Before you shut things out of your <u>life</u> completely, do you <u>examine</u> their <u>merits</u> objectively as they pertain to you? Do you <u>explore</u> your options before shutting the doors of <u>opportunity</u> in your life? Shut is an awfully <u>finite</u> <u>word</u>, implying that something is closed off from the rest of the world. Work hard to keep an open mind rather than a closed one, and an open door for the problems of friends and family rather than a closed one. Do you carefully and rationally regard things before you shut things out of your life?

**Shy**: <u>Timid</u> and ill at ease with other people. What reason do you have to be shy? Do you find that a <u>fear</u> of embarrassment from saying the <u>wrong</u> thing at the wrong time keeps you from saying anything at all? The only way to get over this fear is to put yourself out there. It will be hard at first to leave your comfort zone and put more of your <u>personality</u> on the table for all to see, but rest assured, it gets easier the more you do it. The more <u>practice</u> you have at relating your own experiences and feelings to other people, the easier it gets to <u>approach</u> and meet new people who you know nothing about. What do you really have to <u>lose</u>? No one can fault you for being <u>good</u> natured and outgoing, and if they do, it is a <u>personal</u> <u>problem</u> on their part. It may be a long <u>process</u>, but it will be worthwhile; start thinking of strangers as friends you haven't met yet. Many people are concerned about what is thought of them because they are hypercritical of others. You will be surprised at how much less judged you feel when you exit a judgmental mind-set yourself. Do you take opportunities to meet new people?

**Sick**: Ill; unwell. From complex <u>physical</u> ailments and <u>emotional</u> disorders to simply being emotionally sick of someone or something, sickness is debilitating and unpleasant. Remember this when dealing with <u>sick</u> friends and family; they cannot always <u>control</u> unpleasant <u>behavior</u> and cope with the burden of sickness simultaneously. Do you try to be forgiving and supportive in these instances? Do you <u>recognize</u> the necessity of <u>support</u> and <u>love</u> in the face of sickness of any type?

**Side**: In <u>life</u>, there are more than just two sides to every situation. It is easy to distinguish between black and white, right and <u>wrong</u>, but our world is far too diverse and multifaceted to divide things by sides. Just as it is more exhilarating to be in the middle rather than watching from the side, it is important to <u>consider</u> those unrepresented who find themselves in the <u>middle</u> of a two-sided <u>battle</u>. Do you ever find yourself on the sidelines of life?

**Sight**: One of the five <u>senses</u>; also describes something experienced with this sense. Do you <u>trust</u> your sense of sight, or do you <u>judge</u> based on <u>appearance</u> <u>alone</u>? The way you <u>experience</u> the world is based on a <u>marriage</u> of your five senses, <u>consciousness</u>, and <u>intellect</u>. Do you understand your sense of sight as a cog in the grand machine that is your conscious <u>reality</u>?

**Sign**: An <u>object</u>, act, or occurrence that suggests the presence of or stands for something else. Some <u>signs</u> are overt and obvious, such as street signs; others take a host of knowledge to discern signs of mental disorders. Signs tell us what to expect of a given <u>situation</u> or what to expect in the future. Are you as observant and perceptive as possible and prepared for what is to come? Do you pay <u>attention</u> to signs in all of their forms?

**Significant**: <u>Important</u>; noteworthy. Do you <u>evaluate</u> your priorities thoughtfully

---

*"We'd get sick on too many cookies, but ever so much sicker on no cookies at all."*
— *Sinclair Lewis*

and often? There is a tendency to assign more significance to the glaring aspects of a situation. Taking a step back from a situation will allow you to observe your priorities on an equal playing field without placing undue significance on certain stressors. Significance rests in the sensors of the beholder. What is significant in your life?

**Silence**: What exists in the absence of noise? Silence was never written down nor was it uttered. Silence is underrated in our modern era. We are assaulted so thoroughly and constantly by noise that silence can make us uncomfortable. Awkward silences are only so if you refuse to see silence as an appreciation of and reflection on your circumstances.

Let silence relax you rather than press you for something to fill it. Do you appreciate silence?

**Silver**: In competitive arenas, silver is a precious metal and indicator of second place, constantly overshadowed by the esteemed ranking of gold. Similarly in life, we can often feel that we are being overshadowed, perhaps by an older sibling or a competitive peer. In these times, do you choose to continue to settle for second best or do you pick yourself up by the bootstraps and run for the gold? Are you content in being second-rate, or do you strive to achieve all you are capable of and more?

**Simplicity**: The state, quality, or an instance of being simple; having freedom from complexity or intricacy. Simplicity can be difficult to find in life. In today's fast-paced environment, simplicity seems almost impossible to capture when life seems to fly by us. It is a gift to not overcomplicate things. Simplicity can be found in many different things: a piece of chocolate, a quiet room, or a caring friend. While simplicity is most often a positive thing, we should be careful not to oversimplify things lest we forget to take into account something important. Where do you find simplicity in your life?

**Simulate**: Simulations of reality are dangerous when we are unable to distinguish the difference between what is fake and what is real. Current technologies like social media, mobile devices, and video games can contribute to this threat in that they can give us a false sense of connection, belonging, or simply distract us from everyday life. Stay vigilant so that when you are confronted with simulations you will recognize them. Have you ever encountered a simulation that mimicked something real?

> *"Sometimes the questions are complicated and the answers are simple."*
> — *Dr. Seuss*

**Sincerity**: o be sincere is to not be hypocritical or deceitful but rather open and genuine. Do you strive to be sincere, that is, honest and real with those around you? Positivity can come from sincerity because we leave everything on the table and nothing to be desired. However, this requires vulnerability and can cause one to be hurt or criticized in certain circumstances. Are you a sincere person?

**Sin**: To sin is to break a religious rule or law, typically on purpose. There is a certain feeling of exhilaration that comes with breaking the rules; however, the consequences of such actions are never worth it. When was the last time you sinned? What consequences did you face because of it?

**Sing**: To sing is to vocalize melodically. Are there moments in your life that give you so much joy that you just want to sing? Is it easier for you to sing what you feel if your emotions cannot be expressed in any other way? When was the last time you felt like singing?

**Single**: Solitary or not in a relationship. Although there are times when we should focus on trivial or singular things, it is the ability to instantaneously connect with the spirit or being of another human that sustains life. Man was not meant to be alone as we are social creatures whose creativity and life force feed off interaction with one another. Do you enjoy being single? Would you prefer to be single your entire life?

**Single-hearted**: To be single-hearted is to be honest, sincere, and faithful. A single-hearted person sticks completely to his or her purpose in life and never falters from this determination. A musical artist may be poor and starving, but he is single-hearted in his attempts to create something meaningful and beautiful to share with others. Are you a single-hearted person? What single-hearted purpose drives you to achieve your dreams?

**Skill**: The ability, coming from one's knowledge, practice, or aptitude; to do something well. Skills come in many different shapes and forms in life. Whatever your skills may be, they are what make you the best version of you. Have you identified your skills? This is the first step to realizing what you want to do and how you will do it. If you cultivate your skills and improve upon them, you will have plenty of opportunities to make an impact on this world. What are your skills and how do you apply them?

**Skin**: Your skin is a marker of your racial heritage and your personal identity. Do you take care of your skin? It is the first thing people notice when they see you. Maintaining a positive and healthy lifestyle will make your skin look brighter and healthier. Are you comfortable in your own skin? Do you judge people according

to the content of their character and not the color of their skin? Take care to discern skin-deep beauty from all-encompassing inner beauty.

**Sky**: The sky can take on an infinite number of combinations of colors and tones; blue on a clear day, gray on an overcast and dreary day, and any number of pinks, purples, oranges, and reds every day when the sun sets. It is easy to forget that the sky, in all of its beauty, is not a large colorful ceiling on our world but rather a visual representation of an infinite space.

**Slander**: Anything spoken that harms the reputation of someone or something. Do you slander on purpose? Do you verify claims before you spread them?

**Slaughter**: To kill animals or people by butchering them in large numbers. Some believe that killing animals for food is as morally wrong as genocide and elevate all animals to the human level. Human slaughter is always wrong, and though most agree some animals must be killed for food, they don't believe in causing them undue suffering. Then the question becomes *how* are animals being slaughtered? Though it is increasingly taboo to discuss the hunting and killing of wildlife, it is worth knowing how the animals you eat have been treated. Do you know how your meat ended up on your plate?

**Slave**: When one person is owned by another and has no individual freedom. Slavery is never justifiable or acceptable. Human rights are of the utmost importance, and when they are swept under the rug it represents a societal turn for the worse. Do you recognize violations of human rights?

> *"Be not the slave of your own past - plunge into the sublime seas, dive deep, and swim far, so you shall come back with new self-respect, with new power, and with an advanced experience that shall explain and overlook the old."*
> — *Ralph Waldo Emerson*

**Sleazy**: Low in quality and can be applied to objects or people. Do you steer clear of sleazy things and save for the higher-quality product, or do you waste smaller amounts of money at more frequent intervals?

**Sleep**: The state of rest of the body and mind. Sleep allows our bodies and minds to recharge and recuperate after taxing events. Do not underestimate the value of sleep; your mental and physical health suffer as a direct result of not getting enough of it. Do you get enough sleep?

**Sloth**: The condition of being opposed to work or activity of any kind. Rest is necessary but in moderation; if you find yourself opposed to all activity regardless of intensity or type, reevaluate your life and look inward to seek answers as to why you are being unnaturally inactive. Do you rest, play, and work in moderation?

**Slouch**: Your posture and how you carry yourself reflect what type of person you are. Though you should never judge a book by its cover, certain body languages have come to connote certain attitudes; slouching has come to represent disinterest and laziness. Yes, it is possible to slouch and still be successful, but why not present yourself in a positive light, no matter what you are trying to accomplish? Are you slovenly or on top of things?

**Slow**: Moving at a low speed. A word with an increasingly bad connotation, though slow and steady wins the race. In this day and age, "fast" is generally equated with "better." Take care to give all your activities the time they deserve, and be patient with yourself and others; not everything will move as quickly as you want it to. Do you appreciate things for more than the speed at which they are presented to you? Time moves slowly when we are consciously aware of being in an unpleasant situation and extremely fast when we become immersed in life. As life goes on, time moves less and less slowly; appreciate it before it is gone.

*"Don't cry because it's over, smile because it happened."*
*— Dr. Seuss*

**Smell**: One of the five senses that we use to experience the world around us. Our sense of smell has the strongest tie to memory. A simple scent can transport us across time and space; to entire years of our childhood or to a very specific and distinct instance. Be aware of and trust your senses; they bring the world around you to life and allow you to become embroiled in your environment rather than isolated as a distant observer. Do you use your sense of smell to appreciate the world around you?

**Smile**: To show pleasure or approval by turning up the corners of one's mouth. Smiling is an easy way to make those around you feel more comfortable. Smiles are contagious and extremely meaningful; sometimes this simple facial action can say more than words ever could. It is how you show someone that you love them, that you are happy to see them or that you think that they are witty or humorous. Do you make an effort to exude positivity?

**Smoke**: Many harmful things are marked by smoke. Pollution often is visually represented by it and poisons our atmosphere. Smoke from destructive forest fires asphyxiates animals and humans alike, and tobacco smoke causes disease both in the smoker and those around them. Humans have evolved into diverse and versatile body types that can accomplish a myriad of different tasks; filtering smoke with our lungs is simply not one of them. Though it is of course possible to do on a regular basis, it is not a sustainable activity and will lead to the degradation of our bodies just as pollution and fire degrade our environment. Are you conscious of what smoke, in all of its forms, can do to your body?

**Smother**: To smother something implies its eventual demise. This is the goal when one smothers a fire to put it out, but one can be smothered by positive things as well; moderation is key. Affection and support are indispensable assets to have in your life, yet when you are smothered by people who mean well, the results are not so positive. Do you make an effort to give and take in moderation?

**Smug**: Self-satisfied to an aggravating degree. Smugness is selfish and unproductive; if your thoughts or behavior are dominated by justifications and appeal to your greatness, take a second look at your life. Those who are truly great do not need to convince others of this; self-confidence is a positive thing, but smugness precludes insecurity and muddled priorities. Are you suspicious of those who are smug? Do you look for causal insecurities when you encounter smugness?

*"I love Virginians because Virginians are all snobs and I like snobs. A snob has to spend so much time being a snob that he has little time left to meddle with you."*
— *William Faulkner*

**Smut**: Dirty or low-quality talk or writing. Smutty media represents sensationalism in the worst way possible; smutty talk or writing attempts to highlight unpleasantness in order to shock and disgust people into reading or listening in order to turn a profit from morally starved events. Do you recognize smut for what it is?

**Snarl**: To become entangled with something, either literally with rope, or figuratively with situations in life. Do your best to avoid snarls; foresight and planning will help you in this endeavor. Life is like a rope in that when it becomes snarled, tugging on the first bit of loose rope you see rarely solves the problem. You must look at the knot from all sides before you know which bit of rope to pull on; circumvent your problems before you take action. Do you handle the snarls of life with cognizance and tranquillity?

**Sneer**: An ill-intentioned smile with a smug connotation. While smiles are meant to represent and spread joy, sneers are facial expressions of scorn or sarcasm meant to make the recipient feel worse. Do you avoid sneering?

**Snob**: Someone who is arrogant and smug. A snob believes that their own intelligence and taste are items of utmost importance, trumping the feelings and opinions of all others. Snobbishness breeds close-mindedness, the most debilitating impediment to progress in any realm. Do you listen to others and measure other opinions against yours using rationality and reason rather than automatically valuing your own above all else?

**Snoop**: To sneak about in order to obtain information you are not meant to have. Don't be surprised when you are met with disdain and anger when you invade the privacy of others. Do you try to gather as much information as you can before making decisions? The personal affairs of others often supersede the realm of useful information and enter that of useless gossip fueling smut. Snooping around a factory to see if a company is exercising proper environmental protection standards is very different from snooping in a colleague's medicine cabinet during a party to see what kind of embarrassing ailments they have. Are you aware of the consequences of snooping?

**Snooze**: A short rest. A full night's sleep is always preferable to a series of disjointed spats of sleep, but sometimes naps are unavoidable, not to mention quite enjoyable. A nap can sometimes be a healthy tool that gives you the extra brainpower or relaxation you need to make it through the day. That being said, if you find yourself taking multiple naps a day or taking extended, afternoon-encompassing naps, reevaluate your sleep schedule and possibly your life. The symptom of not wanting to get out of bed is associated with depression. Unfortunately, it is a symptom that compounds upon the other effects of the disease; when you stay in bed to avoid facing your problems, they will almost surely become worse, leading you to spend more time in bed, eventually becoming frozen as a result of the fear of these growing problems. Do you snooze responsibly and healthily?

**Snub**: To slight or treat someone with scorn or unfriendliness. What reason would someone have for snubbing you? Causes could be prejudice, jealousy, or just a generally bad attitude. Whatever the case, when someone snubs someone else, it says more about them than it does about the unfortunate recipient of their snubbing. Before you face scorn with unfriendliness, do you use critical thinking to try to understand why you are being scorned? If the person has a legitimate reason, you can learn from their unpleasant behavior at the very least; if they don't have any rational grounds for their snubbing, they can be ignored entirely as their problem is a personal one. Do you regard antisocial behavior with curiosity rather than anger?

**So**: To such an extent. Avoid exaggerating unnecessarily; your future claims will only degrade in credibility, and if you persist, no one will trust anything you say. Do you make sure you always say what you mean and mean what you say, or do you sensationalize for attention? Doing so will hurt your standing as a trustworthy individual.

**Society**: A society is only as good as the intellect and character of its individual members. Does your social system render you dependent on and monetarily beholden to other individuals, conforming in life to rules that were established by that very same social system? It is important to understand our need to gather within the realm of a common cause, even something as simple as living productively, peacefully, and harmoniously as possible. By maintaining balance within the six constants of life, a society can achieve equilibrium. The six constants include changing differences, conflict, resource usage, corporacracy, dependency, and cultural enigmas. How do you achieve stability in your life and strive to be a productive member of society? Social rules or laws also help maintain a sense of balance, but they vary from society to society and can be of the utmost rigidity or extremely relaxed. No matter their levels of flexibility, law and order can be considered the backbone of any society. Different societies function in drastically different ways; keep this in mind when you are visiting new places for the first time. Do you behave with social responsibility? What defines your role in society?

**Sojourn**: A temporary stay or visit. Our time on Earth is but a tiny part of its history; recognizing ourselves in the context of this grand history is humbling and thought provoking. Each of us only gets a certain amount of time to make our mark on Earth, so make it a positive one. Do you make the best of your time on this planet?

**Solace**: Relief or comfort. When times are rough, take solace in friends and family and give solace whenever possible. Even when it seems as if your life is dominated by negative forces, it is important to appreciate and be thankful for what you do have. Never lose hope and you will never be lost. Do you give solace where it is needed?

**Solar System**: A solar system consists of a sun and all objects that are in its orbit. Our solar system includes our sun and our eight planets. It is certainly a humbling experience to imagine how small we are in comparison to our solar system. It is likewise humbling to imagine the millions of other solar systems in the universe. Do not let this enormously vast universe intimidate you, but rather let it dwarf your problems; in the grand scheme of things, your problem may not be as big or serious as you think. How do you maintain a perspective that takes into account the big picture? Not every snafu in life is the end of the world.

**Soldier**: A person who fights for something, most typically in an army of some kind. A soldier of fortune is one that will fight for any cause as long as the price is right. Adhere to your moral compass and stand up for what you believe in; a soldier of fortune only fights for short-sighted selfish reasons. Do you stand up for what you believe in?

**Solemnize**: To celebrate formally; to mark by traditional practices. Are you aware what the ceremonies in your life represent?

**Solicit**: To ask or seek to obtain something from someone else. What do you solicit from others? Do you try to give more than you take? Solicit help from those you trust and be ready to give support when it is solicited from you.

**Solidarity**: Unity in action or feeling. When times are rough, it is very beneficial to have a support group of people who understand your problems. When you are feeling alone and lost, do you seek out like-minded or similarly burdened people? Those who fight tooth and nail to keep the power in the hands of only a few individuals at the expense of the rest of the population are aware that their only hope of doing so is to maintain division between similarly disenfranchised groups; social issues cannot be conquered without solidarity. Do you feel a sense of solidarity in your life?

**Solidify**: To make or become solid or rigid; reinforce. Like learning a new skill by muscle memory, living in new circumstances and situations requires some practice; to solidify good habits we must be consistently correct our behavior. Do you solidify positive ideas and good habits by practicing them consistently?

**Solitude**: Existing or done alone. Solitude can provide you with time to be alone with your thoughts and to relax and just be. Separating yourself from the opinions and actions of others is beneficial in moderation but detrimental if you use it to avoid facing your problems. Solitude should be used as a tool to meditate on your life and yourself, not as an avoidance mechanism. How do you benefit from solitude in your life?

**Solution**: The explanation or answer to a given problem. Keep in mind that the larger the problem, the less clear-cut the solution is bound to be. Sometimes it is valuable to stop looking for a fix-all solution and start looking for ways to compromise in order to accomplish your goals. Solutions are not always well defined or obvious; sometimes they are riddled with compromises and concessions that may not satisfy all of your desires. Do you reach solutions via critical thinking and rationality? Furthermore, do you only look for solutions in the physical world, or do you search elsewhere for answers in emotional, spiritual, or other realms? Can changing

> *"If I had an hour to solve a problem I'd spend fifty-five minutes thinking about the problem and five minutes thinking about solutions."*
> — *Albert Einstein*

or mixing the elements of a problem become the solution for solving that problem? Do you seek solutions in remodeling your creed?

**Solve**: Your problem solving repertoire is the most valuable set of skills that you possess and takes a lot of practice to build, so be patient. What methods have you developed over time to solve your problems?

**Somber**: Sad and gloomy. Avoid having a somber attitude whenever possible as it can escalate to depression. Even when things seem dismal and hopeless, having a positive attitude can only help and having a somber one can only hurt the situation. Do you make every effort to avoid being somber?

**Some**: Of a certain unspecified number, amount, or degree. Most view this word as insignificant when it is actually important. Why? By using the word "some," you can be ethical about the claims you're making and avoid overgeneralizations that are incorrect.

**Something**: A certain thing that is unspecified or unknown. We are all looking for something in life; it is not the thing that matters as much as how we go about getting it. Material goals should be sought after as a means or by-products to your achievements and that which take on the forms of feelings. Happiness and love are perfectly acceptable "somethings" or goals to gear your life toward. Just because your goal is vague does not mean that it is silly or not worth fighting for; you just have to find out how to make it happen. What are you searching for in life, or what goals do you want to achieve? Do you have a plan in mind to accomplish them?

**Song**: A piece of music, usually employing a verbal text. Songs can express ideas, feelings, and vibrations in ways that no other medium can. What is it about certain musical notes that, when put together, pleases our ears and our minds and makes our hearts swell out of our chests? Music is incredible in its universality, and songs can be extremely powerful and unifying catalysts of social change as well as delightful and light entertainment. Sing your own song loudly and proudly, and do not let anyone stifle it. Do you value song for its incredible ability to express and convey ideas and feelings?

**Soon**: Within a short amount of time. It is easy to procrastinate in accomplishing your goals; tomorrow will always be an easier option simply because it is not right now. Quit saying "Soon I will do this," and start saying "Now I will do this." Do not let problems weigh you down unnecessarily. Accomplish what you can while you can, and do not be weighed down by things you cannot change. Do you use soon as a goal rather than an excuse?

**Sophisticated**: Able to comprehend and interpret complex issues; wise in the ways of the world. Sophistication comes from many years of having an open mind and a willingness to learn. Ask questions, try new things; do not mistake sophistication for pride or arrogance; it is much more valuable and useful for that matter. Do you approach every day with curiosity?

**Sordid**: Disgusting, dirty. Literally sordid objects are far less dangerous than sordid ideas; corrupt and evil notions have a way of spreading like wildfire when they catch on in a certain way and are propagated by powerful and clever enough people. Resist them at all costs, and let reason and logic be your beacons of hope. Do you avoid sordid ideas?

**Sore**: Aching or giving pain in some way. Just as muscles become sore after a hard workout, your heart and psyche become sore after emotionally taxing events. The same is then true for both: They rebuild and become stronger than they were before. Think of soreness as growing; concentrate not on how much it hurts but where it will take you. Learn from your emotional or physical soreness and you will be able to prevent it in the future. Do you let soreness weaken you, or use it to gain strength for the future?

**Sorrow**: Sometimes life can seem bleak and hopeless. Concentrate on the positive points in your life instead of problems you cannot solve. Can you solve the problem you are sad about? If you can, do so and move on. If you cannot, learn from it and move on. Instead of wallowing in a pit of sorrow, construct a ladder. Let your friends and family act as the sturdy rails and your accomplishments and ambition as the rungs. It could take a while before you make it above ground, but be patient and do not let go of your ladder. Do you look at sorrow as an end or a beginning?

**Soul**: The part of one's being which is regarded as the center of moral and emotional consciousness and sense of identity. One washes the body in vain if one does not wash the soul. Humans are imperfect, and you must know of and accept the presence of weakness, failure, and negative attributes in order to find your soul. How do you define the soul, and how do you cleanse it? Different people have different conceptions of what constructs it. You must

> *"A room without books is like a body without a soul."*
> *— Marcus Tullius Cicero*

understand your own soul to comprehend the soul of life.

**Sour**: Sharp, acidic taste. Our sense of taste can tell us when something is unsafe to ingest and therefore protect us from illness. In this same way, bad situations can leave us with a figurative sour taste in our mouths, discouraging us from repeating our actions.

**Sow**: We sow the plants that feed us all across the world. But in life, we sow more than plants; we sow knowledge, wisdom, and dreams as well. Do we think in terms of starting or consciously creating life rather than growing? What do you cultivate and share with the world?

**Space**: A vacuum. Space encompasses all known material in the entire universe. We cannot see space, but it is always surrounding us, tethering us securely to Earth's surface. Despite space's unlimited expanse, we feel stifled when we are not allowed enough space. Do you need more space to operate?

**Spare**: It is always a helpful practice to keep a spare of something important around in case of emergencies. Some spare money, a spare tire, an extra change of clothes—we find that we need these more often than we think. Sparing is preparedness with the focus on saving time and effort. What things do you spare or keep spare?

**Speak**: He who speaks sows, and he who hears harvests. The manner in which we speak is a prime indicator of who we are and how we present ourselves to the outside world. The spoken word has the power to tear down and to exalt. We can compose gentle and kind words that comfort and uplift our audience; we can spew out verbal abuse that inspires hatred as well. Sometimes in speaking, we form generalizations in our mind because we already know the specifics and fail to express them. Do you express your thoughts well through speaking? Do you think before you speak?

**Special**: To be special is to have some discerning quality about your character or decorum that separates you from everyone else. Your best and most unique quality is the one that makes you special. No matter how obscure your quality or skill, if it is unique, beneficial, and productive, it is special. What is your special quality?

**Specialty**: Your specialty is simply the way you apply your special skills or abilities to your everyday life. Often it can be difficult to discover exactly what your specialty is. Your specialty is determined by who you see yourself as and the goals you set to get to that point. What is your specialty? Is it beneficial and productive in society?

**Species**: Your species is the biological group that determines to whom you are similar and with whom you may reproduce. In our case, this is the human species. Though we belong to the same group, not every individual we come across will be a potential partner, but it is still important to treat others with respect. Do you treat all humans like you treat your companions?

**Specific**: Specified, precise, or particular. The specifics of any undertaking are important when setting out to do something. When architects and engineers build great monuments or skyscrapers, you won't hear them say, "Well, we need a 2.35 feet bar, but this one is 2.3 feet. Same thing, right?" That construction would be doomed from the start if attention to detail and specifics are not top priority. How can you pay more attention to the specifics in your life? Do you find that you concentrate too heavily on the specifics?

**Spectacle**: A spectacle is any large or noisy public demonstration in which one uses pomp and performance to convey some urgent message. When does an object of interest become a marvel or a curiosity? How often does an object or

> *"Earning happiness means doing good and working, not speculating and being lazy. Laziness may look inviting, but only work gives you true satisfaction."*
> — Anne Frank

> *"People demand freedom of speech as a compensation for the freedom of thought which they seldom use."*
> — Søren Kierkegaard

scene exposed to the public gaze become a spectacle?

**Spectator**: A spectator is merely a bystander watching the events transpiring before him or her. In life, there are times when it is appropriate to watch, but there are times when it is important to act. Are you more than a spectator? Do you passively sit back and observe or do you choose to actively participate?

**Spectrum**: Life can be considered a large prism that when peered through reveals a shining light illuminating multiple paths to take in our lives. What path or paths do you foresee yourself taking in the future?

**Speculate**: The contemplation or consideration of some subject. Speculation is an important process for any person faced with making decisions. Meditating on our thoughts and actions will allow us to make better, more informed decisions. However, we should not speculate so much that we miss opportunities. Do you make rash, impulsive decisions or carefully considered decisions? Do you take time to speculate on a daily basis?

**Speech**: A form of communication in spoken language, made by a speaker before an audience for a given purpose. A well-delivered speech has the power to unite enemies, create social change, or even incite wars. The key to any speech is how it caters to what the audience wants to hear. When we blaspheme or speak negatively about someone, does it not manifest itself as a speech to the audience?

**Speed**: Speed is only a positive until it is used in excess. We should strive to do what we do with speed and skill; however, when we speed up too fast, we leave ourselves vulnerable to mistakes and missed opportunities. Speed is a gift that some are granted genetically, while others get faster through training, hard work, and performance. Do you find that you move through life too quickly or too slowly?

**Spend**: To pay out, disburse, or expend; dispose of (as in money, wealth, or resources). Spending is a dangerous habit in this day and age. Everything seems to be at our fingertips and we can burn holes in our pockets more quickly than ever. Instead of spending money, spend time with the people and things that you love. How do you spend your time, money, and energy?

**Sphere**: The Earth is the all-encompassing sphere of life in which everything comes full circle. We are born into this great sphere and leave as an eternal part of it. Within the planetary sphere, we can partake in public and private spheres of influence. Do you actively participate in your sphere of interest or influence?

**Spill**: To cause or allow to run or fall from a container, especially accidentally or wastefully. An oil spill is one classic example of how negligence and waste can destroy the world around us. How do you avoid spills?

**Spin**: To cause to turn around rapidly, as on an axis; twirl; whirl. Life can seem to spin out around us at times. Sometimes we experience a state of mental confusion when things spin out of control or take a turn for the worse. The dizzying effects of a spin-out can be hard on our minds and our bodies. How do you recover from your spin-outs? How do you avoid them?

**Spirit, Spiritual**: The spirit is the principle component of conscious life. It is that ethereal, vital being that animates the body and mediates between body and soul. Our spirit is our personality and individuality. It is our motivation, our vigor, and our drive to achieve our dreams. The spirit is akin to a fire that burns inside us all. In life, the fire that is our spirit becomes extinguished at times of great despair or when we face the unknown. Human interaction has the power to rekindle that fire, so in these trying times, reach out to someone close to you and reignite that fire. How do you let your spirit flourish? Because each of us has a spirit, humans are unique in that we bridge the gap between the corporeal world and spiritual realm. Is the spiritual world a superior, parallel world within another dimension that comprises the universe in an energy charged aura of positives and negatives? How do you access your spiritual world? *Is our spirit the only connection with God?*

**Split**: To separate persons or groups, disunite; to divide and share; to become broken or ripped apart, especially from internal pressure; to become divided as a result of discord or disagreement; to make trivial distinctions, to quibble; a breach or rupture in a group. When and why did you separate yourself from a group or another person? Was it voluntary or forced? Could it have been avoided, or how would you avoid a similar situation in the future?

**Spoil**: To diminish or impair the quality of; affect detrimentally. Sometimes the best-laid plans are spoiled by circumstances out of our control, but most often it is caused by negligence or a lapse in judgment. Are you the type who stays organized and keeps everything intact, or are you the type who lets the details slip through the cracks and allow things to spoil?

**Sponsor**: A sponsor is someone who vouches for you and supports you in times of need or desperation. Your sponsor is like a mentor and represents the <u>character</u> and decorum that you aspire to achieve. Who would you consider your sponsor? Would you be a sponsor for someone in need?

**Spontaneity**: Coming or resulting from a natural impulse or tendency; without <u>effort</u> or premeditation; natural, unconstrained, and unplanned. Spontaneity is impulsive and <u>fun</u>, but can get out of control quickly when we make spontaneous decisions. Much like most things in <u>life</u>, spontaneity is best when used in moderation. Do you live your life spontaneously? Has your spontaneity ever gotten you in trouble?

**Sport**: Throughout our <u>history</u>, sport has been an important cultural phenomenon that has recently skyrocketed to the apex of human attention. Sports began in ancient times as a test of physical fitness and survival capability. Nowadays, sport exists as a pastime and is a source of <u>entertainment</u> for just about everybody. There is honor in engaging in sports, and sports provide a sense of esteem and confidence in both physical and mental aspects of vitality. Do you find enjoyment, entertainment, or passion in sport?

**Squabble**: We get involved in squabbles all the time; <u>arguments</u> and small fights are impossible to avoid in life. Bickering about petty things usually won't do us any <u>good</u>, but having a go every once in a while can be a healthy way to get our thoughts out on the table and make our feelings known. The only way to <u>solve</u> <u>problems</u> is to <u>work</u> through them, so squabbling can be a positive at times. Do you find yourself squabbling about trivial things? Is it a healthy way for you to

> *"Life is a series of natural and spontaneous changes. Don't resist them; that only creates sorrow. Let reality be reality. Let things flow naturally forward in whatever way they like."*
> — *Lao Tzu*

express your feelings and opinions, or does confrontation intimidate you?

**Squalid**: To be squalid is to be dirty and utterly repulsive. You might find yourself in a squalid <u>state</u> after not showering for a few days. Squalidness is negative because it tells others that you lack self-respect. Do you <u>respect</u> yourself, and how do you maintain a constant feeling of self-respect?

**Squeeze**: To extract from by applying pressure; to extract by dishonest means; to oppress with burdensome exactions. Sometimes we "squeeze out" or <u>force</u> others to reveal <u>information</u> to us that they would otherwise deem as private or prefer not to. Have you ever pressured another to disclose information to you? How did it make you feel, and did you regret it afterward?

**Stable, Stability, Stabilize:** Resistant to sudden <u>change</u> or deterioration. Steadfast, as in character or purpose; dependable. Stability is important to find in <u>life</u>. Stay firm in your position and steadfast in your <u>character</u>. Stabilize your <u>mind</u> and <u>body</u> as a foundation on which to start any project, even one as simple as waking up and beginning your day. Where do you find stability in your life?

**Stage**: It has been said that all the <u>world</u> is a stage where we perform our roles as the audience watches. A stage is a resting place on the journey of life; it is a blank canvas at a crossroad where we paint a picture of what we want for the next stage of our lives. What is your stage and how do you use it?

**Stagnant**: To be inactive, sluggish, or dull. <u>Often</u> <u>life</u> can seem stagnant when we don't have enough excitement or we don't experience any changes. Stagnancy can be a <u>positive</u>

for those who oppose change, and it can be a negative for those who welcome new opportunities. Do you find that your life is feeling stagnant? Do you view it as a positive or negative? If negative, how do you infuse energy into your life?

**Stain**: To bring reproach or dishonor upon; to blemish. A stain on a permanent record is something we all take care to avoid. When we run afoul of the law or the rules, we imprint a stain upon our moral character, personality, or reputation. Do you have any stains? Do they define you? How did you clear your name, if at all?

**Stalemate**: A stalemate is a crossroads in which no move can be made by anyone. It is a complete and utter stop in the progression of an action or process. When stuck at a stalemate in your life, how do you wriggle free from what tethered you?

**Stall**: When you don't give an engine enough gas after shifting gears, it stalls or comes to a standstill and is brought to a stop. In life, we also have moments where we run out of gas and hit a stalling point. In these times, we must restart our engines and get back on the road. When was the last time you hit a stalling point? How did you get going again?

**Stamp**: We all have the power to imprint our stamp onto whatever experiences we encounter. Your stamp is your individual flair and panache, your joie de vivre. Put your stamp on everything you do. What kind of stamp do you imprint on people?

**Stale:** When something is stale, it is unpalatable, dry, tedious, lacking in originality or efficacy, or has lost its freshness. Usually, this term is used in relation to food. When food gets too old, many times it loses its flavor and becomes unpleasant to eat. Is there anything in your life that you once enjoyed but has now become stale? Things that we do often can become boring and tedious after a while, so it is important to try to find new things to keep life exciting. Do you seek out new adventures in your life, or do you keep to your normal schedule? Stale can also be used to refer to the loss of efficacy. If you don't act on situations, it is possible that you can lose the power to effect the outcome. Are there any situations in your life that you feel like you've lost the power to control? It's not too late to take back that power. If you know what you want to do, you must take action to accomplish it. If you do this, the power to control your life is back in your hands. Do you let other people control your life?

**Stand**: Taking a stand for something you believe in is the most noble and courageous act a person can commit. To stand is to exude confidence, to claim honor, and to show poise under fire. We must take a stand when we are oppressed by powers that stifle our creativity or our opinions. We must stand tall in the face of adversity when the cause is just and noble and the effort is true. What calls you to take a stand?

> *"Someday you will be old enough to start reading fairy tales again."*
> — *C. S. Lewis*

**Standard**: An average or normal requirement, quality, quantity, level, or grade. A standard can also be a rule or principle that is used as a basis for judgment and measurement of morals, ethics, or habits. Standards are in place for a reason. They keep us in line and in form. They allow us to erect great monuments and to make strides in technological and scientific advancements. You can also set standards for yourself; it is important to conduct yourself within the bounds of your personal and moral principles. What series of standards have you created for yourself?

**Star**: In the past, stars were symbolically known as gods who were to be revered and idolized. Today, we appropriate that same adoration to celebrities. Wide-scale adoration can be dangerous when we don't hold stars to the same standards as everyone else; however, stars who don't abuse their power deserve their reverence. Who do you idolize? How many stars are in the universe?

**Stare**: A stare is long, inquiring glance at something that captures the interest of its audience. We might find ourselves staring at something very beautiful or very strange. We should take care not to be caught staring at others in order to avoid making them feel uncomfortable. What grabs your attention?

**Start**: Even great towers start at ground level. In the course of a lifetime, we will experience a number of new starting points at which new opportunities will present themselves. The starting line of life is that moment in time and space where we must be prepared to face everything that is about to face us. When do you see yourself making a fresh start?

**State**: A state is a supreme public power within a sovereign political entity. A state requires its citizens to be loyal, for they are the backbone of the political body that represents them. Feelings of nationalism are inspired by the state, and they call upon their citizens to follow the standards of the state as outlined when the state was founded. States are meant to be defended, and this is also the responsibility of the state. How do you honor your state? A state, or state of being, can also be a condition of a person or thing, as with respect to circumstances or attributes; status, rank, or position in life. Your state can be physical or emotional. Where or what is your state of being? Are you happy, sad, wealthy, or healthy, ill, or handicapped? of control either over you feel in control of your other people? poor? Physically, are you One can also be in a state themselves or others. Do life, or do you try to control

> *"I wore black because I liked it. I still do, and wearing it still means something to me. It's still my symbol of rebellion—against a stagnant status quo, against our hypocritical houses of God, against people whose minds are closed to others' ideas."*
> *— Johnny Cash*

**Statue**: A statue is a symbolic monument erected to pay tribute to someone or something that had a tremendous and meaningful impact. The Statue of Liberty symbolizes freedom and opportunity for the USA. What do statues mean to you?

**Stay**: To hold out or endure, as in a contest or task. Staying the course is important to accomplish any goal. When it comes to any plan, you have to stay dedicated to making a positive impact on what you do. Do you know when to stay the course and when not to stay the course? Do you stay with the positives or succumb to the negatives?

**Status**: Status is the comparison of your social situation to the social situations of all others. We use status to assist in determining who the important people in our society are. Measuring status is controversial as it has a tendency to discriminate the marginalized minority. What do you consider to be your status?

**Steady**: Everyone knows the adage "Slow and steady wins the race." We need to keep our aim steady and true in order to accomplish what we set out to accomplish, though we should not let steady become stale. Do you maintain a steady and positive lifestyle?

**Steal**: To take (the property of another or others) without permission or right, especially secretly or by force. Stealing is an affront to the decency of the human race. Stealing robs people of more than just their possessions. When you steal from someone, you steal their confidence and sense of safety. You open them up to vulnerabilities and cause them to lose self-respect. What causes a person to commit such a negative, immoral act? What is the motive to steal?

**Steer**: To guide the course of (something in motion) by a rudder, helm, or wheel. As teenagers, we learn how to drive a car, and the most important part of that learning process is operating the steering wheel. In life, we have to take the wheel in making all decisions. Where is the next place to which you will steer yourself?

**Step**: We take baby steps when learning a new skill or task. When we make a game plan or a business plan, we follow steps to ensure that we cover all the bases and get the job done. What is your next step in life?

**Stereotype**: Stereotypes are generalizations made about a specific group of people. They can often be employed to tease or to oppress a minority. Stereotypes should never be used to discriminate against others. Have you ever been discriminated against with a stereotype? Have you ever stereotyped others?

**Stifle**: To suppress, curb, or withhold. Life can be overwhelming sometimes, and it can seem to stifle our creativity and vigor for living. When life seems to stifle you, try looking at what you're doing from a different perspective. How do you avoid being stifled?

**Stigma**: A stigma is a brand of infamy, disgrace, or reproach. It is typically handed down for committing some terrible crime, such as the red "A" forced upon Hester Prynne in Hawthorne's *The Scarlet Letter*. Do you bear any stigmata?

**Still**: To be still is to be free from turbulence and silent. Stillness is tranquillity in a fast-paced life. Where do you go when you need stillness? Where is your beach?

**Stimulus**: Something that incites action or exertion or quickens action, feeling, or thought. A stimulus is like a shot of adrenaline straight to the heart. It has the power to resurrect that which is dying. There is any number of stimuli in the outside world, but the most important stimulus comes from within. What is your internal stimulus?

**Stink**: A stink is a particularly awful odor that offends all the senses. A corrupt government office might be said to have a certain "stink" to it. Does anything in your life stink?

**Stock**: The quantity of something accumulated, as for future use. We keep a stock of products for safekeeping in case of an emergency. It is important to always have a backup plan in case of an emergency. What sort of things do you keep in stock?

**Stoic**: A stoic person is seemingly indifferent to or unaffected by joy, grief, pleasure, or pain. Stoicism is positive only when it is appropriate not to show emotion; otherwise, we should not purposefully hide our emotions but rather allow them to be seen and heard. Do you find that you bottle up your emotions or let them out?

> *"So we shall let the reader answer this question for himself: who is the happier man, he who has braved the storm of life and lived or he who has stayed securely on shore and merely existed?"*
> — *Hunter S. Thompson*

**Stone**: Stone is the basis for all construction. Humans have been working with stone for thousands of years. We have erected great monuments and developed <u>tools</u> and weapons with stone. Do you realize the major impact that stone has on your everyday <u>life</u>?

**Stop**: What causes someone to ask you to stop? They might be uncomfortable or offended by something you've done. The key is to <u>know</u> when and why. Do you stop when you are told to do so?

**Store**: We go to the store whenever we <u>need</u> something; stores have made our lives incredibly easy in the last hundred years or so. But are we too dependent on them?

**Storm**: A storm is a veritable flurry of turbulence and violence in which one can get caught up. Storms are frightening, but we can take <u>comfort</u> that the storm does not last forever. Have you weathered a storm in your <u>life</u>?

**Story**: The story is the benchmark of human literacy and <u>progression</u>. We recount great tales of myth, as well as maintain a family history to pass down through the generations. As a <u>life</u> form, we are all telling a story. How do you appraise your life's story?

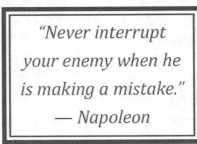

*"Never interrupt your enemy when he is making a mistake."* — *Napoleon*

**Straight**: Keeping a straight line or a straight <u>path</u> is an expedient way to get what you want. The shortest distance between point A and point B is a straight line. If you know what you want and where you must go to get it, the straightest path is your <u>best</u> bet. Do you walk a straight path in your life?

**Strain**: To be subjected to great <u>stress</u>. We all experience strain and create strain on others in our life. We must learn to balance the negatives and positives of life so as not to put an unnecessary strain on the world around us. Does your lifestyle strain the community, the environment, or even those close to you (family, etc.)?

**Strange**: Things we <u>consider</u> strange are often just unfamiliar to us. Have you ever reacted poorly to something you <u>thought</u> to be strange only to later find you simply had misunderstood it?

**Strategy**: A plan, method, or series of maneuvers or stratagems for obtaining a specific <u>goal</u> or <u>result</u>. Any good life plan needs a strategy to be effective. What is your strategy? How do you approach the obstacles in your life to effectively solve them?

**Stratify**: To lie in beds or layers. Many spend their <u>lives</u> stuck on single plane of existence. Do you ever feel yourself to be stuck? How can you widen your <u>perspective</u>?

**Stray**: To stray is to deviate from a <u>course</u> that is regarded as right or <u>moral</u>; to deviate from the subject matter at hand, digress. It becomes easy to stray when you lack any real <u>goals</u> and ways of achieving those goals. How can you develop a more specific life plan to help you avoid straying? Were there ever moments in your life where you strayed?

**<u>Strength</u>**: Together is strong; exude it, don't feign it. Strength can be <u>found</u> in other people and our <u>ability</u> to <u>work</u> together. Where do you find strength, and how do you show that strength? Do you exude it or feign it when you have not yet attained it?

**<u>Stress</u>**: <u>Mental</u>, <u>emotional</u>, or <u>physical</u> strain or tension. Stress can be caused by a myriad factors, both environmental and self-induced. What causes you stress? How can we <u>learn</u> to understand and recognize the causes and effects of stress so that we can avoid it? *How lethal is stress to your health and well-being?*

**Stretch**: To draw out or extend to the full length or extent. How far can we stretch to the point of breaking beyond limits? What can we stretch? The truth can be stretched and turned into a lie by distortion and omission. But our abilities can also be stretched, pushing us to accomplish things we didn't know we were capable of. Do you expand your skills in life?

**Strike**: Strikes are a formal way of registering discontent; they are a right that was fought for by labor unions in the nineteenth and twentieth century. But sometimes these venues are not enough. Especially now, with government interests looking to curb what little power labor unions exert, what are the viable alternatives?

**Stringent**: To be stringent is to be rigorously binding and exacting; it is being sever and strident in your views. While stringency can be a virtue in many respects, how can it also be a burden? How can a stringent perspective or worldview make for a closed mind, unwilling to listen to the worldviews of others?

**Strive**: To make strenuous efforts toward any goal. We strive for many things in life, but not all are positive and necessary. What do you strive for? Is it the necessary things in life, or the fleeting ones, the selfish, shallow, and ephemeral?

> *"I don't believe in colleges and universities. I believe in libraries because most students don't have any money. When I graduated from high school, it was during the Depression, and we had no money. I couldn't go to college, so I went to the library three days a week for ten years."*
> — *Ray Bradbury*

**Strong**: We must be strong for ourselves, but perhaps even more so for others—those who cannot be strong or that society has made weak. The weak need others to defend them and make sure their voice is heard when those in power would choose to ignore it. There is strength in numbers, as well; only together can change be conceivable. Do you feel strong? How do you employ strength in your life and others' lives?

**Structure**: Mode of building, construction, or organization; an arrangement of parts, elements, or constituents. Structures are inescapable; they mediate our every interaction in the world, surrounding us in various social, political, and physical forms. While these structures can at times feel oppressive, is there a sense in which they might be necessary? How do structures give us grounding, showing us how to act? And if these structures are in fact oppressive, how can we change them from the inside?

**Struggle**: To contend resolutely with a task or problem. Every person deals with struggle in their life. But how can we surpass these struggles and move forward in our lives? How do you react when faced with struggle—do you capitulate or press on with determination?

**Stubborn**: Unreasonably committed to your own opinion, even in the face of contrary evidence. Adhering to your principles is admirable, but refusing to use reason and critical thinking to improve and adapt your principles is ignorant and counterproductive. Do you care more about finding the truth or being right?

**Student**: A learner. When you open your mind to the teachings or advice of others, you become a student. Formally, we are recognized as students until we cease going to school, but one should never stop being a student of the world. Never stop learning just because you are not officially a student. What can you do to learn new things?

**Study**: The devotion of <u>time</u> to attentive scrutiny and <u>learning</u>. What in your life do you study? Never stop learning and exploring the world that you live in. There is more information available currently than you could ever learn in a lifetime; boredom with the world is a poor <u>excuse</u> used by lackluster people to justify their dullness.

**Stumble**: To trip and almost fall; to briefly lose your <u>balance</u>. You will figuratively stumble at many junctures in <u>life</u>; the important thing is that you keep walking or maybe jog for a second to recover and avoid embarrassment. It may take extra <u>work</u> to recover from more severe stumbles, but nonetheless you must press on with the <u>knowledge</u> you have gained about the sidewalk you happen to find yourself on; the more times you stumble the more you will <u>learn</u> about yourself. Are you afraid to make mistakes, or do you embrace them and learn from them? When in life have you stumbled?

**Stunt**: A stop or hindrance in <u>growth</u> or development. Beware of things that inhibit your growth as a person. Reevaluate your <u>life</u> thoughtfully and often in order to determine what in your life is helping you grow in the right direction and what is inhibiting <u>positive</u> growth. Do you distance yourself from growth-stunting activities?

**Stupid**: <u>Slow</u> to understand; worthless. People throw around this word a lot, using it to condescend to others. Everyone <u>learns</u> in different ways; just because your way may be slower or require more information does not mean that you are stupid. To be truly stupid is to concede to what other people say you are and as a result stop trying to learn or <u>understand</u> new things. Face your <u>problems</u> head on, study, and work until you understand topics that elude you. Do you believe that someone else cannot tell you what or who you are?

**Stylish**: Wearing clothes that conform to whatever is currently considered to be fashionable at a given time. The key word here is conform; you can be considered stylish if you *conform* to whatever random trend everyone seems to find cool and new and exciting at a given time. Do not <u>waste</u> too much time chasing this elusive goal. What is 'stylish' changes often with random ferocity and in the end, how cool is it to try to be exactly like other <u>people</u>? Do you <u>appreciate</u> your uniqueness?

**Suave**: Smooth; charming. Suaveness is a useful attribute to add to your repertoire, but you must take care and use it to lubricate <u>social</u> situations and make others more comfortable, not to deceive or <u>manipulate</u>. Beware of those who are ill intentioned but hide behind a façade of suaveness or use it to further their own evil doings.

**Subconscious**: Pertaining to the part of the <u>mind</u> that we are not completely aware of, yet that influences our <u>feelings</u> and <u>decisions</u>. Get in touch with your subconscious; what feelings do you have that you can't quite explain? Scrutinize your behavior and try to separate overtly conscious <u>decisions</u> from subconscious influences.

**Subculture**: Do not be fooled by the prefix of this word; it does not refer to an inferior culture but rather a smaller one existing within a larger one. If variety is the spice of life, subcultures help to create a culinary masterpiece out of otherwise homogenous social landscapes. The existence and acceptance of subcultures provides a context for new <u>ideas</u> to flourish and take form. What subcultures interest you? What can you do to learn more about them?

**Subcutaneous**: Directly below the skin. This word is important not in its literal application of the biological matter exactly under your skin, but rather for its description of what is important in life; we should <u>judge</u> people by what is inside their <u>mind</u> and <u>heart</u>, not what color their skin is. Racial <u>differences</u> are only skin deep and should be recognized as such. Do you make subcutaneous judgments based on the color of someone's <u>skin</u>?

**Subdue**: To bring under <u>control</u>. What in your life subdues you and what sets you free? Some limits are good and <u>moderation</u> is key in a balanced life but unnecessary limits can be harmful and intellectually emotionally stunting. Do not let anyone subdue your <u>curiosity</u> or <u>passion</u>. As long as you are not hurting anyone else, you should be allowed to do and think what you want.

**Subject**: The topic at hand; a <u>person</u> who holds allegiance to a specific someone or something, or to <u>cause</u> to undergo. Who or what do you hold allegiance to?

**Subjective**: Proceeding from or influenced by personal <u>sentiments</u>, <u>opinions</u> and tastes. Everyone lives within their own subjective reality; we are all the stars of our own show. <u>Understand</u> the difference between subjective opinion and objective fact; be wary of those who attempt to put their own views forward as <u>fact</u>. Appreciate and explore your subjective view of the world; it is yours alone. Do you value your subjectivity?

**Subserve**: To <u>promote</u>, be useful to, or further. What purposes do you serve? Only promote things that you can align your own personal set of

> *"All things are subject to interpretation. Whichever interpretation prevails at a given time is a function of power and not truth."*
> — *Friedrich Nietzsche*

> *"Success is not final, failure is not fatal: it is the courage to continue that counts."*
> — *Winston Churchill*

morals with. What would the world be like if we were all subservient to one another?

**Substance**: Solid or real; a substantial <u>quality</u> or character. Seek out those with substance and stay away from those who display superficial values. Your thinking <u>power</u> and <u>abilities</u> to reason and rationalize are what make you unique and valuable; do not compromise them for anything or anyone. Do you base your <u>judgment</u> of yourself and others on substantial rather than superficial criteria?

**Substitute**: A replacement. Do not substitute excuse for <u>achievement</u>. Face your <u>failures</u> for what they are; learn and grow from them instead of ignoring them. Do you accept <u>responsibility</u> for your actions and avoid making excuses for failure?

**Subterfuge**: Deception used to further a goal. Be aware of the use of subterfuge in all of its forms. Those with morally starved <u>goals</u> know that their selfishness is not palatable in others, so they must instead <u>deceive</u> in order to get the <u>help</u> or take the advantage that they need from others. Do you avoid using subterfuge and playing into it when it is present?

**Subversive**: Intending to overthrow an established organization or institution in some way. Beware of those who <u>wish</u> to end organizations which are for the good of the <u>public</u>. Know the difference between subversion and reform; do not let those who sit comfortably in an unfair institution tell you that you are harmful and subversive when you attempt to enact <u>positive</u> change. In what ways do you try and bring about positive change?

**Succeed**: To accomplish what is attempted or intended. We should want to succeed but not in something that is <u>negative</u>. Do not move on simply for the sake of moving on; make sure your progress is in the right direction. Do you succeed with positivity?

**Success**: How do you <u>measure</u> your success? Before deeming something successful or not, examine the criteria you are using to do so. It is possible to fail in your expressed <u>goal</u>, but to still come out on top. Life is a learning <u>experience</u> and should be regarded as such. Begin to consider lessons learned from your mistakes as successes.

**Succumb**: To give in. Do not give in to anything. Make conscious <u>choices</u> based on what is best for you personally and stick to these choices. Sacrifices must be made sometimes, but they should be calculated choices rather than the relinquishing of all <u>control</u> to an external force. Are you determined to accomplish your goals?

**Suffer**: To feel <u>pain</u>, physically or emotionally. If you cannot prevent the suffering of others directly, try to understand it. Suffering can cause people to <u>act</u> not like themselves, so be patient and supportive. Suffering brings out a range of <u>emotions</u>, so be ready for anything from self-hatred to <u>apathy</u> and <u>anger</u>. Forgive yourself for not being able to explain your emotions while suffering. Do you understand the special circumstances which suffering creates?

**Sufficient**: <u>Adequate</u>; enough. Are you self-sufficient? How much do you depend on others to live your daily life? What material objects are sufficient for you to <u>live</u> a happy life? Note the difference between necessities and desires. If you <u>begin</u> to believe that your ideal conception of life is the only way to live, you will never be happy. Instead, boil your life down to your absolute necessities, and look at everything else as a bonus.

**Suffocate**: This word literally means to kill or <u>die</u> because of a lack of oxygen, but can be extended in a figurative sense to the stifling of creativity or <u>imagination</u>. What in your life attempts to suffocate your personal <u>expression</u>? What can you do to avoid suffocating forces?

**Suggest**: To <u>recommend</u> or imply. How do you handle suggestion? Suggestion is a subtle <u>art</u>, as doing so with too much force can rub people the wrong way. How do you handle suggestions? Being able to <u>process</u> constructive criticism calmly and rationally is a valuable <u>skill</u>. Tact is absolutely necessary when making suggestions; bear in mind that some do not take well to advice.

**Suicide**: Killing oneself intentionally. Suicide is the result of <u>mental</u> instability caused by trauma or chemical imbalances. Those who are suicidal must deal with one of the worst ailments imaginable—the <u>brain</u> wants to kill the body. Take signs of self-hatred and hopelessness seriously when you <u>observe</u> them in others. How do you cope during dark times and moments of self-doubt, hate, or pity?

**Sulk**: To remain <u>silent</u> or hold oneself aloof in a sullen, ill-humored, or offended <u>mood</u>. Do not <u>waste</u> time with negativity. Sulking keeps you from moving forward and accomplishing anything. Many people sulk for <u>attention</u>. Why not come clean with someone you trust and explain your problem instead?

**Sullen**: Bad-tempered; gloomy. What does being apathetic and sad <u>accomplish</u>? Deal with disappointment or sadness in healthy ways which propel you forward instead of holding you back. The disappointment of a letdown in <u>life</u> will only abate with the passage of time. In the meantime, take <u>care</u> of yourself; exercise, talk to close friends about your problems, eat well and in <u>moderation</u>. Do you <u>fight</u> sullen moods proactively with healthy behavior?

**Summit**: The top or highest point of a given object. It takes ambition and determination to reach the summit of a mountain, just as it takes these things to reach the figurative summit of your goals. Some parts of the climb may be rocky and treacherous, but with an open mind and a willingness to learn, it will get easier as you go on. What will it take to reach your summit?

**Sun**: Without the sun, life on Earth could not exist. It is humbling to realize that every star in the night sky is the size of the sun—and many of them are bigger than it. The sun serves as a reminder of the tremendous amount of energy outside of our galaxy and the potential for other life forms somewhere in the universe.

**Sunday**: How do you use your Sunday every week? Some use it for rest and relaxation, and others use it for religion. Regardless of what day of the week it is, you should set aside time to reflect and do things for yourself. Do you get sufficient rest and relaxation on a weekly basis?

**Super**: Very pleasant or good; especially. What are you particularly super at? Value your unique skills. Superlatives denote "the most" of something. You are the MOST, the supreme, the best at something, even if that thing is being you. How do you value your unique qualities and life experiences?

**Superiority complex**: A mask of arrogance and elitism put on by those who are compensating for low self-esteem and self-worth. Do you recognize the need to be better than others just for the sake of it as unhealthy?

**Superficial**: situated or occurring near the surface. Distance yourself from superficiality in any form; consumerism, vanity, and prejudice based on appearance should all take a back seat to individual substance and experience. Do your achievements and goals reflect your substance?

**Superstition**: A superstition is a myth or an old wives' tale. Superstitions span all walks of life, but the reasoning behind the belief in a myth differs. Do you override the reality of life? Do you act unreasonably based on superstition?

**Supplant**: To replace. Before you replace someone or something, do you think critically about the role being filled? Sometimes replacements end up being mere hollowed-out shells of the original; make sure you know the difference. Have you replaced something in your life and then regretted it in hindsight? On the other hand, have you replaced something only to have it help you in the long run?

**Supplement**: To enhance by addition. Always go the extra mile to ensure that you are getting the most out of your experiences. Supplemental information will always give you more insight, which will therefore allow you to derive more utility from the situation. Do you go beyond what is put in front of you?

**Supplicate**: To humbly ask or beg for something. It is best to swallow your pride when asking for something; making demands or acting aloof when you truly need something comes off as arrogant and entitled. Do you acknowledge what others do for you with both your language and behavior?

**Suppose**: To draw conclusions based on probability or evidence without unequivocal proof. A large amount of guesswork is involved in life; it is impossible to know every piece of information and every variable orbiting an issue, so instead of being paralyzed by a lack of knowledge, we must infer things about life. What do you infer about? Are your inferences usually correct or off base?

**Suppress**: To inhibit the development or expression of something. It is unhealthy to suppress your feelings. Be honest with those around you instead of bottling up emotions and issues. Express anger and frustration in proportion to the situation at hand; too much built-up anger will result in it boiling over at a disproportionate and inappropriate time. Do you express rather than suppress?

**Supreme**: Superior to all else. What is your supreme goal or priority in life? Once you achieve this goal, what next? What is on the other side of your climb to the top? Supreme goals could reflect desires for quality of life, not material goods.

**Sure**: To be sure is to be confident with no doubt. Sureness is of utmost importance in your everyday decision making. Being sure of yourself and your decisions exudes confidence and poise. Are you sure in your decisions and actions?

**Surge**: A surge is an increase in movement and can be improved upon by a natural force. We all have times where we have the opportunity to surge out from our current spot in life. It's in our nature to want something different, but don't let your emotions force you to surge out of your current situation. Rather, make your surge rational and logical. Where do you feel the need to surge? Is it simply to get away for relaxation or for an entirely new start?

**Surgery**: To have surgery is to have an operation to help heal or repair a physical or

> *"Ethically they had arrived at the conclusion that man's supremacy over lower animals meant not that the former should prey upon the latter, but that the higher should protect the lower, and that there should be mutual aid between the two as between man and man. They had also brought out the truth that man eats not for enjoyment but to live."*
> — *Mahatma Gandhi*

mental ailment. There are a large amount of benefits and risks involved in surgery today. While surgery is a positive when we are able to cure illnesses or fix broken body parts, it can be very dangerous as well. Do you find the benefits of surgery to be worth the risks? If you ever opted out of surgery, do you wish you had given yourself the chance to improve your bodily situation?

**Surmise**: To surmise is to assume an outcome or a cause-effect relation without the evidence to do so. It can be dangerous to jump to conclusions in this fashion, but our society continuously resorts to assuming something rather than collecting all of the solid evidence and information that is needed first. How quick or how often do you infer without sufficiently conclusive evidence? How much do we rely on it?

**Surpass**: To surpass is to exceed or be greater than what people expect out of you. Humans have an internal drive to better their situations and skills. It is our nature to attempt to increase our position in life, to improve our qualities, and to surpass our very potential. How can you surpass your expectations and better yourself? Does the pressure from others in wanting you to surpass your expectations prove troublesome?

> *"One of the advantages of being disorganized is that one is always having surprising discoveries."*
> — *A. A. Milne*

**Surprise**: A surprise is an unplanned and unexpected event, and is usually followed by a feeling of shock. Surprises are typically only funny and enjoyable at birthday parties. The <u>nature</u> of a surprise is to mislead and rouse someone without any warning. Surprises are negative when they are done with <u>ill</u> <u>intentions</u>. Have you ever been unpleasantly surprised?

**Surrealism**: The definition of surreal is difficult to pin down precisely because it contains all that is outside of the real. It's difficult to come to grips with surrealism simply because it's too bizarre and unbelievable to be true. <u>Life</u>, however, is supposed to be bizarre and somewhat <u>strange</u>, so don't let those surreal <u>moments</u> in life throw you for a loop. What surreal moments have you witnessed in life? Did they seem way too good to be true?

**Surrender**: To surrender to someone is to cease resistance and relinquish your authority. Surrender is a <u>negative</u> when we are <u>forced</u> to give up something that we once stood for or when we find that we are too <u>weak</u> to continue in the <u>fight</u>. However, surrendering yourself in order to <u>spare</u> others is perhaps the most courageous and noble task a person can perform. Would you surrender something of yours in order to help someone else?

**Surreptitious**: Surreptitious means sly and often deceitful. We should <u>strive</u> for <u>transparency</u> in our <u>efforts</u> and endeavors. Have you been a <u>victim</u> of surreptitiousness? How can situations like these be avoided?

<u>Surround</u>: To surround is to be enclosed within a specific area. The <u>opportunities</u> that you come across are often a result of those with whom you surround yourself. It is important to surround yourself with people who will <u>benefit</u> you just as you benefit them; it should be a give-and-take <u>relationship</u>. Are you aware of whom our <u>leaders</u> surround themselves with? Is this good, bad, or indifferent?

**Surroundings**: Surroundings are the things around us. The surroundings in which we live have a major part in making us who we are. Ideal surroundings are <u>safe</u> and comfortable, and allow you to <u>express</u> yourself freely. In what <u>environment</u> do we place ourselves? Do we place ourselves in an environment that may be out of our jurisdiction?

**Surveillance**: To keep under surveillance means to have a keen eye, especially regarding a search for a spy or criminal. Vigilance is a key in keeping yourself and your <u>possessions</u> <u>safe</u>. The <u>necessity</u> of surveillance has come to us at a price; it means that crimes are taking place and we can't seem to stop them. What do you keep under surveillance? Do you rely on surveillance too much?

**Survey**: When we survey, we take into account all factors of that into which we inquire. <u>Observation</u> is the most important part of any survey; we must always keep our eyes fully open and <u>view</u> our <u>world</u> from as many angles as possible. What do you observe and survey? Is your survey of the world based on your opinions and views or others?

**Survival**: Survival describes the ability to continue living despite some sort of obstacle. The drive to survive is something that pushes all living things to <u>improve</u> their positions. Is survival a true and real factor in *your* <u>world</u>? If so, what are you surviving from? Is it actually survival or <u>perseverance</u>? What does <u>life</u> or <u>death</u> survival mean to you?

**Suspect**: A suspect is the person whom the evidence points to as having committed a crime. We should hope through proper decorum and <u>morality</u> that we never find ourselves as the suspect in a <u>crime</u>. Have you ever suspected someone of committing a crime that you couldn't prove? Have you ever been suspected of a crime that you had absolutely no business with?

247

**Suspense**: Suspense can be described as a feeling of anxiousness and uncertainty. Life is full of suspenseful moments, but when they seem to <u>control</u> our life, it can become a very negative thing. Suspense is fun at movies, but in life it would be a horrible <u>existence</u> to always be <u>anxious</u> and looking over one's shoulder. Do you enjoy a suspenseful life or a life of peace and harmony? Do you personally add suspense to your own life or simply let life's events take care of that?

**Suspicion**: To have suspicion is to have the intuition that something might possibly happen. Suspicion is a <u>positive</u> when it causes us to think critically and <u>rationally</u> in order to solve a problem. However, it becomes a <u>negative</u> when suspicion is borne of paranoia or gullibility. Suspicion should always be checked and backed up by solid <u>evidence</u>. How do you deal with your suspicions? Are they often right or far too exaggerated?

> *"When angry, count four. When very angry, swear."*
> *— Mark Twain*

**Sustain, Sustainable;** To support or strengthen. Food sustains us <u>physically</u>; we need to take in the right kind and amount at regular intervals for our <u>bodies</u> to continue to <u>function</u>. What sustains you in less tangible ways? Through rough times, our sustenance comes in the form of <u>support</u> from friends and family and hope for better times to come. Do you take it upon yourself to obtain the right kind of sustenance?

**Swap**: To trade one thing for another. We swap <u>money</u> for goods and <u>services</u> on a regular basis; this is the obvious <u>tangible</u> presence of trading in our life. Think about the less tangible things that you swap. Many people swap their present <u>happiness</u> for the hope of a better <u>future</u>, while others swap their future for instant gratification. Think about the intangible elements of life you swap on a daily basis. Do the swaps and sacrifices you make in life reflect your goals and sentiments? Do you swap too much, only to get little in return?

**Sway**: To swing into position, incline in the direction of change, or to exert influence to elicit this inclination. Whether it's obvious or not, people will try to sway you to make a <u>decision</u> in their favor. Therefore, it's important to <u>examine</u> the <u>motives</u> of those who try to sway you. Are they doing it as a result of expressed or ulterior motives? Are you easily swayed or stubborn and decisive?

**Swear**: To take an oath or to use profanity. Though profanity is just a form of expression through <u>words</u>, people have varying <u>degrees</u> of skin thickness when it comes to swearing. Take care to know your <u>audience</u> before you <u>risk</u> offending with your words. Regarding the other meaning, do not make promises that you cannot keep. Do you think ahead before you act? Is swearing part of your regular <u>vocabulary</u>?

**Sweet**: A positive stimulus to our senses. The most literal connotation is with <u>taste</u>, yet this word has expanded to encompass <u>pleasure</u> in all of our senses; sounds and sights can be described as sweet. Sweetness can be addictive, yet extremely <u>rewarding</u>, so it's ideal to have it in moderation. Do you take time to <u>appreciate</u> and examine the sensory input you are faced with?

**Swell**: To become larger in size. When you are feeling especially <u>proud</u> or good about something, it can feel almost as if your chest is <u>growing</u> in size. Feed off this feeling; let it be your incentive to <u>accomplish</u> more of your <u>goals</u>. At the same time, don't let this feeling get too out of control that it rubs people the wrong way. Swelling because of the collection of fluid in an area is also our <u>body</u>'s response to injury; in this case, take swelling as a <u>signal</u> that you should not repeat a behavior. Do you interpret swelling and act accordingly?

**Swerve**: To deviate from a path or change direction. In life, the key is <u>knowing</u> when to swerve and when to stay the course and weather the storm ahead. Do you get all the information you can about a given event in the <u>future</u> before you <u>decide</u> whether to embrace or avoid it?

**Swindle**: To use deception to steal from others. Beware of those who wish to relieve you of your hard-earned <u>money</u> or possessions. Do not be rushed into <u>decisions</u>; always get all the <u>information</u> you can, and be wary of those who wish to withhold information about an investment. Are you wary of swindlers in all of their forms? What can you do to combat swindlers?

**Swing**: This describes an oscillating movement. We can swing <u>objects</u> with our <u>body</u> or our body itself. Can you <u>express</u> yourself with body language and creative <u>movements</u>? Can you swish, swipe, and swirl to release pent-up <u>energy</u> or to deliver a message? Of course, not literally, but do you swing from place to place, or job to job without realizing the good <u>opportunities</u> in front of you?

**Sycophant**: Someone who flatters in order to benefit themselves in some way. Beware of people who pour fuel into your self-<u>confidence</u> in order to get into your good graces to <u>accomplish</u> ulterior <u>motives</u>. Do you accept flattery for what it is without allowing yourself to get carried away by it? Are there any sycophants in your life that only seem to take and not give?

<u>**Symbol**</u>: A symbol represents or stands for something abstract. Symbols are omnipresent in our lives. Every day we are confronted with symbols on various levels. Street signs contain <u>instructions</u>, <u>rules</u>, and <u>warnings</u>, which we <u>understand</u> without thinking because we have been culturally acclimated to them. The very letters that form these words are symbols that represent different things to people who speak other <u>languages</u>. Every aspect of our lives is laden with symbols; do you look beyond the symbol to its intent and origin? What are the symbols in your life that represent something?

**Sympathize, sympathy**: When you sympathize for someone, you feel bad for them and, among others, offer your condolences. Your <u>ability</u> to put yourself in someone else's shoes will help you <u>relate</u> to people and <u>help</u> them as effectively as possible. Those without the capacity for sympathy should be regarded with suspicion; the fact that someone is incapable of empathizing means that they will not think twice about hurting you. Do you sympathize with others? Do you have the capacity to put yourself in someone else's shoes and experience their <u>pain</u> with them?

> *"No man needs sympathy because he has to work, because he has a burden to carry. Far and away the best prize that life offers is the chance to work hard at work worth doing."*
> — *Theodore Roosevelt*

**Symptom**: To have symptoms is to have an indication of an injury or illness. Be <u>aware</u> of your <u>body</u>; take all ailments seriously as possible symptoms of a larger <u>problem</u>. Do you know how to identify <u>behaviors</u> that are symptomatic of problems in friends and family? When examining problems in your life, try to see the big picture. What could this minor problem be symptomatic of on a grander scale?

**Synergism**: When two or more things act together in such a way that it results in a product that would not have been possible with the individual elements alone. Being able to work <u>together</u> effectively with other people is an invaluable <u>skill</u>. It is always <u>valuable</u> to bounce your ideas off friends even if you are working alone. It is synergy that makes two heads better than one. Who do you have synergy with? Has your synergy with an individual or group led to success?

**Synopsis**: A synopsis is a brief recap about an event, oftentimes highlighted in a novel. It can be distressing to think in these terms; seeing your <u>life</u> <u>accomplishments</u> boiled down into a paragraph can seem belittling. It simply does not do your hard <u>work</u> any justice. Still, a synopsis can serve as a quality baseline for how you want to <u>improve</u> your life. What would a synopsis of your life look like? Is it fair to break down your life through a synopsis?

**Synthetic**: To be synthetic is to be not genuine or insincere. We live in an age that is characterized by <u>imitation</u> in many forms. It is okay to accept synthetic <u>alternatives</u>; just make sure you are aware of what they are missing when compared with the original. Synthetic materials are often cheap and poorer in <u>quality</u> than what they attempt to emulate. Do you recognize synthetic things and interact with them accordingly? How much of <u>life</u> in general is not genuine, artificial, or devised? How much of your life is superficial and fake?

**System**: A system is a structure made up of connected <u>parts</u> to form a whole. All of <u>life</u> is a part of a grand system that has an almost infinite number of variables and moving <u>parts</u>. Thinking in terms of systems allows us to see the big picture that comprises a <u>complex</u> network of individual parts. Try to think in this <u>manner</u> by attempting to see and <u>examine</u> things in your life as they fit into larger frameworks. Do you see all life in terms of systems? What systems are you a part of?

# T

**Tabloid:** When we go to the gas station or the supermarket, we are always confronted with tabloids reporting unbelievable headlines about celebrities. Tabloids are essentially gossip stories designed to give the masses cheap entertainment. While tabloids can provide some fleeting, attention-grabbing fodder, people often confuse them with reality. Should we try to avoid gossip even though it can be interesting and conversational? Do you tend to enjoy such diversions or do you strive to focus on more worthwhile endeavors? Have you considered how the subjects of such gossip feel? Recall a time when you were the subject of rumors. How did you internalize that experience and how did it feel?

**Tabular:** When we tabulate things, we organize them into lists, much like a to-do list. We can tabulate the progression of life in a similar way. Do you take the time to remain organized? How could such an approach to living hinder us? Does it little to an obstinate worldview? Do you attempt to find a balance between organization and flexibility?

**Tacit:** A tacit gesture is understood but not heard, giving it a secretive and alluring quality. A wink, a thumbs-up, or the flash of a smile are some heavily utilized silent expressions. This word also applies to the realm of politics; our silence regarding the actions of our government are seen as license for them to continue. This is called "tacit consent." It would behoove us, however, to consider that our silence in such matters can be just as damaging as governmental action itself. Do you speak up when political leaders make poor decisions? Do you do so even when it doesn't directly affect you? What kind of tacit gestures do you make, and to what end?

**Tact:** Tact is one of life's most important skills. Having tact means you know how to deal with people in delicate situations without causing anger or hurt feelings. Knowing the right thing to say or the right thing to do in certain situations is one of the most difficult skills to master. Consider times when you've witnessed an embarrassing or alarming situation that was diffused because somebody knew the right thing to do or say. What did they do? How can you emulate their behavior so that you can handle tough situations with a higher level of tact and understanding?

> *"I have no special talents. I am only passionately curious."*
> — *Albert Einstein*

**Take:** Life is full of giving and taking, and sometimes we find ourselves on the taking side. Humans have been taking what they've wanted for as long as history has been recorded. The concept of war began because a group of people wanted something that they couldn't have and resolved to join together in order to take it for themselves. When we take something, it feels as though we've won it, and we feel a great sense of accomplishment. However, if we come to depend on the people we take from, we will become dependent and lazy. Balancing the taking with some giving will make each act much more fulfilling. In what ways do you give back? Do you only give back to those you love or to your community as a whole?

**Talent:** A talent is a special skill that you are born with and develop during your lifetime. Everyone has a talent, even if he or she doesn't realize what that talent is yet. The key is to know who you are and what you want to do. With this knowledge, your talent will become more and more evident as you grow. Do you know what your talent is? How did you develop it? How will you apply your talent for the betterment of yourself and others? It is important to remember that even though you may be talented, you must be humble and willing to learn. Talent can only take you so far; it must be combined with skill and hard work. Do you stay humble regarding your talents? Do you seek out those who may know more than you in that field?

**Talk:** The gift of speech is one of the most important human abilities. Talking is how we communicate our thoughts to one another, and humankind is characterized by this phenomenon. Talking carries a much more personalized tone than writing ever can. Without talking, we could never discuss or debate with one another, overtly display our emotions, or capture the attention of a large audience in a single instance. Humans have developed thousands of different varieties of speech in order to vocally express their thoughts, feelings, and attitudes about the worthwhile things in life. Think about how difficult life would be if humans could not talk with one another. How has speech influenced your life? How can you use the power of the spoken word to make an impact on the lives of others? Additionally, when is silence the better option? If you ability to listen to others. Be conversations; the words of your own. Do you take time to the words of others the same

*"The reason I talk to myself is because I'm the only one whose answers I accept."*
— *George Carlin*

are always talking, you lose the cautious and avoid dominating others are just as valuable as listen to others? Do you give value as yours?

times? Do you seek excitement in order to break this?

**Tally:** Tallies are used to record a score or keep a count. We organize and track things using tallies, especially when keeping a record of monetary transactions. Outside of this, we keep records of wrongs committed against us by others. While we must be cautious to avoid toxic relationships, at a certain point holding onto such negative emotions only poisons our own lives. It's a fine line to walk, and the goal of both sides should be self-preservation. Do you find yourself holding grudges for long periods? How does that affect you? Do you think it affects you or the other person more?

**Tamper:** Meddling in the affairs of others often has unforeseen consequences. Even when the one doing the tampering has good intentions, the fact that he or she was secretive or dishonest hurts those affected. When attempting to interfere or repair something, honesty and transparency are always the best choice. Do you meddle in the lives of others? Has your life been tampered with? What was the outcome of either of those situations?

**Tame:** Human nature is, like that of most creatures, inherently wild. Through the centuries, we have tamed that nature as 'we've developed laws and societies that outline appropriate behavior. This word can also describe things that are boring or inoffensive. Does your life feel tame at

**Tangible:** Everything that we can touch, feel, and understand easily is tangible. The tangible things in life are much more fleeting and unfulfilling in comparison to the intangibles like love, trust, or faith. However, we do need some tangible things in our life, such as shelter and food. It is comforting to have something that you can hold in your hand, feel its weight, and know that it's real without any confusion. What tangible things do you need in your life? Do you ever get so caught up in attaining such things that you lose sight of the big picture?

**Tantalize:** The word comes from the name Tantalus, a king in ancient Greek myth. He angered the gods, so they punished him by forcing him to stand in a pool of water up to his chin. Each time he tried to drink the water, it would move away from his lips. When he attempted to reach the fruit branches hanging above him, they would move just beyond his reach. This anecdote is a perfect illustration of the surprising and heart-wrenching effects that tantalization can have on the soul. When we want something that seems to dangle in front of us out of our reach, it can be devastating and drive us to insanity. What or who tantalizes you? How have you coped with the things that tantalize your senses?

**Tantrum:** As children, we all threw our fair share of tantrums, whether or not we admit to them. They are incessantly annoying and elicited unwanted attention for our parents. As adults, tantrums become unacceptable, and when we don't get what we want, throwing a tantrum is not the answer. The problem in both cases is a lack of maturity, and while children have an excuse, adults do not. Do you find it difficult to keep your temper? Do you recognize when your anger is not justified? How can you keep your temper in check and peacefully resolve your conflicts?

**Tardy:** Timeliness is one of the most simple and important qualities one should possess. Even so, it seems timeliness is very difficult for many people. Everyone has been late to something—classes, meetings, etc. Being

*"Desire, even in its wildest tantrums, can neither persuade me it is love nor stop me from wishing it were."*
— *W. H. Auden*

late is embarrassing and unprofessional, and it can make a horrible first impression. No matter where you're off to in the race of life, be sure you get there on time. Lateness shows an inherent selfishness that is incredibly off-putting to others. Do you strive to keep your commitments and appointments? Do you make sure others know they are important to you by showing up when you say you will?

**Target:** In human terms, a target is someone who is attacked in a malicious manner. If you find yourself being targeted by someone, consider both sides of the situation and attempt to come to a resolution. If that is impossible, distance yourself from that person to avoid further confrontation. Have you ever felt targeted in your life? Have you ever unfairly targeted someone else? If so, how could you have resolved the situation better?

**Task:** A task is something one has to do or is told to do whether they want to or not. When we have a task at hand, it becomes the central focus of our day until we accomplish what we set out to do. Much as we may not want to do the tasks assigned to us, it is our responsibility to fulfill them completely. Whatever task you need to accomplish, give it 100 percent of your energy so that you complete it with the highest level of satisfaction. Do you commit yourself to your work completely? Do you procrastinate when you 'shouldn't?

**Taste:** Taste is both flavor and preference. As one of our key senses, taste allows us to determine the quality of the things we eat. As humans, we have cultivated a keen sense of culinary aptitude through our explorations of taste and texture. Taste invokes pleasure, comfort, and desire. At the same time, taste is the ability to know and judge what is beautiful and proper. Good taste requires a time-consuming process to determine what things you like and dislike. What would you consider your tastes to be? How do those tastes compare with the tastes of your peers and others? Is good taste objective, or is it at the mercy of the individual? Even though something may be to your tastes, don't frown on others whose interests differ from yours.

**Tattle:** A tattler tells the secrets of others and is generally an untrustworthy person. Avoid tattling at all costs because it is childish and underhanded. If you've ever been tattled on, how did it make you feel? By contrast, however, when does tattling become necessary? When others are committing egregious wrongs, do you have a responsibility to say something? We may want to hide the sins of those we care about in order to save their reputation, but at what point are we hurting them more than helping them?

**Taunt:** Mocking and taunting are excruciatingly harmful to the confidence and well-being of the one being taunted. Taunting is just as childish as tattling, but it is often more hurtful and malicious.

> *"A child can teach an adult three things: to be happy for no reason, to always be busy with something, and to know how to demand with all his might that which he desires."*
> — *Paulo Coelho*

Have you ever been taunted? How did you feel—embarrassed, hurt, or foolish? What measures can you take to eradicate taunting and other mean-spirited acts?

**Tawdry:** At the fair of St. Audrey, once held each year in England, one could buy cheap, showy garments. The name St. Audrey was shortened to tawdry and is now used to describe things that appear gaudy and overly flashy. It can be fun and exciting to dress or be tawdry, but be sure that such behavior is done in appropriate situations. That which is tawdry lacks depth and value in a greater sense; do you find yourself drawn to such things? Is diversion more important to you than it should be?

**Tax:** Taxes, along with death, are one of life's unavoidable thorns always sticking in your side. If you don't pay them, you will be thrown in jail. Without taxes, we wouldn't have common luxuries like a police force or roads. Despite most everyone's loathe for taxes, they contribute to our society, which is like a large pie that requires heavy resources but everyone gets a slice in the end. Do you keep yourself informed as to how your tax dollars are spent?

**Teach:** A teacher has a quieting effect on our minds. A teacher makes the way easier. A teacher is more helpful than any scripture or book. But this is only the case with a good teacher, and that cannot always be expected, unfortunately. Software mogul Bill Gates, in a 2010 interview, noted that there are too many bad teachers in America rather than bad kids. Gates believes that teaching is so much more than imparting knowledge to young children. They need to be engaged and captivated, and related to rather than looked down on. In order for children to learn properly and gain confidence, teachers must use knowledge to empower them rather than using it to measure one against another. We must also keep in mind that regardless of age, we can always be taught. This requires us to not only find those who can teach us, but also lower our pride to make learning possible. Do you have teachers in your life now? Do you continue to seek out the wisdom of others? Who do you teach?

**Team:** A team can be many things, ranging from teams at work, in sports, or the military. The one thing these various groups have in common is their purpose—a collection of individuals gathered together for a common goal, becoming greater as a unit than the sum of their parts. As the poet John Donne wrote, "No man is an island." Results are achieved quickly through collaboration; the perspectives and actions of others may be exactly what are needed to move forward when our own sight or abilities are limited. Additionally, a team provides a sense of community, echoing and reminding us of the roles we can play in larger communities, whether they be families, neighborhoods, countries, or the Earth itself. Do you try to collaborate with others, providing a contribution that encourages and propels your team to success? Do you take an active part in the other communities in which you exist, or do you passively allow choices to be made?

**Tear:** Separation is difficult, but it is often necessary for us to grow as individuals. There are times when we are faced with decisions where we have no choice but to separate from our friends, loved ones, or careers in order to improve our own lives. At these moments, do not fear the unknown but rather use your past to guide yourself into the future. Do you consciously remove negative elements from your life or hang onto them because of nostalgia?

**Tease:** Much like taunting, teasing can be painfully annoying at times. However, there is a playful side to teasing that makes it more light-hearted than taunting. We've all heard the old saying "you only tease the ones you love," and this may or may not be true. As well intentioned as you may be, are you aware of all the effects of your teasing? Are you mindful to tease only those who can take it and enjoy it?

**Technique:** Skill and artistry combine to form technique. Technique is the precise method with which you get things done. Good technique requires practice, diligence, and determination. It is the embodiment of patience, prowess, and grace under fire. Whatever your expertise, how can you hone and develop your technique? Do you find yourself relying on talent rather than developing skill?

> *"It has become appallingly obvious that our technology has exceeded our humanity."*
> *— Albert Einstein*

**Technology:** Living in the Information Age makes it nearly impossible to escape the influence of technology. We are constantly bombarded by new gadgets as companies attempt to turn profits off our desires. At the heart of these desires is a craving for life to be made easier through technology. What's the final result of such desires? Do our lives need to be made easier? How has technology impacted your life? Where do you see technology going, and is it a bright or dark future?

**Tedious:** Some things in life are so boring and monotonous that they make us want to tear our eyes out. Although it seems that we can't avoid the tedious things, we should take comfort in knowing that slogging through the boring things in life is precisely what makes the more enjoyable things exciting. Do you focus on your work, even when it feels tedious? Do you shirk responsibility in favor of that which is exciting?

**Telecast:** A telecast is simply something that is aired over the television. Yet television programs can be made by those with insidious intentions, and so we should be careful with what we watch on television. Even news programs need to be meticulously scrutinized because they rarely provide unbiased facts. Just like anything that anyone tells you in life, examine what was said from all angles and decide for yourself the validity of the statement. How much of your life is spent watching television? What are some more productive ways you could spend your time?

**Telepathy:** Have you ever felt so connected to someone that it seems like you know what they're thinking? We can't truly know if the power of telepathy exists, but everyone has experienced a moment when they've felt as though it was happening. What does this say about the power of human connection? Has someone ever been so connected to you that they've experienced this?

**Telephone:** The telephone is one of the most important inventions in modern history; it gave rise to the global telecommunications market in which we live today. By allowing people to instantaneously converse with one another, this invention vastly accelerated the speed at which information travels. Telephones play an enormous role in our daily lives,

especially now that they have become mobile and extremely accessible. When was the last time you went a full twenty-four hours without using a telephone? How has our dependence on telephones influenced the way we communicate?

**Television:** Nearly the same as the telephone, the television is the overachieving younger brother. Instead of just transmitting simple noise, the television also provides a picture to accompany the sounds. Many people will argue that television has destroyed our sense of imagination, that it has brainwashed us into believing everything that we see. While this notion is a bit far-fetched, the things shown on television should always be scrutinized for their truthfulness and reality. How does television influence your perception and everyday life? Are you mindful about maintaining a balance between television and other forms of diversion?

> *"I find television very educating. Every time somebody turns on the set, I go into the other room and read a book."*
> — *Groucho Marx*

**Tell:** The ability to tell others what we are thinking is one of the most spectacular gifts that humans possess. We have relied on telling for the entirety of human existence. Without the telling of stories, we would have no history and no blueprint for our customs and preferences. Narration has played a major role in the creation of culture, government, customs, and morality. Aesop is an excellent example of a person who has brought the power of storytelling from antiquity to the modern day. His fables, which date back to 600 BC, express worldly wisdoms that can act as a guide for living an honest and good life. His stories have been told to generation after generation and have helped to form the basis for all law and tradition as we know it today. How have the things told to you by your parents, teachers, and advisors shaped or influenced your thoughts, attitudes, and beliefs? What do you pass on as you tell those who learn from you about the world? Do your actions tell a story as much as your words?

**Temper:** What mood would you consider to be your default mood? Are you always elated, worried, or even just apathetic? Your temper determines how others think of you and how they will act when they are around you. If you can keep your temper stable in stressful situations, you will be able to think more clearly and make better decisions. Temper

is all about emotions, so if you don't let your emotions drive your behavior, and you might discover a new sense of happiness or inner peace. Do you manage to keep an even mood? Are you prone to volatile reactions? How have those reactions affected situations?

**Temperance:** Temperance is moderation, and moderation is one of the most <u>important</u> things in life. <u>Keeping</u> your urges, <u>actions</u>, appetites, and <u>emotions</u> in check is incredibly <u>essential</u> to functioning in a meaningful way as you <u>progress</u> through life. The trailblazer for the original democracy, Athenian lawmaker Solon, is famous for saying "Keep everything with moderation." These words still ring true today. Do you <u>maintain</u> balance in your life, <u>avoiding</u> excessive <u>focus</u> on any one thing? When have you lost sight of this balance, ignoring critical <u>parts</u> of your life?

> *"I can resist anything except temptation."*
> *— Oscar Wilde*

**Temporal:** Temporality is <u>time</u>; it is everything that is bound to the <u>Earth</u>. As mortal beings, we are temporal, bound by time, until our <u>deaths</u>. We should not lament that we have such limited time on this <u>planet</u>; in fact, we should rejoice this very <u>fact</u>. Having a <u>sense</u> of urgency is what <u>motivates</u> us as humans to get our work done. We would have nothing even close to what we have today if we were not under the constant and immutable <u>pressure</u> of time. Do you make sure to <u>value</u> the time you have here? Do you make the most of the time you do have?

**Temporary:** Many things in life are temporary or require some sort of temporary fix. The impermanence of what is temporary <u>suggests</u> an <u>opportunity</u> for a new <u>beginning</u>. What things in your life are temporary? When the temporary <u>ends</u>, did you <u>gain</u> a <u>new</u> <u>perspective</u>?

**Temporize:** To temporize is to act in a way that one <u>believes</u> will be popular or advantageous rather than a way that is <u>right</u>. <u>Avoid</u> temporizing yourself at all costs. If you temporize your <u>behavior</u> in <u>order</u> to be liked, it will never <u>end</u> well because others will detect your insincerity. Are your beliefs <u>genuine</u>? Do you say one thing to people but really think

another? If you've known others who are like this, how did it <u>affect</u> your <u>opinion</u> of them?

**Temptation:** <u>Religions</u>, constituting much of our <u>societies'</u> <u>moral</u> fiber and fortification, completely abhor temptations, preferring rather to be "delivered from evil." Temptations are most often sinister and insidious. They creep up on us and before we even have the <u>chance</u> to <u>realize</u> their presence, they have a firm grasp on us. All humans are tempted. There is no person that can't be broken down, <u>provided</u> with the right temptation. Whatever your temptation is, <u>find</u> the <u>support</u> to keep it at bay and you will be set <u>free</u> from it. But <u>remember</u> that it is not always weakness that yields to temptation. As Oscar Wilde said, "There are terrible temptations which it requires strength and <u>courage</u> to yield to." What things in life tempt you to the point that you can't control yourself any longer? What is the apple to your Eve, and more <u>importantly,</u> who is your serpent? When is it permissible to give in to temptation? Are there not moments in which we are tempted to <u>trust</u> others even if past <u>experience</u> has left us guarded? In this <u>sense</u>, isn't yielding to temptation the nobler <u>choice</u>?

**Tenable:** Something tenable is something that we can grasp firmly and <u>defend</u> forcibly. For humans, shelter and <u>family</u> are perhaps the most tenable and <u>sacred</u> things. What things in life do you hold close to you? What things would you defend so strongly that you would give your life for them? <u>Consider</u> beliefs as well as <u>physical</u> examples.

**Tenacity:** Tenacity is <u>mental</u> toughness. It is determination and will to hold and <u>protect</u> yourself and what is <u>rightfully</u> yours. What things bring out the tenacity in you? What are you willing to hold onto at any cost?

**Tendency:** Our tendencies often <u>define</u> who we are in the eyes of others. Tendencies can make us seem predictable at <u>times</u>, but they also embody the things that we <u>value</u> in life. Tendencies are <u>created</u> by repetition and <u>result</u> in <u>comfort</u>. What things in life do you tend to do more often than others? Are those tendencies <u>healthy</u> and <u>beneficial</u> to those around you? What reputation do you have based on your tendencies? Do others <u>view</u> you with <u>respect</u>?

*"I love sleep. My life has the tendency to fall apart when I'm awake, you know?"*
— *Ernest Hemingway*

**Tender:** Tender means soft, malleable, sensitive, and <u>new</u>. As <u>children</u>, we are said to be at a tender <u>age</u> because we are impressionable and gentle. When life seems to harden you with its many <u>challenges</u>, try to ease up and retain your childlike tenderness. Be cautious to <u>avoid</u> callousness with <u>friends</u> and <u>loved</u> ones, as tenderness is <u>needed</u> to convey empathy. Are you tender with those you love? Is it a challenge for you to lower your guard?

**Tenet:** A tenet is very similar to a <u>creed</u>, the focal point of this <u>work</u>. A tenet is a specific <u>rule</u> that one <u>promises</u> to observe. It is most typically <u>religious</u>, but it certainly does not have to be restricted by such definitions. A tenet is simply a <u>truth</u>. This truth has been passed down through generations and has come to be <u>accepted</u> and held <u>sacred</u> by a person or <u>group</u>. What tenets do you live by? Do you examine the <u>tenets</u> of your beliefs completely? Are you open to <u>change</u> if your tenets become doubtable?

**Tense:** How do you <u>react</u> when you are in stressful or anxious <u>situations</u>? Do you tense up and get nervous, or do you thrive on the pressure?

*"It is clearly absurd to limit the term 'education' to a person's formal schooling."*
— *Murray N. Rothbard*

It is most likely that the majority of us will get nervous and tense. When you <u>experience</u> tension, be sure to <u>breathe</u> deeply and regain your composure before <u>responding</u> to the situation. While it's impossible to <u>avoid</u> tension, we shouldn't let anxiety cloud our <u>judgment</u>. What makes you tense? How have you dealt with it in the <u>past</u>? How could you deal with it better in the <u>future</u>?

**Tentative:** When one is tentative, they <u>pause</u> before going after what they <u>want</u>. While sometimes it is <u>beneficial</u> to be tentative in a dangerous <u>situation</u>, do not let a tendency to be tentative keep you from <u>accomplishing</u> what you want. Are you ever tentative when you shouldn't be or rash when you should be tentative? Has your hesitation made situations worse for you in the <u>past</u>?

**Tenure:** Holding tenure implies that you have <u>successfully</u> dedicated yourself to your life's <u>work</u> and are now being rewarded for it. Tenure affords <u>freedom</u> and <u>security</u>. It is an honor reserved only for those who have committed themselves completely to a singular <u>cause</u>. Does your career stimulate you enough that you want to stay there for life? Are you <u>applying</u> yourself as you should, or do you get complacent? If so, why? If not, why not? Should it be possible to <u>achieve</u> such security in a position, or does it <u>encourage</u> complacency?

**Term:** A term is the amount of <u>time</u>, fixed by <u>law</u> or rule, in which a contract or <u>agreement</u> lasts. Everyone is bound to the terms of a <u>contract</u>, and sticking to those terms is a mark of integrity. Do you fulfill your contracts with integrity? Do you hold <u>true</u> to your <u>word</u>?

**Terminate:** Inevitably, everything that once was <u>alive</u> is terminated. The finality of termination can be frightening and comforting at the same time. For some, it is the end of a long and hard journey; for others, it is the beginning of a new, ethereal existence. What do you need to accomplish before termination? What will happen when we leave this life?

**Terrestrial:** As humans, we are terrestrial because we are bound to the Earth. Despite our capabilities in the water, we live and thrive on solid ground. How are we dependent on our earthly environment in ways we often don't realize? Could we benefit from a greater level of respect for our environment?

**Terrible:** What causes you great fear, terror, or dread? The terrible things in life can be hard to bear, such as injuries, death, loss of a job, etc. When terrible things happen, stay strong and fight the fear; perhaps it won't be so terrible when you've conquered it. What coping techniques have you developed to deal with terrible events? Do the unfortunate events in your life make you stronger in the end?

**Terrific:** According to the dictionary, terrific has the exact same meaning as terrible. We've come to know terrific to mean exactly the opposite through conversational use. Every so often, certain words are appropriated to the point that they are unrecognizable. Terrific is just one example of how the meanings of words can change drastically over time and colloquial usage. What terrific experiences have you had in your lifetime?

**Terrify:** Everyone is terrified of something. It can be anything, something as small as a spider or as big as thunder. The important thing is how we deal with what terrifies us. Try to expose yourself to what terrifies you then cope with it inside the situation. Who knows? It might not be so terrifying after all, and exposure to what terrifies you will build resilience against it. Do you face your fears,

or do you allow them to control you? What are you terrified of?

**Territorial:** Our natural disposition as biological creatures is to protect our home. Our territory is our life, our family, and our fortification. Our territory protects us from harm, and we become territorial when we are called to protect our territory just as it protects us. What things in life make you territorial? Have you ever been unjustly possessive over people or things?

**Terror:** Terror affects all of us in life. This sad realization has crept closer to home in recent years, as technology has allowed for horrific attacks against the innocent. Terror is not so much the direct cause of fear but rather the fear itself. Terror is living in fear, constantly looking over your shoulder. No one should have to live in fear, but it is the reality of Earth today. Do you live in fear of something? How do you deal with it on a day-to-day basis? Does it change the way you live, or do you carry on despite the possibility of disaster?

**Terrorism:** Terrorism is a dreadful method of using threats and fear to force a large group of people into obeying completely. Terrorism is a scourge on society and must not be allowed to remain a viable option for those seeking power. It is a bit utopian to call for a world without terrorism, but as long as we don't impart the practices of terror to our children, a world free of terrorism is a distinct possibility. How has recent terrorism affected your life? Are you concerned about terrorism in your country?

**Terse:** Terse comes from a Latin word meaning "clean." We've come to know this word as meaning short and to the point. Speaking tersely is advantageous in life because when you convey your ideas in a short and accessible fashion, people will be more inclined to value your opinions. Instead of rambling and stumbling through your thoughts, try to synthesize your ideas into a few words that better express your thoughts. Are you concise in your explanations?

**Test:** A test is the ultimate deciding factor in determining the fitness of a specific thing. For humans, tests are mostly associated with determining the fitness of the mind, measuring what you've learned and how well you can apply that knowledge. All tests boil down to one of two options: pass or fail. While it seems cruel to reduce hard-fought efforts into such categories, such is the way of humanity forever breaking down and categorizing until we can understand with absolute clarity. We grow up with people telling us that tests will decide our paths for the rest of our lives. Some people will tell us that our entire lives are a test for some unknown judge. However you value tests, always remember to prepare properly and give them your all. When you are tested, do you weather the storm? Do you handle the pressure well and rise to the task?

> *"Nearly all men can stand adversity, but if you want to test a man's character, give him power."*
> — *Abraham Lincoln*

**Testament:** A testament is a statement of beliefs that are intended to be passed down through the generations. We know testaments from the Bible quite well; they represent many stories and lessons compiled into one complete set of beliefs. What are the testaments that govern your life, and how did they come to be? Do your beliefs truly dictate how you live your life, or are you a hypocrite?

**Testimony:** When someone gives a testimony, they are swearing to tell the truth about something that has happened in the past. Often, a testimony comes in the form of an eyewitness account or a product review. In these times, we call on others to give us an accurate description of what happened or how well something worked. Always be wary of testimonies, but not totally untrusting, as they can be incredibly helpful. When your opinion is asked do you offer the most honest perspective possible? Do you do so even if it hurts someone else?

**Than:** We use this word to make comparisons between two things. Typically, the positive side of the comparison is on the front half—better than; smarter than; faster than; stronger than. If you're on the right side of the comparison, keep up the good work. If you're not, how can you improve yourself to outstrip the competition? Do you think you are better than others? What are you good at?

**Thank:** Thanking is the most common expression of gratitude. To thank someone is to show appreciation for a gift, service, or even just good company. A simple thank-you is one of the easiest and most courteous gestures one can make. Always offer your thanks when something nice is done for you. Do you thank others frequently? Do you enjoy when others thank you for nice gestures you have made?

**Theme:** The word theme comes from a Greek word meaning "what is laid down." A theme can be thought as having been put in place or laid down as the foundation of a piece of writing or music. Theme is most known as the broad idea or message conveyed in art and literature, and this idea can be applied to life as well. What is your theme? How do you convey your message to the world? What theme would you like to have for your life?

**Then:** This adverb has a number of separate, colloquial meanings, but for our purposes, we can concentrate on the temporal aspect of then. The word then is used to signify that something took place at a specific time in the past. We know the classic adage "that was *then*, this is now." So we can come to understand *then* as a reflection of our past experiences. By reflecting on *then*, we determine the now and the future. What part of you is left in the past? How does your *then* influence your now?

> *"One man's theology is another man's belly laugh."*
> — Robert A. Heinlein

**Theocracy:** A theocracy is a state governed by a church that is regarded as having immediate contact with and receiving guidance from some divine presence. Theocracies have, for the most part, been eradicated from the Earth, with Vatican City remaining the only true exception. Why is a theocracy not appropriate? Would you enjoy being governed by a theocracy?

**Theology:** Theology is the study of religion, derived from the Greek *theologia* and defined by Plato in the fourth century BC as "discourse on god." For example, the theology of Christianity studies the interworking of the Trinity—Father, Son, and Holy Ghost. Christian theology is centered on the transcendence of humans to a state that reflects God. This is a very similar theme that we see all over the world. Islam and Judaism are most similar in their theologies, but Eastern religions like Buddhism and Hinduism are also focused on reaching a higher level of existence based on love, compassion, and goodwill toward others during our time as mortals. In a 2008 speech, Pope Benedict XVI stated his interpretation of theology when he said, "We are called to be the forces of unity. Let us be the first to seek inner reconciliation. Pray for a renewed sense of unity and purpose. Let us be the first to demonstrate humility and purity of heart. Let us go forth as heralds of hope." Some more recent scholars have taken issue with theology. American revolutionary Thomas Paine, in his book *The Age of Reason*, describes theology as "the study of nothing," and he continues, "It is founded on nothing; it rests on no principles; it proceeds by no authorities; it has no data; it can demonstrate nothing; and it admits of no conclusion. Not anything can be studied as a science, without our being in possession of the principles upon which it is founded." Whatever your views are on theology, always stand up for what you believe in and never take your beliefs for granted. What do you believe in? Do you find religion and its history to be interesting? Would you study religion?

**Theory:** A theory is something like an educated guess, although it typically holds a bit more weight. We use theories to attempt to explain how or why things happen the way they do. The most common misconception about theories is that they are facts. Theories are gateways to discussions about things that we don't fully understand, such as the nature of the universe or the process through which human life was born. Theories are a perfect representation of the thinking process that humans go through every day. We are always wondering about the nature of things, and theories are how we explicate these wonderings. What are some theories that you have come up with to explain the world around you? How do they relate to the theories of others? How can you apply them to your everyday life?

**Therapy:** Depending on your situation, therapy can be a very useful and safe outlet to express your thoughts and work through whatever is troubling you. It's always healthy to have a shoulder to cry on. The most important thing about therapy is trust. If you can't trust the person helping you, then they are no help at all. Have you ever used therapy to cope with an emotionally troubling problem or to heal from some physical disease? Was it effective for you?

**Thesis:** A thesis is a statement that is defended by a solid argument. We use theses to argue for or against points of contention, and they are typically formal and academic in <u>nature</u>. When you argue, whether in writing or in speech, do you have a <u>clear</u> thesis encapsulating your argument? Do you excel at <u>creating</u> thesis statements?

**Thief:** A thief steals what he wants without detection. Even though some people, like Robin Hood, <u>claim</u> to be righteous thieves who steal from the rich and <u>give</u> to the poor, thievery is still <u>considered</u> a very serious crime no matter the <u>intent</u>.

**<u>Think</u>:** There are three components <u>opinions</u>. When we think, we we see and feel to develop the

> *"Most people are other people. Their thoughts are someone else's opinions, their lives a mimicry, their passions a quotation."*
> — *Oscar Wilde*

Theft comes in many <u>forms</u>; one can steal material objects, but also an <u>idea</u>, even a significant other. Have you engaged in theft in any <u>kind?</u> What were the eventual consequences, and what do we really <u>lose</u> when we steal?

**Thing:** The most ambiguous <u>word</u> possible, a thing can be anything, and it's no coincidence that thing is found in the words anything and everything. A thing is a tangible <u>object</u> that <u>exists</u> in <u>reality</u>. What things are most <u>important</u> to you?

of thought: <u>decisions</u>, <u>ideas</u>, and <u>analyze</u> the components of all that <u>power</u> of <u>reasoning</u> integrate facts, and seek the truth. Thinking is rationalizing our emotions and <u>desires</u>, and has its source in the ego. Thinking can be used to make life easier for the ego by causing the <u>world</u> to ease its pull on our <u>attention</u>. Then our attention can be better directed to the Self. Correct thinking is thinking that leads us to good <u>conditions</u> of health and supply, then to mental traits of love and peace, and finally to oneness, where, there being no other, thought is impossible and all is in <u>harmony</u>. Taking it from the top, the most correct thinking is 'no thoughts.' Truth is in the realm of knowingness. It is when all thoughts are stilled that we remove the blanket covering the omniscience that we all have now. We can liken thinking to diving into an enormous vat of <u>questions</u> and swimming around in search of <u>answers</u>. Thinking is a <u>process</u>; life is created with <u>positive</u> thoughts, while negative thinking destroys life. Do we learn to think or is thinking a <u>natural</u> process? Do you strive to push yourself mentally? Are you aware of the directions your mind goes? Do you recognize trends in your thinking, especially negative <u>trends</u>? How can you stop yourself from going down that path?

**Thirst**: Nearly all <u>living</u> things need <u>water</u> to survive, and that most certainly includes humans. Just as we need water to survive, we have other <u>needs</u> and <u>desires</u> to be fulfilled. Thirst is a strong <u>passion</u> for something that we can't live without. What are you so passionate about that you thirst for it? Does that desire lead to <u>healthy</u> situations, or do you sometimes desire that which harms you?

**Thorough**: To be thorough is to have <u>finished</u> something in the most careful and exact way

with nothing left out or undone. We should strive to do everything in life in a <u>complete</u> and thorough <u>manner</u>. Thoroughness is important in all facets of <u>life</u>; without it, nothing would ever get done the right way or in a timely fashion. What things in life require your engaged, unbridled <u>attention</u>? Do you commit yourself fully to the <u>projects</u> you engage in? If a <u>job</u> is worth doing, isn't it worth doing right?

**<u>Thought</u>**: If one is fixated on multiple <u>subjects</u> at one time, most people limit their thought <u>process</u> and shut out new or unrelated thoughts. Thought, when combined with different information and <u>emotion</u>, produces different results that culminate in classifications of humankind into categories like criminals, <u>scholars</u>, introverts, professionals, etc. Idle thought can be considered as thinking that <u>rationalizes</u> only the moment in which the thought came to be. We think, "What is affecting only me at only this instance in <u>time</u>." This is thinking that relies on a <u>false</u> <u>security</u>; thinking that is only steered by momentary convenience. We can also refer to this mode of thought as <u>shallow</u> thought. Do you, while holding your own thoughts closely, respect the thoughts of others? What is required to respect the thoughts of others even when you disagree with them? Do you feel comfortable having others disagree with you even when they <u>respect</u> you, or is feeling right more important?

**Thoughtful**: A thoughtful person is one who thinks of the comfort or well-being of others, often by intuiting ahead of time what they might need or want. Thoughtfulness is one of the best qualities to have. It is an unselfish gesture that has the power to brighten a person's day. When was the last time somebody did something thoughtful for you? How did that make you feel? Did you pay it forward?

**Threat:** A bad <u>omen</u>, a signal of something <u>violent</u> to come, a threat has the <u>power</u> to instill great fear into the hearts of many. Threats are an <u>assault</u> on our <u>person</u> and <u>senses</u>. While they usually don't inflict any physical <u>harm</u>, they often do much worse damage psychologically. Threats <u>force</u> people to live in <u>fear</u>, a paralyzing state to which none should ever be subjected. Have you felt threatened in the <u>past</u> or <u>present</u>? The threat doesn't need to be physical to be damaging; one can live in fear of losing their job. Has this happened to you? How did you cope with the situation, and what could you have done differently?

**Thrift:** Thriftiness is a great <u>skill</u> to have in life. Most of the time it's fun to spend our <u>money</u> on frivolous things that we really don't need. However, saving money will allow us to have the funds to live our <u>dreams</u> in the <u>future</u>. Thriftiness will save not only our precious dollars but will also deliver us from <u>greed</u> and all its individualistic, trivial pursuits. How can you take steps toward maintaining a thrifty lifestyle? The answer could be simple as cooking at home more often, but the money saved will be more substantial than you think.

**Thrill:** The word comes to us from an Old English word meaning "to pierce." Nowadays, we've come to understand thrill as though some strong feeling of joy or wonderment has pierced us. To be thrilled is the ultimate happiness: a potent cocktail of surprise and awe. What thrills you in life? Is there ever a risk in pursuing thrills?

**Thrive:** To thrive is to <u>grow</u> and <u>prosper</u> in a <u>healthy</u> and successful manner. Thriving is all about <u>environment</u>. In order for you to find personal <u>success</u>, you need to surround yourself with people who share your <u>dream</u> for the <u>future</u>. It is impossible to grow and prosper in a <u>toxic</u> environment. Are you in the right setting and surrounded by the right <u>crowd</u>? What do you need to do to put yourself in a position where you thrive? Is it just about the environment, or does your own work ethic play a role?

<u>**Through**</u>: When we move through, we go in one side and come out the other. I imagine a tunnel on a highway. It looms low and dark as I approach; I can't see what lies ahead and the unknown scares me. I hit the mouth of the tunnel with speed, plunging into the darkness. Alas, the tunnel is not an empty pit of nothingness as my <u>eyes</u> <u>adjust</u> to the dimness. As I pass through the tunnel, I become increasingly familiar until it seems that I am now driving the car instead of the other way around. A light <u>shines</u> at the end of the tunnel, and I feel drawn to it. Speeding toward the bright light, I feel <u>accomplished</u> for having braved the tunnel and successfully navigated its turns. The light accepts me

as I burst forth into the shining void. Much the same can be said about our passage through life,

*"The fear of death follows from the fear of life. A man who lives fully is prepared to die at any time."*
— *Mark Twain*

wouldn't you agree? Are something you know you must?

**Time:** What is the true is complicated. The time that solely based on machines. We that we have a meeting in five taking off in two hours. But are only accurate because to read the same thing. Time is a number. Strictly scientifically, but time goes so much further

you afraid of going through How can you conquer your fear?

nature of time? The answer governs our everyday lives is use our watches to remind us minutes or that our plane is those two hands on the clock everyone else's clock happens not a standard measurement or time is a physical mechanism, beyond this. Time is a chief

element of a human's life and psyche. Every person is aware that they do not have an infinite amount of time in this life. Without any sense of urgency, perhaps Alexander the Great would have never thought it important for his legacy to conquer the Near East; Michelangelo would have never painted the Sistine Chapel; Mozart would have never composed a note. With the clock ticking, go out in the world and discover your own experiences, for choosing well what you do with your time on Earth is of the utmost importance. Do you make valuable use of your time? Do you ever feel you wish you had more time? Consider ways that you can plan better in order to make the most of what time you have.

**Timid:** Timidity is akin to weakness when we visibly display fear or shyness. Fear and shyness are signs to others that you lack confidence and self-assurance. If you are a timid person, displace yourself from you comfort zone and try to adapt to unfamiliar situations. You'll find some truth behind the saying that there is really nothing to fear but fear itself. Has timidity held you back in the past? Have you considered that situations you once thought crippling weren't so bad?

**Tired:** Fatigue means we have accomplished a hard day's work. Each night after a long day, we tire out and need sleep to refuel. Ending the day tired after accomplishing what needed to be done is a rewarding feeling, and sleep is the ultimate trophy for a day's work. On the other hand, if we feel tired easily without having accomplished much, perhaps your body is telling you something is wrong. Maybe you need to adjust your diet or exercise more. If these changes don't fix the problem, perhaps you should consult a doctor. Do you find fulfillment after a long day's work? Do you take care of your body in order to maintain your energy daily?

**Titanic**: The famously massive boat was called *Titanic* for exactly that reason—it was enormous and powerful. The *Titanic* made one mistake, though, and it caused the entire enterprise to come crashing down into the sea. When you have a monumental task to complete—your *Titanic* crossing the Atlantic—be sure to consider all the possibilities so that you don't get sunk by the tip of a hidden iceberg. Always remember that arrogance is the surest way to failure. Do you examine historical situations like this one in order to grasp what lessons they might offer? Do you learn from those lessons?

**Titillate**: What titillates your senses? Whatever excites or pleases you, maintain it and enjoy it as much as possible. Keep in mind that the best thing in life is moderation, so don't saturate yourself with the things that titillate you. Instead, enjoy them only so often that they continue to titillate you each and every time. Is it difficult for you to resist giving into the temptation of those things you enjoy? Do you maintain balance in your life?

**Tobacco**: One of the major sharecrops that helped shape the Southern colonies of the nubile United States, tobacco is now better known for its misuse. Tobacco can be habit forming, and it is most certainly harmful to one's health, but it is also seen as a pleasuring retreat.

**Today:** Today is the day to get going, to make a new start, and to have some fun! Today is all about living in the now, concentrating on the next few hours of daylight, and making it as productive as possible. What can you accomplish today?

**Together**: Life is so much more enjoyable when you have the opportunity to share it with someone. Doing things together with somebody you care about will enliven the experience as a whole. Who do you want to be together with?

**Tolerance**: In a world that is increasingly more aware of differences between people and cultures, tolerance has become a hot-button issue in all societies. We should always uphold a standard of maximum tolerance that is afforded to all. Ignorance can be bliss at times, but it also breeds intolerance. Do those who lack awareness have more tolerance for the things that happen to them because they are unaware of the alternatives?

*"If you can cultivate the right attitude, your enemies are your best spiritual teachers because their presence provides you with the opportunity to enhance and develop tolerance, patience, and understanding."*
— *Dalai Lama XIV*

**Tomorrow**: What will tomorrow bring? This biting question has nagged at the human soul forever. While it is impossible to be certain of what tomorrow holds, we humans have mastered the art of planning, which makes tomorrow a bit less unpredictable. Whatever your plans, embrace the enigma of tomorrow and live each day as though it were a surprise.

**Too**: Too much of a good thing can be bad. We've all heard our mothers drilling this into our heads as kids when we are begging for candy or whatever other desires we have as kids. Once that phrase sounded ridiculous and implausible, but as we grow and mature, it makes a lot more sense. What can't you get enough of? Have you ever had too much? How can you teach yourself moderation?

**Tool:** A tool is used to carry out a particular function or task. Look out at the world around you, and you'll find there are several tools to help you achieve in your life and yield as much success as you want. The problem lies in the fact that some are not immune to such tools. Why is this? Are too many people giving them wrong advice and hiding necessary tools from them? How have you used the tools in your world to improve your life?

**Topic**: A topic is a matter, issue, or theme that is being discussed. Topics being discussed generate a lot of opinions on both sides of the issue. However, in this day and age, those opinions rarely meet in the middle to gather and share fair and adequate solutions regarding the topic at hand. What topics lately have been burning in your mind? Do you have a strong, one-sided opinion on an issue? Do you try conceding with other opinions to eliminate any discretion?

**Torment**: Torment suggests that one has been bothered or treated harshly over and over again. In ancient Greek mythology, the Furies were the embodied representation of torment. They would fly down and peck at the bodies of those who were doomed to their horrible punishment. Negative emotions and violent actions are quite similar to the Furies when they bite at our mind and soul. The only thing that we can do is to ensure that we never subject others to torment and hope that torment doesn't reach us. But also be aware of how we can torment ourselves. What demons do you inflict upon yourself?

**Torture**: Slightly different from torment, torture suggests such great pain in one instant that the body can barely stand it. Torture is one of the most inhumane acts a person can inflict on another person. Torture has become something of an issue recently with the reports of heinous acts committed at American military bases against detainees. How can we put a stop to the injustice that is torture?

**Total**: The whole is much greater than each of its parts. Sometimes it's difficult to see the total picture, but when we consider each part the picture becomes clearer. Once we've developed an image of the grand scheme in our mind, we can accomplish what we set out to accomplish with the parts at our immediate disposal. What does the total picture look like in your mind?

**Totalitarian**: A totalitarian government is one in which a single political party holds control over all power and outlaws any other government to even have a presence. Totalitarian governments should be eradicated from the Earth if we are to truly have a global society based on freedom to preach and practice what we will. How can we avoid such situations? When we give up freedoms—even small ones—are we creating a political climate in which these governments exist?

**Touch:** Touch is the only one of our five senses that covers our entire bodies. We see and believe, and in order not to make a mistake, we touch. It combines the feelings of hot and cold, rough and smooth, wet and dry, soft and hard, as well as pain and pleasure (sub-senses). Much like our household animals, who love to be petted; touch. A touch is a comforting connectedness, sympathy, or both in proximity and in magical quality about touching. shake someone's hand. We feel big hug. Some shy away from a fear the touch of another person. much more easily just from the touch play in your relationships? come to understand the world from it?

> *"Every heart sings a song, incomplete, until another heart whispers back. Those who wish to sing always find a song. At the touch of a lover, everyone becomes a poet."*
> — *Plato*

humans delight in a soft, caring way to express feelings of care, gratitude. A touch is familiarity relationship. There is a certain We make a connection when we the warmth that is provided by a friendly touch, but we shouldn't We can get to know one another slightest touch. What role does Is it an essential part of how you around you, or do you shy away

**Tough:** We should all strive to be tough, whether it's physically, mentally, or emotionally. Toughness allows us to be more vigilant and more receptive to the myriad options that life throws at us. Toughness implies experience, so get busy living and you will become tougher and more resilient in whatever you do. Do you stand up well under physical and mental pressure? Additionally, this word can be used to describe those who are too stern in their approach to dealing with others. Do you try to make yourself easy for others to work with?

**Toxic:** Many things in life can have toxic or devastating effects on our bodies and minds. Drugs and alcohol are the most obvious toxins to which we <u>subject</u> ourselves; however, our environment can often be the most toxic element in our lives. <u>Success</u> in life is all about the people with whom you surround yourself. If you hang around with the <u>wrong</u> people or find yourself turning up in the wrong places, it can be incredibly toxic to your <u>goals</u> and <u>ambitions</u>. Are you mindful of toxic elements in your life? Do you excise those portions of your life that poison you?

**Track:** What track are you on in your <u>life</u>? We can visualize our lifetime as though it is wrapped around a race track. We <u>start</u> with a bang and then slowly even out until we hit our cruising stride. When we hit the <u>finish</u> line, we should have the assurance that everything we had to <u>offer</u> the world was left on the track. Is your life on track?

**Trademark:** A trademark is a special thing that defines what is <u>unique</u> or interesting about you. A trademark can be a special <u>skill</u>, a quirky <u>fact</u>, or well-known attribute. Whatever your trademark is, own it and <u>flourish</u> it in all its glory.

**Tradition:** Traditions are an integral part of human life. We would have no common <u>history</u> and no <u>sense</u> of <u>identity</u> or importance without traditions. Humans have relied on the passing of customs and beliefs through <u>word</u> of mouth for all our history. <u>Cherish</u> your traditions, for they are truly what make you who you are. Yet at the same time, don't be afraid to depart from tradition when they no longer suit your life in the present; learn to strike the <u>difficult</u> balance between tradition and innovation.

**Tragedy, Tragic:** Tragedy as an art form first came to us around two thousand five hundred years ago with the ancient Greeks.

> *"A love for tradition has never weakened a nation, indeed it has strengthened nations in their hour of peril."*
> — *Winston Churchill*

Shakespeare then made tragedy even more famous some two thousand years ago. Much like those great works, our everyday lives are riddled with tragedies both great and small. Tragedies, though always ending on a sad note, are not the end of the play that is our <u>lives</u>. When tragedy strikes, do the curtains <u>close</u>, or do we emerge from it stronger than we once were? We may question our <u>faith</u> in the face of random <u>acts</u> or <u>events</u> of <u>destruction</u>. We may wonder why such events happen to the <u>innocent</u> —why things are taken from those who deserve <u>abundance</u>, why lives are cut short, why <u>prevention</u> eluded us. In the face of this, however, should we let tragedy define us, or should we let our actions in the wake of such events define tragedy? It's the strength of <u>spirit</u> of those who survive—their <u>perseverance</u>, <u>generosity</u>, and <u>courage</u>—that shows how deeply we are connected as <u>humans</u>.

**Training:** Training is a <u>learning</u> process. We must go through training <u>exercises</u> in order to get our bearings when we enter a new phase in our <u>lives</u>. We train for new jobs, we train to excel physically, and we train from <u>birth</u> to be productive and courteous members of <u>society</u>.

**Trait:** Our individual qualities are known as traits. Our personality can be broken down into individual traits like sense of <u>humor</u> or <u>compassion</u>. Nurture your traits and your <u>true</u> colors will <u>shine</u> through.

**Traitor:** <u>Betrayal</u> is the ultimate mark of the traitor. Perhaps the most famous traitor of all comes from the Bible, as Judas betrayed Jesus to the Romans. It is inevitable that traitors will roam among us unknowingly. We must remain <u>vigilant</u> against traitors and <u>liars</u> lest we are to be betrayed and wounded by their harmful words and deeds. Have you ever been betrayed? How did that <u>experience</u>, no matter how difficult, help you to grow into a better person?

**Trance:** Are you a daydreamer? We all have those moments when we seem to get <u>lost</u> inside our own minds. Idle time and an <u>idle</u> mind can breed inattentiveness. Avoid falling into an unfocused trance by remaining <u>busy</u> and <u>active</u> in respect to both body and mind.

**Tranquillity:** <u>Free</u> from the tree of <u>silence</u> hangs the fruit of tranquillity. Tranquillity is <u>peace</u> and quiet, like an untouched mountain spring. As humans, we relish tranquillity, and we even make special trips just to get a piece of tranquillity. But you need not go to the mountains to find tranquillity; you must rather cultivate within yourself, making it an internal place you can return to wherever you may be.

**Transcend:** Transcendence is truly the definitive <u>ambition</u> of human <u>progression</u>. To transcend is to go beyond the limits of human <u>capability</u>, to create something that has never been seen before, to surpass what is known into a <u>new</u> realm. We should all strive to reach transcendence in whatever we do. <u>Society</u> will benefit invaluably from any form of art or innovation that has the ability to progress us to a new level of knowledge or beauty.

**Transform, Transformation:** In <u>life</u>, we go through many different transformations, both physically and mentally. From puberty as a teenager to that motorcycle you bought on your fiftieth birthday, it's <u>healthy</u> and cathartic to strip away <u>old</u> layers of ourselves and rebuild something completely <u>new</u>. What will be your next transformation?

**Transient:** The transient things are so often the sweetest; however, the things that stick around for a while are much more meaningful. Summer <u>love</u> is quite a delight for a sprightly eighteen-year-old until <u>fall</u> brings imminent heartbreak. Before getting wrapped up in life's transient wonders, <u>cherish</u> those things that stay near you above all else.

**Transparency:** We should aspire to live our <u>lives</u> openly without <u>secrets</u>, <u>lies</u>, or any other form of dishonesty. How can you be more transparent in your life?

**Trash:** There is a lot of trash out there in the <u>world</u> today, and I don't mean the kind that ends up in a landfill. We should be cautious when absorbing the enormous amount of <u>information</u> being spewed at us from the <u>television</u> or computer screen. With some obvious exceptions, a lot of what you might find on the Internet or television is complete garbage.

**Treason:** Benedict Arnold was a noted traitor, and he was duly hanged for his <u>crimes</u>. Treason is one of the foulest crimes a <u>person</u> can commit. To go against one's country is to go against one's self, <u>family</u>, and <u>dignity</u>. But there are subtler forms of treason, sometimes as simple as a lack of <u>effort</u> when you know more is needed of you. Have you committed treason, even in smaller forms?

> *"The difference between treason and patriotism is only a matter of dates."*
> — *Alexandre Dumas*

**Treat:** Treats are the perfect way to treat someone. Giving a <u>gift</u>, such as a treat, is a wonderful way to show someone <u>appreciation</u> or <u>support</u>. How can you treat someone deserving today?

**Tremble:** A tremble can be caused by both <u>fear</u> and excitement. I distinctly remember the <u>moment</u> I was opening my college acceptance letter. I was extremely scared to be rejected by the school I had loved my entire life. But at the same time, I was so incredibly excited at the <u>opportunity</u> of attending there. As my fingertip slipped beneath the corner of the envelope, my entire <u>body</u> trembled with nervous anticipation. Thankfully, I was <u>accepted</u>, but I will never forget that trembling feeling. When did you last tremble with <u>nervous</u> anticipation?

**Tremendous:** When I <u>imagine</u> tremendous, I envision a great urban sprawl much like New York City or Hong Kong. Tremendous, to me, means becoming a <u>part</u> of something that is so much larger than just you. A tremendous city has its own breath, style, and pulse. When you <u>allow</u> yourself to be engulfed by a tremendous city, you become a tiny blood <u>cell</u> within the massive <u>body</u>; without the function that you and all others bring to city, it dies and is no longer greater than the sum of its parts. How can you allow yourself to be engulfed by a tremendous outside force while still maintaining your autonomy?

**Trepidation:** Trepidation is a feeling of great <u>fear</u>. Fear can play a great <u>role</u> in our decision making <u>processes</u>. We should never let fear grab hold of our <u>moral</u> compass, but rather recognize fear for what it is and overcome it. By remaining <u>strong</u> and steadfast, you can overcome your fears and take control of them.

**Trial**: Everything new needs a trial run before it can be fully adopted. When we buy new shoes, we try them on first. When we buy a new car, we drive it around the block a few times. Trial and <u>error</u> is one of the most fundamental scientific <u>methods</u>. It's always <u>worth</u> giving something new a try when you have the reassurance that you can decide whether you like it and want to keep it. What new things in your <u>life</u> are still awaiting trial?

*"If tribulation is a necessary element in redemption, we must anticipate that it will never cease till God sees the world to be either redeemed or no further redeemable."*
— *C. S. Lewis*

**Tribe:** In the ancient and medieval Middle East, Arabs placed heavy emphasis on the tribe to the extent that the entire tribe was considered one's immediate family. Nowadays, our notion of tribe has dissipated into smaller 'household' family units, but the <u>connection</u> felt between its members has not changed in the slightest. Whether you consider your tribe to be your <u>family</u>, your <u>friends</u>, or your coworkers, keep them close and protect them in the same manner that you would expect from them.

**Tribulation:** Tribulations are simply a fact of <u>life</u>. We all have troubling <u>issues</u> with which we must cope. At times, they may seem unbearable, but take <u>heart</u>—there is always a light at the end of the dark tunnel. What tribulations have you overcome successfully, and what have they <u>taught</u> you?

**Tribute:** A tribute is a show of <u>respect</u> to someone who has done something worthy of great gratitude. We pay tribute to our parents by respecting their rules and to our teachers by respecting their guidance. Who are the people in your life to whom you have not yet paid tribute?

**Trillion:** One trillion is the equivalent to one thousand billion, a number that is staggering even to try to <u>imagine</u>. Yet there are things in the volume of trillions that <u>exist</u> all over the <u>earth</u>—insects, for instance, or even the trillions of cells alive and at <u>work</u> inside your own <u>body</u>. How can you better comprehend such things that are <u>difficult</u> to conceptualize?

**Trinity:** The Trinity of the Christian belief describes three separate entities—the Father, Son, and Holy Ghost—<u>united</u> as one divine being. A trinity can also simply mean anything that comes in a <u>group</u> of three but is introduced as one. An equilateral triangle, with its three sides, is the strongest geometric shape. With that being said, many good things come in threes, and three has been considered an almost mystical number throughout history. In my experience, the third time usually is the charm. What <u>role</u> does the number three play in your life?

**Trite:** The word trite comes from the Latin meaning "to wear out," and we still use that meaning today. Trite statements are typically clichés that have <u>lost</u> their luster, such as "the bee's knees." While trite sayings can seem corny, they can provide some <u>laughs</u> when used casually. Are there any funny sayings that you use that are no longer considered fresh?

**Triumph:** <u>Success</u> and victory precede triumph. Triumph is that gratifying emotional celebration after competing and winning whatever endeavor had to be <u>fought</u> for. Personal triumphs are good for the soul; they bring added <u>confidence</u>, but too much triumph can breed an oversized <u>ego</u> and <u>greedy</u> mentality. No matter what level of personal success you find in your life, remain humble in the <u>celebration</u> of your life's victories.

**Trivial:** Some things in life are not worth a second of our <u>time</u>. These things would be regarded as trivial, the way trivia is considered to be <u>knowledge</u> of completely useless <u>facts</u>. Don't get too wrapped up in the small, unimportant things in <u>life</u>; otherwise, the big <u>picture</u> will be rightly skewed. What trivial things in your life are you currently paying too much <u>attention</u> to?

**Trouble:** Trouble is <u>worry</u>, annoyance, or <u>suffering</u>. Trouble can come about in many forms, and it can often be hidden in disguise or sneaking in the shadows like a sly fox waiting to pounce. Trouble is much like the little demon that sits on your shoulder and whispers into your ear. Trouble is <u>tempting</u> and often <u>promises</u> <u>fun</u> and excitement, but beware, for there are always unseen <u>consequences</u> that can have devastating effects on you and those around you.

**True:** The most <u>genuine</u> word known to <u>man</u>; that which is true is <u>loyal</u>, exact, rightful, and most importantly, real. Strive to be the truest form of you as possible, for being untrue to yourself is equivalent to being untrue to everyone else. In the <u>absence</u> of what is true, we become mere shadows of ourselves, clouding the distinction between what is real and what is made up. If we allow this <u>false</u> presence to occur, we lose all <u>sense</u> of our <u>identity</u> as lies pile on top of lies. We may know of certain truisms that will forever remain correct. However, it is the task of each individual to recognize these truths as they manifest themselves around us at all <u>times</u>. Individuals do not make his or her own truth; they must perceive themselves from an outside perspective in <u>order</u> that they might know and embrace their true nature.

**Trust:** Trust is often so easily taken for granted, and it must not be this way. Trust is something that must be earned and maintained. Trust should never be granted or gifted without first being tested; otherwise, we leave ourselves susceptible to trickery and falsity. Trust is a defining point in any <u>relationship</u> between two <u>individuals</u>. When trust is awarded to us, we must never abuse it. Trust is all about <u>intuition</u>, and it starts with the <u>self</u>. If you trust your own intuition and ability, you will have a much easier time discerning who is worthy of your trust and who is only feigning <u>loyalty</u>. To be trusted is even more fulfilling than being loved.

> *"I'm not upset that you lied to me, I'm upset that from now on I can't believe you."*
> — *Friedrich Nietzsche*

**Truth:** Truth is not a quest or something we must find; it is sitting right in front of us just waiting to be recognized. Truth is that which never changes, and it cannot be taught or created; it simply is. Truth can be approached on an intellectual level, an emotional level, and an intuitive level. Truth must be perceived through realization. This is the unique characteristic of truth: It must be seen by each individual through his or her own perception. The individual that lives in accordance with the truth will find supreme happiness as his or her limitations slowly fade away and he or she discovers a natural, inherent state in which all power and knowledge reside. As O. Anna Niemus penned, "Truth is self-luminescent. It is reality, self-evident, needing no external defense. It is immediately recognized by resonant hearts. It can be hidden for a short time… but inevitably truth conquers all." Where do you find truth in your life?

**Try:** Trying is all about patience. When we try something new, we are bound to have a strange or awkward experience with it. Remember learning how to ride a bike? After a few scraped knees, you may have wanted to give up, but you didn't and now riding a bike is almost second nature. A good rule of thumb is this: Give everything a solid, honest try at least once. If you live your life snubbing experiences and opportunities, you'll surely regret it later. What in your life is waiting for you to give it a try?

> *"Secrets, silent, stony sit in the dark palaces of both our hearts: secrets weary of their tyranny: tyrants willing to be dethroned."*
> — *James Joyce*

**Turbulence:** Turbulence is a part of life. There will always be times that are a bit bumpy and wild. Working through the turbulence is a necessary experience, and having dealt with it once, you will be more prepared to deal with it in the future. A little hardship makes the smooth cruising that much more enjoyable.

**Turn:** Life is full of twists and turns, and we often don't know where they will take us next. In order to navigate the turns that life throws at us, we can surround ourselves with others who have the experience and wisdom to help guide us through the twists.

**Tutor:** A tutor is a mentor in his or her own right. Tutors are extremely helpful for someone who is struggling with a specific subject because they work one on one with the student. Tutors do more than just teach; they also guide and help shape the student to be a better and more productive member of school and society.

**Type:** People come in all shapes and sizes, but we don't necessarily consider similar people as conforming to a specific type. Personalities are much more classifiable as types, leaving each person regardless of color, age, or sex to be their own individual. Whether you or others consider you to be funny or serious, warm or cold, embrace who you are and perhaps you can shatter the stratification that comes with placing individuals into types. When you nourish all facets of your personality, there is nothing typical about you.

**Tyranny:** A tyranny is an unjust form of government that cruelly uses its overwhelming power to punish its subjects into submission. Tyrannical leadership comes about when greed is factored into the equation. Those leaders who lust after power at the expense of their citizens should be removed from power. It is up to the citizens subjugated by that terrible leader to take action and reclaim the power that they rightfully deserve.

# U

**Ubiquitous:** To be <u>present</u> everywhere at the <u>same</u> <u>time</u>; to be <u>omnipresent</u>. In today's <u>world</u> of <u>technology</u> and <u>mass media</u>, one can <u>interact</u> with almost anyone in any place at any <u>hour</u>. This can be exciting and overwhelming, <u>advantageous</u> and <u>dangerous</u>. Take a <u>moment</u> to <u>consider</u> the things in <u>life</u> that surround us at all times, such as <u>faith</u>, <u>crime</u>, <u>nature</u>, and <u>desire</u>. How can we distinguish the <u>positive</u> <u>forces</u> in our <u>lives</u> from the <u>negative</u>? Is life becoming an existence where everything is <u>happening</u> at the same time in many places? Do you <u>feel</u> the <u>need</u> to be <u>constantly</u> updated with what everyone is doing?

**Ugly:** We have a propensity to <u>think</u> of ugly as a descriptor of undesirable <u>physical</u> features. Just like <u>beauty</u>, ugly is highly <u>subjective</u> to the eye of the beholder. Perhaps we can consider ugly as an <u>opportunity</u> for <u>improvement</u>. An ugly <u>house</u> <u>presents</u> an opportunity to fix it up; an ugly painting presents an opportunity to hone one's <u>skills</u>. One of the <u>most</u> <u>sacred</u> <u>human</u> <u>condition</u> is the <u>ability</u> to <u>create</u> opportunity from <u>failure</u>, to create beauty from ugliness. Which is more <u>significant</u> to you—inner or outer ugliness? Who <u>decides</u> what is ugly? How can we think of ugly as a <u>positive</u>? Do you <u>find</u> yourself to be beautiful on the inside and outside?

**Ulterior:** We often have undisclosed <u>desires</u> and <u>motives</u> that we <u>wish</u> to keep hidden from others. These desires and motives can be malicious, <u>embarrassing</u>, or expedient. Whatever the <u>reason</u>, we must <u>consider</u> the repercussions of <u>secrecy</u> when collaborating with others. Ulterior motives and desires are irrefutably <u>negative</u> in <u>human</u> <u>interaction</u>.

We must <u>constantly</u> engage in <u>discussions</u> to <u>reveal</u> our <u>personal</u> desires and motives in order to <u>achieve</u> <u>goals</u> for the <u>public</u> <u>good</u>. Do you have ulterior motives? How do you <u>portray</u> yourself when you have an ulterior motive?

**Ultimate:** The <u>final</u> <u>stage</u> of <u>development</u>, the <u>most</u> <u>fundamental</u> and basic <u>level</u>* of <u>human</u> <u>nature</u>, the highest or farthest <u>point</u> we can <u>reach</u> in terms of our aspirations. To be the ultimate is to be the <u>best</u>. We should <u>strive</u> to reach the ultimate level of any <u>task</u> we set out to <u>accomplish</u>. What is your ultimate <u>goal</u>? How do you <u>plan</u> to reach your ultimate goal? Have you already reached an ultimate goal?

**Ultimatum:** <u>Final</u> demand on which an <u>agreement</u> or the <u>success</u> of a <u>relationship</u> is contingent upon. Be careful when issuing ultimatums. Before giving an ultimatum, <u>think</u> <u>clearly</u> about the <u>consequences</u> that may transpire from making certain demands. When dealing with <u>disputes</u>, set an ultimatum for yourself before <u>threatening</u> others. By holding yourself to the same <u>standard</u> as your <u>opponent</u>, a <u>compromise</u> can be <u>reached</u>, and the dispute can be <u>resolved</u> <u>positively</u> without the threat of escalation. Do you attempt to compromise before <u>issuing</u> ultimatums? Have you issued an ultimatum before? Why?

**Ultra:** We must <u>strive</u> to go beyond the usual <u>expected</u> limits of <u>human</u> capability. By pushing ourselves to <u>achieve</u> beyond what is expected, we can become ultra-humans. How can we go beyond what is expected of us or what we expect of ourselves? Do you strive to be an ultra-human? Do you <u>exceed</u> expectations?

**Un:** We <u>use</u> this to denote things that are not or things that are the <u>opposite</u>. We often use un-<u>words</u> to explicate the <u>characteristics</u> of ourselves and others. These can be both <u>positive</u> and <u>negative</u>. If you are unbiased, it can be positive because you have a neutral and more <u>valid</u> <u>opinion</u> than someone who is <u>biased</u>. At the same time, if you are unbiased, it can be negative because you lack the fortitude to take a <u>stand</u> on a particular <u>side</u> of an <u>issue</u>. When using un- words with negative connotations like 'unable,' analyze the way these words reflect our <u>sense</u> of <u>self</u> and <u>consider</u> painting yourself in a more positive <u>light</u>. Have we taken the <u>time</u> to consider the ways we convey our <u>personalities</u>, <u>attitudes</u>, and <u>thoughts</u> with un- words?

**Unanimity:** <u>Complete</u> <u>agreement</u> in your <u>life</u> can be exceedingly frustrating. We want our <u>family</u> and <u>friends</u> to agree with our <u>own</u> <u>behaviors</u> and <u>attitudes</u> in life. A <u>state</u> of unanimity is elusive, as <u>disagreements</u> are virtually unavoidable. Seek a state of unanimity within your inner <u>circles</u> of family and friends, but don't be <u>surprised</u> when some disagreements still arise; instead, <u>choose</u> your battles. Do you work to restore and <u>maintain</u> <u>harmony</u> among your family and friends? In what <u>groups</u> do you have unanimity?

**Unanimous:** Be of one <u>mind</u> with your <u>community</u> and those who <u>care</u> for you. When we <u>agree</u> as a <u>whole</u>, we can transcend the <u>power</u> of the <u>individual</u> mind. A collective <u>body</u> of the same mind can <u>achieve</u> more collaboratively and surpass the constraints of one <u>person</u> in isolation. How might a unanimous <u>decision</u> be <u>harmful</u> to a <u>group</u>? Do you make unanimous decisions in groups you are a part of?

**Under:** To be below something or someone else, whether <u>physically</u> or <u>mentally</u> below the curve of a score and the <u>success</u> of another <u>person</u>. What <u>times</u> in your <u>life</u> were you underappreciated others or have felt underwhelmed? How might we <u>transform</u> our under <u>experiences</u> into <u>positivity</u> that can <u>help</u> us surmount <u>barriers</u>? How often do we sell ourselves short or <u>perform</u> below our <u>potential</u>?

> *"If you can't explain it to a six-year-old, you don't understand it yourself."*
> *— Albert Einstein*

**<u>Understand, Understanding</u>:** To comprehend something or what someone says. It is <u>important</u> to understand <u>tasks</u> you are assigned in <u>order</u> to be <u>successful</u> in <u>completing</u> them. If you do not understand something, you should ask <u>questions</u> to <u>clarify</u> it. The only way to <u>truly</u> understand a <u>person</u> or <u>subject</u> is to <u>follow</u> the trail of logical, critical thought; this process begets wisdom. In <u>life</u>, we often miss certain social cues or <u>misunderstand</u> messages. We should <u>listen</u> carefully, engage and confer our <u>own</u> <u>opinions,</u> and then gather both viewpoints to <u>create</u> understanding with others. Do we understand the <u>meaning</u> of life? Have we taken the <u>time</u> to try to understand it? In <u>perceiving</u> other life, do we understand it? When we understand something, do we not <u>define</u> it first and then <u>discover</u> its meaning? How can we <u>improve</u> the way we <u>interact</u> and empathize with others? Do you easily understand others? Are you easy to understand?

**Unhappiness, Unhappy:** The <u>opposite</u> of <u>happy</u>; to be <u>sad</u> or disappointed in yourself, someone else or how a <u>situation</u> <u>developed</u>. It is <u>important</u> to be <u>positive</u> because <u>attitude</u> affects how <u>events</u> play out. Try to stay positive through hard <u>times</u> and <u>reach</u> out to those you <u>love</u> for <u>comfort</u>, guidance, and reassurance. Are you easily made unhappy? How do you <u>overcome</u> unhappiness? How can others overcome their unhappiness? Are you comforting to those who are unhappy?

**Unique:** It is essential to develop your own sense of self before trying to impact the lives of others. Cultivate your skills, pursue identity, and be proud of your person has the potential to stereotypes, as well as stand out are you unique? Who defines unique if you are? What skills more unique?

your interests, create your distinctive character. A unique defy expectations and shatter and become successful. How uniqueness? Do you enjoy being could you cultivate to become

> *"We need more light about each other. Light creates understanding, understanding creates love, love creates patience, and patience creates unity."*
> — *Malcolm X*

**Unite, Unity, Unification:** A people who share the same We all live on the same planet humans, most of us strive to that nurtures the soul and From this viewpoint, we can be of unification is inherent

feeling of oneness with many aims, interests, and feelings. and breathe the same air. As achieve some form of happiness promotes the common good. unified in purpose. The concept in all. Because of changing

differences, it is difficult to find true unification. Consider the effect of diversity on unity. Introduce yourself to your neighbors, invite an interesting stranger for coffee, or support your local businesses. In seeking unity, do you look for cohesiveness and equality that can be linked to a purpose or cause? Do you consider the logistics of distant unification? Is it possible that salvation can be achieved in unification? Does unification simplify life? Through interaction, relationships, and shared experience, can we find true unity? Who do you feel a sense of unity with?

**Universal:** Something that is common throughout the world, not just in one particular country. The advancement of our civilization has opened new gateways for more universal communication. We can express ourselves through new media, making global connections never before possible to create a universal society. If we engage in a universal discourse, we come to see ourselves as important pieces in the universal puzzle of society. By connecting our experiences with others, we can improve ourselves and our universal society. However, we should be careful to preserve all cultures instead of trying to assimilate. How can we make sense of our individual experiences in a connected world?

within which we live, the universe as a whole may seem unthinkable. Instead of pondering unanswerable questions, focus on the way we, as humans, function in space and time. We are not simply insignificant cogs in some massive machine controlled by an omniscient puppet master. Every human has roles, responsibilities, and gifts that he or she should share with the universe. Our universe is defined by what we achieve within it. It begins at the individual level and ends at the collective understanding and functions of humankind. All that we do, say, think, and feel, collected into one comprehensive body, creates the universe that we know. We are all connected in the cosmos, so how do we comprehend and succeed at our role within it? What is the true nature of the universe? Can you imagine what else is out there in the universe that we have not discovered?

**Universe:** Since we can only speculate about the origins and movements of this vast expanse

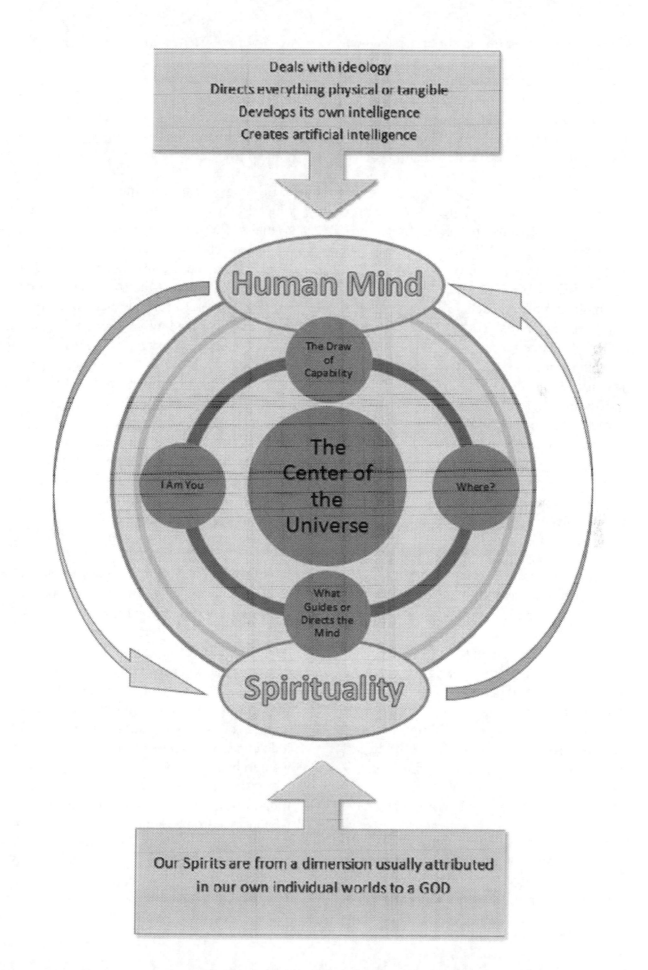

**Unknown:** Something that is not <u>understood</u> or <u>discovered</u>. It is <u>difficult</u> for <u>humans</u> to know the <u>answers</u> to every <u>question</u>. We do not fully understand all the <u>phenomena</u> in this <u>world</u>. Therefore, much of it is unknown to us. What is unknown to you? What do you <u>wish</u> you could understand? What do you <u>want</u> to discover?

**Up:** We all <u>strive</u> for <u>advancement</u> whether in our careers, <u>relationships</u>, or <u>identities</u>. Picture the process of living <u>life</u> as climbing a ladder. Each <u>accomplishment</u> moves you up another rung. At each rung, we gain <u>valuable</u> life <u>experiences</u> that act as <u>stepping</u> stones moving us upward. What rung of life's ladder are you at in your career, relationships, and <u>sense</u> of <u>self</u> at this <u>moment</u>? How high is your ladder, and what are the <u>goals</u> you <u>hope</u> to <u>achieve</u> at each rung along the way? What do you <u>need</u> to do right now to <u>move</u> yourself up to the next rung?

**Upset:** To be <u>emotional</u> about something, whether it be disappointment, <u>anger</u>, <u>sadness</u>, or too much <u>stress</u>. Everyone gets upset once in a while and you should <u>comfort</u> those who are upset. In the <u>moment</u>, everything seems <u>difficult</u> and like nothing is <u>right</u>. Do not <u>worry</u>; things will get <u>better</u>. The sooner you see the <u>positive</u> things in <u>life</u>, the sooner you will be <u>moving</u> <u>forward</u>. It is <u>important</u> to stay positive because <u>attitude</u> is everything. Do you get upset easily? What makes you upset? How do you comfort those who are upset? How can we <u>avoid</u> getting upset?

**Urbanity:** To be courteous or polite. Work to <u>associate</u> yourself with <u>sophistication</u> and <u>suavity</u>. <u>Expand</u> your worldview by traveling, <u>reading</u>, and <u>interacting</u> with all <u>different</u> <u>types</u> of <u>people</u>. <u>Cultivating</u> a cosmopolitan <u>personality</u> will illuminate your <u>life</u> with a

<u>wealth</u> of <u>knowledge</u> and <u>experience</u>. Seek refinement in your <u>tastes</u>, and people will <u>honor</u> your insights. Do you have the <u>quality</u> of being urbane? Can you think of someone who is very urbane? How can you become more like him or her? Is it <u>possible</u> to be too polite or too courteous?

**Urge:** Basic <u>instinctual</u> and <u>inevitable</u> drive, which is a <u>true</u> reflection of our <u>emotional</u>, <u>animalistic</u> <u>desires</u>. Whether you <u>crave</u> chocolate bars or chocolate martinis, always <u>stay</u> grounded. Do not let the rush take over or cloud your <u>judgment</u>, and get spiraled into <u>addiction</u>. Indulging in your <u>pleasures</u> is far from a <u>problem</u>; in fact, it's <u>healthy</u> to find enjoyment in your <u>life</u>. The <u>key</u> is to <u>control</u> your urges. Keep your <u>mind</u>, <u>body</u>, and <u>soul</u> satiated by treating yourself in small doses. What urges do you have? Have you been addicted to feeding your desires? Do you know anyone that is addicted? How can we <u>overcome</u> our addictive <u>habits</u>?

**Urgency:** We <u>feel</u> a <u>sense</u> of urgency in our <u>lives</u> as <u>people</u> <u>constantly</u> remind us how short <u>life</u> is and how you only live once. In today's fast-paced, globalized <u>world</u>, it may feel like we have no <u>option</u> but to stay in constant motion lest we <u>fall</u> behind or fail to <u>accomplish</u> our <u>goals</u>. It is <u>important</u> to live with a sense of urgency to the extent that the impetus of <u>motivation</u> does not succumb to indolence. Push yourself to get where you <u>want</u> to be in life, but take a few <u>moments</u> to <u>rest</u> along the way. If you <u>move</u> through life too fast, you might miss the beauty and wonderment to be found in the smallest things. Is your life very fast paced? Do you have a <u>sense</u> of urgency with everything you do? Do you have a list of activities you <u>want</u> to do during your lifetime?

> *"A life spent making mistakes is not only more honorable, but more useful than a life spent doing nothing."*
> *— George Bernard Shaw*

**Use:** To use is a foundational human action. Our ability to use things for specific purposes defines who we are, what we do, and how we do it. We've adapted the way we use things so well that we can build skyscrapers and fly around the world. Use your knowledge and life experiences to determine your path in life. Apply the skills you've acquired through those experiences, and use the proper tools to accomplish what you set out to do. In order to be, you must do, and in order to do, you must use what you have. What tools do you possess? How do you use them? How do you use things in your daily life? How do you apply your mind? What can you do with your hands? Do you use people to get what you want? Do you use any drugs?

"Literature is
my Utopia"
— Helen Keller

**Utopia:** This ideal state is elusive and perhaps unattainable. The scope of the idea is intended to be pervasive and holistic. However, the fruition of the utopist state is unrealistic to expect in this life. Instead, we can seek out utopia on a localized scale. Find paradise inside the confines of your home. Be harmonious with your family and friends. A utopia doesn't have to be worldwide. We can achieve utopia when we are at peace with ourselves. What is in your ideal world? What state or country would be a utopia for you if you lived there?

# V

**Vacant, Vacancy:** To be vacant is to be <u>empty,</u> or unoccupied. A vacant mind is one set apart from <u>reality</u>. It can lead to one's own conclusions from what it sees in the world around them, rather than having to succumb to outside influences. Distancing ourselves from life's troubles can be a <u>tempting</u> prospect, but is a life which is centered on <u>detachment</u> and disinterest conducive to <u>happiness</u>? Is it easier to be anything you want to be in a virtual cyber world than in the new world? Is this supposedly without risk *or not*?

**Vacuous:** Something or someone devoid of substance or <u>essence</u>, being mindless. In an increasingly <u>virtual</u> world, it's easy to forget the <u>beauty</u> of physicality, and the <u>substance</u> that face-to-face interaction can add to all of our lives. It's important to make efforts to seek out <u>real</u>-life interaction to add further depth and <u>meaning</u> to our lives, which will only help you become a better person in all facets of life. How can you add more substance to your life?

**Vague:** Not being specific or direct. Vagaries are best avoided in most <u>aspects</u> of life, as they are surrounded with gray area. <u>Specificity</u> can make your goals an accessible and <u>tangible</u> <u>reality</u>, thus reducing any sort of stress that might come about because of vagueness. However, vagueness is not something to be shunned altogether. Is it unrealistic to expect to <u>quantify</u> everything? Artistic and abstract work and thought thrive with some amount of vagary, allowing others to observe your ideas in their own manner. How can you balance the positive qualities of vagary with the benefits of detail? Is there a certain amount of vagary that needs to be a balanced with details?

> *"There comes a time when you look into the mirror and you realize that what you see is all that you will ever be. And then you accept it. Or you kill yourself. Or you stop looking in mirrors."*
> — Tennessee Williams

**Vain:** Vain can be seen in someone <u>possessing</u> a high degree of <u>confidence</u>, or admirableness, about themselves, whether that be with their appearance, possessions, or abilities. Can excessive concern about one's own <u>appearance</u> or <u>achievements</u> lead to arrogance or <u>conceit</u>, and thus create the paradox of <u>futility</u>, becoming *in vain* and thus rendering the <u>vanity</u> useless or without real <u>value</u> or worth? Why do people feel the need to be vain? Is it to justify themselves within the societal rank or merely because they are insecure about themselves and, therefore, need reassurance from others?

**Valid, Validate:** Serving as an acceptable and suitable supporter to an intended claim or point. What makes something valid? Whether or not someone or something is constituted as being "valid" may depend upon personal <u>opinion</u>, rather than <u>fact</u> or evidence. A valid <u>argument</u>, for example, is one that is sound and <u>true</u>, while also carrying the weight of being <u>logical</u> and effective as well as credible, but what makes a valid human being? This is a far more complex question to address. It's fair to say that most people feel the need to be "validated" or to have their worth and value acknowledged. Does this need to have our accomplishments approved stem from inherent selfishness, or is it simply a basic human trait, deeply woven into every person's life? Does everything in our life need to be validated or simply the things that mean the most to us?

**Valor:** Strength, courage in times of weakness. Valor in the face of danger or despair, though an archaic concept, is just as important today as it was centuries ago. Should fear control our everyday actions and becoming self-defeating affect our everyday decision making? Will it have dire consequences down the road? To be petrified by our anxieties leaves us stuck and unable to progress as individuals in the direction we desire. Indeed, it can be incredibly difficult to overcome our fears. It takes practice, perseverance, and valor. What do you do to overcome your fears in order to present more valor?

**Value:** Assigning meaning to something that is denoted by being important or beneficial. What do you value in your life, and why do you value it? These questions require contemplation and self-reflection to truly answer. What we value ultimately shapes who we are, and consequently, acknowledging the things we prize can help us to better understand ourselves. Does your true meaning of value relate to money or to your moral principle? The real question comes down to what is "worth" valuing. In an economic sense, valuing material items can be a benefit in living a comfortable life, but such things are transitory, and making an effort to acknowledge this fact can open our eyes to more important and meaningful facets of life. Money 'can't buy happiness, nor can it vault you to have more value in your life; you have the capability to assign value, and it does not need the help of distractions. *Value can be found in everything.* Sometimes it takes a lot of digging to find it. Does greed override value in a detrimental way? Though we are in a constant state of change when it comes to what we cherish, it is imperative to recognize the value in both ourselves and our relationships with others, and should never be overlooked. Take a few moments out of your day to ask yourself what you truly value. *Are the things you value contributing to a meaningful existence*? Do you wish you had more value in your life, or are you content with the value around you?

> *"Try not to become a man of success. Rather become a man of value."*
> — Albert Einstein

**Vanity:** Possessing excessive pride. In an exceedingly materialistic world, it's easy to become fixated on our physical appearance, but to what extent should we judge ourselves based on what we see in the mirror? What constitutes true beauty is a far more complex equation than what meets the eye and should involve analytical observation. Excessive vanity can turn our thoughts toward ourselves, leading to a life of increasing self-obsession and indulgence. Thus, it creates further separation between you and the outside world, leading to a strong sense of disconnection. Instead of working toward covering up our alleged inadequacies with a layer of makeup or a suntan, better time can be spent working on long-lasting and genuine beauty. Does vanity lack real value or worth?

**Vantage:** Viewing from a good or satisfactory place or position. How we observe certain aspects of life is oftentimes more important than what we see. From a low or obstructed vantage point, a landscape may not look as impressive as it would from a more elevated perspective. Our experiences and attitudes shape our perspectives, but finding the right vantage point in life can be difficult and takes practice. However, finding that right vantage point, whatever or whenever it may be, can lead to an array of new viewpoints for the world around us. In what ways can we work to improve our vantage point and gain an <u>advantage</u>? How do vantage points help or hurt our everyday life?

**Variation:** Variation can be described as instilling <u>change</u> in a variety of realms. Variety is the spice of life. A world without variation would be a dreary place indeed. Unique people, places, and things we come across every day add their own diversity to our daily lives. Society, however, has a tendency to promote uniformity and single-mindedness. Should people who have more variation in their life be considered outsiders in our society, or should we greatly welcome variation throughout? Keeping this in mind, it's important to expand our interests and passions in order to ensure that our lives are full of diversity and variety. What do you do to create variation in your life?

**Varicolored:** Consisting of multiple or an array of colors. Imagine a life without colors. What a bland and dreary picture. Thankfully, we live in a varicolored world. People from all walks of life bring <u>diversity</u> to the colorful mixture that is humanity, making for an incredibly rich and vibrant world. Art galleries and museums boast several pieces of <u>art</u> that are varicolored, which immensely triggers our attention to various pieces more than it would with black-and-white art. Take time to appreciate the beauty found within the "colors" of our lives. What different and unique colors can we paint onto the ever-growing mural of our world? Specifically, would you describe your life as varicolored or simply black and white?

**Varlet:** A young butler; an unprincipled being. Most notably derived from the French Renaissance ages, a varlet is something that you don't want to be, even in today's society. "Varlet" can also be used to describe an <u>individual</u> who is undisciplined and unreliable in his practices. Are you undisciplined? When one is undisciplined, their life is completely a mess; they lie' to others and are unable' to keep their things tidy. Take a deep breath and try to imagine being more disciplined in your day-to-day actions. It must be a good feeling to visualize your life being "cleaned" up.

**Vary:** A <u>change</u> or difference in some form from the original. In the absence of variety, life stagnates. Why is this the case? Varied people, places, and attitudes all contribute to the <u>complex</u> and ever-changing entity that is our world. From day to day, we must work to vary ourselves by making modifications to the way we think, act, and behave in order to grow as people. Without a drive to set ourselves apart from the masses, we surrender ourselves to mediocrity and predictability, akin to the constant of changing differences. Like a tree changes the hue of its leaves to adapt to its environment, we can change our own selves as needed. Moreover, it enhances artistic abilities and expands species. Make an effort to vary yourself as a person every day; one small change can make a big difference in the grand scheme of things.

**Vehement:** To feel strong, passionate, or intense toward. What do you feel strongly about? To feel vehemently about someone or something requires immense <u>passion</u> and <u>investment</u>. In turn, your <u>effort</u> level regarding whatever 'you're vehement about increases dramatically in positive fashion. It's good to have intense feelings toward one thing or another, so long as we don't voice our opinions so loudly that we drown out the views of others. Should there be concern for <u>extremism</u>? Where do you draw the line between being vehement and completely over the top?

**Venal:** From the Latin word meaning "for sale," to be venal is to be easily bribed to do wrong. Though it is not flattering, history is rife with examples of such behavior. Even today, especially within the field of commerce, we see questionable <u>behavior</u> made in the name of <u>money</u>. How much would it take to convince you to disobey your <u>value</u> system? Is it your responsibility to call out those who are venal or their own? Would any amount of money justify harming ourselves, others, or our planet?

**<u>Venerate</u>:** A venerable character is one who deserves the <u>respect</u> of others and is highly regarded by them as well. Whether they are our <u>leaders</u>, elders, or simply valued friends, a select few people in life will succeed in capturing our adoration. Inevitably, differing <u>cultures</u> maintain their own sets of criteria for what makes a respectable character. This brings about the question: What types of <u>traits</u> demand the respect of others? Wealth? Age? <u>Family</u> lineage? Strength of character? Who we respect and why we respect them ultimately comes down to personal choice. It's critical that we maintain some amount of <u>skepticism</u> in regards to our "venerable leaders" lest they abuse their stature. What sorts of traits demand your respect? Do you see any of these traits in yourself? Do we have the capacity to deem ourselves venerable?

**Vengeance:** Gaining revenge through punishment exacted by injury or wrong. Be careful of the <u>power</u> of vengeance. At some point in our lives, we will find ourselves wronged by others. Is <u>revenge</u> a way to rectify this wrong? The answer is usually a resounding no, but in what situation can it actually rectify a wrongdoing? Vengeance is ultimately self-defeating, forcing us to commit the same wrong that drove us to revenge in the first place. What are some better ways to deal with harm done to ourselves by others? Is retribution as <u>evil</u> as the action that precipitated it?

**Vent:** "To let out freely in <u>words</u> or <u>action</u>." When <u>stress</u> or <u>pain</u> builds within us, it can feel as if we're about to rupture. Never mistake the power of talking with others about your <u>problems</u>. Though it may be difficult to open up to someone else about your troubles, most likely you'll find that the relief of letting your thoughts out far outweighs any anxieties about revealing your innermost turmoil. Are there any happenings in your life right now that require discussing with someone else?

> "If an injury has to be done to a man it should be so severe that his vengeance need not be feared."
> — *Niccolò Machiavelli*

**Venture:** A <u>journey</u> with a certain amount of risk involved. Life is full of ventures. Whether it is a <u>business</u> venture or a <u>personal</u> journey, there is always some <u>risk</u> associated with starting a long <u>endeavor</u>. Certain <u>risks</u> will always be present in achieving our <u>goals</u>, and it's easy to let <u>negative</u> <u>thoughts</u> cloud our <u>judgment</u> before setting our sights on the future. Be <u>prudent</u>, but not overly so. Don't let your personal ventures be crippled by a paralyzing fear of uncertainty because those are simply minuscule short-term obstacles in your long-term journey. What are some ventures you can undertake right now in order to improve your life?

**Veracity:** The quality of being truthful. Never underestimate the <u>power</u> of <u>truth</u>. It is a <u>fundamental</u> <u>guiding</u> principle in life. We lose the essence of our actual selves the moment we begin lying to ourselves and others, with distractions around us forcing us to lie more frequently. Are you following a truthful path in life, or has <u>deceit</u> become habitual? It can be difficult to maintain a sincere and honest attitude in a very dishonest world, but only through truth can someone truly discover themselves and their true purpose.

**Verbal:** The forming of words orally that are enunciated to one person or a group of people. Never mistake the unparalleled power of words. Of the many forms of communication, our ability to verbally convey ideas, thoughts, and feelings is one of the greatest abilities available to us. Words are a tool that can be used to express pain, pleasure, hope or despair. Regardless of your strength in vocabulary, it's important to ensure that you're using your verbal power in a positive way. Many great things have been, and are yet to be accomplished, with the power of verbal communication, though simple acts of kindness are no less significant. Write a letter to someone telling them how much you care for them. Express your feelings through songs or writing. Make a list of everything you're thankful for in life. How can we make the world a better place through the use of words?

**Verge:** Being on the brink or border. Do you ever feel as if you're "on the verge" of some thing or some realization in life? Standing on the edge of change in life can be a terrifying prospect, though it is in these times where we grow the most as people and realize the true makeup of our identity. Imagine yourself standing on the edge of a cliff, the clear water far below. You're deathly afraid of heights, but you muster the courage to jump anyways. The water hits you hard as you plunge the cold depths, but you emerge from the lake as one who has conquered fear and turned a new page in life. What kinds of verges are beckoning, and more importantly, what could help you finally take the plunge into a newfound outlook on life?

**Versatile:** Being able to adapt to a variety of functions, activities, and people. Have you ever had a conversation with someone who only talked about one topic? It's a very confining and frustrating situation to be in, and this is due to that person's lack of personal versatility. Are you one of these people? It's never too late to change! In order to get the most out of life, take time to try new things, master new art forms, and expand your horizons. By adding facets such as these to your personality, it's likely that you will be able to interact with and enjoy the company of a much richer variety of people. How can you make yourself a more versatile individual today? Can versatility be inspired

> *"That's what I like about film— it can be bizarre, classic, normal, romantic. Cinema is to me the most versatile thing."*
> *— Catherine Deneuve*

and taught to others? Is it strictly constrained from coming about internally rather than externally?

**Version:** A differing form or report, stemming from something previously established. Do you find yourself forming different "versions" of yourself according to the situation? Indeed, we act differently among our friends than we do at work or the proctologist; just be sure that you aren't masking your true identity to appease others. There are many different types of people out there, each of which has their own point of view of the world in which they live. Keep this in mind when dealing with others, as they probably don't see things exactly as you. Finally, ask yourself, just what version of the world you see, and is it conducive to your growth and happiness? Is it best that you build upon versions from several different entities in an attempt to culminate together to form your own?

**Verve:** To have "verve" is to be full of energy and enthusiasm. Keeping a positive and upbeat attitude can make a world of difference in anyone's life, but it takes a lot of practice, especially considering the unpredictability of our daily lives. Oftentimes life throws us unexpected curveballs, making it difficult to stay upbeat and energized in the face of sadness or fear. Our mind-set precludes our outcomes and a positive attitude will likely lead to positive results, including a healthier mind and spirit. Take a moment to assess how you are seeing the world. Is the glass half full?

**Vex:** "To make someone feel annoyed, frustrated, or worried." Life's little vexations, or annoyances, can add up. Whether a coworker is late to a meeting or a family member makes a mess without cleaning up, don't sweat the small stuff. How do you deal with life's vexations? Do you tend to bottle them up inside you, prolonging the frustration and worry, or quickly and swiftly resolve the issue?

**Vibrant:** The word vibrant evokes thoughts of bright blue skies and shimmering waters, colorful things that bring about good feelings. The world is a vibrant place, if you know where to look. Appreciate the vibrancy surrounding you every day and emit your own light. Are you doing your best to be a rich and vibrant individual? What changes need to be instilled to make that possible?

**Vicariousness:** "Felt or enjoyed through imagined participation in the experience of others." Living life through another, for whatever reason, can be a dangerous prospect. Though it's easy to get caught up in the lives of the rich and famous, doing so can sell you short in your own life, causing you to lose a bit of your own selves. In our current media-rich environment, the images of these individuals are especially prominent, but it is crucial to avoid these distractions and create your own identity and persona. Do you lead your own life, or do you imagine your life through the eyes of another? Besides wealth, what else drives you to being vicarious?

**Vice:** Pertaining to sloth, lust, and waste; immoral behavior. At one point or another, we all indulge in behavior that isn't considered "acceptable" by society's standards. We each have our own weaknesses in character to one degree or another. What's important is how we go about addressing them. Whether it is a smoking, something less easily defined, unmoral conduct in a manner happiness is an essential part of are your vices in life and are routine? If not, fretting over the necessary in the first place. *If us from reaching our potential*, to be addressed. Recognizing our personalities, and ultimately recognizing and dealing with locking yourself in an endless demons, try acknowledging that your own personality and accept to fix them. Notice what types troubling behavior, and from

> *"The problem with people who have no vices is that generally you can be pretty sure they're going to have some pretty annoying virtues."*
> — Elizabeth Taylor

gambling, or drinking habit, or learning to approach our conducive to our individual living a meaningful life. What they interfering with your daily occasional bad habit may not be *certain habits are in fact keeping* then there is a problem that needs that our weaknesses are part of ourselves, is a key first step in our character flaws. Rather than and ferocious battle with your these flaws exist as aspects of them as such before attempting of situations are leading you to there decide on the best way to approach your flaws. Do you have a matter-of-fact attitude toward them? What vices are controlling you now? Is it time for a change? Do you have the desire to change?

**Vicious:** Being spiteful or deliberately cruel. Our world, sadly, is filled with a lot of hateful and vicious acts, whether they involve violence or not. Kids are being bullied on the playgrounds; homosexuals and minorities are ridiculed for their identity. Where does this viciousness come from? Have you ever been vicious toward someone or had someone be vicious toward you? Did you rise up in rebellion or succumb to the vicious actions?

**Victim:** Someone who has been harmed or even killed as a result of a handful of events; they are usually identified as a target. What are we victims of in life? Our surroundings? Our circumstances? Ultimately, many aspects of our lives are out of our hands, making it easy to feel as if we're victims to the whims of fate. It's not a pleasant feeling to be out of control, subject to the forces of some external entity. Therefore, it's necessary to fight back when confronted with situations which make us victims and to grasp our fates with our own hands. Are you feeling victimized at this very moment? More importantly, do you feel as if you could be victimizing another? Are you the perpetrator of a crime and thus the creator of a victim? With or without remorse?

**View:** Having an outlook or perspective on something from a particular place, including tangible and intangible. How we view the world around us is one of the most significant reasons for the way we feel, think and act. Moreover, our views on life and living it shape our opinions and who we are as people. Viewing our surroundings in one way can inspire and uplift; conversely, another viewpoint can corrupt and degrade our spirit. The endless variety of viewpoints, held by individuals across the globe, is one of the reasons the world is such a diverse place. The question is, how are we viewing our lives, and is our viewpoint inspiring or limiting our daily lives? Does our world have enough viewpoints or are we too close minded?

> *"The devil can cite Scripture for his purpose.*
> *An evil soul producing holy witness*
> *Is like a villain with a smiling cheek,*
> *A goodly apple rotten at the heart.*
> *O, what a goodly outside falsehood hath!"*
> *— William Shakespeare, The Merchant of Venice*

**Vigor:** Possessing physical strength, toughness, and good health. Where do you display vigor? A vigorous mind-set is one inspired by passion and intensity. To be so passionate about a goal that we pursue it with vigor is not only healthy, but a necessity in life. After all, it's important to care about what you do, especially if that care inspires powerful energy. But it's important not to indulge too much in improving upon your vigor to the point where you become far too intense and enthralled with the task at hand. Moderation will effectively field this necessity in life.

**Vile:** Being unpleasant or foul to a great degree. What do you find to be vile? For some action to be despicable so as to be considered vile, it must go against the very foundations of our being and the morals that make up our code of ethics. Not surprisingly, something considered vile by one person can just as easily be called beautiful or admirable by another. What we find to be unpleasant can tell us quite a bit about ourselves and what kind of moral code by which we live our lives. *How do you handle vileness?*

**Villain:** A wicked or evil person. Just as our personal code of morals guides our judgment of things or actions, it also applies to our view of others (and the standards in which they live by). Who we declare as "villainous" says a lot about our ethical makeup and the morals that we hold dearest. How can we take further steps to combat villainy? Given that society has defined villain as a wicked or evil person, do you consciously choose the opposite posture of goodness and spiritual guidance, or do you succumb in some way to evil forces?

**Vindication:** The state of being vindicated; used for an excuse or defense. Does vindication ride in the same vehicle with <u>forgiveness</u>? Sometimes we travel down the road of life unsure of where we are going or how things will turn out. Do we take the times to alleviate suspicions or justify defenses against opposition? When things do turn out pleasantly, we can be glad we started in the first place. Moments of vindication inspire us to carry on and serve as reward for our personal risk and uncertainty. In what parts of your life are you hoping to see vindication in the near future?

**Vindictive:** Inclined to respond to harm with more harm. Do you seek <u>vengeance</u> before you seek a <u>solution</u>? Consider that <u>retaliation</u> does not accomplish anything except for the most <u>selfish</u> of goals. We must work to maintain our <u>composure</u> when we are wronged and strive to seek <u>justice</u> rather than malicious revenge. Why do you feel the need to be vindictive? Do your <u>emotions</u> ultimately take hold of the situation, leading to a stagnant resolution?

**Violate:** To break or disturb, most notably including rules, laws, and regulations. We must aim not to break the <u>rules</u> that are established in order to secure the safety and well-being of the collective <u>society</u>. Violating the <u>regulations</u> that have been previously established stems from lack of <u>respect</u> for those orders. In order to prevent the violation of rules, we must know and honor them. We must be <u>aware</u> of which <u>actions</u> are construed as violations and why. Do you know what constitutes a violation in the context of your life? Have you violated the rights of others and life forms with or without remorse?

**Violent, Violence:** The act of being physically aggressive with the goal of harming, hurting, or killing someone or something. Do you make an effort to solve <u>conflicts</u> diplomatically and peacefully, or do you justifiably rationalize the use of improper force? Violence is never an <u>answer</u> unless you are acting in self-defense. Those who must wield violence to accomplish their <u>goals</u> are on the wrong side of <u>history</u>, rubbing shoulders with the most selfish and shortsighted of leaders past. Why do you feel people immediately resort to violence to settle issues and problems? Are you able to cope with the destructive forces of <u>nature</u>?

**Virgin:** Untouched; pure, fresh. This word implies innocence and inexperience. We must be aware of those who are less experienced and worldly than us and work to bring them up to speed or cushion them from blows which they cannot <u>understand</u>. Respect and maintain your own <u>innocence</u> and child-like <u>curiosity.</u> What is the status and significance of virginity in 'today's <u>society</u>? Has it diminished since what it used to mean to society, or does its status and significance give you a personal new outlook on the topic?

**Virile:** Strong, powerful, forceful; equated with <u>ideals</u> of manliness. This word is based upon an archetypal conception of a <u>man</u> and a woman; these gender roles are <u>socially</u> constructed. Yes, biologically there are many differences in the proportions of men and women on average, but there are always exceptions to rules based on blanket generalizations. Do you recognize the potential of both genders to have qualities that are typically equated with the opposite? Can virility cross over to egotistical behavior? What does this do for the social spectrum of women? Do they adapt this manliness to fit in within society, or do they try to disassociate themselves with it completely or be somewhere in between?

**Virtual:** When something is almost what it is described as. We often hear about "virtual reality" in which we as a society are spending an increasing amount of time. <u>Computers</u> and the Internet offer a <u>wealth</u> of <u>knowledge</u> and windows of <u>opportunity</u>, but they are insufficient and limited when compared with real-life hands-on experiences; these are the types of activities that we should strive to participate in. The virtual reality contained by the Internet has many obvious benefits but also serves as a buffer between people and the real world which leaves people lazy and reluctant to go out and have real experiences when they could have pseudo- experiences through others from the comfort of their couch. Plus, interpersonal relationships are negated by the anonymous identity that is available on the Web. Is this an overwhelming problem for our society? Do you recognize virtual reality for the valuable but limited tool that it is? Are distinctions between real and virtual becoming blurred?

**Virtuality:** It is what I make it to be at this moment in my world. People put too much emphasis on the parameters of their virtual world and try to replicate as close to their real life as possible. It's fun to think about life in the virtual world because it gives us a renowned sense of imagination, but it shouldn't entirely funnel your thinking. There is simply more to life than a computer screen and keyboard. How much of your thoughts refer to the virtual world?

> *"Courage is the most important of all the virtues because without courage, you can't practice any other virtue consistently."*
> — *Maya Angelou*

**Virtue:** Morally right action and thinking; goodness, nobility exists in virtue. Virtues are synonymous with, but not limited to: prudence, charity, honest, humility, kindness, chastity, patience, integrity, righteousness, modesty, morality, and truth. We must be the guide of our own moral compasses; it can become muddled and biased by the moving parts of life, but we must take care to maintain its orientation to the "true north" of morality. Do you value moral actions over material goods? Can you recognize morally starved decisions or actions when they are at play? You must work to maintain patience and peace in your life. Rushing through things can cause you to make decisions based on convenience and availability rather than according to your moral fibers and being engaged in conflict of any kind has a way of shoving morality into the backseat of the decision making vehicle. Do you make an effort to live a virtuous life by acting with regard to morality and surrounding yourself with those who do the same?

| | | | | |
|---|---|---|---|---|
| **V** | … | *Virtuous/Morally Pure* | … | **Chastity** |
| **I** | … | *Inclined to Benevolence* | … | **Charity** |
| **R** | … | *Reserved* | … | **Prudence** |
| **T** | … | *Trustworthy* | … | **Honesty** |
| **U** | … | *Unassuming and Unpretentious* | … | **Humility** |
| **E** | … | *Enduring* | … | **Patience** |
| **S** | … | *Spiritually Sympathetic* | … | **Kindness** |

| | | | | |
|---|---|---|---|---|
| **V** | … | *Vagrancy, Vile, Vulgar* | … | **Sloth** |
| **I** | … | *Immoral, Impure* | … | **Lust** |
| **C** | … | *Contempt, Corruption* | … | **Hate** |
| **E** | … | *Envy, Enmity* | … | **Jealousy** |
| **S** | … | *Slander, Scandal* | … | **Spite** |

**Virulent:** Deadly, poisonous or very harmful. What things in your life do more harm than good? We must stay away from things that are toxic, whether literal or figurative. Corrupt ideas and sentiments can be as poisonous and harmful as diseases if they are propagated effectively. Be wary of those who wish to spread virulence in any of its forms. Is it ever accidental or does it truly only stem from pure intention?

**Virus:** An organism that is capable of multiplying in living cells and is smaller than bacteria. Viruses hold enormous potential for destruction; as they make humans and animals the vehicle for their warpath nothing is safe. Beware of contagions—viruses that threaten to rob our body of its ability to function normally. Can you take on the aspect of a virus in 'today's society?

**Visualize:** To create a picture in one's mind of something. We must visualize our goals before we can achieve them; without a vision, our goals 'don't have any existence. Even if you do not know exactly where you want to end up, visualize the best direction for your interests and general goals, and take a step in that direction. Your initial visualization is not an automatic ticket to achieving your goals, but it can be successfully complemented with hard work, determination, and perseverance. Language gives us the power to visualize ideas, objects, and situations from a series of sounds that others make—a truly incredible concept when boiled down. The ability to visualize is the foundation of imagination; new ground would never be broken if people could not dream bigger than reality. Do you visualize how you can improve your life and the world you can live in before you act? Do you find yourself visualizing a goal and believe you cannot achieve it? What can you do to overcome that initial sign of struggle?

**Vital, Vitalize, Vitality:** Strength of mind and body; energy, vigorousness. Do you behave according to how your vitality can best be maintained? Maintaining a healthy body and mind are cornerstones of living a long and fruitful life. But this is a lot harder said than done, as it requires an immense amount of discipline in sticking to a life filled with vitality. Do you have the capacity for survival and endurance? Do you give life and energy outside of your world?

**Vitiate:** To corrupt or taint the goodness of something. Can you recognize when something good has become vitiated? Good intentions can be muddled, sacrificed, and eventually forgotten as a result of greed; the only way we can be sure that good intentions translate into beneficial actions is to educate ourselves about what is going on around us. Do not take someone else's opinion as the only one; compile the facts yourself and draw your own conclusions. As a majority, has our society succumbed to being more vitiate, especially in the realm of politics and business?

**Vivacious:** Full of life; animated. People are drawn to those with spirit and vitality; do your best to approach each day with enthusiasm. Find something that you are passionate about, and let it fill you with excitement about life. Everyone wins when you attempt to be lively and pleasant in your interactions: it is contagious, usually producing a friendly response in others, and even if it doesn't, you can feel good about trying your best and giving them the benefit of the doubt. The beauty of this is surrounded around the fact that there are endless opportunities for your life to be filled with vivacious. Are you lively and enthusiastic on a regular basis? Are you dull and boring?

**Vivid:** Distinctive, strong and bright. The most vivid colors and images are the most powerful. Vivid stories and descriptions make your own imagination more accessible and relatable to others. Does it also make stories and descriptions more credible and reliable? Work on your attention to detail and appreciation of nuggets of detail provided by the experience of others. Does it lead to better understanding?

**Vocabulary:** All the words used by a particular person or persons. Do everything you can to expand your vocabulary; the more extensive it is, the more ideas you can explain, and the more people you can appeal to. It also makes you more astute and articulate if you are able to communicate in a free and swift manner. Miscommunication is a rampant problem that ruins relationships and incites serious conflict on much larger scales. Having a larger working vocabulary will allow you to get to the bottom of every argument you are presented with; in order to keep people honest, you must hold them accountable for exactly what they are saying as language is often used to obscure the intention and motives. Can vocabulary be adulterated into negativity and evil by the use of slang and swearing?

**Vociferous:** Loudly outspoken; unusually loud in making one's opinion known. Trust opinions based on the merit of their content, not on the volume at which they are expressed. Don't be fooled by those who attempt to replace rationality with sensationalism. Do you regard ideas with a discerning eye no matter how they are presented to you? Are you more attentive to someone's boisterous opinions because of their voice inflection?

**Voice:** The act of putting one's sentiments into words; the figurative vehicle that we all have to express our thoughts in any medium. A voice can reflect a

> *"If you're not ready to die for it, take the word 'freedom' out of your vocabulary."*
> — *Malcolm X*

> *"Reading is the sole means by which we slip, involuntarily, often helplessly, into another's skin, another's voice, another's soul."*
> — *Joyce Carol Oates*

collective effort from like-minded individuals who all rise up to speak or express support or contempt for the same thing. The freedom to express ourselves is an invaluable force of positive change which should not be taken for granted and should be utilized often. Do you premise that everybody has the right to express their opinion? What form does your "voice" take on? What do you use your voice to express or accomplish?

**Voluble:** Talkative; describes one who finds it easy to express themselves by talking. This is a good quality to have to lubricate social situations and make strangers feel more comfortable, but like any other, extreme quality is best used in moderation. Being overly talkative about trivial things will cause people to tune out the more important things. Make sure you listen at least as much as you talk, and try to keep your ideas grounded in the situation at hand. Do you talk too much? Do you find yourselves not listening to someone else because you're too caught up in what you want to say next?

**Voluntary:** Utilizing your own free will. Before you allow yourself to feel crushed and trapped by your responsibilities, take a moment to consider what is absolutely mandatory that you do. Of course, some responsibilities trump all else, but a large majority of your life is up to you, at least to a certain extent. Explore your options. Are things given freely most appreciated?

**Voluptuary:** Someone who is devoted to lavish personal pleasure and rich living. Obsession with status and wealth is unhealthy and shallow; those who care only about these things lack real meaning in their lives and are naïve to the beauty of <u>life</u> around them. <u>Desire</u> is rampant in today's <u>society</u>; people sometimes only seem to want things because they are valued and coveted by others, not because they have any real direct positive <u>impact</u> on their life. What are your priorities and goals in life? Are they shallow or meaningful? Do you have rich belongings simply because of the status they yield, or do they truly add real value to your life?

**Voluptuous:** Characterized by seeking or giving sensual <u>pleasure</u>; a <u>sexually</u> attractive woman. Oftentimes, it is acceptable to feel that someone is good looking; it's <u>human</u> nature. But it comes into conflict when individuals exploit and become obsessed with another individual's <u>sexual</u> features, leading to awkwardness and uncomfortableness. Have you ever felt you are going over the top about an individual's voluptuous figure or characteristics?

**Voracious:** Having an eager, desirous approach. <u>Greed</u> should never <u>motivate</u> your <u>actions</u> in life. Does greed overrule most, if not all, of your actions? Do not trust those whose desires cease to be encompassed by mere <u>ambition</u> and enter the realm of unnecessary excess. Do you have morally grounded goals?

**Vote:** To vote is to express a preference between two or more choices. Voting in the United States is a distinct privilege; other countries simply cannot boast that they reserve the same freedom for their citizens. Still, there are countless Americans who decide not to voice their opinion and have their vote be counted toward garnering the results. Why is this the case? Do you look forward to voting in an election or a referendum?

**Vouch:** To promise or guarantee something by using one's word as collateral or proof of its <u>validity.</u> There are two schools of thought on vouching for someone: You do it out of the <u>kindness</u> of your heart in an attempt to truly help out the other individual, or you do it with the mentality of expecting something in return. Do you vouch for things only when you <u>trust</u> them completely yourself? Do you vouch in good <u>faith</u>, never taking advantage of someone's trust in you?

**Vow:** A promise or oath to a prescribed course of action. In life, is it important to carry out those tasks that we have promised in <u>good</u> <u>faith</u> to perform? Beware of those who break <u>promises</u> or use them to <u>justify</u> <u>immoral</u> <u>actions</u>. Do you keep your promises?

**Vulnerable:** Being susceptible to physically or emotionally damaging situations. To feel <u>exposed</u> either physically or <u>emotionally</u> can be disconcerting and <u>anxiety</u> producing. When feeling vulnerable, we must keep those we <u>trust</u> the closest; where we are too weak to defend ourselves, they will bear the brunt of our troubles. Do not take those who try to help you in <u>contempt</u> simply because you are feeling vulnerable and weak; put your <u>pride</u> aside. Do you allow others to help when you are feeling vulnerable? Do you work best when you face vulnerability alone?

> *"Waking up this morning, I smile. Twenty-four brand new hours are before me. I vow to live fully in each moment and to look at all beings with eyes of compassion."*
> — *Thích Nhất Hạnh*

# W

**Wait:** We often have to wait for the things we want in life. Patience can be excruciatingly frustrating, but it is a valuable practice. Waiting affords us the time to reflect on our decisions. The virtue of patience will grant us the wisdom to shape our perspectives. What do you have to wait for in life? Are you capable of being patient and waiting?

**Wake:** There are moments in our lives that seem to shake us at the core. These awakenings can come from the smallest coincidence to a cataclysmic experience. The day-to-day grind of life can often lull us to sleep; some days it may seem impossible to even get out of bed. Make a concerted effort to wake from a life of mundane existence. Living life wide awake will open your world to new experiences that you could have easily missed. What makes you awake? What new experiences would you like to try? Are you stuck in a routine that you want to change?

**Wander:** We often feel stuck in one place during our lives. There is some value in wandering, but only to the extent that we are on journey of discovery. Wandering implies that we have a destination that is yet to be defined. The moment that you find where you want to be in your life, your wandering is over. But until you reach that destination, stay curious, for not all who wander are lost. What prompts you to wander? When do you wander? Where does your mind wander? Where do you want to be? What have you found or experienced when you have wandered?

**Want:** Our desires shape our and motivations. However, many want or how to obtain it. Focus family, friends, and colleagues— want for themselves and for you. how the things you want in life peers will help guide you toward you understand the difference do you want for yourself? What What do you want for the shared work to earn what you want? Is as good (or bad) as you want it to

> *"If you want your children to be intelligent, read them fairy tales. If you want them to be more intelligent, read them more fairy tales."*
> — *Albert Einstein*

behavior and drive our ambition of us mix confusion with what we on your surroundings —your and consider the things that they Gaining a renewed perspective on reflect the things desired by your your ultimate goals in life. Do between a need and a want? What do you want for your loved ones? future of mankind? Do you anything you do only going to be be?

**Wanton:** Something done carelessly or unjustifiably, without regards to what is right. Have you ever acted carelessly? Do you regret what you have done? How can we help and positively impact others who act in this manner?

Wanton as you dare
To live unchained; go forth now,
Leave regret behind.
The end draws near when
Present greets past; of life now
Memories remind.

So frolic about,
Flourish your soul; keep the faith

That time will be kind.
And when the bell tolls,

Save the times you lived truly,
Wanton as you dared.

**War:** Death, destruction, and constant conflict between two or chronicler Herodotus once fathers. In war, fathers bury concise observation serves as a tragedy that is war. On the face distinctly human behavior borne to defend our property, pride, war to such a level of banality Italian Renaissance philosopher not to be avoided, but is only put Machiavelli's wisdom stands the nature of warfare today, a nature

> *"Love does not begin and end the way we seem to think it does. Love is a battle, love is a war; love is a growing up."*
> — *James Baldwin*

desolation resulting from more groups. The great Greek said, "In peace, sons bury their their sons." This hauntingly chilling reminder of the human of it, war may appear to be a by an evolutionary tendency and way of life. Reducing should be a crime in itself. Machiavelli laments that "war is off to the advantage of others." test of time and illustrates the in which we find the United

States arming Afghanis to fight Soviets, only to turn around twenty years later and aim the bullets back at the Afghanis. One individual can incite a war, but it requires a nation united, acting as one individual to stop it. Whatever outside force compels you to war, consider the reasons for which you fight, because war does not determine who is right—only who is left. Do you choose your battles carefully? Do you employ diplomacy and compromise before using force to achieve your goals? Are wars fought by the infiltrator or by the perpetrator? Are they fought by the misguided, uniformed, those with false pride and unbalanced convictions? Has present-day warfare evolved to nothing more than leadership incitement, over religious bigotry and resource control, primarily supporting excessive monetary gain for the elite few? What is worth fighting for? If it takes an army to fight a war, do you want to be a part of the army?

**Wariness:** It is good to keep on your toes, but not to be cripplingly overcautious. To be wary is not to fear; it is the opposite in fact. To be wary is to be alert, apprehensive, and aware in the face of the unknown. Always remain wary in the course of your life, but be sure to welcome the unfamiliar; in order to tread with caution, you must first take a step in a new direction. What in life are you wary about? Are you ready to progress in your life?

**Warm:** Freshly baked cookies, a fluffy parka, an inviting smile, an autumn forest—warmth can come from so many places in our lives. We equate warmth with comfort. Warmth radiates through our bodies when we share tender moments. Think about what makes you feel warm in your life and strive to keep it. What makes you warm inside? How do you make others warm?

**Warning:** Heed warnings in their most obvious and overt forms as well as in their more subtle forms. Warnings are so often swept aside that they have lost authoritative weight. Warnings most often come from our parents and teachers—the same people that drive us insane during adolescence. For this reason, warnings are often stripped of their inherent, sanguine quality: caring advice. The paradoxical conflict of the warning is derived from the fact that you cannot know what you do not experience. However, if you honor warnings as a form of loving guidance rather than a restriction to live life on your own terms, you could leapfrog over those mistakes that others have made and will inevitably keep making. Do you scrutinize warnings you are given? Have you warned others?

**Waste:** Humans follow their internal clocks religiously and cannot stand <u>time</u> wasted, but often don't blink when Earth's <u>resources</u> are wasted for personal benefit or ease. The ultimate <u>goal</u> in human advancement should center on the maximization of the <u>use</u>, reuse, maintenance, and restoration of the <u>natural</u> resources we need and even ones that do not directly <u>benefit</u> us but that face extinction nonetheless. This sustainable <u>utopia</u> will not come easily, as it necessitates <u>sacrifices</u> in lifestyle and <u>comfort</u>. Regaining and balancing a bucolic sense of sustenance with the allure of urban sprawl will be an important step in human <u>progression</u>. If we fail to make sustainability and conservation a part of our <u>culture</u>, will the <u>Earth</u> be laid waste by humans, who ultimately will be the victims of their own <u>ignorance</u>? Do you make <u>efforts</u> to reduce the waste that you <u>produce</u>? How wasteful are you? Would you consider yourself a sustainable person? How could you be more sustainable?

**Wasteland:** Barren land that is uncultivated. Land can become barren because of disastrous floods and other <u>natural</u> occurrences or because <u>humans</u> have not <u>treated</u> the land <u>well</u>. What have you <u>done</u> to contribute to the destruction of land? How can we keep more land from becoming barren?

> Man looks upon the deeds he's done,
> Having destroyed all but the sun;
> No fruit to behold,
> Man's heart will grow cold;
> Of land laid waste, no damage undone.

**Watch:** <u>Consider</u> moments packed with so much <u>suspense</u> that we simultaneously can hardly bear to watch and yet cannot remove our eyes from the spectacle. Despite paying hundreds for great seats at the football game, when it comes down to the last scoring <u>chance</u>, half the people in the stadium bury their faces in their <u>hands</u>. As <u>humans</u>, we crave these moments. When it seems <u>life</u> is <u>moving</u> too fast, watch for ways to slow it down and treasure those moments that make you look twice. What is the greatest moment you have been able to watch? Is there any event you <u>wish</u> you could have watched?

**Water:** Water is an <u>element</u> and is the single most dominant and constant entity on this <u>planet</u>. It is the root to all life. <u>Humans</u>, <u>animals</u>, plants, and all living things are dependent on it. It is required for nearly every process, from <u>complex</u> webs of international macroeconomics to the basic <u>functions</u> of a single cell. Water is the one staple that humans can simply not do without. Water is <u>natural</u> purity, a parsimonious molecule, a <u>building</u> block of life, and an overwhelmingly powerful <u>force</u>. Bodies of water have a mystical quietude about them. Though they are repositories for much of what is unknown to man, bodies of water have the <u>ability</u> to help us <u>transcend</u> our fear of the <u>unknown</u> and offer in its place <u>serenity</u> and reflection. Water determines where cities are built, where people live, and where crops are grown. Our planet would cease to <u>exist</u> without water, so we must take care to <u>preserve</u> it as best as possible and always respect its awesome <u>power</u> to give and take life. Do you appreciate the shared responsibility we have to <u>maintain</u> the finite <u>resources</u> we still have? Are you aware of how much water you use daily, for drinking, washing, showering, and <u>cleaning</u>? How can you decrease the amount of water you use each day?

> *"Start writing, no matter what. The water does not flow until the faucet is turned on."*
> — *Louis L'Amour*

**Waterfall:** A slope in which <u>water</u> rushes over it and pools at the bottom. Waterfalls are <u>beautiful</u> sights to see and many people <u>enjoy</u> traveling to see them. Do you enjoy looking at waterfalls? What do you enjoy looking at?

> On high, so elegant a wat'ry wayAbides above the growth and gaping glen, Whose melodies oft whispered sweetly sway With

tempered gait, she turns to Earth again. What furtive danger lurks 'round yonder bend? Still, she appears; yet swifter does she flow, And drinks of insights currents did append; Endowed she vows to teach what now she knows. The edge aflame in red horizon's glow, Cascading down she gasps her final breath, With wisdom reaped still seeds abound to sow, For life fulfilled is never lost in death. When comes the day of your demise, recall: Your soul endures in those who lay your pall.

**Way:** Two exemplary <u>measures</u> of <u>character</u> are <u>defined</u> by the <u>path</u> you choose and the method you take to traverse it. Way encompasses both, for the way in which you <u>move</u> through life is <u>determined</u> by the path on which you move through <u>life</u>, and vice versa. In order to <u>stay</u> in your lane as you drive, you must <u>constantly</u> grip the steering wheel to <u>navigate</u> the vehicle. Likewise, in life, you must <u>maintain</u> a firm grip on what *BB*and method. The <u>*creed*</u>, or way, is sometimes more <u>important</u> than the destination. Do you have a <u>clear</u> and defined way of doing things? Have you <u>lost</u> your way? How do you plan to reach your <u>goal</u> or destination?

**Wayward:** To be wayward is to be stubbornly <u>lost</u>, <u>changing</u> directions erratically to no avail. Some are more familiar than others with <u>fear</u> and <u>insecurity</u> that comes from being lost in the <u>world</u>. Being wayward can be similar to being a pioneer. It is okay to be fearful of what you meet, but you should utilize your <u>skills</u> and <u>resources</u> to find your way. Embark on your <u>journey</u>, stay

**<u>Wealth</u>:** We can amass wealth on and a societal level. Though many disagree, wealth is not only to be possessions. We may measure or even imagination. Throughout <u>perceive</u> until we have a wealth Wealth will come from whatever what you will and <u>gain</u> as much as in <u>friendships</u>, experiences, and

> *"Books are the treasured wealth of the world and the fit inheritance of generations and nations."*
> — *Henry David Thoreau*

determined, and when you inevitably lose your way, enjoy exploration and <u>personal</u> discovery. Do you <u>enjoy</u> exploration? What personal discoveries have you made recently?

**We:** A complex web of <u>shared</u> interests, shared <u>history</u>, and proximity to others breeds collective thinking and <u>motivations</u> and prompts <u>individuals</u> to coerce into something greater than a sum of its parts. We <u>naturally</u> place ourselves into <u>groups</u> with others who share some characteristic that we <u>value</u> intrinsically, socially, or idealistically. The phrase "you and I" becomes "we" in that <u>intimate</u> moment when we share a <u>part</u> of ourselves with another person. Share yourself and your <u>experiences</u> with the people around you; you'll <u>understand</u> the <u>power</u> that "we" holds. What can we <u>accomplish</u> together that you cannot alone? What groups are you a part of?

**Weak:** We all have weaknesses whether or not we <u>admit</u> to them. A weakness is not something that you cannot do; rather, it is something that presents an <u>opportunity</u> for <u>improving</u> your shortcomings. The first step is <u>recognizing</u> and coming to terms with those areas in your life that you are weak in. Many people have weak <u>public</u> speaking <u>skills</u> due to various social anxieties. Obviously, public speaking is not <u>impossible</u>, and recognizing weakness in this <u>aspect</u> of life affords us the opportunity to improve at it. What can you improve upon in your life? What is your weakness? How can you <u>overcome</u> your weaknesses or at least improve them?

a <u>personal</u> level, a familial level, in our society today would likely <u>measured</u> in <u>money</u> and <u>material</u> wealth in wisdom, skill, prestige, life, we collect everything that we of <u>experiences</u> to impart to others. <u>motivates</u> you in life, so pursue possible from it. Do you let wealth <u>knowledge</u> guide your <u>actions</u>

before mere money? How do we measure wealth? Is your sole focus to acquire as much wealth as you can? What will you do with your wealth?

**Weary:** Life can be frustrating sometimes; it is possible to grow exhausted and frustrated with our daily scene. When you grow weary or impatient, take a step back and relax for a minute or two. Taking some time for self-reflection is healing. It will help you gain some insight into what aspects of your life make you weary and how to improve them, avoid them, or take steps to make yourself better suited to deal with them. What wears you down and why? What can you do to pick yourself back up and progress forward?

**Weather:** It is opposing unpredictability. Weather is responsible for natural disasters as well as our bounty of food and quality of life. It possesses the uninhibited malice to destroy the human race as we know it. It possesses the gentle beneficence to inspire the transcendent thought in the human mind. Weather has no empathy and cares not for the plight of humans; it acts more as a dominating force that shapes and defines human civilization without mercy. In confronting weather, maintain a humble respect and learn from your experiences. How has weather affected your life? What negative experiences have you had with weather?

> *"You are the sky. Everything else—it's just the weather."*
> — *Pema Chödrön*

**Web:** The web of a spider is one of the strongest structures in the world; per square inch, it is stronger than steel. The web is an equally strong metaphor for human interaction. People operate in several webs; it's how we meet new people, find new jobs, and experience new things. Much like the spider's home, the bigger your web is, the stronger you are. People with strong connections are likely to find more success, more happiness, and more opportunity. Engage with the people present in your everyday life; you will strengthen your web and enrich your life. What does your web look like? The Internet? What do you do to make your web grow bigger?

**Wedding:** A ceremony in which two people tie their lives to each other. During a wedding, two individuals make a vow to each other, at which family and friends help the couple to celebrate. Are you married? Do you plan on getting married sometime in the future?

**Weigh, Weight:** Often the most important things in life are the heaviest and most difficult to deal with. However, the things that weigh you down in life and the things that weigh on your mind have the potential to be the most rewarding as well. When life weighs heavily on you, keep exercising your body and mind with the faith that soon you will be rewarded; those things that once seemed so heavy will be lighter than a feather. What is weighing you down? Can you share the burden with a friend or loved one? How do you weigh responsibilities against pleasures to manage your burdens in life?

**Weird:** Weird comes from an Old English word and means "having to do with fate or destiny." When we come across things that we don't understand or when certain things happen for mysterious reasons, we consider that our fate has brought on these things. Remember, every new idea is "weird" at its inception. Nowadays, "weird" has taken on the connotation of something that is odd or out of place. Perhaps instead of going through life passing on what is weird, embrace what is outside of the ordinary. Nobody makes a statement without doing something peculiar. Do you value your weirdness? What weird experiences have you had?

**Welfare:** Health and happiness make up your welfare. Your well-being is your essence; it is your core and determines who and what you are in every aspect. As you grow, educate yourself thoroughly, and cultivate a life that fulfills your health and happiness. Do you make healthy choices? What makes you happy?

**Well:** To be well and to do well go hand in hand in the process of living your life. Before you can help others be well and do well, it is essential that you know exactly what it is that you do well and what makes you feel well. Reflect on these important questions and welcome a life to be lived well. What do you do to help others? What do you do well? What makes you feel well?

**What:** A common word used to ask a question in which the answer describes something. What is your life composed of?

**When:** This question poser suggests an answer of time at, time which, and time within which. As humans, we depend on time to tell us when to do things and to remind us when we've done things. Although time is a manmade concept, it is so essential to our daily lives that time seems to exist outside of us. When helps us quantify and categorize our memories and our motivations. When were you most happy? When are you happy nowadays?

**Whence:** Whence describes who you are and how others perceive you. Be sure to know from whence you came. If you do, there are no limits to where you can go and what you can achieve. Do you know from whence you came— your origins, your heritage, and your shared history?

> *"Whisky, gambling, and Ferraris are better than housework."*
> — *Françoise Sagan*

**Where:** Much like whence, the questioner where determines location. The difference is in the direction: "whence" moves backward, whereas "where" also encompasses the present and moves forward. Where are you right now? Where are you going? Where will you end up?

**Whether:** The word functions as a fork in the road by introducing two distinct paths, doubt between two options that we must use inquiry and investigation to illuminate enough to make a decision. We are confronted by this question every day. The decisions we make are guided by this thought, and it often implies ambivalence. Weigh your options with the word "whether." Sometimes the decision is already made whether or not you do something. What hard dilemmas have you had to face? Should I do this or should I do that?

**Which:** We must make decisions where we must choose between a set of options. Which path will you take?

**While:** Another word derived from man's irresistible drive to quantify time. Especially in today's fast-paced world, we are aware of events happening simultaneously all around the world. I do this while they do that while we do this while you do that. What are you doing while the world spins infinitely?

**Whim:** A wish or desire that springs into your mind without warning or reason. Living life spontaneously is exciting but it can be risky as well. A good middle ground is necessary to find. Doing things on a whim will add some spice to your life, but remember: the key to excitement is moderation. Do you fly by the seat of your pants when the situation calls for it?

**Whimsical:** We have odd notions and silly thoughts all the time. To be whimsical is to be a <u>dreamer</u>, an innovator, and a discoverer. How will you <u>apply</u> your whimsical thoughts to your everyday life? How do we <u>separate</u> the <u>good</u> from the <u>bad</u> or the <u>relevant</u> from the irrelevant? Are you a whimsical person?

**Whine:** Whining is a <u>worthless</u> activity and is one of life's many annoyances. Some kids whine to <u>parents</u> about things that they want to have or don't <u>want</u> to do. But when we <u>grow</u> older, we realize that whining is not the <u>answer</u> (at least most of us realize this). <u>Avoid</u> whining at all costs, it doesn't help in any <u>situation</u>. Do you consider whining to be unacceptable in anyone's <u>behavioral</u> repertoire? Do you whine to others?

**Whiskey:** The word "whiskey" comes from the Irish Gaelic word <u>meaning</u> "water of life." I wouldn't <u>recommend</u> taking that definition literally, though; if you drink whiskey like water, you'll be closer to <u>death</u> than anything else. It is an alcoholic drink that people must acquire a <u>taste</u> for in order to <u>enjoy</u>. Do you enjoy whiskey? What drinks do you enjoy?

**White:** A light <u>color</u> that reflects all the colors of sunlight and <u>represents</u> purity or <u>heaven</u>. What do you picture when you think of the color white? What is your favorite color?

**Who:** The <u>ultimate</u> and most basic question of <u>identity</u>, "who" envelops all of us with a single three-letter word. Who is how we introduce one another and how we inquire about one another. It is <u>information</u> and adoration; it is you and me and he and she and they and we. *Who are we?*

**Whole:** To be whole is to be full of the things that make you <u>happy</u> and peaceful. Our <u>experiences</u> fill us up, but we are never truly full. This is what drives our <u>motivations</u> and <u>hopes</u> so that one day we might have all that we <u>desire</u>. Always <u>remember</u> that the whole is greater than the sum of its parts. What <u>completes</u> you and makes you whole? What fills the void in your life?

**Why:** As <u>children</u> cultivating inquiring minds, we are taught to <u>ask</u> "why?" at a relentless pace. Asking why is the most <u>essential</u> question to mankind. Everything we've ever known and everything that we will know comes from asking why. We are driven by <u>wonder</u>; we need to know why things are the way they are and why they do the things they do. The <u>truth</u> is out there <u>waiting</u> to be found, and asking why will <u>lead</u> you to it. Why are we here?

**Wicked:** Wickedness can be something big like a tyrannical ruler or something small like a hateful <u>act</u> or a hurtful <u>word</u>. <u>Watch</u> for wickedness and do everything in your <u>power</u> to <u>prevent</u> wickedness from spreading. The less hatred and <u>evil</u> we can live with in this the <u>world</u>, the better our lives will be. Do you resist wickedness? Or do you <u>create</u> wickedness?

**Wide:** Looking out on the <u>world</u> from atop a mountain will give you a new <u>appreciation</u> for how massively wide our planet is. This <u>perspective</u> can be overwhelming and inspiring simultaneously. Once we are able to take in the vast expanse that <u>nature</u> has to offer, we can open our <u>minds</u> to the wide <u>variety</u> of <u>experiences</u> and <u>knowledge</u> that is available. Do you search far and wide for what you want in life?

**Wield:** To be skillful in the <u>use</u> of something. More pertinently, to wield is to <u>exercise</u> that <u>skill</u> for a specific, expedient <u>outcome</u>. The weapons you wield, no matter their <u>form</u>, must remain sharp, so nurture your skills and <u>practice</u> them often in order to wield them as well as <u>possible</u>. What skills or <u>tools</u> do you wield and why?

**Wild:** At <u>times</u> in life, we can become so boxed in to our <u>situation</u> that we <u>feel</u> like robots. It is <u>healthy</u> to cut loose every now and then. <u>Think</u> about what it feels like to be a bird, to be wild and <u>free</u> with endless <u>opportunities</u> and endless curiosity. What makes you feel wild? Do you enjoy the feeling of being wild? Are you too wild?

**Wile:** Being willing to take any measure to lure someone or something into a trap. Someone who enjoys trickery and deceitfulness. We must be alert in order to protect ourselves against the challenges that wile can throw in our path. What forms of wile do you avoid on a daily basis? Do you enjoy tricking others or being deceitful?

> *"What is now proved was once only imagined."*
> *— William Blake*

**Will:** Will is the power of the mind to decide and control one's own destiny. The human will has a fixed purpose that is sought after with keen determination. The story of pianist Leon Fleisher is an inspirational tale that illustrates the power of will. Fleisher was a master pianist who was diagnosed with focal dystonia, a neurological disorder that led to the paralysis of his right hand. As a pianist, many thought Fleisher's bright career had hit a permanent road block. However, Fleisher was not ready to give up the instrument that he loved so dearly. Fleisher was determined to play piano even with only his left hand, and through this process he experienced an epiphany about his instrument. He realized that playing the piano was not only about fierce discipline and instrumentation. Those qualities faded away as he rediscovered music for what music truly is: its substance, content, and emotion. Fleisher continued to play with one hand for nearly forty years until modern advancements in medicine afforded Fleisher the opportunity to regain the use of his right hand. After rigorous rehabilitation, Fleisher was able to play piano fully once again. Fleisher's will and determination carried him through his career and never allowed him to give up or make excuses. We should all strive to live to the standard set by Leon Fleisher, whose exemplary strength of will gave him the fortification needed to push passed the obstacles and live out his dream. How do you exert your will? *Can you will healing?* What are you motivated and dedicated to do?

**Willful:** To be willful is to be stubborn in order to get your way. We start life as infants who cry when we don't get what we want. As children, we often don't understand why we can't have what we want at all times. As we grow older, we come to terms with the fact that we don't always get what we want. And finally, as fully grown adults, most realize that true happiness comes from giving others what they want. What makes you willful in your life? What ways can you alleviate your own stubbornness, sacrifice your wants, and help others?

**Willing:** Be willing to help others and leave your comfort zone. Those who are willing are the adventurers, the trailblazers, and the open minded. Don't fear new opportunities or experiences; embrace them and be willing to learn what you can from them. People who say yes more often than no often have much richer lives. What are you willing to do to achieve your goals? How willing are you to help your family, friends, and neighbors achieve their goals? Are you willing to donate your money or time to help others?

**Willpower:** Willpower is an essential life force. Our willpower is our strength of mind and our strength of purpose. The stronger your willpower is, the better your decision making skills and sense of self will be. Many things in life require our willpower to guide our choices. Vices such as drugs, alcohol, gambling, or sex can challenge our willpower. Even bad habits like nail biting or impulse shopping can weigh down our willpower. Our willpower is tested on a daily basis; we must face vastly more desirable things on a given day than we can afford (monetarily and healthwise) to indulge in. Test your willpower in the other direction: Challenge yourself to do something that seems out of your league and see how far your willpower takes you. Testing your willpower gives you strength for the <u>future</u>; you will never know what you are capable of until you have exerted every last bit of willpower you have to achieve a <u>goal</u>.

**Win:** Winning is a rewarding and <u>fulfilling</u> <u>experience</u> to all humans. To win requires a combination of <u>skill</u>, timing, poise, and diligence. Winning also encompasses the persuasive <u>process</u> of gaining one's <u>favor</u>. Winning favor, glory, or anything means that you put in the hard <u>work</u> and stayed <u>motivated</u> long enough to <u>achieve</u> your <u>goal</u> and be recognized for your accomplishments. A competitive <u>attitude</u> is not always appropriate, but keeping an edge and striving for achievements will prove that you are a <u>valuable</u> asset to whatever you set your <u>mind</u> to. What have you won in your life? Are you a competitive person? Do you u<u>nderstand</u> when a competitive attitude is not appropriate?

**Wince:** When we wince, we <u>draw</u> back and twist up our face, usually in <u>pain</u> or in fear. Anything from a <u>bad</u> smell to a scary moment can <u>cause</u> us to wince. Wincing is a subconscious defense

mechanism; be aware of the message it is sending. If someone poses an unsavory or foolish <u>idea</u>, be careful to <u>control</u> your expression. A wince can often offend others and <u>create</u> the image that you <u>feel</u> you are above the other person in some <u>aspect</u>. Think about what you would feel if someone else winced when you asked a question or offered an <u>opinion</u>. Do you have a <u>habit</u> of wincing at others? Are you an expressive person?

**Wink:** In the split second that it takes to wink, we <u>send</u> and receive much deeper <u>messages</u>. A wink is a punch line to a joke, a sensual invitation, and a <u>quiet</u> affirmation. If you've ever been winked at, then you know the warm <u>feeling</u> it brings. Find that person that spikes your <u>interest</u>, flash them a wink, and see what happens. Do you <u>like</u> to wink? Who do you wink at?

**Winsome:** To be <u>attractive</u> in a sweet and pleasant way is advantageous and <u>desirable</u>. We should all aspire to be affable and winsome. <u>Maintaining</u> a winsome personality will <u>benefit</u> you, and more <u>importantly</u> will benefit others. Do you make an <u>effort</u> to be pleasant? Is it <u>difficult</u> for you to be pleasant to certain people?

> *"Knowing yourself is the beginning of all wisdom."*
> — *Aristotle*

**Wisdom:** Wisdom comes from <u>knowledge</u> and <u>experience</u>; it comes from living your life with good <u>judgment</u> and a critical, discerning eye. We should <u>seek</u> to live in accordance with our <u>world</u> through empirical and critical thought. Living <u>harmoniously</u> with the world around us is a key component of wisdom. If we live at odds with <u>reality</u>, fighting it, obscuring it, or ignoring it, we are surely doomed. If we cultivate an agreeable <u>relationship</u> with reality, we will find true <u>happiness</u> and peace. Humans everywhere, at all times, have had at least an inkling of this notion. There's a Chinese proverb that says, "Wisdom is <u>avoiding</u> all thoughts that weaken you and embracing those that <u>strengthen</u> you." Your <u>mind</u> is a fortress and a temple. Every <u>individual</u> life experience, no matter how minute, <u>helps</u> fortify your mind against harmful external <u>forces</u>. Each bit of knowledge gained is nourishment for your mind. Does wisdom require a strong, <u>open</u>, and agile mind, thinking with <u>C.L.A.R.I.T.Y.</u> in order to discover reality's most sacred <u>truths</u>? Do you <u>seek</u> wisdom? Do you <u>respect</u> wisdom? Are you wise?

**Wish:** We often <u>find</u> ourselves stuck wishing for something to happen or for someone else to take <u>action</u>. A wish is a <u>positive</u> thing only

until it inhibits tangible forward <u>progress</u>. Wishes can turn into dream states when they take the place of <u>reality</u>. Don't sit back and passively wish for things—get out in the world and actively pursue your goals. The best wish is one that is no longer a wish but rather a reality. Dreams do come true. What do you wish for in life? What are your desires, dreams, and passions? What do you wish for your future? For your family's future?

**Wit:** A funny anecdote or silly quip can cheer others up in a heartbeat. After all, laughter is the best medicine. Let your wit shine through and spread it to everyone you encounter because laughter is contagious. Are you funny? Do you find humor in everyday life? Do you enjoy others who make jokes and have a good sense of humor?

**With:** When we meet new people and invite them into our lives, they are with us. When we learn new things, if we review them, they remain with us forever. Everything that happens in life, we carry with us. Do you respect the burdens others carry with them? What things or people do you want to be with? What do you carry with you?

**Withdraw:** Sometimes we have to withdraw our hand from the game, so to speak, in order to move away from it. When we withdraw from or give up certain things, we remove that influence from our lives. Bad habits and bad company are good to withdraw from. It is when you begin withdrawing from healthy activities you usually enjoy that you should take a step back and examine your situation. What are some areas in your life that you have withdrawn from? Have you ever had to give up something against your will?

**Wither:** To shrivel away, which may be due to age. Do you have a garden with withered plants? Do the elders you know seem to wither away with age?

Weak and withered
Beneath the fire I burn
With droopy eyes closed;
Some symphony splits the sky
Pouring life to ground at last

**Within:** We often live our lives within our comfort zones, where we know what to expect and how to deal with it. To be within something implies security, membership, and acceptance. The things that we keep within are ours alone to decide who to share them with. What places do you find yourself within? What things do you hold inside? Do you judge others according to what is within their heart rather than superficial criteria?

**Witness:** We witness millions of things happening every day. Some events we don't notice; others we can't take our eyes off of. Though we relish in seeing events that are out of the ordinary, we should pay closer attention to the things that are commonplace, but overlooked in everyday life. Something as small as a smile, so often unnoticed, has the power to reverse a bad mood and enliven a day. What have you borne witness to that which has changed your life? What do you hope to witness in your lifetime?

**Woman:** The counterpart to man. As the life-bearer, the woman holds a highly sacred place in the history of humankind. Throughout human history, women have been an inspiration for everything from beautiful works of art to massive warfare. Despite the tendency of some men to try to protect and stifle them, women have the power to accomplish anything that men are capable of. Women should be cherished, not coveted, and they should never be discounted from the likes of men, for without them, none of us would exist. Do you have equal respect for men and women?

> *"In three words I can sum up everything I've learned about life: it goes on."*
> — *Robert Frost*

**Wonder:** Wondering leads to learning and often, learning leads to a sense of wonderment. It is normal to wonder about the nature of things. It is also a good way to recapture the rush of excitements and awe of your youth. Consider the things in your life that give you an enchanted feeling and strive to find more of those things. What fills you with wonder? What things in life are so extraordinary that you can't help but stare in amazement? What makes you curious and causes you to stop and think?

**Wont:** We all have habits or practices that become embedded into our everyday lives. Some are healthy habits and others are more unsavory. Whatever it is that you do habitually, consider its consequences on your health and well-being, as well as its effects on the people around you. What good and bad habits do you have? Are you fully aware of your habits?

**Word:** Wounds from the knife are healed, but not those from the tongue. Words are only as effective as the understanding and meaning derived from their collective composition. Words serve as a window between our inner dialogue and the outside world. A series of sounds made with our larynx and mouth can convey abstract thoughts about anything we want. Squiggles on a page can hold complex meanings as well. The spoken word can vary drastically from the written word. We often speak hastily without thought, directing our emotions toward a target. However, written words can be developed slowly and with due diligence. Words can be written and spoken in many different languages. How is the written word different from the spoken word? Do we regret what we have said more so than what we have written? Do you think before you speak? Will the words in this book guide you to a better life if you do not want them to do so? Are you able to use your words well?

> *"To be yourself in a world that is constantly trying to make you something else is the greatest accomplishment."*
> *— Ralph Waldo Emerson*

The most selfish one-letter word:
  "I"—Avoid it.

The most satisfying two-letter word:
  "We"—Use it.

The most poisonous three-letter word: "Ego"—Overcome it.

The most used four-letter word: "Love" —Value it.

The most pleasing five-letter word: "Smile"—Keep it and practice it.

The fastest spreading six-letter word: "Gossip"— Ignore it.

The hardest working seven-letter word: "Success"—Achieve it.

The most enviable eight-letter word: "Jealousy"—Distance yourself from it.

The most powerful nine-letter word: "Knowledge"—Acquire it.

The most valued ten-letter word: "Friendship"— Maintain it.

**Work:** Hard work is the means by which you achieve your goals. Put in the effort and keep your nose to the grindstone; you may be shocked at what you can produce. Producing a quality product will give you a great sense of accomplishment and will boost your self-esteem. It may also give you motivation to work harder in the future. Always give 100 percent to your work, and you will get back more than you put into it. Do not sell yourself short; never give up without putting in sufficient work first. What do you work at? What could you work on? Are you motivated to work hard at everything you do?

**World:** We all live in our own little worlds, in our own specific location, and in our own way according to societal influences. starts with thoughts emanating only when we are aware responsibilities of living life in unity and harmony with but not all events that affect the forms. The world comprises that make up communities of world is very much alive even It's difficult to imagine our world tucked-away corners have yet Aside from our humongous local meaning when you think an individual. Your personal friends, family, and colleagues. that you normally go: home, house, etc. Through broadening reap the benefits of knowledge, It is located in our brains and from our minds. Life balances of, identify, and fulfill the outside our own bubbled world others. We are exposed to some, planet we inhabit and other life a massive web of connections all types of living things. The though we can't always see it. in its entirety, because so many to be discovered and explored. planet, the world takes on a more about the world you live in as world is made up of your It is confined to the places work, grocery store, grandma's your personal world, you will experience, and skill that the larger world has to offer. Is your conscious awareness and attention span limited (for the most part) to your personal world? How can you expand your understanding of the world around you? Have you taken advantage of every opportunity the world has thrown at you? How has the world benefitted you, and how can you benefit the world? *Are you worldly motivated or universally motivated?*

> *"What Is love? I have met in the streets a very poor young man who was in love. His hat was old, his coat worn, the water passed through his shoes, and the stars through his soul"*
> — *Victor Hugo*

**Worldly:** We should strive to be wise to the ways of the world. Knowledge has the power to make us worldly and erudite. To be worldly, you must be open minded, accepting, and interested in the multitude of cultures and modes of thought that the world has to offer. What efforts can you take to broaden your horizons, seek out unfamiliar experiences, and become wise to the ways of the world? Are you able to cope with the worldly constants and conditions that are part of the total picture?

**Worn:** Everything in life eventually gets worn down, including our minds and bodies. Although being worn out is not pleasant at the time, it is an indicator of hard work and good use. Your favorite pair of jeans gets worn out only because you loved them so much that you'd rather wear than anything else. So when you get worn out, take a rest and reflect on the hard work that got you there, and then get back at it again. Are you easily worn out? What causes you to be worn out?

**Worry:** Worry comes from the Old English word meaning "to strangle" because a worried person feels as though he or she is being choked to death by their intense feelings of concern. Humans are constantly worrying about things due to life's unpredictable and complex nature. Worrying is typically considered an unsavory quality; but the fact is that people worry about the things they care about. Parents will worry about their children; workers will worry about their projects, and so on. Put the energy you spend worrying about something into the actual process of achieving what you want from it. Choose your battles, so to speak. If you cannot change something, what will worrying accomplish? What do you worry about? How can you overcome the stress of worrying and apply it to something practical?

**Worse, Worst:** To be the worst at something means that you are the <u>final</u> <u>measure</u> of ineptitude, a comparative mark to which all others <u>strive</u> never to sink. At some <u>point</u> in every person's life, they've either been the worst or at least felt that they were the worst at some specific thing. If you <u>consider</u> yourself the worst at something or if people only see the worst in you, do not <u>despair</u>. The areas that seem to be your worst are not doomed for all eternity; they are simply <u>opportunities</u> for <u>improvement</u>. Before you <u>trust</u> someone when they say you are the worst, <u>examine</u> the <u>character</u> of whom is telling you this and scrutinize the <u>reasons</u> they cite. What areas of your life or <u>personality</u> do you or others find unsatisfactory? How can you take <u>advantage</u> of this <u>realization</u> and improve?

**Worship:** We worship many other things besides our <u>personal</u> <u>god</u>(s). We worship the sanctity of <u>family</u> and the mysterious <u>power</u> of <u>nature</u>, among other things. The things we <u>love</u> and adore on <u>Earth</u> are worshipped just as gods are. We often associate worship with <u>religion</u>, but is worship limited to only the divine? What do you worship, and how do you show proper <u>respect</u> to the things that you worship? *Do you worship foolishly?*

**Worth:** Worth is a <u>measure</u> of <u>value</u>, but it is not restricted to <u>monetary</u> value. The most <u>important</u> things in life—trust, honor, <u>love</u>, patience—are what truly make up your worth as a human being. How do you measure your worth? How do your peers value you?

**Wrath:** There are many stories about the imminent wrath of <u>God</u> who will cleanse the <u>Earth</u> in a catastrophic <u>storm</u> of rage. The word wrath evokes a certain apocalyptic flare that takes normal <u>anger</u> to the next <u>level</u>. When you're feeling extremely angry, take a step back and think about other ways to handle your <u>problem</u> before you exert wrath on others. Do you think before you <u>act</u>? How can you <u>control</u> your wrath?

**Wreck:** There are <u>times</u> in life when we <u>feel</u> like a total wreck. At these <u>moments</u>, we have to resurrect ourselves and begin to fix the <u>problems</u> that have <u>damaged</u> our life. The most classic <u>feature</u> of a shipwreck is the buried treasure on the seabed. So when you feel wrecked, let the dust settle and <u>find</u> the buried treasure that reveals the <u>mistake</u> from which you must <u>learn</u>. Even when you are a wreck, are you confident in your <u>ability</u> to bounce back? How are you able to bounce back? Have you learned from your mistakes?

**Wrestle:** We all wrestle with the <u>problems</u> and <u>decisions</u> we face in life. In hindsight, battling with our problems becomes a <u>learning</u> <u>experience</u>. What things do you wrestle with in your life? What have you learned from past wrestling matches?

**Writhe:** We writhe when we see something that scares us or makes us <u>feel</u> uncomfortable. Writhing is a <u>physical</u> signal that something is not right. What things in <u>life</u> are so awful that they make you writhe? How do you <u>react</u> when others writhe in discomfort?

*"There is nothing to writing. All you do is sit down at a typewriter and bleed."*
— *Ernest Hemingway*

**Writing:** Writing is a <u>communication</u> <u>tool</u> that has allowed us to preserve our thoughts and <u>memories</u> permanently in great <u>detail</u>. Without writing, we would be horribly disorganized since <u>laws</u> and <u>history</u> would be <u>constantly</u> <u>changing</u> as they are passed through generations. The <u>ability</u> to write is one of the most <u>essential</u> <u>skills</u> that a human can possess. Writing is a distinctively human <u>quality</u> that <u>allows</u> us to record and store our knowledge for others to learn. <u>Consider</u> how widespread writing is, how does writing play a role in your life? What will you write in your lifetime that will <u>serve</u> as your legacy? *Does writing guide our way of life (<u>creed</u>)?*

**Wrong:** Sometimes we have to eat crow and <u>admit</u> that we are wrong. While no one likes to be wrong, it is inevitable that you will be <u>wrong</u> about tons of things in the <u>course</u> of your life. This isn't such a <u>bad</u> thing after all, because every time we are wrong, we <u>learn</u> from our <u>mistakes</u>. How have you dealt with being wrong? Did you learn anything from it? Do you <u>admit</u> when you are wrong?

# Y

**Year:** A year is a time period that consists of 365 days. While a year is undoubtedly a long period of time, people have the feeling it goes too fast or too slow. Why is this? Largely, time moves faster when we are involved with more things and moves slower when you aren't as busy. However, it is possible to become far too preoccupied in the sense that you don't have any grasp of how much time has elapsed over the days, weeks, and months. Moreover, your mind can spiral out of control when you have too much time on your hands. Throughout a given year, it's important to stop, smell the roses, and realize the true beauty of the world around us. How do you spend your year? Do you find yourself losing track of time as your life moves on?

**Yearn**: Yearning equates to an intense longing and/or desire for something. Life is much richer when we fill ourselves with an impassioned longing for something. What are you passionate about? What are your desires and adorations? Whether it's your career, your family, or your favorite sports team, living your life with passion is essential to finding real happiness. You have the power to achieve anything, but first you must know for what it is you yearn. Uncalculated passion is often wasted. Remain vigilant and strive to know your passion fully, and then apply yourself to fulfilling it. When you yearn, do you take action? What do you yearn for that you haven't been able to take action on?

> *"Youth is happy because it has the capacity to see beauty. Anyone who keeps the ability to see beauty never grows old."*
> — *Franz Kafka*

**Yes**: Yes is a mind-set, a philosophy. How often do you say yes instead of no? The word "yes" has unlimited potential. Active participation improves the quality of your life, and saying yes is the key that unlocks the doors to experience. Use the word "yes" as much as possible in your everyday life. Who knows? You just might discover an entirely new world. What have you said "yes" to that has changed your life in a small or big way? Is it easy for you to say yes even if you're uncomfortable about the possible outcome?

**Yet**: Something that has not happened in the present, but has the possibility to happen in the future. It can also be used as a conjunction. What haven't we been able to achieve yet? What comes next in life? Human progress is determined by what we haven't done yet. Anything involving progress is a process that won't happen overnight, but the more hard work that gets put into it, the less bleak the future looks. Consider your goals in life. What haven't you done yet? Where do you need to be? What will tomorrow bring? Fulfill your life by continuously setting goals for the future. What you do today can be measured by what you do tomorrow, so make an impact today and evaluate what yet must be done.

**Youth**: Youth relates to a group of individuals who are in the early stages of their life. Age is but a number. We can't keep our youth in respect to physical appearance or ability, but we can always keep a youthful mind and a youthful soul. Staying young requires curiosity and an open mind. Be the discoverer of new experiences, and youth will remain in you. In the words of Tennyson, "Though much is taken, much abides; and though we are not now that strength which in old days moved earth and heaven; that which we are, we are; one equal temper of heroic hearts, made weak by time and fate, but strong in will to strive, to seek, to find, and not to yield." What keeps you young? Do you actively try to stay young no matter how old your age says you are? Are you offended when someone thinks you are older than you actually are, ultimately dissipating your youth?

# Z

**Zeal**: When you possess zeal, you have great deal of passion and excitement for a cause or an objective. Like a preacher to his word, we should live with an <u>enthusiasm</u> for <u>life</u>. Cultivating a sense of enthusiasm for what you do and how you do it will <u>improve</u> your experiences dramatically. We thrive off enthusiasm, especially when our peers express an eagerness to achieve a goal. Living and working with zeal will improve the <u>quality</u> of your life and, more importantly, will positively impact the quality of others' lives and their <u>relationships</u> with you. What are you zealous about? Do you share the same zeal about certain topics and issues as the people around you?

**Zest**: The word comes from the French for a piece of orange peel added to a dish to give flavor to the food. In <u>life</u>, we can figuratively add orange peels to whatever we do to spice up our experiences. Adding <u>excitement</u> to our lives will provide a greater sense of <u>enjoyment</u> and <u>happiness</u>. We will have better <u>relationships</u>, and others will want to participate in our interesting experiences. Add some orange peels to your life and spice things up. In the end, you'll have a more fulfilling life and, I guarantee, the best pub stories around. What do you add zest to in your life? Is it ever possible to be too full of zest?

> *"As flowerlets drooped and puckered in the night turn up to the returning sun and spread their petals wide on his new warmth and light—just so my wilted spirits rose again and such a heat of zeal surged through my veins that I was born anew."*
> — *Dante Alighieri*